soup

A WAY OF LIFE

also by Barbara Kafka

ROASTING: A SIMPLE ART

PARTY FOOD

THE OPINIONATED PALATE

MICROWAVE GOURMET HEALTHSTYLE COOKBOOK

MICROWAVE GOURMET

FOOD FOR FRIENDS

AMERICAN FOOD AND CALIFORNIA WINE

as editor

THE JAMES BEARD CELEBRATION COOKBOOK

THE FOUR SEASONS

THE COOK'S CATALOGUE

THE CUISINE OF TOULOUSE-LAUTREC

soup

A WAY OF LIFE

BARBARA KAFKA

COLLAGES BY Ann Field
PHOTOGRAPHS BY Gentl & Hyers

ARTISAN NEW YORK

Grateful acknowledgment is made for permission to reprint recipes for
Jean-Georges Vongerichten's Chicken Soup with Cocount Milk and Lemongrass (page 128)
and Jean-Georges's Chicken Stock (page 351) from *Jean-Georges* by Jean-Georges Vongerichten
and Mark Bittman. Copyright © 1998 by Jean-Georges Vongerichten and Mark Bittman. Used by
permission of Broadway Books, a division of Bantam Doubleday Dell Publishing Group.

Published in 1998 by Artisan
A Division of Workman Publishing, Inc.
708 Broadway
New York, New York 10003

LIBRARY OF CONGRESS CATALOGING-IN-PUBLICATION DATA

Kafka, Barbara.
Soup, a way of life
p. cm.
ISBN 1-57965-125-9
1. Soups.
TX757.K26   1998
641.8′13—dc21   98-6964
CIP

PRINTED IN THE UNITED STATES OF AMERICA

10 9 8 7 6 5 4 3 2 1

First printing

Book design by Vertigo Design, NYC

contents

swimmers in soup

For Openers • Shellfish Soups • Fish Soups •
Hearty Meals

"oats, peas, beans, and barley grow..."

Fresh Bean Soups • Dried Bean Soups •
Soups with Legumes • Lentils • Grain Soups

the soul of soup

The Basics of Stock • Bird Stocks • Meat Stocks •
Sea Stocks • Gelled Jems • Vegetable Stocks • Soup Bases

from stock to soup
noodles, dumplings, meatballs, sauces, and other good things

Noodles and Filled Pastas • Dry Noodles • Fresh Egg Noodles •
Filled Pasta • Bobblers and Sitters with Soup • The Somethings Extra •
Sauces for Big Soups • Ecuadorian Ingredients • Vegetables

Acknowledgments

As the years pass, the list of those to whom I owe much has grown beyond decent boundaries; but that, I feel, is the reward of a life, both personal and professional, well-lived. Sadly, I will not be able to mention all of these wonderful people.

I have had for some twenty years now a loving, supportive, and talented editor who makes beautiful books, Ann Bramson. Through her, I have come to have the marketing and communications support and friendship of Kimberly Yorio and the editing and copyediting of Deborah Weiss Geline and Judith Sutton. Ann's assistant, Tricia Boczkowski, has been unfailingly helpful and cheerful. Ann introduced me to the Workmans, both of whom are a pleasure. What cookery writer could not love a publisher who, when told there were to be three tripe soups in this book, said, "Wonderful"? I wonder what he will think of the eel soups.

Esti Marpet has been in my corner for ten years, Sarah Carey has been testing, tasting, organizing, and mastering the computer throughout this book. I have had the joy of knowing Chris Styler for eighteen years, and he has worked with me on and off for many of them. I sometimes think he knows my culinary mind as well as I do. Many of these recipes have been developed in years past and a panoply of gifted assistants have helped me do what I do, starting with Susan Grodnick, who worked on *Food for Friends,* where some of these soups first greeted the public, and going through Stephana Bottom, who worked on *Roasting,* where some of the stocks in this book had their formal beginnings.

Before Artisan, there was for many years William Morrow. I am grateful to those who helped me there and who still publish *Roasting, Party Food,* and *Microwave Gourmet.* Lisa Queen has been a particularly good friend. Bill Wright has been impeccable and Pam Hoenig generously let me go.

I have had many supportive and generous editors at *The New York Times.* Recently, Rick Flaste, Michalene Busico, and Pat Gurosky have found a place for me in their pages. In previous years, I had a home at *Gourmet,* where Gail Zweigenthal, Alice Gochman, and Zan Early Stewart permitted me to ramble on about Russian and Ecuadorian soups and polished my prose. Above all, there was Jane Montand, who brought me there.

Special thanks are due to Stubbs's godmother, Pat Adrian, for glasses of Champagne at the ballet and warm help and support for my books, and to Buddy's family, who gave me breathing and writing time.

There would have been no career without Leo Lerman, who started it all by getting me to write about food for *Vogue* and getting *Vogue* to publish me. I loved him and I miss him. I still love Gray Foy.

I am lucky to love so many of those I owe: Joe Baum, who taught me about restaurants; Jim Beard, who shared passions for Scotch and time-ravaged cookbooks and research and food and long conversations. Corby Kummer has been a consistently helpful eye for my writing. Tom Margittai supported me through the Four Seasons project and is a dear. Jacques Pépin and Gloria were some of my earliest friends in the food world.

I thank Barbara Tropp for her love, knowledge of Chinese cooking, and the passion for research she shares with me; Paula Wolfert for many shared hours in the kitchen and opening up the world of Morocco; Suzanne Hamlin, who has encouraged me.

No food writer invents everything from out of the mind. I owe thousands of writers who came before me and those who are living and working now. I owe as well the many chefs who have given me marvelous food. Flavors and ideas are the food of what I do.

More specifically, the following have lent me recipes with great goodwill and generosity or through historical availability: Adele Adato, Pelligrino Artusi, Rick Bayless, Vatcharin Bhumichitr, Lillian Langseth Christensen, Alberto Ciarla, Elizabeth Craig, Remy Dorotan, Nathan Fong's mother, Jaume Fàbrega, Francesco Ghedini, Copeland Marks, Mark and Kim Millon, Namita Panjabi, Mai Pham, Doug Rodriguez, Piero Selvaggio, John Martin Taylor, Shizuo Tsuji, Jean-Georges Vongerichten, and Patricia Wells. They should not be held liable for the current manifestations of their brain children.

Other food writers have been sources of information, inspiration, and, better yet, conversation: Chester Aaron, Colman Andrews, Elizabeth Andoh, Michael Batterbury, Vincenzo Buonassisi, Irena Chalmers, Shirley and Alf Collins, Louis Diat, Susan Friedland, Diana Kennedy, Diane Kochilas, A. J. Leibling, James Nassikas, Fred Plotkin, Jon Rowley, Jeffrey Steingarten, and Eileen Yin-Fei Lo.

Books are not made just of words. The beautiful photographs are the work of Gentl & Hyers and the food was prepared by Rory Spinelli. The collages are by Ann Field. The designer who put it all together is Renata De Oliveira from Vertigo, with art direction by Artisan's Susi Oberhelman and production by Nancy Murray. I am grateful to them all.

Prologue

Soup is the solvent of memory. For many of us it is love. When I am tired and want comfort, when I want to share happiness, or when I want flavor, my first desire is soup.

The pots and bowls and cups of soup contain the sensations of childhood, the heritage of families, the identities of peoples, the inspiration of land and water, and cooks' inventions. Every culture has its soups and the soups may be said to represent them. Groups of culinary cultures may be defined by their use of fat or starch, but soups are more particular to smaller groups. A Chinese meal may have many soups, but will certainly have two: one to drink during the meal and one as the conclusion. Every Japanese meal, including breakfast, will have a soup. In Ecuador (see pages 319–321), the meal is defined by the soup. Mexicans equally will have a soup in every meal, let alone the Germans, French, Turks, and Russians. Aside from vegetarian cultures, chicken soup in one form or another is endemic.

When I am trying to think what I want to eat, the answer is often soup. It may be as a snack, as an accompaniment for a sandwich, as an opener of a meal, as the main course of a meal, or as an entire meal or party.

My own culinary culture is defined by the soups that I revel in making. I am Jewish and Russian. My husband is Viennese. I grew up eating and cooking French food. Since then, in New York, my home, and during my travels around the world, I have grown to love the soups of many cultures. For me, soup is often the meal, and any meal is better for having a soup in it. There are cold crisp soups as simple as salad, clear gelled soups that soothe the throat, simple soups to begin a meal, soups that nourish, soups that are festive events, and hangover soups to help us recover from too much festivity.

I am not an expert in every culinary culture, and this book is perforce Eurocentric. Pleasure has led me to learn some of the vast array of the world's soups and where I am less than comfortable, I have turned to experts whom I trust, writers of books and friends. However, I have tested and tasted, and the soups all work and please me or they wouldn't even be in the book—even for a fantasy of completeness.

No book on soups can be comprehensive, especially as each city block or turning in a country lane where there is a home or a restaurant will provide a new recipe or a variant of a known one. There is no definitive recipe, no single authentic one.

Soup is easy food, easy for the eater and easy for the cook. Aside from a few basically restaurant soups, traditional and complex, a little variation in ingredients or technique will only personalize the soup rather than causing disaster.

My definition of soup is flexible. I like to eat with a spoon and can often be found scooping up all the sauce, lamenting that there is no more and leaving part of my meat or fish behind. I like lots of sauce, but not lots of thickeners. My recipes often move in the direction of a true goulash (page 182), more soup than stew.

Confession, they say, is good for the soul. I have shocked more than a few purists by starting with commercial broth. I consider that sharing the soup is more important than perfection; but I also think I cheat intelligently. No one knows there is a bought base unless they spot a can in the garbage. When I don't have the long simmering time for the chicken broth, I disguise and enjoy. (See page 347.)

Some of the soups are what I call big or two-piece soups. The liquid is served first and the solids are a separate course, or even several. Pot-au-Feu (page 221) and Bouillabaisse (page 268) are examples. Still other soups are festive events at which a group of friends can sit around cooking or mixing and matching, those such as Shabu-Shabu (page 190) and Tortilla Soup (142).

As a convicted roaster, I usually have the making of stock on hand and, for me, a freezer full of stock is as comforting as a security blanket, for I know that I always have the makings of a meal. Yet many of my soups are made without stock, or are comfortable using commercial stock, say from a can, or Garlic Broth (page 86) or vegetarian stock (pages 380–383), for vegetarian friends.

Soups are thrifty food, many of them the subsistence food of poor people. There are the vegetarian, agriculture-based soups of Italy, the bean soups, the spelt soups, and the minestrones, soups for which no one could afford to kill an animal. There are the soy- and the noodle-based soups of Japan, the leftover-rice soups of China. There are the corn-based soups of the Americas. There are the tomato soups based on plentitude and ingredients that could be preserved. Remember the invaluable root vegetables, potatoes, carrots, turnips, parsnips, and celery root, that, like cabbage, keep through long winters.

For people on the edge of the sea, fish, particularly what used to be known as trash fish—the ones with lots of bones the fancy folk didn't want whole, like rascasse—were left for the fishermen. Inland, there were eel, pike, perch, and tench, also with lots of bones, which provided gelatin to give the soups silkiness and body.

I have some of all of these soups and a few elegancies for special dinner parties. Sadly, I cannot invite all of you to my house, but I think there is a full array of recipes here for happiness.

How to Boil Water

Soup is easy. Anyone who can boil water can make soup. If that seems problematic, put the water or other liquid, which is mainly water in any case, in a pot (see page xiv) and fill no more than two thirds of the way. Over high heat, with a lid on—use a cookie sheet if there isn't a lid—bring to a boil. Steam will begin to escape. The temperature will be slightly different depending on whether the water is salted or not and the altitude. It won't make any difference to the result. The recipe, soup, can begin.

Soup is water flavored by meat or bones, or vegetables or legumes, herbs and spices, and almost everything else the human race is known to eat. The soup may have pieces of all these things in it.

There are other temperatures of liquid besides boiling. All liquids should be brought to a full boil—not just bubbles around the edge, but with lots of bubbles all over the top—before timing begins, since otherwise it is impossible to tell what the temperature actually is. Normally, the heat is then reduced. A lid may be put on ajar or an *otoshi-buta* (a Japanese wooden lid that fits inside the pot, leaving an inch [2 cm] of space all around) so that the heat may be controlled and not rise behind the cook's back from retained steam.

The temperature of the liquid may go down as much as to a very low heat where the surface shimmers and wiggles but no bubbles break, to a gentle simmer where there are occasional bubbles, or to a simmer where bubbles break fairly constantly but there is not a boil; this last is a medium simmer.

"Medium" when used about the heat source is much easier. It is halfway between low and high and usually refers to frying or sautéing.

Many, but by no means all, soups start with stock. Most of the stock recipes, including various chicken stocks, fish stocks, and vegetarian stocks, can be found in The Soul of Soup, starting on page 339, along with more explicit instructions on the procedure of boiling: what temperature to start at, skimming, and much more. However, Beef Stock is in The Meat of the Matter, on page 165.

Stock is really the only time-consuming element of soup making. I have confessed to using commercial chicken stock and I also make quick stocks that are unlike my normal unseasoned stocks that cook for many hours. They cook for as little as half an hour. See Fake Beef Stock (page 168) and Fake Chicken Stock (page 347).

Soup is also easy in that it is rarely demandingly exact. A little more or a little less of an ingredient will not ruin the dish. That is why I rarely give specific weights for vegetables, but instead describe them as small, medium, or large. Those desiring more exactitude can see what is meant by looking at page 447. In the same way, the amount of a soup created may vary from batch to batch; there may be more or less of an ingredient or the cooking temperature may have varied, producing more or less reduction. Taste, correct if need be, and enjoy.

Soup not only is easy and forgiving; it also requires very little special equipment. What do I use? A colander, sieves, a food processor, a blender (liquidizer), a food mill, a mortar and pestle, pots and pans (discussed on page xiv), pot lids or an otoshi-buta (page xii), a little string, cheesecloth, coffee filters, and pot holders.

 A large colander is useful for pastas, beans, and large amounts of stock when the liquid is being separated from a substantial amount of solids. Sieves are useful for draining smaller quantities and, if fine, for removing particles from stock, or for refining purées. A food processor is useful for sauces and purées. A blender will make smoother purées. A mortar and pestle are chosen by the pesto maker and are good for pulverizing a small amount of dry spices— a coffee mill can be used instead. A food mill is not in the repertoire of every kitchen, but it is a wonderful thing. It removes seeds, pits, and skins while puréeing. The best kind is large and comes with three different discs to give different finenesses of purée. I don't like my potages as fine as my bisques. The latter can be puréed in a food processor or in a blender.

 Those who do not have a food mill can remove the solids from the liquid of a cooked potage (page 15 and pages 99–103) with a slotted spoon or ladle and process in batches until there is still a nubbly texture—not a fine purée.

 The string will hold herbs together so that they are easy to remove after cooking. The cheesecloth makes for a good filter or herb bag. Coffee filters are also useful for straining. Pot holders, slotted spoons, wooden spoons, and knives are self-evident.

The size of the pot will make a great deal of difference to the result. Tall narrow pots—stockpots—rotate the liquid over and around the ingredients for maximum flavor extraction. The diameter of any pot will also result in a specific amount of evaporation. A pot that is large enough to hold all the ingredients comfortably without spreading them out too much is ideal. These are what I use.

My preference is for stainless-steel pots with a good mild-steel sandwich on the bottom or lined-copper pots. Glazed earthenware and heavy enameled iron can be used. Aluminum is a no-no except for large amounts of stock without wine or vegetables.

POT AND PAN SIZES

Roasting pans
Large: 18 × 13 × 2 inches (45.5 × 33 × 5 cm)
Medium: 14 × 12 × 2 inches (35.5 × 30.5 × 5 cm)
Small: 12 × 8 × 1½ inches (30.5 × 20 × 4 cm)

Saucepans
Small: 1-quart (1-l), 5½ × 3 inches (14 × 7.5 cm)
1½-quart (1.5-l), 6½ × 3 inches (16.5 × 7.5 cm)
2-quart (2-l), 6¾ × 4 inches (17 × 10 cm)

Medium: 3-quart (3-l), 7½ × 4 inches (19 × 10 cm)
4-quart (4-l), 8 × 5 inches (20 × 12.5 cm)

Stockpots
Medium: 6-quart (6-l), 10½ × 4 inches (26.5 × 10 cm)
8-quart (8-l), 10½ × 6 inches (26.5 × 15 cm) or 10 × 7½ inches (25 × 19 cm)

Large: Tall narrow 8-quart (8-l), 9 × 8½ inches (23 × 21.5 cm)
9-quart (9-l), 9½ × 7½ inches (24 × 19 cm)
12-quart (12-1), 11 × 8 inches (27.5 × 20 cm)

Large: Wide 9-quart (9-1), 11 × 5 inches (27.5 × 12.5 cm)
Huge braisers, diameter of more than 12 inches (30 cm)

Look up any ingredients about which there are questions in the Index. I use kosher salt (page 226) for which medium sea salt or gros sel may be substituted, large eggs, unsalted butter, black pepper fresh out of a mill, yellow onions, unless otherwise specified. The olive oil is extra virgin, but I save the strongest for adding to the soup once it is cooked. Always use extra virgin olive oil, but save the best for last—to add to cooked soup just before serving. Use tamari soy sauce if possible.

In this book, I have given metric conversions for almost everything. They have been rounded off to be sensible. Those looking for capsicums should find bell peppers; for aubergines, find eggplant; for courgettes, find zucchini; for witloof or chicory, find endive; for Batavia, find escarole.

I often serve my soups straight from the pots they were cooked in and choose my pots accordingly. I put the pot down on the table, or better yet, a serving table, protecting the table with a mat or trivet. Sometimes I use tureens. I have several and they are festive. A ladle will be required in any case.

Two-piece (big) soups will often require a platter for the meat and a carving knife and fork. Little soufflés, custard cups, Chinese or Japanese teacups, or any small decorative dishes can be used for ingredients that are self-served at the table. I have one presentable grater that I use for people who want to add extra cheese. I am not so assured that I don't put saltcellars and peppermills on the table. My guests have a right to their own palates. I do object—to myself—when they add seasonings without tasting first.

I like to use rimmed soup bowls, the kind that look like dinner plates but with a deeper center, for stew-like soups or other substantial soups. These merit large oval soupspoons. Sometimes I will use mugs, particularly out of doors in the country. They don't need to match and usually don't require spoons; but a teaspoon may be just the right size. For gelled soups, I often like to use glass bowls. Disused finger bowls are often perfect. Consommé cups and bowls have two handles. The cups are smaller and look like teacups. They are usually used for double consommés. The spoons for these are round. In more ornate times, there were two sizes of these spoons, a smaller one for consommé and a larger one for cream soups.

Serving temperatures: There are people who have an absolute fetish about hot soups being served at the boil. I don't. If the soup is too hot, it burns the tongue, and if it is too cold, it cannot be tasted. Mine is more the style of the Italian peasant soups that are served much closer to room temperature. People should choose their own style.

If really cold or hot soup is desired, serving tureens or individual bowls should be warmed with boiling water or in a low oven or chilled in the refrigerator before being used.

Accompaniments: I almost always serve some kind of bread, whether it be a crunchy French loaf, an Italian peasant bread, an Indian flat bread, or a tortilla. When sauces or croutons are called for, there are recipes. I need salad and I love wine. Good friends and laughter are the best seasonings.

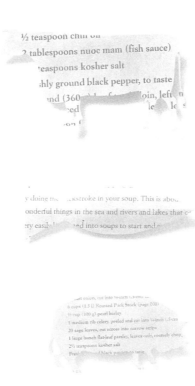

soup

A WAY OF LIFE

Family soups

FOR ALL OF US, no matter where we come from, the soups we have had with our family as children and, later, as adults are those we return to with a special pleasure. I have many friends and I have enjoyed the soups that I have made for them and those that they have made for me; but the family soups still hold a special place for me, the soups of love.

I have been lucky in my family, my husband, the family that came before me, and the one that follows me. I cannot speak of all of them; but here are the most immediate and the soups that I associate with them.

Dora

DORA SHAPIRO, MY MOTHER'S MOTHER, started the soup tradition that means most to me—which is odd, as she was by all accounts a bad cook. After her husband died, she was very sad. To cheer her up, my oldest uncle on that side of the family, Irwin Shapiro, took her out for a drive. Looking for a place to eat, he pulled into the driveway of a restaurant. Faced by a large sign, FOOD LIKE MOTHER USED TO MAKE, he accelerated out and away. She laughed. My younger uncle, Abe Shapiro, as a child went off to camp. He refused to eat the chocolate pudding; he thought it was funny, no lumps.

She was, however, a generous woman though poor, and if one of her children asked if a friend could come to dinner, she answered, "Yes, I can always put more water in the soup." It cannot have improved the soup, but it certainly improved life.

I hope I am a better cook and my life has certainly been easier; but I learned from her that a pot of soup is warmth and welcome for family and friends alike.

This is my improved version of the soup I think she made. I may think so because a version of chicken soup has proverbially been made by grandmothers the world over. For others, see pages 124–134.

chicken soup

THERE ARE as many ways to make chicken soup as there are grandmothers. Some are more intense and start with stock. Others start with pieces of chicken. I like to use the bones from a cooked chicken to make a stock. That way I can skin the cooked chicken and cut it into pieces of edible size. Even when I use the bones from a cooked chicken, I will start with stock if I have it on hand.

I like to skim all the fat from the soup; but there are those who will swear that the soup doesn't taste right without some golden globules of fat on the surface.

Leave the chicken pieces whole for chicken in the pot. If stock is on hand and chicken is needed as well as vegetables and noodles, simply poach some chicken breasts in the stock before making the soup; this should take about 12 to 14 minutes at a simmer.

Avoid mushy vegetables by cooking them just until tender. Stir the cut-up chicken in at the end.

I like dill in the soup, but tarragon is a good substitute. Cooked noodles (pages 392–393) of any size or Matzo Balls (page 13) can be added.

for the chicken and stock

One 5-pound (2.25-kg) chicken, skinned or not, cut into pieces, and 12 cups (3 l) water; or 8 cups (2 l) Basic Chicken Stock (page 345) or commercial chicken broth

for the soup

2 cups (90 g) medium egg noodles

2 small carrots, peeled, cut in half lengthwise and across into ½-inch (1-cm) lengths

2 small onions, cut into ½-inch (1-cm) cubes

2 small ribs celery, cut in half lengthwise and across into ½-inch (1-cm) lengths

1 medium leek, white part only, cut in half lengthwise, washed well, and cut across into ¼-inch (.5-cm) slices

1 small turnip, peeled and cut into ½-inch (1-cm) cubes

1 small parsnip, peeled and cut into ½-inch (1-cm) cubes

1 clove garlic, smashed and peeled

Stems from 1 bunch parsley, tied together with string

2 teaspoons kosher salt, or less if using commercial broth

½ cup (15 g) loosely packed dill sprigs, chopped

IF MAKING STOCK, in a tall narrow stockpot, bring the chicken and water to a boil. Lower the heat and simmer for 30 to 35 minutes. Remove the chicken and allow to cool slightly.

Remove and discard the chicken skin, if left on. Remove the meat, tear into bite-sized pieces, and reserve for this soup or another use. Return the bones to the pot. Simmer for 3 hours and 30 minutes, skimming occasionally to remove impurities and fat.

Strain the stock through a fine-mesh sieve, and reserve. There should be about 8 cups (2 l).

For the soup, in a small saucepan, bring 3 quarts (3 l) water to a boil. Season lightly with salt. Add the noodles and cook until tender. Drain and reserve.

In a medium saucepan, bring the stock, carrots, onions, celery, leek, turnip, parsnip, garlic, and parsley stems to a boil. Lower the heat and simmer for 10 to 15 minutes, or until the carrots and turnips are tender. Remove the parsley stems.

Stir in the salt, dill, noodles, and, if using, the reserved chicken. Heat through.

MAKES 11 CUPS (2.75 L); 5 TO 7 MAIN-COURSE SERVINGS

Sara

BY THE TIME I knew my father's mother, Schimke Peteskey, she was old and had long before given up cooking; but I credit her with any culinary genes I have. In Russia, she supported her scholarly husband and thirteen children from a variety of marriages by running a bakery and an inn with a restaurant.

She nourished her children with a fierce love of good food and drink and created a lifelong nostalgia for the foods of their youth. Prominent among them were herrings and soups that were meals. My mother's mother gave me an attitude toward food. My father's mother inspired me to try to re-create the foods of memory.

vegetarian borscht

THERE ARE MANY different kinds of borscht (page 176). The very first recipe I wrote for print was an attempt to make one that my father spoke of (page 178). This borscht takes into account the many fasting days on the old Russian calendar and also the Jews who liked to use sour cream but couldn't include it if the soup had a meat base. The flavor is still so intense that I don't miss the meat.

If the beets are nice and small and the greens look good, wash them, cut them across into narrow strips, and add them to the soup along with the cabbage. A small, whole boiled potato can be added to each bowl of soup.

> 1 ounce (30 g) dried porcini mushrooms (cèpes)
>
> 2 tablespoons vegetable oil
>
> ½ pound (225 g) white mushrooms, trimmed, wiped clean, and sliced ¼ inch (.5 cm) thick
>
> 1 large onion, cut into ¼-inch (.5-cm) dice
>
> 10 small or 7 to 8 medium beets (about 1½ pounds; 675 g), with green (see Headnote), peeled, quartered, and cut across into ¼-inch (.5-cm) slices

2 medium carrots, peeled and cut across into ¼-inch (.5-cm) rounds

1 medium parsnip, peeled and cut across into ¼-inch (.5-cm) rounds

1 very small or ½ large celery root (about ¾ pound; 360 g), peeled and cut into ½-inch (1-cm) cubes

1½ pounds (675 g) mashing potatoes, peeled and cut into ½-inch (1-cm) cubes

½ small white cabbage (about ¾ pound; 360 g), cored and shredded

3 large cloves garlic, smashed, peeled, and very finely chopped

3 tablespoons tomato paste

1 medium bunch dill, fronds only, coarsely chopped

¼ cup (50 g) sugar

½ cup (125 ml) cider vinegar

2 tablespoons kosher salt

Freshly ground black pepper, to taste

for serving

Coarsely chopped dill

Sour cream

Boiled potatoes, optional

SOAK THE DRIED MUSHROOMS in 1 cup (250 ml) hot water for 15 minutes. Drain, reserving the liquid, and squeeze out the excess liquid. Strain all the soaking liquid through a fine-mesh sieve. Reserve the liquid (there should be 1 cup; 250 ml) and the mushrooms separately.

In a tall narrow stockpot, heat the oil over medium heat. Stir in the fresh mushrooms and cook, stirring occasionally, for 4 minutes. Stir in the onion and cook, stirring occasionally, for 8 minutes.

Add the beets, carrots, parsnip, celery root, 8 cups (2 l) water, and the mushroom soaking liquid. Bring to a boil. Lower the heat and simmer for 5 minutes. Stir in the potatoes, cabbage, garlic, and, if using, the beet greens. Dissolve the tomato paste in ½ cup (125 ml) of the liquid and stir it back into the soup. Return to a boil. Lower the heat and simmer for 5 minutes. Stir in the reconstituted dried mushrooms and simmer for 5 minutes, or until all the vegetables are tender.

Remove from the heat. Stir in the dill, sugar, vinegar, salt, and pepper.

Pass bowls of chopped dill and sour cream at the table.

MAKES 19 CUPS (4.75 L); 8 MAIN-COURSE SERVINGS

Lillian

MY MOTHER, LILLIAN POSES, like her mother before her, could not cook. She was an enormously accomplished woman, a lawyer, an engineer, and a social worker. There wasn't much space in which I could shine; but her lack of culinary skills gave me a little chink. In it, I have made my life.

She was a very competitive woman, but it didn't matter to her that she couldn't cook any more than it mattered that she couldn't type. Those were jobs that typecast women as girls. She had broader goals.

She gleefully told the story of a day early on in her marriage when she set out to make split-pea soup according to a recipe given to her by a friend. She followed the recipe and then proudly served it to my father and waited for applause. Upon tasting it, he pursed his mouth and declared that he would eat it if he had to but *she* shouldn't by any means. She had used laundry starch. The borscht grandmother declared her brilliant, as my father immediately hired a cook and my mother never cooked again.

The cook, Rachel Wellman, who came when I was four and stayed until I was sixteen, had an unpromising background for a cook. She was a black Canadian woman who had been raised by the Salvation Army. By the time I ate her food, she was a superb cook and could produce almost anything that was described to her. I didn't learn to cook from her—she rarely tolerated me in the kitchen—but I did have the flavors of good food in my mouth. She didn't make split-pea soup.

I, in turn, had my own troubles with split-pea soup. I went to a school where girls and boys alike were taught to cook. Lo and behold, the very first recipe we were given was split-pea soup. Triumphant, I came home and declared that I knew how to make it and insisted that I do so.

It was ghastly. I cooked it too long and let it sit so that it turned into sludge. Although my parents were very nice about it, it was years before I could bear the smell of pea soup. Today, I think I know how to make a good one and I even enjoy eating it.

split-pea soup

I DON'T LIKE sliced frankfurters on top of pea soup, but they can be added. Instead, I top the soup with crisp cubed croutons for satisfying and contrasting crunch.

> 1 pound (450 g) split peas
> 1 small smoked ham hock (10 ounces; 300 g)
> 12 cups (3 l) Basic Chicken Stock (page 345) or commercial chicken broth
> 2 bay leaves
> 3 tablespoons vegetable oil
> 4 medium carrots, peeled and cut into ¼-inch (.5-cm) dice
> 2 medium ribs celery, peeled and cut into ¼-inch (.5-cm) dice
> 1 large onion, cut into ¼-inch (.5-cm) dice
> 2 cloves garlic, smashed and peeled
> Kosher salt, to taste
> Cubed Croutons (page 430)

IN A TALL narrow stockpot, bring the peas, ham hock, stock, and bay leaves to a boil. Lower the heat. Simmer for 1 hour and 30 minutes. Remove the ham hock and allow to cool slightly. Remove and discard the skin. Tear the meat into bite-sized pieces.

While the soup is simmering, in a large frying pan, heat the oil over medium heat. Stir in the carrots, celery, onion, and garlic. Cook, stirring, for 8 minutes.

Stir the vegetables into the soup with the meat from the ham hock. Return to a boil. Lower the heat and simmer for 30 minutes. Remove the bay leaves. Season with salt.

Sprinkle some croutons on each portion, or pass them.

MAKES 10 CUPS (2.5 L); 8 TO 10 FIRST-COURSE SERVINGS

Jack

MY FATHER, JACK POSES, LOVED TO EAT. To my mother's dismay, he would gnaw the steak bones at the end of a meal. He had prejudices. Fruit—remember, this was the era of broiled grapefruit—had no place at the start of a meal. Protein, by which he meant meat, poultry, seafood, and cheese, was good. Aside from copious amounts of salad and potatoes, vegetables were uninteresting. Smoked fish, braised as well as roasted meats, and soup all were good. Dessert didn't matter. I think I have adapted many of his ideas except that I like beans, legumes, and all sorts of vegetables, particularly when I grow them.

Part of my learning to cook was to please him. He certainly pleased me with visits to restaurants. My mother liked restaurants as well. Her favorite was Lafayette in Greenwich Village. One entered through a bar with a tile floor and elderly men playing chess at special tables. The dining room was more formal, but the food was bistro. Mother's favorite dish was moules marinière. Sometimes I would join my parents.

The most exciting restaurant visits, the ones that made me a restaurant addict, were made by me alone with my father when my mother went to Washington to do war work for the government. As if in revenge, my father would take me to wonderful places like Le Chambord, in the shadow of the Third Avenue El. There in a kitchen displaying an enormous batterie of copper pots behind a glass wall, the chef would make any dish from the classic repertoire. There was a fabulous prewar wine list. I remember vividly that my father allowed me to be the taster for a 1919 Lafite, which was nineteen dollars, a fortune at the time. The entire restaurant came to a halt. Heady.

It was there that I tasted the upmarket version of mussel soup for the first time. I have loved it ever since.

billi bi

THIS SOUP can be made ahead until the mussels are added back; however, the flavor gets stronger and may need some milk. Hot or cold, with tarragon or curry, it is a scrumptious, old-fashioned treat.

1 medium bunch tarragon; or 1 tablespoon (15 g) unsalted butter and 1 teaspoon curry powder

1 bottle (750 ml) dry white wine

4 medium shallots, finely chopped

3 pounds (1.3 kg) mussels, well scrubbed and debearded

4 egg yolks

1 cup (250 ml) heavy cream

1 tablespoon kosher salt

Freshly ground white pepper, to taste

IF USING THE TARRAGON, strip the leaves from half the sprigs. Reserve the leaves to top the soup. Discard the stems. In a large wide pot, bring the wine, shallots and the remaining whole sprigs of tarragon to a boil.

If using the curry, in a large wide pot, melt the butter over medium heat. Stir in the curry powder and cook, stirring, for 2 to 3 minutes, until aromatic. Stir in the wine and shallots. Bring to a boil.

For either version, lower the heat and simmer, uncovered, for 10 minutes. Stir in 1 cup (250 ml) water. Return to a boil. Stir in the mussels, cover and simmer for 5 to 6 minutes, or until all the mussels are open. Remove from the heat. Remove the mussels from the liquid and allow to cool slightly. Strain the liquid through a damp-cloth–lined sieve and reserve.

Remove all but 6 mussels from the shells and reserve. The soup can be made several hours ahead to this point.

In a medium saucepan, return the mussel liquid to a boil. Reduce the heat to low. Whisk together the egg yolks and cream. Whisk about half of the simmering liquid into the egg yolk mixture, a ladleful at a time, then whisk it back into the simmering broth. Carefully, bring back just to the boil, stirring constantly. As soon as the soup begins to foam, remove it from the heat and stir in the mussels that have been removed from the shell. Continue stirring for about 2 minutes, until the mussels are heated through. To serve cold, refrigerate for up to 2 days.

Season to taste. Divide the soup evenly among 6 bowls and lay 1 mussel in the shell in the center of each. For the tarragon version, top with the reserved whole leaves.

MAKES ABOUT 6 CUPS (1.5 L); 6 FIRST-COURSE SERVINGS

The Kafkas

WHEN I MARRIED, I sat at a table new to me set with huge linen napkins and tablecloths embroidered by my mother-in-law, Hanni Kafka, and her mother and grandmother. Today, their napkins and large Austrian soupspoons sit on my table, a constant reminder of their legacy. Knowing them, I had a new set of soups to re-create, those of my Viennese mother-in-law. It was a risky business. In-laws' recipes always are, especially when the in-laws are good cooks. There were some strange results, as can be seen from the matzo balls ahead. Even so, I had a few outright successes. I managed to make a good Beef Stock (page 165), which was one of my mother-in-law's star turns, without turning the beef into old laundry. I learned about liver dumplings (page 419) and putting thin strips of crêpes rather than noodles in broth (page 396).

One day shortly after I was married, my new and shiny husband requested matzo balls. I had never made them. Shaking slightly, I turned to the back of the box of matzo meal and carefully followed the recipe. I was elated when they turned out just as I thought they should, fluffy but round and holding together. When I served them, my husband asked me what they were. I didn't understand the question until a year or so later when his mother had us over to dinner and served matzo ball soup.

There, sitting unrecognizable to me in a wide-rimmed soup bowl in a small sea of beautiful broth, were five dark ivory balls the size of shooting marbles. I tried to cut one with the edge of my spoon. It bounced slightly. Looking at my new relatives, I saw that they were spooning the whole marbles into their mouths. I quickly did the same and discovered that these were matzo balls, dense and chewy.

When I told the story in amazement to others, sometimes I discovered that that was also their family's idea of a matzo ball. It still isn't mine.

matzo balls

I HAVE MADE only a few changes to the classic matzo balls. Mine are smaller, so there is no chasing them around the soup bowl and splashing all over the table. I add parsley for flavor as well as looks and pepper for a small burst of flavor.

Those who want chewier matzo balls do not need to change the ingredients. They should cook them uncovered and for less time. Matzo balls are traditionally served in chicken broth, seasoned with salt and pepper and a sprinkling of chopped parsley or dill. Cooking the matzo balls in the stock will cloud it slightly. Those who want impeccably clear stock should cook the matzo balls in salted water, as described here, before adding them to the soup.

Chicken fat is rendered in the same way as duck fat (pages 402–403), although an onion is often added to the chicken fat as it renders. Those who are not worried about their diet can increase the chicken fat to 2 tablespoons.

2 eggs
1 tablespoon rendered chicken fat or vegetable oil
3 tablespoons club soda (or, for Passover, cold water)
½ cup (55 g) matzo meal
¼ cup (15 g) finely chopped parsley
1 teaspoon kosher salt
Large pinch of freshly ground black pepper

IN A SMALL BOWL, beat the eggs, chicken fat, and club soda or water until thoroughly blended. Stir in the remaining ingredients until just blended. Don't overmix. Refrigerate for 20 minute, or up to 1 day.

With moistened palms, roll the matzo mixture into balls, using level measures of 1½ teaspoons, 1 tablespoon, or 2 tablespoons.

Bring a large pot of lightly salted water to a boil. Add the matzo balls; work in batches if necessary so the pot will not be crowded. Return to a boil. Lower the heat and simmer, partially covered, for 15 to 20 minutes for small balls, 20 to 25 minutes for medium balls, or 30 to 35 minutes for large balls.

MAKES ABOUT 32 SMALL, 16 MEDIUM, OR 8 LARGE MATZO BALLS; 6 TO 8 FIRST-COURSE SERVINGS, EACH SERVED IN 1 TO 1½ CUPS (250 TO 375 ML) SEASONED BROTH

Childhood

My own children, Michael and Nicole, were raised on soup. It is only a short step from puréed vegetables to potage (pages 99–103). I could make pots of soup and have them frozen in portions to use as need arose. I must admit that the full virtues of these vegetable soups were only revealed to me on our first family trip to Europe, when my son was a mere eighteen months old and my daughter three and a bit. They ate lunch with us; but dinner in French hotels was too late and too formal for American children. (I always wondered how the French got their children to sit quietly at table through long meals and to eat with silverware.) I discovered that there were no meals especially for children, but that someplace in the kitchen there would be a potage that the children could eat with chunks of good bread and pleasure.

Just as, at one time in America, it was pie for lunch and pie for dinner and pie for supper, in France, for the poor, potage and bread was a three-times-a-day habit.

Today, potage still makes a good meal with a salad, some cheese, and a glass of wine.

For vegetarians, the soup is a good one if made with Garlic Broth (page 86) in place of stock.

I have met children who wouldn't eat their vegetables, but they all love this soup, and the vegetables sneak in.

mixed vegetable potage

THIS SOUP IS FLEXIBLE and the ingredients can vary. I usually scan the refrigerator and see what I have on hand before I go shopping. It's amazing what can happen with a slightly wilted bunch of watercress, some carrots from last night's dinner, and other items on hand.

Good chicken stock will make better soup, but I have often made this with commercial stock, frozen or canned, which is perfectly adequate. Stock cubes are very salty and should be avoided if possible. Garlic Broth (page 86) is a good alternative for vegetarians. Omit the garlic in this recipe if using the broth. This is a great soup to make in large quantities because it freezes and reheats well.

Stir in 1½ teaspoons butter for each portion right before serving (do not add the butter before refrigerating or freezing).

> 1¾ pounds (785 g) spinach, stemmed and washed well
>
> 2 pounds (900 g) mashing potatoes, peeled, halved lengthwise, and cut across into slices
>
> 12 medium carrots, peeled and sliced
>
> 2 medium onions, cut into chunks
>
> 10 cups (2.5 l) Basic Chicken Stock (page 345) or commercial chicken broth
>
> 3 cloves garlic, smashed and peeled
>
> Kosher salt, to taste
>
> Freshly ground black pepper, to taste
>
> 3 tablespoons (45 g) unsalted butter

IN A TALL STOCKPOT, bring all the ingredients except the salt, pepper, and butter to a boil. Lower the heat and simmer for 30 minutes, or until each vegetable is easily pierced with the tip of a knife.

Pass the soup through the medium disc of a food mill. Or skim the vegetables out of the liquid, pulse to a coarse purée in a food processor, and recombine the vegetables and liquid. Season with salt and pepper. The soup can be refrigerated at this point for up to 3 days or frozen for up to 2 months.

Bring the soup to a simmer. Stir in the butter just before serving.

MAKES ABOUT 4 QUARTS (4 L); 12 FIRST-COURSE SERVINGS OR
ENOUGH FOR SEVERAL SEPARATE MEALS

Michael

MY CHILDREN GREW, and while they did not discard the soups of kindergarten years, their tastes expanded. Michael Kafka went on to Bouillabaisse (page 268), and a myriad of Provençal fish soups followed. He doesn't think my bouillabaisse is as good as the one at Tetou's restaurant in Cagnes-sur-Mer; but he does love my fish soup, especially when accompanied by a bowl of Rouille (page 433), Croutons (page 429) to be rubbed with extra peeled cloves of garlic, and, sometimes, sliced boiled firm potatoes and grated cheese, sometimes Parmesan, usually Gruyère.

He has become an easy cook, a husband, a delicious father, and an interesting man.

michael's fish soup

ONCE when a grown and married Michael was coming to dinner, I was caught a little short. I devised a soup based on the prepared ingredients in the freezer. Here is a reward for having made fish stock and tomato base some months before. The only limitation is that it really is better made with a food mill; but the solids can be skimmed out and puréed in a food processor.

If desired, a fish fillet per person can be slipped into the puréed soup to cook for 5 minutes, or until opaque.

While the fish soup can be served as a first course, with all the added attractions, it can be a meal. It can be multiplied as often as your freezer provides ingredients.

1 medium onion, cut into ¼-inch (.5-cm) dice

½ cup (125 ml) olive oil

8 medium cloves garlic, smashed, peeled, and coarsely chopped

1 teaspoon pure chili powder

½ teaspoon cayenne pepper

½ gram saffron threads (two and a half .25-g packages)

½ cup (125 ml) white wine, preferably acidic

3 cups (750 ml) Chunky Tomato Base (page 385), drained and lightly
    crushed canned (not plum) tomatoes, or sterile-pack chopped tomatoes

5 cups (1.25 l) Double-Rich Fish Stock (page 363)

¼ teaspoon dried thyme

½ bay leaf

1½ teaspoons kosher salt, or to taste

Freshly ground black pepper, to taste

½ cup (125 ml) dry anise liquor (not liqueur; see page 247)

IN A MEDIUM STOCKPOT, cook the onion and oil over very low heat, stirring occasionally, for 12 minutes. Stir in the garlic and cook for 7 minutes, until both the onion and garlic are very soft but not brown. Stir in the chili powder and cayenne pepper. Cook, stirring, for a minute.

Meanwhile, soak the saffron in ¼ cup (65 ml) wine.

Add the saffron-wine mixture, the tomatoes, stock, thyme, and bay leaf to the onions. Bring to a boil. Lower the heat and simmer for 45 minutes. Remove the bay leaf.

Pass the soup through a food mill fitted with the medium disc. Return to the pot and season with salt and pepper. The soup can be made ahead up to this point and refrigerated.

If it has been refrigerated, reheat the soup. Flame the anise liquor and pour into the soup. Stir in the remaining wine. Bring to a boil. Serve immediately, with chosen accompaniments.

MAKES 7 CUPS (1.75 L); 4 MAIN-COURSE SERVINGS

Nicole

Our daughter, Nicole Kafka Foote, was our firstborn. She has grown into a loving, accomplished woman, a surgeon, a wife, and a good cook who cherishes our house in Vermont. She has enthusiastically taken over the vegetable garden, which looks better now than it ever did when I was in charge. She still plants for me an inordinate amount of salad greens and most of the other things I love. A few years ago, she grew an assortment of potatoes and carefully kept track of those we liked best so that they could be planted again.

She chases through the Vermont woods with her father searching for mushrooms. In the fall, we find coral mushrooms (*Clavaria*), usually all at one time. They make an aromatic, elegant soup.

white coral
OYSTER MUSHROOM SOUP

When picking mushrooms, always know what to pick. If there is any question, check with an expert. There is a way to make this soup with store-bought mushrooms. It is very important to pick coral mushrooms (*Clavaria*), with the aid of a small, sharp knife in order to avoid as much dirt as possible, especially as the mushrooms tend to grow on beds of pine needles. Even with careful picking, cleaning coral mushrooms can be very difficult, because all the leaves and pine needles most likely will not come out. They will float to the top during cooking and can be removed. The mushrooms will separate into thin strips when cleaning.

If there is a larger haul of mushrooms than can be used for the day's soup, the remainder can be made into a base with less broth and frozen. Add 5 cups (1.25 l) of stock all at once for soup, or only 2 cups (500 ml) for the base. For a large haul, multiply the base ingredients as need be to make the base. Come a cold winter's day, the base can be defrosted, the remaining amount of broth added, and the soup produced.

Those who cannot find *Clavaria* can make the soup with wild or domestic oyster mushrooms (*Pleurotus oestreatus*). Wild oyster mushrooms grow on trees and should be cut away, leaving the base of the mushroom attached to the tree. Soak these wild mushrooms briefly in salted water to force out any small bugs. Cut off the stems as they tend to be fibrous. The stems can be used to make Mushroom Broth (page 382).

If the egg yolks seem to make this soup too rich, it can be made using only the cream.

8 tablespoons (120 g) unsalted butter

½ pound (225 g) cleaned coral mushrooms or stemmed and cleaned oyster mushrooms

2 cups (500 ml) Basic Chicken Stock (page 345) or commercial chicken broth to make a mushroom base, or 5 cups total (1.25 l) to make the soup

1 tablespoon kosher salt

Freshly ground black pepper, to taste

1 cup (250 ml) heavy cream

3 egg yolks

IN A MEDIUM SAUCEPAN, melt the butter over medium heat. Stir in the mushrooms. Cook, stirring, for 10 minutes.

To make a mushroom base, stir in 2 cups (500 ml) stock (this will make 5 cups [1.25 l] base); remove from the heat and refrigerate for up to 2 days, or freeze for up to 3 months. If making the soup, stir in 3 more cups (750 ml) stock. (Or if using the premade base, add the 3 cups [750 ml] stock.) Bring to a boil. If using coral mushrooms, some little pine needles or bits of soft leaves may float to the top; skim these off. Season with the salt and pepper. Lower the heat and simmer for 15 minutes.

In a small bowl, whisk together the cream and egg yolks. Slowly whisk a few ladlesful of the hot soup, one at a time, into the cream mixture. Whisk this mixture back into the soup. Simmer gently, whisking constantly, until the soup is slightly thickened. Remove from the heat and serve immediately.

MAKES ABOUT 7 CUPS (1.75 L); 6 FIRST-COURSE SERVINGS

Jill

WHEN MICHAEL MARRIED the beautiful and delightful Jill Gaydosh, we acquired another discriminating eater and good cook. She has by far the best hands for pastry in the family. She is also involved with work that benefits schools and children—admirable. She is a splendid mother to Oliver, the next generation of happy Kafka eaters. She loves this oyster soup and I now make it every year for Thanksgiving. It is festive but light enough to go before the large meal.

oyster soup with broth

ALTHOUGH THIS SOUP is very simple, start it early on the day of the meal, which only means putting the shucked oysters in a large sieve so that their liquor, or juice, drains into the soup pot.

The recipe can be divided or multiplied at will, according to need and the willingness of the market to shuck the oysters and send them in their juice. Order ahead.

4 cups (1 l) Basic Chicken Stock (page 345)

5 pints shucked oysters, drained, liquid reserved

2 medium shallots, finely chopped

½ teaspoon hot red pepper sauce

About 1½ tablespoons kosher salt (exact amount depends on the saltiness of the oysters)

Freshly ground black pepper, to taste

1 medium bunch flat-leaf parsley, leaves only, coarsely chopped

2 medium bunches scallions, green part only, thinly sliced across

3 tablespoons fresh lemon juice

IN A MEDIUM STOCKPOT, bring the stock, oyster liquid, and shallots to a boil. Lower the heat and simmer for 20 minutes. Stir in the hot red pepper sauce, salt, and pepper. Simmer for 5 minutes. Stir in the parsley , the scallion greens, and lemon juice, followed immediately by the oysters. Return to a boil for 1 minute. Serve immediately.

MAKES 12 CUPS (3 L); 10 FIRST-COURSE SERVINGS

Richard

NICOLE MARRIED RICHARD FOOTE, whose elegant and lovely mother, Jerry, made goose every year for Christmas. I love Richard, so I roast goose for him. I usually roast an extra one so he can have leftovers to take home. I keep the carcasses and make stock. If there is a little meat left over for me, I use it in the soup; otherwise, I use the goose confit I have made much earlier, or I put in good duck confit that I can buy from D'Artagnan (280 Wilson Avenue, Newark, New Jersey, 07105; telephone: 1-800-DARTAGN or 973-344-0565; ext. 0).

cabbage and goose
CONFIT SOUP

THIS SOUP using winter vegetables is very good on the first day, but better on the second. If you have enough stock and ingredients, double the recipe. Any extras will freeze well.

4 cups (1 l) Goose Stock (page 353)

¾ pound (360 g) Jerusalem artichokes, peeled and cut into ¾-inch (1-cm) dice

1 pound (450 g) white cabbage, cored, tough outside leaves removed, and cut in ½-inch (1-cm) squares

7 sage leaves, cut across into narrow strips

1 teaspoon kosher salt

3 pieces Quick Goose Confit (page 404) or purchased confit, meat removed from the bones and torn into ½-inch (1-cm) pieces (1½ cups, 270 g), or leftover cooked goose

Freshly ground black pepper, to taste

IN A MEDIUM SAUCEPAN, bring the stock to a boil. Add the Jerusalem artichokes. Return to a boil. Lower the heat and simmer for 5 minutes. Stir in the cabbage, sage, and salt. Return to a boil and cook for 5 minutes. Stir in the goose confit or goose and pepper. Heat through.

MAKES 6 CUPS (1.5 L); 4 GENEROUS FIRST-COURSE SERVINGS

Ernie

MY HUSBAND, ERNIE, COMES to his love of duck by way of his father, Adolph Kafka, who was born in Vienna of Czech parents and used to take the family out to a sokol, a sort of part patriotic group, part athletic organization. When I knew it, there were pictures of the Czech heroes Masaryk and Beneš on the walls, an implicit resistance originally to the Germans and then to the Soviets. These photographs hung in an otherwise stark dining room that served wonderful food, the crispest duck, large dumplings that were sliced and served with duck-broth gravy to moisten them, red cabbage, potato pancakes, and spaetzle. We always ended the meal with palacinky, thin crêpes spread with apricot preserves, melted chocolate, or hazelnut purée, rolled, and dusted with powdered sugar.

For years I tried to duplicate that duck. I think my recipe in *Roasting* does the job. It also produces lots of good stock that gets stronger each time ducks are cooked.

I do give a duck stock for those who don't cook duck my way.

I'm not sure my duck meets my husband's memories. I do know he thinks this is the best soup he has ever eaten.

winter duck soup

THIS IS A MEAL in a bowl. If there are guests who will not be happy cutting up their duck in the bowl, remove the pieces when the soup is cooked, skin them and cut the meat from the bone, and return to the soup.

One 5-pound (2.25-kg) duck, cut into 14 pieces (see page 122; back, neck, and wing tips reserved for stock)

1 medium yellow onion, cut into ¼-inch (.5-cm) dice

3 medium cloves garlic, smashed, peeled, and very finely chopped

8 cups (2 l) Duck Stock (page 353), Basic Chicken Stock (page 345), or commercial chicken broth

1 bay leaf

1 large carrot, peeled and cut into ½-inch (l-cm) dice

½ small celery root, trimmed, peeled, and cut into ½-inch (1-cm) cubes

1 small turnip, peeled and cut into ½-inch (1-cm) cubes

¾ pound (360 g) mashing potatoes, peeled and cut into ½-inch (1-cm) dice

1 medium parsnip, peeled and cut into ½-inch (1-cm) dice

1 medium bunch parsley, leaves only, coarsely chopped

1½ tablespoons kosher salt, or less if using commercial broth

Freshly ground black pepper, to taste

IN A LARGE FRYING PAN, starting with the skin-side down, cook the duck pieces over high heat until they are golden in color and have lost their raw look, 7 to 10 minutes per side. Remove from the pan and place in a colander to drain.

Spoon 2 tablespoons of the fat from the pan into a large tall stockpot (reserve the remaining fat for another use). Stir in the onion. Cook for 3 minutes over medium heat. Stir in the garlic and cook for 2 minutes.

Add the stock and bay leaf and bring to a boil. Add the duck, carrot, celery root, and turnip. Return to a boil. Lower the heat and simmer for 15 minutes, skimming off excess fat as needed. The soup can be made ahead up to this point and refrigerated for up to 2 days.

If refrigerated, reheat. Add the potatoes, parsnip, parsley, and salt to the soup. Return to a boil, lower to a simmer, and cook for 15 minutes, or until the duck and vegetables are tender. Season to taste with pepper.

MAKES 12 CUPS (3 L); 6 TO 8 MAIN-COURSE SERVINGS

Barbara, young

I HAVE ALWAYS COOKED for friends and family to give pleasure and to draw people together. There came a time, well after I had been writing and getting printed, when I began to consider myself a professional. James Beard was an important force in my change of perspective, as he was for so many others. One day he told me that he was going out of town and he wanted me to teach a course in a week of assorted teachers, among whom were Madhur Jaffrey and Maida Heatter. The courses were to be taught twice, once in the evening to the high-powered types and once during the day to loyal followers of Jim's.

The evening course came first. I had never taught cooking before and I had a modified disaster. I had chosen to make a bouillabaisse. Jim had installed Corning electric cooktops. I had had the wit to try them to see if they got hot enough that my soup would boil vigorously enough to have all the ingredients come together. Unfortunately, I didn't realize that all of the burners had heat sensors. When the part of food that was at the bottom of the pot got very hot, the burner would not continue at full blast. I had not tried the burner with a really large pot of liquid.

The soup took forever. When it came time to put the white wine in, I found that the students had drunk it (I cannot blame them) and I had to beg Jim's invaluable assistant, Clay Triplett, to provide more wine. The rouille, which I made routinely in the food processor, broke the first time around. By the end of the evening, I couldn't tell if the soup was good or not. I don't think I impressed the class—well.

The next day, the regular students were warm and welcoming. I had figured out the soup problem. When I broke the sauce again, I redid it and explained to the students what I had done wrong. They thought that that was the best thing about the class. I learned to be honest with students, never to cover up. It cannot have been such a disaster, since I went on to teach with Jim for many years.

At this point in my career, I was still mainly making personal adaptations of existing recipes.

gazpacho

I HAVE THE HABIT of beginning my books with recipes that I not only like but that I know my readers like as well. This gazpacho first appeared in a cookbook that James Beard wrote with Carl Jerome for Cuisinart. Jim asked me for a recipe and, flattered, I came up with this. I still like it.

It is the paradigm of a raw soup originally made by farmworkers using what they had in the fields around them as well as a little olive oil. It is not meant to be a purée, but chunky, and for that the food processor, for those as lazy as I am, or a large knife for the vigorous is the best tool. The vegetables here are cut up to process evenly but not to purée. Recently in Barcelona I had a version that was not only puréed, but also sieved. (See pages 32–35 for other refinements in today's textures.) Be sure to make this far enough ahead so that it gets really cold. I often double the recipe.

It is only one of the many Spanish gazpachos, a few of which can be found on pages 32–35. This is probably the most familiar to today's eaters.

> 1 small Bermuda or other sweet onion, cut up
> 2 firm small cucumbers, peeled and cut up
> 2 small green bell peppers, cored, seeded, deribbed and cut up
> 6 medium-to-large ripe tomatoes, cored, peeled, and cut into eighths
> 5 large cloves garlic, smashed and peeled
> Approximately1 cup (250 ml) tomato juice
> ½ cup (125 ml) olive oil
> ¾ teaspoon pure chili powder or 1 small piece fresh chili pepper
> 1 tablespoon kosher salt, or to taste

IN A FOOD PROCESSOR, finely chop the onion, stopping occasionally to scrape down the sides. Scrape into a large metal bowl. Repeat the process with the cucumbers, then with the green peppers, adding each to the onions in the bowl. Process 5 of the tomatoes until finely chopped, but not puréed. Add to the other chopped vegetables.

Process the remaining tomato with the garlic, 1 cup tomato juice, the oil, and chili powder until a smooth liquid has formed. Combine with the chopped vegetables, cover, and refrigerate until chilled.

Before serving, season to taste with salt. If the soup is too thick, more tomato juice or a combination of tomato juice and beef broth may be added.

MAKES ABOUT 6 CUPS (1.5 L); 4 FIRST-COURSE SERVINGS

Grown up

IT WAS MANY YEARS and classes later before I would write a book. I felt that I had nothing original to add to the vast accumulation of the world's cookbooks. I probably wouldn't even have done it then if my upstairs neighbor hadn't been Irena Chalmers, who, at that time, was publishing a series of short, elegant cookbooks. She asked me to write one that would also concentrate on the wines of California. At that time, I knew something about these wines, since I had been doing wine lists for restaurants.

When it came time to do the recipes, I unconsciously turned away from traditional American foods and instead gave my own recipes using American ingredients. I didn't realize then that I was at the beginning of an exciting moment in American cookery. That book turned out to be *American Food and California Wine.* Buckwheat pasta with the newly available golden caviar and a duck with rhubarb were two recipes that I thought were original and of which I was proud.

Today, my food is a combination of my take on the world's favorites and those that I think are actual inventions, such as the veal soup that follows.

veal soup
WITH FENNEL

THIS MAY BE MY most original soup. It's one of my favorites, and it makes an unusual, but good, dinner. This soup takes advantage of an inexpensive cut of veal and doesn't require all that much of it; but it is much better with beef stock.

> 5 tablespoons (75 g) unsalted butter
>
> 2½ pounds (1.1 kg) boneless veal shoulder, cut into 1-inch (2.5-cm) cubes
>
> ¼ cup (25 g) all-purpose flour
>
> 12 small shallots, peeled
>
> 1 teaspoon ground coriander
>
> 2 medium tomatoes, cut into chunks
>
> 5 cups (1.25 l) Beef Stock (page 165) or, in England, imported beef or meat stock; or Basic Chicken Stock (page 345) or commercial chicken broth plus ⅔ cup (180 ml) Glace de Viande (page 355)
>
> 2 bulbs fennel, trimmed, cored, and cut into 1-inch (2.5-cm) chunks
>
> ¼ cup (65 ml) fresh lemon juice
>
> 1 tablespoon kosher salt, or less if using commercial broth
>
> Freshly ground black pepper, to taste
>
> 1 pound (450 g) medium egg noodles, cooked just until tender (see page 394)

IN A MEDIUM STOCKPOT, melt 2 tablespoons butter over medium-high heat. Toss the meat with the flour. Add one third of the veal and brown, about 5 minutes per side. Set aside in a bowl. Melt 1 more tablespoon of butter, add another one third of the veal, and brown on all sides. Transfer to the bowl, repeat with 1 more tablespoon butter and the remaining veal.

Add the remaining butter, the shallots, and coriander. Toss to coat the shallots with butter. Lower the heat to medium and cook for 5 to 7 minutes, shaking the pan frequently, until the shallots are beginning to brown.

Stir in the meat, tomatoes, stock, and, if using, the meat glaze. Bring to a boil, scraping up the browned bits from the bottom of the pan. Skim any foam that rises to the surface. Lower the heat and simmer for 30 minutes.

Stir in the fennel. Return to a boil. Lower the heat and simmer for 30 minutes. Season with the lemon juice, salt, and pepper.

Pass the noodles on the side, or stir into the soup just before serving. When ladling the soup, make sure to get the heavy stuff, as it has a tendency to sink to the bottom.

MAKES 12 CUPS (3 L); 6 MAIN-COURSE SERVINGS

Vegetable
soups

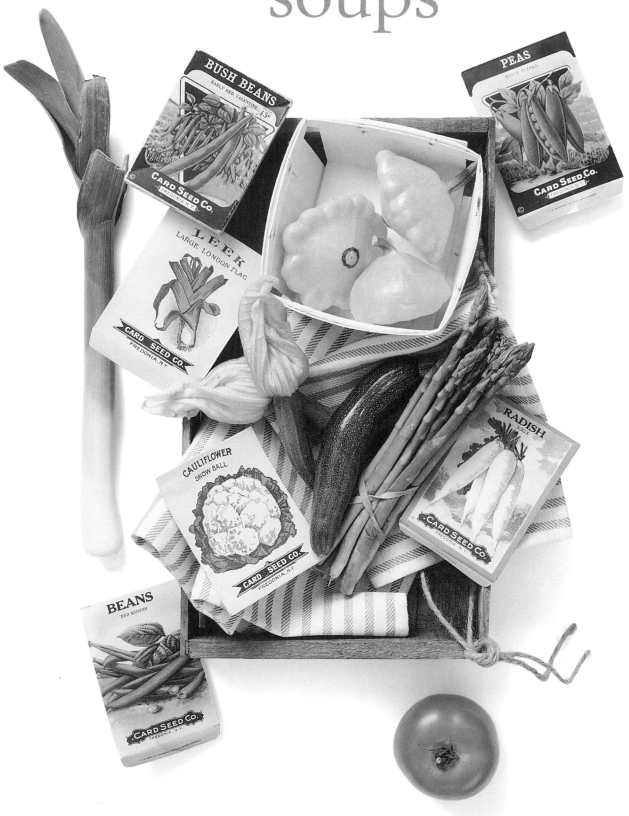

A WALK TO THE GARDEN for herbs or the makings of a salad, a hasty can appealing roadside stand, a backbreaking—there is always too much that I want—trip to a farmer's market, a foray into a Chinese or Indian market, or even a shopping cart expedition around my local supermarket frequently results in a soup. Vegetable soups, icy, steaming, or pleasantly room temperature, may be elegant but are most often direct and peasanty and reflect the seasons' generosity. A soup as basic as a minestrone is a theme whose variations are regional—Genoa, Tuscany, and Milan—and seasonal. They are eaten hot, room temperature, and cold.

Some vegetable soups are vegetarian (see Index), some are truly vegan, without even a hint of butter or cream, and others are lavished with butter, olive oil, eggs, cream, or stock. Others can be made vegetarian by substituting Garlic Broth (page 86) for the usual stock or using vegetable stock (pages 380–383).

There are big soups, whole meals, teeming with vegetables, like Vegetarian Borscht (page 6) or Vegetable Gumbo (page 118), and elegant light first courses like Jellied Borscht with Caviar (page 371). This is not all, for there is a whole chapter full of bean and legume soups that begins on page 291.

No matter how elegant, vegetable soups retain their relationship with the land, owing much of their success to the gardener, even if a commercial one. Seed catalogues provide inspiration early in the year and garden visits later on. There are many kinds of vegetable gardens I would like to have; but the short-summer, cold-winter Vermont year, with the soil's major crop being stones, limits what can be grown.

The fine writer on food and culture Paul Levy's pleasantly disarrayed English kitchen garden erupts in spring. It is set inside sturdy brick walls tall enough to protect the ripening fruit and vegetables from Oxford's chilly late-summer days, invites walks on York pavers next to the espaliered apple and pear trees, thick and gnarled with generations of pruning. Scrambling up the same walls are roses that grow bigger than my cold Vermont winters will allow, and I see unfamiliar vegetables: sea kale, purple-tipped sprouting broccoli, and broad beans, favas, that have wintered over. There is a huge asparagus bed edibly producing a full month before mine.

In summer, orderly as the great château *parterres*, formal in geometries of bedded-out flowers, are the French *potagers* (kitchen gardens), with neat blocks of pale yellow-green, frilly, flat rounds of chicory and tidy rows of carrot fronds waving flirtatiously above dark soil so finely worked it looks sifted.

Each provides vegetables for immediate use in soups and others to put away in dark cellars for winter cooking. The types of potato may vary. I may not even try as Paul does to sprout and blanch the roots of the chicories such as Treviso. My rafters, unlike Italian ones, will not have sprays of drying tomatoes, or ristras of peppers, like the Mexicans. We will all have bunches of herbs drying, tomatoes frozen or packed in jars, and cabbages and onions. Gardens are good for us and to us.

In addition to the vegetable soups in this chapter, a large group of those made with dried vegetables turn up in "Oats, Peas, Beans, and Barley Grow . . . ," starting on page 291. There are still more, the aspics and gelled soups, on pages 367–379.

See pages 447–451 for cooking times of vegetables. Also there are the weights implied by a small, medium, or large vegetable.

World of vegetables, cold

"Soups" usually mean to me cozy soups, comforting soups, as the steamy, robustly flavored soups of winter; but on a hot summer's day when vegetables and fruits are ripe,
nothing is more welcome than an icy soup. When I am eating out of doors and the day
threatens to heat the soup, I sometimes put an ice cube in the center of each dish. Even
in an air-conditioned world, the memory of the heat and its simmering edges impinges
on my day and cold soup is the perfect restorative. It is also salvation for the party giver
in a desert climate or an overheated apartment. Cold soups can be portioned and
served before my guests sit down, which makes life a lot easier.

Some cold soups are silky, creamy, and elegant; others, the clear gelled essences
(pages 367–373), slip down like throat balm; while my favorites are robust and chunky,
using the best produce of the season. Some are wildly easy, needing no cooking at all.
For really chilly serving, a little forethought may be needed to allow time in the refrigerator. Use a metal bowl when combining the ingredients for a cold soup—it will chill
more quickly.

It is a good idea to remember that most flavors and seasonings will be less
intense after chilling. Only lemon and vinegar seem to increase in energy. It is a good
idea to up spicy seasonings slightly when soups are to be chilled and to go easy on the
acid and salt. These last can always be increased just before serving.

Many of the soups in other parts of the book can also be served cold, such as
Radish Soup (page 65), Summer Mushroom Soup (page 73), Carrot and Leek Soup
(page 81), Potato and Leek Soup (Vichyssoise, page 94), Curry Tomato Soup (page 72),
and Green Soup (page 75). Look in the Index for a full listing.

soups without a stove

There are cold soups as spontaneous in the making as a salad and often using the same ingredients, down to the olive oil and lemon or vinegar. The simple Gazpacho (page 25) is perhaps the best known.

They are often the easiest, quickest, and pleasantest soups to make on a steaming summer's day, uncooked, generally country in origin, and strongly seasonal, using the moment's bounty, crushed or chopped and seasoned without a hint of a hot fire. Tomatoes are frequent (see page 68 for information).

Liquid may be added or may come from the chopped or puréed vegetables. The soups used to require time with a knife or a mortar and pestle. Today they are easier, thanks to food processors, food mills, and blenders (liquidizers). Usually they benefit from sitting time in the refrigerator after preparation. The flavors come together as the soup chills.

green gazpacho
WITH CITRUS AND YELLOW SQUASH

THERE ARE SO MANY gazpachos in Spain I thought there could be no objection if I added a slightly freaky one of my own. I love the colors, the rich aroma of citrus, garlic, and coriander; the taste has a rich balance too. If chunks of orange and lemon seem too odd, simply omit them. This soup is spicy. Seed the jalapeños if a milder soup is desired.

1 medium onion, quartered

1 cup (250 ml) Spanish olive oil

3 medium garlic cloves, smashed and peeled

2 small jalapeño peppers, cut into ¼-inch (.5-cm) slices

4 teaspoons kosher salt, or to taste

3 slices soft white bread, crusts removed, torn into pieces

2 medium green bell peppers, cored, seeded, deribbed, and cut into 1-inch (2.5-cm) squares

2 medium cucumbers, peeled and cut up

½ cup (30 g) packed parsley leaves

½ cup (30 g) packed cilantro leaves, or ¼ cup if not using citrus

1 medium yellow squash, trimmed and cut up, optional

2 lemons, scrubbed, optional

1 navel orange, scrubbed, optional

Kosher salt, to taste

IN A FOOD PROCESSOR, pulse the onion, olive oil, garlic, jalapeños, and salt until the vegetables are finely chopped. Remove to a bowl large enough to hold all of the vegetables. Pulse the bread and green peppers in the food processor until finely chopped, stopping occasionally to scrape down the sides of the bowl. Add to the onion mixture. Repeat the process with the cucumber, parsley, and cilantro. Add this mixture to the other vegetables.

If using the squash, in the food processor, pulse until coarsely chopped. If using the citrus, cut 1 (seeded) lemon and the orange into quarters; reserve one quarter of the orange for another use. In the food processor, finely mince the lemon and orange, stopping frequently to scrape down the sides of the bowl. Add to the vegetables.

Squeeze the juice of the remaining lemon into the soup and stir to combine. Add water to adjust the consistency of the soup to the desired thickness. Season with salt to taste. Refrigerate until ready to serve.

After refrigerating, the soup may need to be thinned with more water, since oil thickens as it gets cold.

MAKES ABOUT 5 CUPS (1.25 L) WITHOUT CITRUS AND SQUASH,
6 CUPS (1.5 L) WITH; 4 FIRST-COURSE SERVINGS

cucumber gazpacho

THIS IS A delightfully aromatic soup with the cucumber and mint—very fresh. Purée-ing the cucumbers provides the liquid base, a nice little trick.

> 5 medium Kirby cucumbers, peeled and seeded
>
> 1 medium Vidalia onion, cut into 2-inch (5-cm) chunks
>
> 2 large red bell peppers, cored, seeded, deribbed, and cut into
> 2-inch (5-cm) squares
>
> 1 medium jalapeño pepper, seeded and deribbed
>
> 4 medium cloves garlic, smashed and peeled
>
> 6 slices firm white bread, crusts removed
>
> 2 medium bunches mint, leaves only, 8 small sprigs
> reserved for serving
>
> ¾ cup (180 ml) olive oil
>
> 3 tablespoons fresh lemon juice
>
> 2 tablespoons kosher salt
>
> Croutons (page 429), for serving

IN A FOOD PROCESSOR, purée the cucumbers until very liquid, almost like water. Remove to a large bowl. In the food processor, pulse the onion until coarsely chopped. Add to the cucumbers. Repeat with the red peppers. Add to the cucumbers and onions.

Process the jalapeño, garlic, bread, and ¾ cup (20 g) mint leaves, while slowly pour-ing the oil through the feed tube, until a paste is formed. Stir into the vegetables. Stir in the lemon juice, salt, and 2 cups (500 ml) water. Refrigerate for 2 hours, or until cold. The soup can be made up to 1 day ahead.

Serve the soup chilled, with two croutons and a sprig, or a few leaves, of mint on top of each serving.

MAKES 8 CUPS (2 L); 8 FIRST-COURSE SERVINGS

grape gazpacho

THIS IS A VERSION of a traditional gazpacho. I am cheating the tiniest bit, as the almonds need to be cooked briefly; however, I have simplified the making. By putting the grapes through a food mill, one gets rid of the skin and seeds and obtains a tasty liquid. If melon is stirred into the soup, it is pretty and less difficult than peeling grapes for the top.

⅔ cup (135 g) whole blanched almonds

1 pound (450 g) stemmed seedless green grapes

2 ounces (60 g) crustless French or Italian bread, torn into small pieces

2 to 3 large cloves garlic, smashed and peeled

⅓ cup (80 ml) olive oil

2⅔ (630 ml) cups ice water

3 tablespoons white wine vinegar

4 teaspoons kosher salt

Freshly ground black pepper, to taste

for serving

4 to 5 peeled seedless green grapes; or 1½ ounces (45 g) peeled and seeded honeydew melon, cut into ½ × ¼-inch (1 × 0.5-cm) pieces

IN A SMALL SAUCEPAN, cover the almonds with water. Bring to a boil. Lower the heat and simmer until the almonds plump slightly and are somewhat softened. Drain and set aside.

Pass the grapes through a food mill fitted with the medium disc.

Place the bread in a small bowl. Pour enough of the grape juice over the bread just to cover. Press the bread into the juice so that it absorbs the liquid.

In a blender, purée the almonds, bread, and garlic. With the machine running, slowly pour in 1 cup (250 ml) of the grape juice. Process, scraping down the sides of the jar from time to time, until the mixture is smooth. With the machine running, slowly pour in the remaining grape juice and the olive oil. Scrape the mixture into a large metal bowl. Stir in the ice water, vinegar, salt, and pepper. Refrigerate until cold.

Pour into bowls and top each serving with a grape or some melon.

MAKES 5 CUPS (1.25 LITER); 4 TO 5 FIRST-COURSE SERVINGS

simple celery soup

A SOUP THAT IS in no way a gazpacho, but it is light and refreshing. The three versions of celery—stalks, leaves, and seeds—combine to give an amazing amount of flavor.

2 medium bunches celery, trimmed, leaves reserved, peeled, and cut across into ½-inch (1-cm) lengths

2 cups (500 ml) buttermilk

6 medium scallions, trimmed and cut across into 1-inch (2.5-cm) lengths

2 teaspoons kosher salt

Freshly ground black pepper, to taste

1 cup (250 ml) ice water

Scant ¼ teaspoon celery seed

IN A BLENDER, purée half of the celery leaves and stalks and 1 cup (250 ml) buttermilk. Add half of the scallions and salt and pepper and purée. Scrape the celery mixture into a large metal bowl. Repeat with the remaining vegetables, buttermilk, and seasoning. Stir in the ice water.

Refrigerate for 2 hours, or until cold.

Top each serving with a few celery seeds and a little pepper.

MAKES 6 CUPS (1.5 L); 6 FIRST-COURSE SERVINGS

spicy almond soup

IF MAKING AHEAD and refrigerating, save the final addition of orange juice until just before serving, as the flavor of orange juice gets stronger as it sits.

   1 large bunch cilantro, leaves only

   2 small jalapeño peppers, cut into ½-inch (1-cm) slices, seeds intact

   ⅔ cup (135 g) whole blanched almonds

   4 medium cloves garlic, smashed and peeled

   1 teaspoon ground cumin

   2 tablespoons olive oil

   1½ cups (375 ml) orange juice

   4 slices firm white bread, crusts removed, torn into large pieces

   ½ cup (125 ml) fresh lemon juice

   1 cup (250 ml) ice water

   2 teaspoons kosher salt

IN A FOOD PROCESSOR, finely chop 1 cup (250 ml) cilantro leaves and the jalapeños. Set aside.

In a blender, purée the almonds, garlic, cumin, olive oil, and ½ cup (125 ml) orange juice, stopping several times to scrape down the sides of the jar. Scrape half of the purée into a small bowl. Add half of the bread, 2 tablespoons of the remaining orange juice, ¼ cup (65 ml) lemon juice, and ½ cup (125 ml) ice water to the purée in the blender. Blend until very smooth, stopping once or twice to scrape down the sides of the jar. Scrape into a large metal bowl. Repeat with 2 tablespoons orange juice, the remaining purée, bread, lemon juice, and water.

Stir in the reserved cilantro mixture, the remaining orange juice, and the salt. Refrigerate for 2 hours, or until cold.

If the soup is too thick, thin it a bit with water or orange juice. Pour into bowls and top with the remaining cilantro leaves.

MAKES 4 CUPS (1 L); 4 FIRST-COURSE SERVINGS

southwestern pea soup

THIS IS A PRETTY SOUP, as colorful as the Italian flag, but very American in flavor.

Frozen peas are fine in it. If fresh peas are cooked, it is only a matter of minutes.

6 pounds (2.7 kg) peas in the pod, shelled (5½ cups), or three 10-ounce
    (300 g) packages frozen peas, defrosted in a sieve under
    warm running water and drained (5 cups)

2 cups (480 g) plain yogurt

½ cup (125 ml) olive oil

½ cup (125 ml) fresh lime juice

4 medium cloves garlic, smashed and peeled

1 tablespoon chili powder

2 teaspoons minced jalapeño pepper

2 cups (500 ml) ice water

2 tablespoons kosher salt

for serving

2 plum tomatoes, chopped fine

½ medium red bell pepper, cored, seeded, deribbed, and chopped fine

3 tablespoons cilantro or flat-leaf parsley leaves

IF USING FRESH PEAS, in a small saucepan, simmer the peas in lightly salted boiling water for 8 minutes. Drain and run under cold water to stop the cooking process.

In a food processor, purée all but ½ cup (220 g) of the fresh or frozen peas, stopping from time to time to scrape the sides of the bowl. Add the yogurt, olive oil, lime juice, garlic, chili powder, and jalapeño and purée. Scrape the mixture into a large metal bowl. Stir in the ice water and salt. Refrigerate until cold.

Combine the reserved peas, the plum tomatoes, red pepper, and cilantro. Pass for sprinkling over the top of each serving.

MAKES 7 CUPS (1.75L); 6 TO 7 FIRST-COURSE SERVINGS

cucumber soup

THINK OF THIS as the soup version of raita.

4 medium cucumbers, peeled, quartered, seeded, and cut across
  into 2-inch (5-cm) lengths

1 tablespoon kosher salt

2 large cloves garlic, smashed and peeled

⅓ cup (20 g) packed mint leaves

1⅓ cups (300 g) plain yogurt

2 cups (500 ml) ice water

Freshly ground black pepper, to taste

16 to 20 mint leaves, for serving

IN A FOOD PROCESSOR, chop the cucumbers medium-fine. Scrape into a medium metal bowl. Stir in 2 teaspoons salt. Let stand for 1 hour and 30 minutes.

Drain the cucumber in a medium-fine sieve, pressing lightly. Put the cucumber in a metal bowl.

In a food processor, chop the garlic and mint fine. Add to the cucumbers. Stir in the remaining ingredients. Refrigerate until cold.

Before serving, stir to combine. Top with the mint leaves.

MAKES 4 CUPS (1 L); 4 FIRST-COURSE SERVINGS

The generosity of cows

COWS GIVE US MILK and the wondrous assortment of foods developed from milk: heavy cream, sour cream, clotted cream, crème fraîche, yogurt, kefir, curds, cheeses—fresh and aged—buttermilk, and butter. Almost all of these find their way into one soup or another.

However, there are parts of the world where no one eats milk, probably for reasons of adaptive digestion. There are still others where the only way milk is eaten is as butter or in a cultured form such as yogurt. These are generally oil rather than butter cultures.

Other animals, notably goats and sheep, also give milk from which many of these products are made. The taste of dishes made with these foods will vary with the kind and breed of animal, the feed—grazed or served—as well as the climate. Where cultures are used, the sort of culture will change the flavor as well.

I remember a time when butter was almost always salted to preserve it and, if I wanted to use sour cream in a recipe, I had to call for commercially soured cream. As time has progressed, the foods of many parts of the world have traveled, expanding our larders and, in fact, being replicated in lands far from their origin.

Still, there are choices to make. Foods such as yogurt made with sheep's milk will almost always have a higher fat content than those made with cow's milk, especially as one can buy reduced-fat milk and cream and skim (0% fat) foods. This is no doubt an advantage for the diet and health; but as in the instance of buttermilk, it may result in a sharp diminution of flavor and body. Keeping buttermilk for several days after purchase will tend to produce more body. Foods rich in fat will separate when raised to the boil. When heating them is desirable, they are often combined with flour or used in a cultured—crème fraîche—form. Culturing milks thickens them and gives a silky texture. However, not all cultured milk foods are stable when heated, as in the case of yogurt, for example.

Fatty milk products can often be replaced by curd cheeses such as ricotta and skim (0%) milk cottage cheese without loss of body or risk of separation in the finished soup; but these products are best puréed first in a blender (liquidizer) to eliminate any risk of grittiness.

Finally, I always use unsalted, sweet butter. If salt butter replaces it, there will be more risk of spattering and sticking when sautéing, as the salt retains water; in addition, care must be taken when salting the finished soup. There is a great variation in the tastes of different butters; select according to taste and pocketbook.

sour cherry soup

MY FATHER WOULD have disapproved of a fruit soup to start the meal; but large numbers of people from what was Czechoslovakia, as well as Hungary and Scandinavia, make one version or another of this soup.

If you are in the same camp as my father, try doubling the sugar and replacing the sour cream with a finishing dollop of ice cream or sorbet and serving this as a dessert. Fruit soup desserts have become very trendy in France.

I prefer the soup made without cooking the cherries. The color is better. A food mill is used to get rid of the skins and pits, so a food processor is not a good substitute.

This is a rich soup; a small serving is fine.

1 pound (450 g) sour cherries

½ cup (75 g) superfine sugar

½ cup (125 ml) red wine vinegar

1 cup (250 ml) half-and-half

1 cup (240 g) sour cream

1 cup (250 ml) ice water

1 teaspoon kosher salt

for serving

Sour cream, optional

Ground cinnamon

RESERVE 6 WHOLE CHERRIES. Pass the remaining cherries through a food mill fitted with the medium disc into a metal bowl.

Whisk the remaining ingredients into the cherry juice. Refrigerate until cold.

Pour the soup into bowls and top each serving with a dollop of sour cream, if using, one of the reserved cherries, and a sprinkle of cinnamon.

MAKES 5 CUPS (1.25 L); 5 TO 6 FIRST-COURSE OR DESSERT SERVINGS

ginger peach soup

IF THE PEACHES are really ripe, the skin can be peeled off using a sharp paring knife. If they are slightly less ripe, cut a small cross in the bottom of each peach, blanch them in boiling water for 20 seconds, remove with a slotted spoon, and plunge into a bowl of ice water. The skins will slip right off.

1½ pounds (675 g) peaches

2 tablespoons plus 1 teaspoon fresh lemon juice

1½ cups (375 ml) buttermilk

⅔ cup (160 ml) apple juice

½ teaspoon peeled, grated ginger

1 teaspoon honey

Scant 1 teaspoon kosher salt

4 aromatic geranium leaves, 4 unsprayed rose petals, or 12 to 16 slices peeled, pitted peach, for serving

PEEL AND PIT the peaches, rubbing them with 2 tablespoons lemon juice as needed to prevent discoloration. In a food processor, purée the peaches.

Scrape the peach purée into a medium bowl. Stir in the remaining ingredients. Refrigerate until cold.

Pour into bowls and top each serving with a geranium leaf, rose petal, or peach slices.

MAKES 4 CUPS (1 L); 4 FIRST-COURSE OR DESSERT SERVINGS

cooked but cold

These soups actually require heat and therefore forethought, as they have to be chilled. They can be made ahead, sometimes, as in the Zucchini Gazpacho (page 46), where the base is made at the moment when there is a plentitude of an ingredient, far ahead.

Zucchini is only one of the vegetables that deluge the garden with their ripeness all at one time. Those who do not garden will find that the produce is cheapest and best at these seasons of the year. This is when the risk of glut and feelings of loathing for a lovely vegetable can come upon one. Then I make bases (pages 384–389) to use throughout the year, when they are a blessing. It is following the old model of putting up tomato purée (pages 384–386) for winter use.

moroccan tomato soup

THIS REQUIRES two minutes of cooking, but the rest is easy, providing that the tomatoes are good. It is a lot easier to use a food mill, which removes both skin and seeds. Lacking a food mill, peel the tomatoes. If they are really ripe, this can be done by running the back of a table knife firmly all over the surface of the tomato. It will then be easy to pull the skin away from the tomato. Cut the tomatoes in half and, with a small spoon, scoop out the seeds. Pulse in a food processor until puréed, being careful not to create tomato juice.

5 medium cloves garlic, smashed, peeled, and very finely chopped

2½ teaspoons paprika

1½ teaspoons ground cumin

Large pinch of cayenne pepper

4 teaspoons olive oil

2¼ pounds (1 kg) tomatoes, cored and cut into 1-inch (2.5-cm) cubes

¼ cup (15 g) packed cilantro leaves, coarsely chopped

1 tablespoon white wine vinegar

Juice of 1 medium lemon

5 teaspoons kosher salt

continued

Cilantro sprigs

4 medium ribs celery, peeled and coarsely chopped

3 tablespoons olive oil, optional

IN A SMALL SAUCEPAN, stir together the garlic, paprika, cumin, cayenne, and olive oil and cook over low heat, stirring constantly, for 2 minutes. Remove from the heat and set aside.

Pass the tomatoes through a food mill fitted with the large disc. Stir in the cooked spice mixture, 2 tablespoons water, and the remaining ingredients. Refrigerate until cold.

Pour into bowls and top with the cilantro sprigs, chopped celery, and, if desired, a drizzle of olive oil.

MAKES 4 CUPS (1 L); 4 FIRST-COURSE SERVINGS

red pepper soup

HERE IS ANOTHER soup quickly prepared with a cooked-ahead ingredient, Red Pepper Soup Base. The soup is beautiful and very light.

2½ cups (625 ml) Red Pepper Soup Base (page 389)

1 cup (250 ml) buttermilk

½ cup (125 ml) Vegetable Broth (page 380) or Roasted Vegetable Broth (page 380)

Kosher salt, to taste

Freshly ground black pepper, to taste

PLACE ALL THE INGREDIENTS in a large bowl; whisk to combine. Refrigerate until chilled.

MAKES 4 CUPS (1 L); 5 FIRST-COURSE SERVINGS

vichyssoise

OF RED PEPPER

THIS IS THE MOST glorious color. While it can be sprinkled with snipped chives like an ordinary vichyssoise, consider the violet of chive blossoms. Hold the bottom of a chive blossom in one hand and pull out the individual flowers to sprinkle on the coral-colored soup.

> 5 medium shallots, minced
>
> ¾ pound (360 g) mashing potatoes, peeled and cut into 1-inch (2.5-cm) cubes
>
> 1⅓ cups (325 ml) Basic Chicken Stock (page 345) or commercial chicken broth
>
> 2 cups (500 ml) Red Pepper Soup Base (page 389)
>
> 1½ teaspoons kosher salt, or less if using commercial broth
>
> ⅓ cup (80 ml) heavy cream

PLACE THE SHALLOTS, potatoes, and stock in a small saucepan. Cover. Bring to a boil. Lower the heat. Simmer, covered, for 22 minutes, or until the potatoes are tender when pierced with the tip of a knife.

Combine in a bowl with the red pepper base, salt, and cream. Purée in 2-cup (500 ml) batches in a blender until smooth.

Refrigerate for at least 2 hours, or overnight. If the soup is left in the refrigerator overnight, remove it about 30 minutes before serving, or it will be too thick.

MAKES 4½ CUPS (1.1 L); 4 FIRST-COURSE SERVINGS

zucchini gazpacho

SOMEWHERE BETWEEN a salad and a soup is this cool refreshing thing for the hottest summer days—or, using the zucchini base, to remind you in winter that summer was there.

2 tablespoons olive oil, if not using the zucchini base

3½ cups (800 ml) Zucchini Purée Soup Base (page 387), made with olive oil, or 3 pounds (1.4 kg) zucchini, trimmed, peeled, quartered lengthwise, and cut across into ½-inch (1-cm) lengths

1 medium red bell pepper, cored, seeded, deribbed and cut into ¼-inch (.5-cm) dice

2 small tomatoes, seeded and cut into ¼-inch (.5-cm) dice

1 medium rib celery, peeled and cut into ¼-inch (.5-cm) dice

½ cup (30 g) coarsely chopped basil

Freshly ground black pepper, to taste

1½ tablespoons kosher salt, or to taste

1 tablespoon fresh lemon juice

4 large basil leaves, cut across into narrow strips, for serving

IF NOT USING the zucchini base, in a medium stockpot, heat the oil. Add the zucchini and toss to coat in the oil. Lower the heat, cover, and cook, stirring occasionally, especially at the beginning, for 45 minutes, or until the zucchini is very soft. Remove from the heat. Cool slightly and pass through the fine disc of a food mill.

Combine all the ingredients except the lemon juice and thinly sliced basil leaves in a bowl. Refrigerate overnight.

Add the lemon juice to the gazpacho and pour into bowls. Top each bowl with a little of the sliced basil leaves.

MAKES 5 CUPS (1.25 L); 4 FIRST-COURSE SERVINGS

curried tomato soup

A ZINGY SOUP softened with yogurt, this makes a good first course.

3 tablespoons vegetable oil

2 cloves garlic, smashed, peeled, and very finely chopped

2 tablespoons curry powder

1 teaspoon dry mustard

3 pounds (1.4 kg) tomatoes, cored and coarsely chopped

2 cups (500 ml) cold Basic Chicken Stock (page 345) or commercial chicken broth

1½ cups (360 g) nonfat yogurt

¼ cup (7 g) mint leaves, cut across into narrow strips

2 teaspoons fresh lemon juice

Kosher salt, to taste

6 mint sprigs, for serving

IN A MEDIUM SAUCEPAN, heat the oil over medium heat. Add the garlic and cook, stirring, until soft, about 5 minutes. Add the curry and mustard and cook, stirring, for 3 minutes.

Stir in the tomatoes and 1 cup (250 ml) stock. Bring to a boil. Lower the heat and simmer for 15 minutes, stirring occasionally. In a food processor, purée the soup, working in batches if necessary, or pass through a food mill fitted with the medium disc. Refrigerate for 2 hours, or overnight. The soup will keep, refrigerated, for 2 to 3 days.

Stir in the remaining stock, the yogurt, mint, lemon juice, and salt. Serve chilled, topping each portion with a sprig of mint.

MAKES ABOUT 6 CUPS (1.5 L); 6 GENEROUS FIRST-COURSE SERVINGS

celery-tomato soup

A LOVELY SOUP that is particularly easy if the bases are on hand.

    1 tablespoon olive oil

    1 medium onion, coarsely chopped

    **2 medium ribs celery, trimmed, leaves reserved, peeled,
and cut into ¼-inch (.5-cm) dice, or ½ cup (125 ml)
Celery Soup Base (page 388)**

    **1½ pounds (675 g) plum tomatoes, halved crosswise, seeds removed,
and cut into 1-inch (2.5-cm) pieces; or 2½ cups (625 ml)
Plum Tomato Purée (page 386)**

    **1½ cups (375 ml) Basic Chicken Stock (page 345) or commercial
chicken broth**

    1 bay leaf

    1 teaspoon celery seed

    **3 tablespoons coarsely chopped celery leaves (from reserved leaves,
plus extra if needed)**

    2 teaspoons salt, or less if using commercial broth

    1 tablespoon fresh lemon juice

    ½ cup (125 ml) heavy cream

IN A MEDIUM SAUCEPAN, heat the oil over medium heat. Stir in the onion and, if using, the diced celery. Cook, stirring, until the vegetables are beginning to soften, about 6 minutes. If using celery base, stir it in now.

If starting with fresh tomatoes, stir them in to the onion mixture with the stock. Bring to a boil. Lower the heat and simmer for 15 minutes, or until the tomatoes are very soft. Pass through the medium disc of a food mill, or purée in 2-cup (500-ml) batches in a blender. Return to the pan.

If using the tomato base, stir it into the onion mixture along with the stock and bring to a boil.

Stir in the bay leaf, celery seed, celery leaves, salt, lemon juice, and cream. Heat through to blend the flavors. Refrigerate for at least 2 hours, or overnight.

MAKES 4 CUPS (1 L); 4 FIRST-COURSE SERVINGS

watercress soup

THIS BEAUTIFUL GREEN SOUP with a peppery punch is elegant and should be silky smooth—no food processor, please. This is a good dinner party starter.

4 large bunches watercress, leaves and just enough of the stems
    to measure 2 quarts (360 g)

4 cups (1.5 l) Basic Chicken Stock (page 345) or commercial
    chicken broth

1 tablespoon kosher salt, or less if using commercial broth

4 eggs, lightly beaten

1 teaspoon freshly ground black pepper

1½ cups (375 ml) heavy cream

IN A MEDIUM SAUCEPAN, bring the watercress, stock, and salt to a boil. Lower the heat and simmer, stirring occasionally with a wooden spoon, for 13 to 15 minutes, or until the stems are soft.

In a blender, working in batches of no larger than 2 cups (500 ml), purée the cooked watercress and liquid; or pass through a food mill fitted with the fine disc.

Return to the pan. Gradually whisk 2 cups (500 ml) of the purée into the eggs, then whisk the egg mixture into the remaining purée. Cook over low heat, stirring constantly, especially around the edges of the pot, until thickened, 2 to 3 minutes. Season with the pepper. The cream may be added now or when the soup is chilled. Refrigerate for 2 hours, or until cold.

Before serving, remove the soup from the refrigerator and let sit at room temperature for 10 minutes. Taste for salt.

MAKES 6 CUPS (1.5 L); 6 FIRST-COURSE SERVINGS

pea soup
WITH CURRY

THE GENTLE GREEN color of this soup masks a surprisingly rich flavor. For a somewhat lighter soup, substitute Basic Chicken Stock (page 345) for the oxtail or beef.

1 medium onion, cut into ½-inch (1-cm) cubes

1 tablespoon vegetable oil

1½ tablespoons curry powder

4½ pounds (2 kg) peas in the pod, shelled (4 cups), or two 10-ounce (300 g) packages frozen peas, defrosted in a sieve under warm running water and drained (3⅓ cups)

3 cups (750 ml) Oxtail Stock (page 356), Beef Stock (page 165), or, in England, imported beef or meat stock

1½ teaspoons kosher salt, or more to taste

Freshly ground black pepper, to taste

2 teaspoons fresh lime juice

½ cup (120 g) low-fat yogurt

IN A SMALL SAUCEPAN, cook the onion in the oil over medium heat until wilted. Add the curry powder and cook, stirring constantly to avoid scorching, for 1 minute. Stir in the peas and stock, cover, and bring to a boil. Lower the heat and simmer until the peas are soft, about 8 to 10 minutes for fresh, 4 for frozen.

Pass through the fine disc of a food mill or a fine sieve to remove the pea skins. Season with salt and pepper. Refrigerate for 2 hours, or overnight.

Stir the lime juice and yogurt into the soup. Adjust the seasoning, if necessary.

MAKES ABOUT 5 CUPS (1.25 L); 4 FIRST-COURSE SERVINGS

spinach soup

SCHI

THERE ARE MANY different Russian soups called schi. This pleasantly tart (particularly if sorrel is available), cold version has an added snap from diced dill pickles. If that is too freaky for your taste, just substitute cucumbers for crunch. The beer stands in for kvass (page 177).

2 pounds (900 g) spinach, stemmed and washed well but not dried

¼ cup (15 g) loosely packed dill fronds

1 medium scallion, white and light green parts only, thinly sliced across

½ pound (225 g) good-quality dill pickles, cut into ¼-inch (.5-cm) dice (or substitute peeled, seeded cucumbers)

One 12-ounce (375-ml) bottle beer

¼ teaspoon peeled, freshly grated horseradish

Kosher salt, to taste

1 scant tablespoon (15 g) unsalted butter, if using sorrel

6 bunches sorrel, leaves only, cut across into narrow strips, optional

Use 1½ cups (360 g) sour cream, if using sorrel, or ½ cup (120 g) if not

Use 1½ cups (375 ml) heavy cream, if using sorrel, or ½ cup (120 g) plain yogurt, if not

1 tablespoon cider vinegar

IN A LARGE FRYING PAN, cook the spinach, covered, over medium heat for 10 minutes, stirring once or twice, just until wilted. Drain.

In a food processor, finely chop the spinach with the dill. Scrape the mixture into a metal bowl. Stir in the scallion, pickles, beer, 1½ cups (375 ml) water, the horseradish, and salt.

If using sorrel, in a large frying pan, melt the butter over medium heat. Add the sorrel and cook for 5 minutes, or until the color turns. Remove from the heat. Stir the sorrel, 1½ cups sour cream, and 1½ cups heavy cream into spinach mixture. If not using sorrel, stir in ½ cup (120 g) yogurt instead of the heavy cream and ½ cup (120 g) sour cream. Refrigerate for 2 hours, or until cold.

Just before serving, stir in the vinegar. Season with additional salt, if necessary.

MAKES 8 CUPS (2 L) WITHOUT SORREL, 12 CUPS (3 L) WITH;
8 FIRST-COURSE SERVINGS WITHOUT SORREL, 12 WITH

fennel soup

THIS PALE SOUP has an intriguing sweetness from the ricotta behind the lightly anise flavor of the fennel. It can be served hot as well as cold.

4 cups (1 l) Basic Chicken Stock (page 345) or commercial chicken broth

5 medium bulbs fennel, trimmed (reserve tops for garnish), cored, and cut into 1-inch (2.5-cm) cubes

1 cup (225 g) part-skim ricotta, cottage cheese, or fromage blanc

2 tablespoons fresh lemon juice

1 tablespoon kosher salt, or less if using commercial broth

Freshly ground black pepper, to taste

IN A MEDIUM STOCKPOT, bring the stock to a boil. Add the fennel, cover, and return to a boil. Lower the heat and simmer, covered, for about 25 minutes, or until the fennel is soft. Pour into a sieve set over a bowl. Reserve the liquid and fennel separately.

In a food processor, purée the fennel, stopping once to scrape down the sides of the bowl. Add the ricotta and process until smooth. Add the lemon juice and 2 cups (500 ml) of the reserved liquid. Pulse to combine. Scrape into a large bowl and whisk in the remaining liquid. Season with salt and pepper.

To serve the soup hot, return to the saucepan and heat through. To serve chilled, refrigerate for 2 hours, or overnight.

Coarsely chop the reserved fennel tops and sprinkle over the top.

MAKES 9 CUPS (2.25 L); 8 FIRST-COURSE SERVINGS

string bean

SOUP PUREÉ

A REFRESHING SOUP that takes advantage of tender summer green beans. It may be necessary to thin the soup down with additional chicken stock and/or cream after refrigerating.

¼ cup (33 g) kosher salt, plus additional to taste

2¼ pounds (1.1 kg) string beans, tipped and tailed

3 cups (750 ml) Basic Chicken Stock (page 345) or commercial
    chicken broth, or more if desired

½ cup (125 ml) olive oil

2 tablespoons fresh lemon juice, or more to taste

1 cup (250 ml) heavy cream

1 small Kirby cucumber, thinly sliced crosswise, for serving

IN A LARGE nonaluminum pot, bring 6 quarts (6 l) water to a boil. Add the salt. Stir in the string beans. Return to a boil and cook until the beans are tender but still bright green, about 4 minutes. Drain the beans, then plunge them into a large bowl of ice-cold water. Drain.

Combine the stock, olive oil, and lemon juice in a large measuring cup. In a food processor, finely chop half of the string beans. With the motor running, pour in half of the stock mixture. Continue to process until puréed. Pass the string bean purée through a fine sieve, or a food mill fitted with the fine disc, into a large mixing bowl. Repeat with the remaining string beans and stock mixture. Whisk the heavy cream into the soup and season with salt. Refrigerate for 2 hours, or overnight.

The consistency of the soup may be adjusted, if necessary, with additional stock. Adjust the salt and lemon juice if necessary. Top with the cucumber slices.

MAKES 6 CUPS (1.5 L); 4 TO 6 FIRST-COURSE SERVINGS

chilled zucchini

IF USING THE zucchini purée soup base, this low-calorie soup is ridiculously easy.

> **4 cups (1 l) Basic Chicken Stock (page 345) or commercial chicken broth**
>
> **4 medium zucchini, trimmed and cut across into ⅓-inch (.75-cm) slices, or 2 cups (500 ml) Zucchini Purée Soup Base (page 387)**
>
> **1 medium bunch flat-leaf parsley, leaves only**
>
> **½ cup (120 g) low-fat cottage cheese**
>
> **Few drops of hot red pepper sauce**
>
> **Kosher salt, to taste**
>
> **Freshly ground black pepper, to taste**

IF USING FRESH ZUCCHINI, in a medium saucepan, bring the stock to a boil. Add the zucchini. Return to a boil. Lower the heat and simmer for 12 minutes, or until the zucchini is soft. Stir in the parsley just to wilt. Strain, reserving the liquid.

In a blender, working in batches of no larger than 2 cups (500 ml), purée the solids with the cottage cheese and a little of the liquid. Transfer to a metal bowl and stir in the remaining liquid.

If using the zucchini base, in a medium saucepan, combine the stock and the base and heat through. Stir in the parsley just to wilt. In a blender, purée the cottage cheese with ½ cup (125 ml) of the soup. Combine with the remaining soup.

Season the soup to taste with hot red pepper sauce, salt, and pepper. Refrigerate until ready to serve, at least 2 hours, or overnight.

MAKES 6 CUPS (1.5 L); 6 FIRST-COURSE SERVINGS

sorrel soup

THE VERY BEST sorrel soup is made with wild sorrel, which is smaller, tarter, and a lighter green than French sorrel but has the same shield-shaped leaves.

Sorrel is a pest in the flower garden, particularly in the cultivated soil around roses. When they were little, my children loved this soup so much that a promise to make it was bribe enough to get spring weeding done. Today, I plant French sorrel, which is a perennial. Every few weeks, I shake a little more seed onto the same plot of soil. As long as I cut it back ruthlessly and do not let it go to seed, I have sorrel through to frost.

When sorrel cooks, it loses its bright green color. Some cooks add some spinach for color. I have never found the color obnoxious. However, if an aluminum pot is used, a really revolting mess occurs from the interaction between the sorrel and the pan.

To add color, stir in a sorrel butter at the end. This is made by puréeing 1 cup (30 g) of sorrel leaves with 1½ tablespoons (25 g) of butter. Thank you, Patricia Wells.

This soup thickens in the refrigerator, especially if a high-quality homemade stock is used. If too thick, add cream or stock to thin.

I usually double this recipe, as leftovers stored in a glass jar in the refrigerator disappear as if by magic. In any case, the soup tastes better after a full 24 hours in the refrigerator.

3 tablespoons (45 g) unsalted butter

2 ounces (60 g) sorrel leaves (1 cup tightly packed), cut across into narrow strips

5 cups (1.25 l) Basic Chicken Stock (page 345) or commercial chicken broth

5 egg yolks

1½ cups (375 ml) heavy cream

Kosher salt, to taste

IN A MEDIUM SAUCEPAN, melt the butter over medium heat. Add the sorrel and cook for 2 minutes, or until it has wilted. Add the stock and bring to a boil. Lower the heat and simmer, uncovered, for 20 minutes.

Beat the egg yolks and cream together in a small bowl. Slowly ladle in some of the hot soup, whisking constantly, until you have added about one third of the soup and raised the temperature of the egg yolks. Now, while whisking the soup, slowly pour in the egg yolk mixture. Slowly bring to a boil, whisking constantly, to thicken. Season with salt.

Remove from the heat, and continue whisking as the soup cools. Refrigerate, covered, and whisk the soup occasionally until it is fully chilled to ensure proper consistency; adjust seasoning to taste.

MAKES 6 CUPS (1.5 L); 6 FIRST-COURSE SERVINGS

cold beet borscht

THIS MAY BE one of the world's most glamorous-looking soups. It turns a brilliant magenta as the cream is added to the cooked beets and beet liquid. I like to serve it in a large white bowl surrounded by smaller bowls containing the toppings. I ladle out the soup and invite the eaters to serve themselves with the toppings.

I frequently double or treble the recipe and keep it in the refrigerator. A large bowl of soup plus bread and a salad is an ideal summer lunch.

> 1 pound (450 g) beets, scrubbed well and all but 1 inch (2.5 cm) of stems removed
>
> 2 teaspoons distilled white vinegar, or to taste
>
> 4 teaspoons fresh lemon juice
>
> ¾ teaspoon citric acid powder (see page 371)
>
> ½ cup plus 1 tablespoon (115 g) sugar
>
> 1½ teaspoons kosher salt
>
> ½ cup (120 g) sour cream
>
> ⅔ cup (165 ml) heavy cream

ad-lib toppings

> Chopped onion • Chopped cucumber • Chopped dill • Lemon wedges • Sour cream • Heavy cream • Grated beets • Cold boiled very small firm potatoes • Chopped hard-boiled egg

IN A SMALL SAUCEPAN, bring the beets and 5 cups (1.25 l) water to a boil. Lower the heat and simmer until the beets are tender when pierced with the tip of a knife, about 45 minutes.

Drain the beets in a damp-cloth–lined sieve and reserve the cooking liquid. Run the beets under cold water to cool, then peel. In a food processor, grate the beets with the grating disc (this can also be done on a box grater).

Return half of the grated beets to the cooking liquid. Reserve the rest for topping or for another use. Season the soup with the vinegar, lemon juice, citric acid, sugar, and salt. Chill.

Before serving, whisk in the sour cream and heavy cream. Pass small bowls of the suggested accompaniments.

MAKES 7 CUPS (1.75 L); 6 FIRST-COURSE SERVINGS
(OR MORE, DEPENDING ON THE AMOUNT OF GARNISH USED)

World of vegetables, hot

These are the soups that sustain us in every time of the year, although the repertoire changes with the seasons. There are soups that open a meal and soups to live on. There are vegetarian soups, usually the product of farming thrift, and soups that have a backbone of chicken or meat stock.

Of course, many soups in other chapters have vegetables. There are seafood soups like the clam and kale soup and a plethora of grain, bean, and legume soups. Those included here are the ones where vegetables are the very fiber—double meaning intended—of their essence.

While many of the soups in this chapter are meant to be meals on their own (pages 111–119), there is still a place for hot soups that are meant to start a meal. Of course, I am such a soup eater that I will frequently have a greedy double portion of soup, a salad, a piece of cheese, perhaps some fruit, and a glass of wine and call that a very good meal. I even have friends who are willing to join me.

The soups in this section of the book are first-course soups and they are arranged by season.

When the first greens poke up in the spring and the reappearance of lovage (see Lovage and Potato Soup, page 97) reassures me about the herbs, I go into a frenzy of release from root vegetables and start making soups using the freshness of the season.

miso soup

WITH TOFU AND BROCCOLI DI RAPE

THIS IS A Japanese vegetarian soup, elegant and surprisingly robust.

> **4 cups (1 l) Konbu Dashi (page 383)**
>
> **2 tablespoons dark soybean miso**
>
> **3 ounces (1⅓ cups; 90 g) broccoli di rape, yellow and wilted leaves discarded, tops and leaves only, tops left whole, leaves cut across in ½-inch (1-cm) strips**
>
> **Two 2-ounce (60-g) pieces firm silken tofu, each piece cut across in half**
>
> **2 scant tablespoons hair-thin strips of lemon zest, for serving**

IN A SMALL SAUCEPAN, heat 3 cups (750 ml) dashi just to a simmer. In a small bowl, dissolve the miso in 1 to 2 tablespoons of the hot dashi and return to the pan.

Meanwhile, in a medium saucepan, bring the remaining dashi to a boil. Stir in the broccoli di rape. Bring to a simmer and cook until the rape turns bright green, about 2 minutes. Stir in the tofu and simmer for 1 minute. Turn the tofu pieces over and simmer for 1 minute.

Stir in the miso broth. Heat until little bubbles form around the sides.

Divide the vegetables and broth evenly among four small bowls. Top each bowl with a few pieces of the lemon zest.

MAKES SCANT 4 CUPS (500 ML); 4 FIRST-COURSE SERVINGS

miso soup

WITH DAIKON AND SPINACH

THIS SOUP IS very similar to the previous one, but lighter.

4 cups (1 l) Konbu Dashi (page 383)

One ⅔-pound (180 g) 2½-inch- (6.25-cm-) diameter piece daikon [mouli], peeled, quartered lengthwise, and sliced across into translucently thin slices

3 ounces (90 g) flat-leaf spinach leaves (3 cups), washed well

2 tablespoons dark soybean miso

¼ cup (7 g) very thinly sliced scallion greens, for serving

IN A MEDIUM SAUCEPAN, bring 1 cup (250 ml) dashi to a boil. Stir in the daikon, and return to a boil. Lower the heat and simmer, uncovered, for 14 minutes, or until tender. Stir in the spinach, turning the leaves over a few times to aid wilting. Simmer for 2 minutes.

Meanwhile, in a small saucepan, heat the remaining dashi just to a simmer. In a small bowl, dissolve the miso in 1 to 2 tablespoons of the dashi, and return to the pan. Stir the miso broth into the pot with the daikon and spinach.

Divide the vegetables and broth evenly among four small bowls. Top each serving with 1 tablespoon scallion greens.

MAKES 4 CUPS (1 L); 4 FIRST-COURSE SERVINGS

scallion soup

SCALLIONS OR GREEN ONIONS are up early sometimes, the product of fall planting. They are the makings of the most delicate of the *Allium* (onion) family soups.

> 3½ cups (875 ml) Vegetable Broth (page 380), Basic Chicken
>   Stock (page 345), or commercial chicken broth
>
> 4 medium bunches scallions, trimmed and cut across into 1-inch
>   (2.5-cm) lengths
>
> 4 teaspoons cornstarch
>
> Kosher salt, to taste
>
> ⅛ teaspoon freshly ground black pepper

IN A MEDIUM SAUCEPAN, bring 3 cups (750 ml) broth to a boil. Stir in the scallions. Return to a boil. Lower the heat and simmer, partially covered, for 10 minutes, or until the scallions are very soft.

In a blender, working in batches of no more than 2 cups (500 ml), purée the soup. Scrape back into the pot.

In a small bowl, dissolve the cornstarch in the remaining stock. Whisk the cornstarch mixture into the soup. Bring to a boil. Lower the heat and simmer for 2 minutes, or until the soup is slightly thickened. Season with the salt and pepper.

MAKES 4 CUPS (1 L); 4 FIRST-COURSE SERVINGS

quick pea soup

IF PEA SOUP BASE is not on hand in the freezer, fresh or frozen peas can be simmered and puréed with chicken stock to make the base. Serve with Cubed Croutons (page 430).

> 7 cups (1.75 l) Fresh Green Pea Soup Base (page 388), 6 pounds (2.7 kg) peas in the pod, shelled (5½ cups), or three 10-ounce (300-g) packages frozen baby peas, defrosted in a sieve under warm running water and drained (5 cups)
>
> 4½ cups (1.12 l) Basic Chicken Stock (page 345) or commercial chicken broth, if not using pea soup base
>
> ¾ cup (30 g) loosely packed dill sprigs; or ½ cup (15 g) loosely packed mint leaves plus 3 sprigs dill
>
> Kosher salt, to taste
>
> Freshly ground black pepper to taste

if using mint

> ½ teaspoon freshly grated nutmeg
>
> ½ cup (125 ml) heavy cream
>
> 1 cup (250 ml) milk

IF USING THE PEA SOUP BASE, in a medium saucepan, heat the base over medium heat. Or, to make a soup base, if using fresh peas, in a medium saucepan, bring the peas and stock to a boil. Lower the heat and simmer for 8 minutes. Strain, reserving the peas and liquid separately.

In a blender, working in batches no larger than 2 cups (500 ml) each, purée the cooked fresh or defrosted frozen peas with a little liquid. Scrape into a medium saucepan. Stir in the remaining stock.

If using only dill, stir it into the soup base, season with salt and pepper, and heat through; if necessary, add additional stock to achieve the desired consistency.

If using mint, in a blender, purée the mint, dill, salt, pepper, and nutmeg. With the machine running, slowly pour in 2 cups (500 ml) of the prepared soup base. Whisk back into the pan with the remaining soup base. Stir in the cream and milk, and additional stock if necessary to achieve the desired consistency. Bring to a boil. Lower the heat and simmer for 3 to 4 minutes. Serve immediately.

MAKES 7 CUPS (1.75 L) WITHOUT CREAM AND MILK, 8 CUPS (2 L) WITH; 6 TO 8 FIRST-COURSE SERVINGS

health soup

PRACTICALLY AN INSTANT SOUP, so there isn't really any point in making ahead, although for a party, it can be made a few hours in advance if desired.

8 sprigs parsley, leaves only

10 spinach leaves, well washed

½ cup (30 g) watercress sprigs

4 cups (1 l) Basic Chicken Stock (page 345), commercial chicken broth, or a vegetarian stock (pages 380–383)

4 cloves garlic, smashed and peeled

Kosher salt, to taste

Freshly ground black pepper, to taste

IN A FOOD PROCESSOR, chop the parsley, spinach, and watercress. Scrape into a small saucepan. Stir in the stock and garlic. Bring to a boil. Lower the heat and simmer for 10 minutes. Season with salt and pepper.

MAKES 4 CUPS (1 L); 4 FIRST-COURSE SERVINGS

asparagus soup
WITH CARAMELIZED LEEKS

ONE SPRING DAY, I was at Paul Levy's house outside of Oxford. He and his Aga were making a wonderful soup base from his wintered-over leeks and plentiful supply of asparagus. I promptly stole the notion and made this soup with it. The vegetarian Asparagus Stock base is best made ahead, as it takes quite a long time. I make this base after I have cooked a lot of asparagus for a feast. It can be used as the stock in many spring vegetable soups. Paul makes the stock in the lower oven of the Aga. It can be made in a low oven or a slow cooker. Use the method on page 346. A larger amount of base can even go overnight.

The finished soup cannot be made too far ahead because the asparagus tips and tender stems will shrivel.

2 pounds (900 g) asparagus

4 small leeks, cut in half lengthwise, washed well, green part cut into 2-inch
  (5-cm) lengths, white part cut into 2-inch (5-cm) lengths and
  then lengthwise into hair-thin strips

½ cup (90 g) long-grain white rice

1 tablespoon (15 g) unsalted butter

½ teaspoon very finely chopped fresh tarragon, or a pinch of dried

4 teaspoons kosher salt

Freshly ground black pepper, to taste

BREAK OFF THE woody part of the asparagus and cut into 2-inch (5-cm) lengths; reserve. Peel the remaining tender stalks; keep the peelings with the woody parts. They will be used for the base. Cut the peeled stalks into 1-inch (2.5-cm) lengths and reserve. Reserve the tips separately; the tender stalks and tips will be used for the soup.

To make the Asparagus Stock, in a medium saucepan, bring the woody parts of the asparagus and peelings, the leek greens, and 10 cups (2.5 l) water to a boil. Lower the heat and simmer for 2 hours and 30 minutes. Strain through a fine-mesh sieve, pressing down on the solids to extract as much liquid as possible. There should be about 5 cups (1.25 l).

Meanwhile, in a small saucepan, bring 1¼ cups (300 ml) lightly salted water to a boil. Stir in the rice and cover. Lower the heat and simmer for 13 minutes, or until the rice is almost done. Reserve.

For the soup, in a large frying pan, melt the butter over medium-high heat. Add the whites of the leeks and cook, stirring frequently, for 5 minutes, or until they are nicely browned. Add the peeled asparagus stalks and cook, stirring, for 4 minutes. Stir in the asparagus tips and cook for 1 minute. Scrape into a medium saucepan.

Pour a little of the asparagus stock into the frying pan and bring to a boil, scraping up the browned bits from the bottom of the pan. Pour this over the vegetables. Stir in the rest of the asparagus base.

Bring the soup to a boil. Add the cooked rice and the tarragon. Return to a boil. Lower the heat; simmer for 4 minutes. Season with the salt and pepper.

MAKES 7 CUPS (1.75 L); 6 FIRST-COURSE SERVINGS

light spring soup

WITH PEAS AND ASPARAGUS

NOTHING SAYS SPRING like early peas and asparagus or fiddlehead ferns. In this soup, they shine in all their freshness with little competition from the other ingredients. The colors are pretty too.

5 cups (1.25 l) Basic Chicken Stock (page 345), commercial chicken broth, or Garlic Broth (page 86)

⅓ cup (60 g) long-grain white rice

4 large shallots, finely chopped

2 pounds (900 g) peas in the pod, shelled (scant 2 cups)

1 tablespoon kosher salt, or less if using commercial broth

Freshly ground pepper, to taste

¼ pound (120 g) fiddlehead ferns, washed well; or 1 pound (450 g) medium asparagus, tips only (reserve stems for another use, such as Asparagus Stock, page 63)

IN A SMALL SAUCEPAN, bring 1 cup (250 ml) stock and the rice to a boil. Cover, lower the heat, and simmer for 13 minutes. Remove from the heat and set aside.

In a medium saucepan, bring the remaining stock, the shallots, and half of the peas to a boil. Lower the heat and simmer for 5 minutes. Drain, reserving the liquid.

In a blender, purée the cooked peas and shallots. Return to the saucepan and whisk in the reserved liquid. Season with the salt and pepper. The soup can made ahead up to this point and refrigerated for up to 2 days.

Return the soup to the stove. Bring to a boil. Stir in the uncooked peas and the fiddleheads, if using. Return to a boil, lower the heat, and simmer for 3 minutes. Stir in the asparagus, if using, and the rice and simmer for 2 minutes. Serve immediately.

MAKES 6 CUPS (1.5 L); 4 TO 6 FIRST-COURSE SERVINGS

radish soup

RADISHES, IT SEEMS TO ME, are a sadly neglected ingredient. They show up on our plates mainly raw on their own or as an ingredient in salads. Cooked, they have a mild spiciness and, when treated with a little vinegar, a charming pink color. This soup is also good cold, but in that case, it must be made ahead and refrigerated.

¾ pound (360 g) red radishes, trimmed and thinly sliced across

2 tablespoons red wine vinegar

10 ounces (300 g) mashing potatoes, peeled and cut into 1-inch (2.5-cm) cubes

2½ cups (625 ml) Basic Chicken Stock (page 345) or commercial chicken broth

3 scallions, trimmed and thinly sliced across

Kosher salt, to taste

Freshly ground black pepper, to taste

for cold radish soup with cucumber

1 medium cucumber, peeled, seeded, and cut into ¼-inch (.5-cm) dice

½ cup (120 g) yogurt, optional

TOSS 2¼ CUPS (270 g) of the radish slices with the vinegar.

In a medium saucepan, bring the potatoes and stock to a boil. Lower the heat and simmer for 3 minutes. Add the radish slices in vinegar. Cover and return to a boil. Lower the heat and simmer until the potatoes and radishes are tender, about 15 minutes.

In a blender, working in batches of no more than 2 cups (500 ml), purée until smooth. Scrape back into the saucepan.

Cut the remaining radish slices across into thin strips and stir them into the purée. Bring to a boil. Lower the heat and simmer for 5 minutes. Remove from the heat.

Stir in ½ cup (125 ml) water, the scallions, salt, and pepper.

MAKES 4 CUPS (1 L) HOT, 5 CUPS (1.25 L) COLD WITH CUCUMBER AND YOGURT;
4 FIRST-COURSE SERVINGS

For Cold Radish Soup with Cucumber: Make the soup as above and refrigerate until cold. Stir in the cucumber, the yogurt, if using, and additional salt, if necessary.

celery soup

WITH LIMA BEANS, ASPARAGUS, AND PEAS

THIS USES A NICE fresh-tasting base made from celery. The very ambitious can substitute fresh fava (broad) beans for the limas. Two and three quarter pounds (1.25 kg) in the shell will give 1½ cups.

6 cups (1.5 l) Celery Soup Base (page 388)

One 10-ounce (300 g) package frozen baby lima beans, defrosted in a sieve under warm running water and drained, or 1½ cups shelled favas (see page 293)

1¼ pounds (560 g) peas in the pod, shelled (generous 1 cup)

1 bunch thin asparagus, woody portions of stems snapped off, remaining portions peeled and cut across into 1-inch (2.5-cm) lengths

¼ cup (7 g) very thinly sliced scallion greens

Kosher salt, to taste

Freshly ground black pepper, to taste

2 tablespoons finely chopped celery leaves

2 tablespoons coarsely chopped dill fronds

IN A MEDIUM SAUCEPAN, bring the celery soup base to a boil. Stir in the lima beans or favas. Return to a boil. Lower the heat and simmer for 1 minute. Stir in the peas and asparagus. Simmer for 3 minutes, stirring occasionally. Stir in the scallion greens and simmer for 30 seconds. Remove from the heat.

Season with salt and pepper. Stir in the celery leaves and dill. Serve immediately.

MAKES 7 CUPS (1.75 L); 4 GENEROUS FIRST-COURSE SERVINGS

THE LETTUCE BOLTS in the high heat of summer, but in return we get ripe tomatoes, a fair exchange. Generally, in summer, I will make a cold soup (see the Index), a gelled soup (pages 367–379), or a soup meant to be eaten at room temperature, such as the summer version of Minestrone (page 115). I make an exception for tomato soups, wild mushroom soups, and an occasional hearty soup meal—often seafood—on a, far from rare, brisk Vermont evening.

If the summer season is used to make tomato bases and purées, these soups can be enjoyed all winter.

tomato basil soup

WHAT A DIFFERENCE in flavor a change of tomato variety and a little olive oil will make, as can be seen when comparing this soup to Tomato Soup with Cream or Without (page 69).

3½ cups (875 ml) **Basic Chicken Stock (page 345) or commercial chicken broth**

2½ cups (625 ml) **Plum Tomato Purée (page 386) or drained and puréed canned plum tomatoes**

3 **cloves garlic, smashed and peeled**

2½ **teaspoons kosher salt**

1 **medium bunch basil, leaves only, washed well**

1 **tablespoon olive oil, for serving**

IN A SMALL SAUCEPAN, bring the chicken stock and tomato purée to a boil.

In a blender, or with the side of a large knife on a cutting board, make a paste of the garlic and salt, adding a little stock if using the blender. Whisk the paste into the stock. Lower the heat and simmer, covered, for 10 minutes. Coarsely chop half of the basil. Stir into the soup and continue simmering for 5 minutes. The soup can be made ahead to this point and refrigerated for up to 2 days.

If the soup has been refrigerated, reheat it. Stack the remaining basil leaves, roll them tightly, and cut across into thin shreds. Stir into the soup. Serve immediately, drizzled with a little olive oil.

MAKES 5 CUPS (1.25 L); 4 FIRST-COURSE SERVINGS

Tomatoes

HUGE BEEFSTEAKS, rich and red; sweet orange and yellow; heirloom and almost black, or tiger-striped, or mottled red and green; tiny rounds popping with sweet juice; irresistible shmoo shapes in a spectrum of colors; Italian-style plum tomatoes, meaty and dense; and the crisp green tomatoes rescued before the frost: All are tomatoes, the perfect-tasting food, acid and sweet.

They are best eaten, sun warm, while standing in the garden. They make wonderful salads and ingredients for soups, sauces, stews, and even desserts. It is hard to imagine the world's foods pre-America and the tomato. It has been adopted around the globe from India to Turkey and from Italy to Indonesia. The only place I have never seen a tomato, except in Italian food, is Japan.

Unless plum or cherry tomatoes are specified, all the recipes use ordinary round tomatoes. I use what is ripest and at hand. To substitute tomatoes of another size, see page 451.

Tomatoes preserve well. Whole tomatoes can be popped into individual plastic bags and frozen. They can be dried. The tomato base (page 385) and purées (pages 384 and 386) can be frozen or canned. Tomatoes can be bought as paste—best in tubes—in paper cartons, sterile packed, both chopped and puréed (strained), and in cans. I am odd in that I do not prefer the canned Italian plum tomatoes—they tend to have a taste of the tin and are overly salty—but I use them. I prefer the canned American tomatoes that are round. Canned tomatoes come whole in juice or in purée, crushed, diced, and totally puréed. Each yields a different flavor and texture.

One of the easiest ways of peeling and seeding tomatoes for purée is to cook them whole and then put them through a food mill, which will remove the skin and seeds. If a food mill is unavailable, tomatoes can be peeled by cutting a small cross into the skin of the blossom end, plunging them for a minute into boiling water, and then pulling the skin away with a small knife. Alternatively, if the tomatoes are truly ripe, rub the dull back of a knife firmly all over the tomato and the skin will be easy to remove. In either case, remove the seeds by cutting the peeled tomato in half between the stem and blossom ends. With a small teaspoon or a fingernail, scoop out the seeds. It is possible to cook tomatoes and force them through a sieve to remove the peels and seeds, but it is hard.

There is a whole world of tomatoes, and changing from one to another can vary recipes in sometimes surprising and delightful ways.

tomato soup

WITH CREAM OR WITHOUT

WHAT CAMPBELL'S cream of tomato soup should be, but better. If there is no food mill, peel and seed the tomatoes before cooking. When they're cooked, purée them in a food processor.

    1 tablespoon (15 g) unsalted butter

    1 medium onion, sliced

    3 pounds (1.4 kg) tomatoes, cut into chunks, or 6 cups (1.5 l) Tomato Purée
        (page 384) or sterile-pack strained tomatoes

    1 tablespoon kosher salt

    1 cup (250 ml) heavy cream, optional

    ¼ cup (7 g) narrow strips of basil, optional

    Cubed Croutons (page 430), for serving, optional

IN A MEDIUM SAUCEPAN, melt the butter over medium heat. Stir in the onion and cook, stirring occasionally, for 7 minutes.

If using fresh tomatoes, stir them into the onions, raise the heat, and bring to a boil. Lower the heat and simmer, covered, for 45 minutes. Pass through the fine disc of a food mill and return to the pan.

If using the tomato purée, stir it into the cooked onions and bring to a boil. Lower the heat and simmer for 10 minutes. Pass through the fine disc of a food mill and return to the pan.

Heat the soup through. Season with the salt. If using, stir in the cream and/or the basil.

If desired, sprinkle a few croutons over each serving just before bringing the soup to the table.

MAKES 6 CUPS (1.5 L); 6 FIRST-COURSE SERVINGS

peasant tomato soup

A HEARTY, very good soup, and very quick too, since it uses tomato base or canned or boxed tomatoes and premade stock. A bowl full of the garden's best.

4 small carrots, peeled and cut across into 2-inch (5-cm) lengths
2 small onions, quartered
¾ pound (360 g) bulbs fennel, trimmed, peeled, cut into quarters, and cored
4 medium cloves garlic, smashed and peeled
3 tablespoons olive oil
2 cups (500 ml) Chunky Tomato Base (page 385), lightly crushed canned tomatoes (not plum) with their juice, or sterile-pack chopped tomatoes
1½ tablespoons cornstarch
4 cups (1 l) Basic Chicken Stock (page 345) or commercial chicken broth
5 teaspoons kosher salt, or less if using commercial broth
2 tablespoons fresh lemon juice
Fresh basil leaves, cut across into narrow strips, to taste

IN A FOOD PROCESSOR, coarsely chop the carrots, onions, fennel, and garlic. Scrape into a medium saucepan. Stir in the oil. Cook over medium heat, stirring occasionally, for 4 minutes.

Meanwhile, in the food processor, purée the tomatoes; or pass through the fine disc of a food mill.

In a small bowl, dissolve the cornstarch in a small amount of the stock. Whisk into the rest of the stock.

Whisk the tomatoes and stock into the vegetables. Bring to a boil. Lower the heat and simmer for 5 to 7 minutes. The soup can be made ahead up to this point and refrigerated for up to 2 days.

Reheat the soup, if necessary. Season with the salt, lemon juice, and basil.

MAKES ABOUT 8 CUPS (2 L); 8 FIRST-COURSE SERVINGS

fresh tomato soup

THIS RECIPE IS OUT of my *American Food and California Wine.* If fresh lovage is not available, substitute celery leaves and increase the amount of basil and dill. If the tomatoes are watery, use more tomatoes and less stock.

> 8 cups (2 l) Basic Chicken Stock (page 345) or commercial chicken broth
> 4½ pounds (2 kg) ripe tomatoes, cored and coarsely chopped
> 11 large basil leaves, well washed
> 3 sprigs lovage
> 5 sprigs flat-leaf parsley
> 2 tablespoons coarsely chopped dill
> 1½ teaspoons kosher salt, or less if using commercial broth
> Unsalted butter, for serving

IN A MEDIUM SAUCEPAN, bring the stock, tomatoes, basil, lovage, and parsley to a boil. Lower the heat and simmer until the tomatoes are very soft, about 15 minutes.

In a food processor, purée the soup, then pass through a fine-mesh sieve; or pass through the fine disc of a food mill. The soup can be made ahead up to this point and refrigerated for 2 days.

Scrape the soup back into the pan. Bring to a boil. Lower the heat, stir in the dill, and simmer for 20 minutes. Season with the salt.

For each serving, place a lump of butter in the bowl and ladle the hot soup over.

MAKES 10 CUPS (2.5 L); 8 FIRST-COURSE SERVINGS

curry tomato soup

THIS IS A WONDERFUL SOUP, hot or cold. I always make at least double the recipe. Made with the garlic broth, it is vegetarian.

> 2 tablespoons (30 g) unsalted butter
>
> 1 small onion, finely chopped
>
> 3 tablespoons curry powder
>
> 1 tablespoon sweet paprika
>
> 2½ cups (625 ml) Plum Tomato Purée (page 386), puréed canned Italian plum tomatoes with their juice, or sterile-pack strained tomatoes
>
> 2 cups (500 ml) Beef Stock (page 165) or, in England, imported beef or meat stock, or Basic Chicken Stock (page 345), commercial chicken broth, or Garlic Broth (page 86)
>
> 1 tablespoon salt, or less if using commercial broth
>
> 1 tablespoon fresh lemon juice
>
> Freshly ground black pepper, to taste

IN A MEDIUM SAUCEPAN, melt the butter over low heat. Stir in the onion and cook until it is limp and completely translucent, about 10 minutes. Stir in the curry powder and paprika and cook, stirring constantly, for 3 minutes.

Meanwhile, if using canned plum tomatoes, purée in a food processor. Stir the tomato purée and stock into the onions. Bring to a boil. Lower the heat and simmer for 5 minutes. Stir in the salt. The soup can be made ahead up to this point and refrigerated.

To serve the soup cold, refrigerate for 2 hours, or overnight, then stir in the lemon juice and pepper. Or reheat, stir in the lemon juice and pepper, and serve hot.

MAKES 4 CUPS (1 L); 4 FIRST-COURSE SERVINGS

summer mushroom soup

IT'S THE FLAVORS that make this a summer soup. It can also be served cold.

1 pound (450 g) small white mushrooms, trimmed and wiped clean

2 tablespoons fresh lemon juice

2 tablespoons (30 g) unsalted butter

2 tablespoons sifted all-purpose flour

1 tablespoon cornstarch

4 cups (1 l) Basic Chicken Stock (page 345) or commercial
    chicken broth

½ cup (120 g) sour cream

½ cup (20 g) loosely packed dill fronds

Kosher salt, to taste

Freshly ground black pepper, to taste

for serving

Dill sprigs

Sour cream, optional

THINLY SLICE THE MUSHROOMS and toss with the lemon juice to prevent discoloration. In a medium saucepan, melt the butter over low heat. Stir in the mushrooms and cook, stirring occasionally, until they are softened and give off their liquid, about 10 minutes. Sprinkle the mushrooms with the flour and cook, stirring occasionally, for 3 minutes.

In a large bowl, whisk the cornstarch into a small amount of the stock to dissolve, then whisk in the rest of the stock. Stir into the mushrooms. Bring to a boil, stirring. Lower the heat and simmer, stirring occasionally, for 10 minutes. The soup can be prepared ahead up to this point and refrigerated for 1 day.

If the soup has been refrigerated, reheat it over moderate heat. Remove from the heat and whisk in the sour cream and dill. Season with salt and pepper.

Serve immediately, or chill. Top each serving with a few sprigs of dill and, if desired, a dollop of sour cream.

MAKES 5 CUPS (1.25 L); 4 FIRST-COURSE SERVINGS

corn chowder

THIS MAKES A beautiful bowl—red, green, yellow, and white—of late summer's best.

   1 pound (450 g) mashing potatoes, peeled and cut into ½-inch
      (1-cm) dice

   1 medium onion, cut into ¼-inch (.5-cm) dice

   1 large green bell pepper, cored, seeded, deribbed, and cut into ¼-inch
      (.5-cm) dice

   1 large red bell pepper, cored, seeded, deribbed, and cut into ¼-inch
      (.5-cm) dice

   Kernels from 4 ears corn

   4 medium scallions, trimmed and thinly sliced across

   2 medium ribs celery, peeled and cut into ¼-inch (.5-cm) dice

   1½ cups (375 ml) milk

   ½ cup (125 ml) heavy cream

   2 teaspoons kosher salt

   Freshly ground black pepper, to taste

   Hot red pepper sauce, to taste

IN A MEDIUM SAUCEPAN, bring the potatoes, onion, peppers, and 1 cup (250 ml) water to a boil. Cover, lower the heat, and simmer for 10 minutes.

Stir in the corn, scallions, celery, milk, and cream. Return to just under a boil. Lower the heat and simmer for 10 minutes, stirring frequently to avoid scorching. Season with the salt, pepper, and hot red pepper sauce.

MAKES ABOUT 8 CUPS (2 L); 8 FIRST-COURSE SERVINGS

green soup

THIS SOUP USES lots of good produce. Double it and keep the extra to eat cold the next day. With a vegetarian stock (pages 380–383), it is safe for all but vegans.

2 tablespoons (30 g) unsalted butter (if serving hot) or canola oil (if serving cold)

¼ pound (120 g) tender young mustard greens or kale, cut across into narrow strips

4 cups (1 l) hot Basic Chicken Stock (page 345) or commercial chicken broth

1 cup (60 g) sorrel leaves, cut across into narrow strips

8 egg yolks

1 cup (250 ml) heavy cream

3 small zucchini trimmed and cut into matchstick strips

6 tablespoons Pesto Sauce (page 434)

½ cup (15 g) narrow strips (cut across the leaf) basil

1 teaspoon kosher salt, or to taste

Freshly ground black pepper, to taste

IN A MEDIUM SAUCEPAN, melt the butter over medium heat; or, for the chilled version, warm the oil over medium heat. Stir in the greens, toss to coat with butter or oil, and cook for about 1 minute. Stir in the stock. Bring to a boil. Lower the heat and simmer for 15 to 20 minutes, or until the greens are tender. Stir in the sorrel and simmer for 5 minutes. The soup can be made ahead to this point and refrigerated for up to 2 days.

If the soup has been refrigerated, reheat it. In a small bowl, beat the egg yolks with the cream. Whisk in about one third of the soup, one ladleful at a time, to slowly bring up the temperature of the yolks. Whisk the egg yolk mixture back into the soup. Stir in the zucchini, pesto, basil, salt, and pepper.

Cook the soup, stirring, over medium heat until it is slightly thickened and coats the back of a wooden spoon. Serve immediately, or chill for at least 5 hours.

MAKES 6 CUPS (1.5 L); 4 TO 5 FIRST-COURSE SERVINGS

parsley soup

A MUCH BETTER TASTE comes from this bouquet of herbs than all the health they deliver would imply.

  6 tablespoons (90 g) unsalted butter

  3 large bunches flat-leaf parsley, leaves only, washed well and dried

  3 medium bunches curly parsley, leaves only, washed well and dried

  ¾ teaspoon ground coriander

  3 cloves garlic, smashed and peeled

  3 cups (750 ml) Basic Chicken Stock (page 345) or commercial
      chicken broth

  ¾ cup (180 g) cottage cheese

  Fresh lemon juice, to taste

  Freshly ground black pepper, to taste

  Kosher salt, optional

IN A MEDIUM SAUCEPAN, melt the butter over low heat. Stir in the parsley, toss to coat with butter, and cook over low heat, stirring occasionally, for 5 minutes. Stir in the coriander and garlic. Cook, stirring, until the garlic becomes fragrant, 1 to 2 minutes.

Stir in the stock. Bring to a boil. Lower the heat and simmer for 7 minutes. Remove from the heat and stir in the cottage cheese. Allow the soup to cool slightly. The soup can be made ahead up to this point and refrigerated for up to 2 days.

In a food processor, purée the soup until smooth. Return to the pot and heat through. Season with lemon juice, pepper, and salt, if needed.

MAKES 6 CUPS (1.5 L); 6 FIRST-COURSE SERVINGS

We enter the season of root vegetables, full-grown onions and their kin, and hard-skinned squashes. The potatoes are ready to be dug and put in a dark place. All of these make wonderful soups, many of them straight through the winter. They are often very substantial soups, more meal than starter. See "Vegetables of Substance," page 111.

curried onion soup

THE ONIONS ARE NOT browned in this soup. For a soothing soup, add a cup of heavy cream and additional salt to taste.

> ¼ pound (120 g) unsalted butter, cut into pieces
> ¼ cup (30 g) curry powder
> 4 large onions, cut into chunks
> 4 cups (1 l) Basic Chicken Stock (page 345) or commercial chicken broth
> 3 tablespoons fresh lime juice
> 1 tablespoon kosher salt, or less if using commercial broth
> 1 cup (250 ml) heavy cream, optional

IN A MEDIUM SAUCEPAN, melt the butter over medium-low heat. Stir in the curry powder and cook, stirring, for 2 minutes. Stir in the onions and cook, stirring occasionally, for 10 minutes.

Pour in the stock. Bring to a boil. Lower the heat and simmer for 10 minutes, or until the onions are very soft.

In a blender, working in batches of no more than 2 cups (500 ml), purée the soup until very smooth, stopping once or twice to scrape down the sides of the jar. Scrape the purée back into the pan. The soup can be made ahead up to this point and refrigerated.

Heat the soup through. Remove from the heat and whisk in the lime juice, salt, and, if using, the heavy cream.

MAKES 7 CUPS (1.75 L) WITHOUT CREAM, 8 CUPS (2 L) WITH;
6 TO 8 FIRST-COURSE SERVINGS

onion soup
SOUPE À L'OIGNON GRATINÉ

WHEN MY DAUGHTER WAS A CHILD, she loved a bubbling bowl of cheese-crusted onion soup better than almost anything. For her, I made it without wine. The idea of using Champagne comes from the legend that onion soup was invented by Henri IV one early evening after a hard day's hunting. He was supposed to have stopped at a peasant hut and asked for something to eat. Embarrassed, the wife replied that she had nothing but onions, some stale bread, and a little fat in the house. The king replied that he would make a soup using the Champagne that he had left.

I would use Champagne only if I had some left and getting flat after a party. (Onion soup is a famous hangover remedy.) Usually, I would substitute a somewhat acid white wine—no sweetness, since the onions are so sweet. Any single stock can be used, although I like the balance of beef and chicken. Country people often made this just with water. I remember Jacques Pépin once making a soup (in *A French Chef Cooks at Home*) where he broke the crust of a soup that was almost solid with layered bread and sliding in a ladle filled with egg yolks and Port and swished it around in the soup. Vary at will.

There are pale onion soups, but for this one, it is important to cook the onions slowly so they get very dark but do not burn. When the pan is deglazed, the caramelization, a coating on the onions, comes off into the liquid, leaving the onions clear and the soup very dark. The pan must be large enough so that the onions glaze rather than stew in the juices.

The soup can be served without the bread and cheese (the gratin). If so, it will make more servings; the bread absorbs a great deal of soup.

> **6 tablespoons (90 g) unsalted butter**
>
> **4 large onions, thinly sliced**
>
> **1 cup (250 ml) dry white wine or flat Champagne**
>
> **1 cup (250 ml) Beef Stock (page 165) or, in England, imported beef or meat stock**
>
> **5½ cups (1.4 l) Basic Chicken Stock (page 345) or commercial chicken broth**
>
> **1 tablespoon kosher salt, or less if using commercial broth**
>
> **Freshly ground black pepper, to taste**

for serving

> **Twelve ¾-inch- (1.9-cm) diagonal slices Italian or French bread, toasted**
>
> **5 ounces (150 g) Gruyère cheese, coarsely grated (1½ cups), plus 1 cup (60 g) freshly grated Parmesan; or ½ pound (225 g) low-fat mozzarella cheese, sliced across into 32 slices**

IN A LARGE WIDE POT, melt the butter over medium heat. Add the onions—to keep them from stewing rather than browning, spread them in as close to a single layer as possible. Cook, stirring occasionally, until they are very brown and soft, about 30 minutes; they will need more frequent stirring toward the end.

Stir in the wine and bring to a boil, scraping the bottom of the pan vigorously with a wooden spoon to get up all of the browned bits. Continue scraping while pouring in the beef stock. Then pour in the chicken stock. Season with the salt and pepper. Bring to a boil. Lower the heat and simmer for 10 minutes. The soup can be made ahead to this point and refrigerated for up to 3 days.

To gratiné, preheat the broiler and, if necessary, return the soup to the simmer.

Lay 2 slices of toast in the bottom of each ovenproof bowl or crock, or make two layers of bread in a large earthenware casserole. If using, mix together the Gruyère and Parmesan. Pour the soup over the slices of bread. Sprinkle the cheese mixture evenly over the soup. Or, if using the mozzarella, lay 4 thin slices over the top of each serving or all the slices over the entire contents of the casserole. Place the container(s) under the broiler for 3 to 4 minutes until bubbling and brown.

MAKES 9 CUPS (2.25 L); 6 FIRST-COURSE SERVINGS
IF USING GRATINÉ, 8 IF NOT

creamy carrot soup

BE CAREFUL NOT TO OVERHEAT when cooking the cumin, or it will burn.

2 teaspoons canola oil

1½ teaspoons ground cumin

3 medium carrots, peeled and cut into 1-inch (2.5-cm) lengths

2¾ cups (680 ml) Basic Chicken Stock (page 345) or commercial chicken broth

1 cup (240 g) part-skim ricotta

1 teaspoon kosher salt, or less if using commercial broth

1 tablespoon fresh lemon juice

IN A MEDIUM SAUCEPAN, cook the oil and cumin over low heat, stirring, for 1 minute. Stir in the carrots and stock. Bring to a boil. Lower the heat and simmer for 30 minutes, or until the carrots are very soft.

In a blender, purée the ricotta with a small amount of the cooking liquid. With a slotted spoon, remove the carrots from the pan and add to the ricotta. Blend until smooth. Whisk the purée into the liquid in the pan. Heat through and season with the salt and lemon juice.

MAKES 4 CUPS (1 L); 4 FIRST-COURSE SERVINGS

carrot and leek soup

SIMPLE TO MAKE, this soup can be served hot or cold.

4 tablespoons (60 g) unsalted butter

½ teaspoon ground cardamom

3 medium leeks, white and light green parts only, washed well and
    cut across into ½-inch (1-cm) lengths

5 large carrots, peeled and cut across into thin slices

3 cups (750 ml) Basic Chicken Stock (page 345) or commercial
    chicken broth

½ cup (125 ml) heavy cream

Kosher salt, to taste

Freshly ground white pepper, to taste

IN A MEDIUM SAUCEPAN, melt the butter over medium heat. Stir in the cardamom
and cook, stirring, for 2 minutes. Stir in the leeks. Cover with a lid and cook, stirring occasionally, for 5 minutes. Stir in the carrots and stock. Bring to a boil. Lower the heat and
simmer, covered, for 13 minutes, or until the carrots are tender.

In a food processor or blender, purée the soup. If using a blender, work in batches
of no more than 2 cups (500 ml). Stir in the cream. The soup can be made up to 2 days
ahead and refrigerated.

Remove from the refrigerator and serve cold, or heat through to serve hot. Season
with salt and white pepper.

MAKES 6 CUPS (1.5 L); 4 TO 5 FIRST-COURSE SERVINGS

curried carrot soup

WHILE THE TWO PREVIOUS carrot soups are smoothed together by dairy products, this one is thickened only by puréed vegetables.

3 tablespoons vegetable oil

2 teaspoons curry powder

8 medium carrots, peeled and cut across into thin slices

4 medium ribs celery, peeled and cut across into thin slices

1 medium onion, coarsely chopped

5 cups (1.25 l) Basic Chicken Stock (page 345) or commercial
    chicken broth

1 tablespoon fresh lemon juice

2 teaspoons kosher salt, or less if using commercial broth

Freshly ground black pepper, to taste

IN A MEDIUM SAUCEPAN, cook the oil and curry powder over medium heat, stirring, for 2 minutes. Stir in the carrots, celery, and onion and toss to coat in oil. Cook, stirring frequently, for 10 minutes.

Stir in the stock. Bring to a boil. Lower the heat and simmer for 10 minutes, or until all the vegetables are very tender. Allow to sit for a minute, and remove the grease from the top.

In a blender, working in batches of no more than 2 cups (500 ml), purée the soup. Return to the pot and heat through. Season with the lemon juice, salt, and pepper.

MAKES 8 CUPS (2 L); 6 FIRST-COURSE SERVINGS

parsnip soup
WITH FIVE-SPICE POWDER

THE SWEETNESS OF PARSNIPS that have been in frozen ground is very special. The five-spice powder is an unusual counterpoint.

4 large parsnips, peeled, cut in half lengthwise and then across
    into ½-inch (1-cm) lengths

5 cups (1.25 l) Basic Chicken Stock (page 345) or commercial
    chicken broth

1 teaspoon five-spice powder

1 tablespoon kosher salt, or less if using commercial broth

Freshly ground black pepper, to taste

4 tablespoons (60 g) unsalted butter, cut into ½-inch (1-cm) pieces

3 tablespoons snipped chives, optional

IN A MEDIUM SAUCEPAN, bring the parsnips and stock to a boil. Lower the heat and simmer, uncovered, for 15 minutes. Stir in the five-spice powder and simmer for 5 minutes, or until the parsnips are very soft.

Drain in a sieve, reserving the liquid. In a food processor, purée the solids with a little of the reserved liquid and then whisk the purée into the remaining liquid; or pass the whole thing through the fine disc of a food mill. Scrape the purée back into the pan and bring to a boil. Season with the salt and pepper. Remove from the heat. Stir in the butter and, if using, the chives.

MAKES 5 ½ TO 6 CUPS (1.4 TO 1.5 L); 4 TO 5 FIRST-COURSE SERVINGS

cream of celery root

CELERY ROOT IS VERY UGLY, with dirty brown, coarse, hairy skin. Peeling it is a bit of a problem, requiring a sharp knife and determination. The reward is the aromatic white flesh. If there is a little extra celery root, cut it into matchstick strips and put it in water to cover with a little lemon juice. When the soup is ready to serve, stir in the raw root for a pleasant crunch.

1½ pounds (675 g) celery root, trimmed, peeled, and cut up

2¾ cups (680 ml) Basic Chicken Stock (page 345) or commercial chicken broth

½ cup (125 ml) heavy cream

1 tablespoon kosher salt

Freshly ground black pepper, to taste

Freshly grated nutmeg, for serving, optional

IN A MEDIUM SAUCEPAN, bring the celery root and stock to a boil. Lower the heat and simmer, covered, for 20 minutes.

In a blender, working in batches of no more than 2 cups (500 ml), purée the celery root and stock. Return to the pot, stir in the cream, and heat through. Season with the salt and pepper.

Sprinkle nutmeg over each serving, if desired.

MAKES 4 CUPS (1 L); 4 FIRST-COURSE SERVINGS

Stone soup and garlic

THERE IS AN OLD tale of two very hungry men who enter a town and ask for something to eat. The townspeople very sadly reply that they have no food themselves. The men ask if they have a pot. Yes. "Good," say the men, "because with a pot and water we can make stone soup." The hungry townspeople are fascinated. They bring their pot, put water in it, and set it over a fire. The men wash off three good-sized stones and put them in the water. One of the men asks if by any chance someone has an onion, because stone soup is better with onion. A woman brings an onion. A few minutes later, the same man asks for a carrot. To make a shaggy tale short, after a while there is vegetable soup.

The moral of the tale is that poor people make their food from the minimum of ingredients. They certainly do not kill an animal to make stock. Hence the many stories of the prosciutto bone passed around the village to boil in the soup until there is no flavor left. One has only to look at a Sicilian soup such as Spelt and Lentil Soup (page 330) and Ecuadorian Quinoa Soup (page 334) to see how good minimal can be. My candidate for the Ur basic soup is Garlic Broth (page 86), which uses nothing but garlic, olive oil, and water, and, if desired, salt and pepper. These ingredients are on hand in any Mediterranean home and some version of the soup is made in most.

There are a few versions here; but remember that the broth can be used as a vegetarian alternative in almost any hearty vegetable soup or in place of chicken stock in simple soups such as Brodo con Straciatella (page 127) or its variants.

The following soups do very well with the garlic broth; but remember to reduce the salt as the broth is already salted: Peasant Tomato Soup (page 70), Tomato Basil Soup (page 67), Curry Tomato Soup (page 72), Light Spring Soup with Asparagus and Peas (page 64), Green Potage (page 100), Mixed Vegetable Potage (page 115), Vegetable Curry Soup (to replace the water) (page 116), Bean and Swiss Chard Soup (page 308), Chard and Lentil Soup (page 316), Winter Wheat Soup (to replace the water) (page 332), and White Bean, Chorizo, and Broccoli di Rape Soup (page 309).

garlic broth

THIS IS REALLY a base for other soups that can also be served on its own—but consider adding some jalapeño pepper, cilantro, and lime juice; or diced tomato, chopped parsley, matchsticks of zucchini, and thinly sliced basil; cooked peas and small leaves of spinach; lemongrass, curry leaves, and lime juice; or any other seasoning group that seems enjoyable. See the notes on garlic on page 88.

3 small heads garlic, smashed and peeled
1 tablespoon olive oil
Kosher salt, to taste, optional
Freshly ground black pepper, to taste, optional

CUT THE GARLIC CLOVES in half lengthwise and, if necessary, remove the green germ growing through the center.

In a medium saucepan, heat the oil over low heat. Stir in the garlic cloves and cook, stirring often, until the outside of the garlic is translucent and cloves are soft, about 20 minutes. Don't let the garlic brown.

Pour in 9 cups (2.25 l) water. Bring to a boil. Lower the heat and simmer, uncovered, for 40 minutes. The garlic will be very tender. To eat the broth on its own, season with salt and pepper to taste; or use as a stock.

MAKES 8 CUPS (2 L); 8 FIRST-COURSE SERVINGS

garlic soup

WITH POACHED EGGS

LET THE BREAD sit at room temperature for several hours, or overnight, until dry.

Garlic Broth (page 86)
4 teaspoons kosher salt
½ teaspoon freshly ground black pepper
Eight ¼-inch- (.5-cm-) thick slices French bread, dried
4 eggs
Grated Parmesan cheese, for serving

IN A LARGE DEEP FRYING PAN, combine the garlic broth, salt, and pepper over medium heat. Arrange the bread slices around the edge of the pan, slightly overlapping them and leaving a circle about 6 inches (15 cm) in diameter in the center. Bring to a boil. Lower the heat so the liquid is at a lively simmer. Crack the eggs into the pan so they form a ring, without touching, toward the center of the pan. (If preferred, crack the eggs one at a time onto a saucer and slide them into the broth.) Cook just until the whites and the surface of the yolks are set, 3 to 4 minutes. Spoon broth over the tops of the yolks if they aren't submerged.

To serve, ladle the broth and bread into large warm soup bowls and top each with an egg. Pass Parmesan at the table.

MAKES **4** FIRST-COURSE SERVINGS

Garlic

NOT EVERYBODY LOVES GARLIC as much as I do. In fact, there are those who would prefer the vampire to the garlic. I at least have health information on my side. Garlic helps clear the arteries and acts as a fungicide and a mild antibiotic. For those who fear the odor, I can aver that several sprigs of parsley, chewed, and a Marc de Bourgogne, drunk, after indulging should set all right.

There are many different kinds of garlic. To understand the full spectrum, search out books by Chester Aaron, the American guru of garlic. In America, we mostly find large white heads from Gilroy, California. I prefer the smaller reddish purple heads I get in the South of France or from organic growers here. It is impossible to tell without nibbling a little bit exactly how hot or sweet a given crop of a given variety of garlic will be. Crops vary, depending on the amount of sun and rain the year has had. Use your judgment. Garlic that cooks for a long time has a mellow, somewhat sweet flavor. Raw garlic is sharper. Hence, some recipes add garlic twice.

The easiest way to separate the garlic cloves and to peel them is to put them on a stable surface, cover them with a cloth so the cloves don't jump all over the room, and bring a heavy pot or a large heavy knife down on them with a solid thwack. Lift the cloth. The cloves will be separated and the excess papery skin can be removed. Select just the number of cloves needed and repeat the process. This will loosen the skins from the garlic so that they are easily peeled. If only peeling one or two cloves of garlic, holding a heavy knife in one hand with the palm of the other hand laid flat on the blade of the knife, give the clove a sharp whack with the flat of the blade. (Be sure to keep the fingers holding the handle well back from the work surface.)

There are two advantages, in addition to ease, in this method. First, garlic is a living plant—like a tulip bulb. Whacking it kills it, which prevents it from deploying its self-protective stink. Second, the clove is liable to split open, which makes it easy to see the germ, the central part that turns green and becomes the sprout of the new plant. If the germ (sprout) is heavy or turning yellow or green, it will be bitter and should be removed with the point of a knife.

Garlic soups, however, should never be made with sprouting garlic in the spring. The taste will be nasty.

broccoli di rape

THE SLIGHT BITTERNESS of the broccoli di rape contrasts pleasantly with the sweetness of the garlic. The pasta makes the soup more substantial.

Garlic Broth (page 86)

2½ teaspoons kosher salt

½ teaspoon freshly ground black pepper

¾ cup (135 g) ditalini or other small pasta shape

1 medium bunch broccoli di rape, stems cut off, yellow and wilted leaves discarded, and tops and leaves sliced across into ½-inch (1-cm) pieces

Fresh lemon juice, to taste

Freshly grated Parmesan cheese, for serving

Kosher salt, to taste, optional

Freshly ground black pepper, to taste, optional

IN A MEDIUM SAUCEPAN, combine the garlic broth, salt, and pepper. Bring to a boil. Stir in the pasta and boil for 6 minutes.

Stir in the broccoli di rape and return to a boil. Lower the heat and simmer until the broccoli di rape is tender, about 4 minutes. Remove from the heat and stir in the lemon juice to taste. Check the seasoning and add salt and pepper, if necessary.

Pass grated cheese at the table.

MAKES 8 CUPS (2 L); 8 FIRST-COURSE SERVINGS

garlic soup

WITH TOMATO

THE GARLIC IS ADDED in two lots here to get two different flavors. The first amount is sautéed with other vegetables at the beginning of the recipe in good Italian or Spanish fashion. The second goes in near the end to provide a bite. The tomatoes provide most of the liquid.

> 4 thin slices peasant bread
>
> 3 medium to large tomatoes, cut into chunks
>
> 10 cloves garlic, smashed, peeled, and coarsely chopped
>
> 2 medium bell peppers, red, green, yellow, or a combination, cored, seeded, deribbed, and cut into chunks
>
> ½ cup (125 ml) olive oil
>
> 2 teaspoons kosher salt, or to taste
>
> Freshly ground black pepper, to taste

HEAT THE OVEN to 225°F (107°C; less than #½ gas mark; less than #¼ British regulo). Lay the bread directly on the middle rack and bake for 15 to 20 minutes, just to dry it out.

In a food processor, pulse the tomatoes, half of the garlic, and the bell peppers until coarsely chopped.

In a medium saucepan, heat the oil over medium heat. Scrape the vegetables into the pan. Cook, stirring occasionally, for 5 minutes. Stir in the remaining garlic, the salt, and 2 cups (500 ml) water. Bring to a boil. Lower the heat and simmer for 10 minutes. Season with pepper. The soup can be made ahead to this point and refrigerated for up to 2 days.

If it has been refrigerated, quickly bring the soup back to a boil. Lay 1 slice of dry bread in the bottom of each of four shallow soup bowls. Pour the soup over the bread. Let sit for 10 minutes. Serve.

MAKES ABOUT 6 CUPS (1.5 L); 4 FIRST-COURSE SERVINGS

tomato and bread soup

PAPPA AL POMODORO

THIS IS THE *sopa secca,* or dry soup, version of the soup on page 90. It is usually served at little more than room temperature. It is comfort food to the max.

Four ¾-inch- (2-cm-) thick slices peasant bread

⅓ cup (80 ml) olive oil

3 medium cloves garlic, smashed, peeled, and sliced

1 medium onion, very finely chopped

14 large basil leaves, washed well and cut across into narrow strips

1¾ pounds (790 g) plum tomatoes, peeled and cut into ¼-inch (.5-cm) dice

4 cups (1 l) Basic Chicken Stock (page 345) or commercial chicken broth

2 teaspoons kosher salt, or less if using commercial broth

Freshly ground black pepper, to taste

Good olive oil, for serving

HEAT THE OVEN TO 225°F (107°C; less than #½ gas mark; less than #¼ British regulo). Place the bread directly on the middle rack of the oven. Bake for 20 to 30 minutes, just to dry the bread out; do not brown. Break the bread into large pieces.

In a medium saucepan, heat the oil over medium heat. Add the garlic and onion and cook, stirring, for 5 minutes. Stir in the basil and cook for 1 minute. Stir in the tomatoes and bring to a boil. Cook at a low boil for 13 to 15 minutes, stirring frequently.

Stir in the stock, bread, salt, and pepper. Return to a boil. Lower the heat and simmer, stirring and breaking up the bread with the back of a spoon, for 15 minutes. The bread should break down to a mush. Remove the pan from the heat, cover, and let sit for 10 minutes.

Serve with a few grinds of fresh pepper, and drizzled with some good olive oil.

MAKES 6 CUPS (1.5 L); 6 FIRST-COURSE SERVINGS

The great potato

I HAD NEVER FULLY APPRECIATED the wide variety of the potato, although I have grown many different kinds and was familiar with the fabulous *Dictionaire Vilmorin des Plantes Potagères* of 1947, which lists almost fifty varieties of potato. Among them are varieties that can be dug from late May to October, including types with white, yellow, violet, and bicolored (even red and yellow) flesh.

It took a trip to the Andes of Ecuador to let me see a greater potential. In the Otavalo market, Indians hunker on the ground, fine straw hats on their heads, next to vibrant weavings spread with their home-grown offerings. I have seen as many as seventy-five varieties of potatoes, round and oval, tiny as a jacks' game ball and large as a round eggplant, knobby and smooth, red, pink, blue, white, yellow, golden brown, and almost black. The seller will often sink a thumbnail into a proffered specimen to show how freshly its juices spurt and then break it open to show the crisp flesh. Each potato has its own uses and flavors. We will not find such a splendid variety in our own markets. However, we will find the best and freshest in fall.

For me, potatoes are one of the great gifts to the soup cook. We primarily need what I call "mashing" (floury) potatoes, which tend to fall apart in cooking and give body to soups, and "firm" (waxy) potatoes, which hold their shape and texture as they cook. With these we can make a vast variety of soups, and the flavors will change depending on the potatoes used.

There are round potatoes that describe themselves, and fingerlings are shaped like small link sausages. There are large ovals as big as two fists. Potatoes have always been available in many colors of skin, pale yellow to purple, and flesh—white, yellow, pink, lavender, and blue—and in many shapes and sizes; but those indications alone do not indicate a potato's texture. There are some potatoes with purple or blue skins and lavender flesh that are waxy and others that are floury.

POTATO NAMES

Most of these recipes call for either "mashing" (baking) potatoes, often called floury or mealy; or "firm" (often new) potatoes, often called waxy. If luck provides many kinds, use them on the basis of what the store or experience tells you. Large, older Yellow Finns, for instance, can be used in place of baking potatoes. New, younger Yellow Finns are firm, as are Russian Bananas, or the red fingerlings that make a superior substitution for other new potatoes.

The main mashing potatoes are Idaho bakers, russets, carolas, and mature Yukon Golds. The main firm potatoes are red new, white, Russian Banana, Caribé, and Red Cloud.

POTATO SIZES USED IN THIS BOOK

	Very Small	*Small*	*Medium*	*Large*
Firm	less than 2 ounces (60 g)	4 to 6 ounces (120 to 180 g)	½ pound (225 g)	9 to 10 ounces (270 to 300 g)
Mashing	na	4 to 6 ounces (120 to 180 g)	½ pound (225 g)	9 to 10 ounces (270 to 300 g)

PURÉEING

Since the mashing potatoes are often used in potages and other soups where they are puréed to give body and to hold the soup together much as flour, cream, or eggs act in other soups, it is important that certain things about the way they mash are understood. Mashing potatoes have a high gluten content, which makes them able to hold the vast amounts of milk and butter that are added to them when they are served as mashed potatoes. If they are puréed in a food processor, the gluten will overdevelop and the purée tend to become rubbery. This is all right if the soup is made several hours ahead of time, but disastrous if it is to be served immediately. I use a food mill, but a sieve or potato ricer can also be used.

Conversely, mashed potatoes can be made with firm potatoes, but in that case, they cannot be made ahead or reheated. They will no longer hold all the enriching ingredients.

If possible, follow the indications for potato type and puréeing method given.

potato and leek soup

POTAGE PARMENTIER, IF HOT
VICHYSSOISE, IF COLD

A WELL-REMEMBERED childhood treat was being taken to the old Ritz-Carlton for lunch. Carefully dressed in a pale green wool dress that almost matched the carpet, I was led down a short flight of stairs to a large table. It was a warm spring day and I was served a smooth, creamy, ivory-colored soup sprinkled with green in a two-handled consommé cup. I lifted a round spoonful of the soup to my mouth. Cold and delicious, it slid down comfortingly. This was, of course, Louis Diat's famous invention, vichyssoise. He had based it on his mother's version of the traditional soupe bonne femme, which is known as potage parmentier when it is puréed. In frugal French tradition, he did not use stock but rather hot milk and water. The cold creamed soup had snipped chives on top.

I give my version of the hot puréed soup here. For a chunky version, do not pass through the food mill. In addition to the vichyssoise, which is the parmentier, cold, with some extra cream and chives, I contribute a red pepper version with a taste and rich color all its own—see page 45.

1½ pounds (675 g) mashing potatoes, peeled and cut into 1-inch (2.5-cm) cubes
4 medium leeks, white and 1-inch (2.5 cm) of pale green part only,
    washed well and cut across into ½-inch (1-cm) lengths
4 cups (1 l) Basic Chicken Stock (page 345) or commercial chicken broth
½ cup (125 ml) heavy cream, plus ½ cup (125 ml) for chilled version
Kosher salt, to taste
Freshly ground black pepper, to taste
1 tablespoon finely snipped chives, for chilled version

IN A MEDIUM SAUCEPAN, bring the potatoes, leeks, and stock to a boil. Lower the heat and simmer, covered, for 20 minutes.

In a blender, working in batches of no more than 2 cups (500 ml), purée the soup; or pass everything through the fine disc of a food mill.

Return the soup to the pot, stir in ½ cup (125 ml) cream, and heat through. The soup can be made ahead to this point and refrigerated for up to 2 days.

Season with salt and pepper. If the soup has been refrigerated and it is to be served hot, reheat. If serving cold, stir in the additional cream and top each serving with chives.

MAKES ABOUT 7 CUPS (1.75 L); 5 TO 6 FIRST-COURSE SERVINGS

potato soup

THIS IS A SIMPLER potato soup than the Parmentier (page 94) and is not puréed, but slightly thickened as the potatoes disintegrate. It can be made vegetarian by substituting Garlic Broth (page 86) for the stock.

1 tablespoon (15 g) unsalted butter

1 medium onion, finely chopped

2 pounds (900 g) mashing potatoes, peeled and cut across into
    ¼-inch (.5-cm) slices

6 cups (1.5 l) Basic Chicken Stock (page 345) or commercial
    chicken broth

¼ teaspoon celery seed

Kosher salt, to taste

Freshly ground black pepper, to taste

Buttermilk or extra stock, if desired

IN A MEDIUM SAUCEPAN, melt the butter over medium heat. Stir in the onion, toss to coat in the butter, and cook for 5 minutes, stirring occasionally. Stir in the potatoes and stock. Bring to a boil. Lower the heat and simmer for about 15 minutes, stirring occasionally, until the potatoes are almost cooked through.

Stir in the celery seed and simmer for 5 minutes, stirring frequently to break up the potato slices.

Gently whisk the soup with a balloon whisk so that it becomes a little smoother. There will still be small pieces of potato remaining. Season to taste with salt and pepper. The soup can be made 2 hours ahead and reheated from room temperature, or refrigerated for up to 2 days and then reheated.

If not serving the soup immediately, you may want to add a little buttermilk or extra chicken broth, because the soup will get thicker as it stands.

MAKES 6 CUPS (1.5 L); 5 FIRST-COURSE SERVINGS

celery soup

THIS CAN BE smooth or chunky. Unless very young celery is available, which seems impossible for me to find, the stalks will need to be scraped with a vegetable peeler to remove the stringy, fibrous outer layer before using.

This soup seems too simple and too delicious to be true. Everyone I have taken leftovers to immediately wanted the recipe, so here it is.

8 tablespoons (120 g) unsalted butter

1 large bunch celery, trimmed, peeled and cut into ¼-inch (.5-cm) dice

2 medium onions, cut into ¼-inch (.5-cm) dice

2 pounds (900 g) firm potatoes, peeled and cut into ½-inch (1-cm) cubes

6 cups (1.5 l) Basic Chicken Stock (page 345) or canned chicken broth

Kosher salt, to taste

Freshly ground black pepper, to taste

IN A LARGE SAUCEPAN, melt the butter over low heat. Stir in the celery and onions and cook for 5 minutes. Stir in the potatoes and cook for 5 minutes. Pour in the stock and bring to a boil. Lower the heat and simmer for 30 minutes. Season to taste and serve.

Or, if a smooth consistency is desired, drain through a sieve and reserve the liquid. In a food processor, purée the vegetables. Whisk the purée into the reserved liquid. Season with salt and pepper.

The soup can be made ahead and refrigerated for up to 2 days. Just before serving, heat through.

MAKES 10 CUPS (2.5 L); 8 TO 10 FIRST-COURSE SERVINGS

lovage and potato soup

I LOVE IRELAND and I love lovage. One cold spring day, I had a soup like this in a pub that I probably could never find again. It was a delight. If lovage is unavailable, this shouldn't be made with anything else. Lovage is worth growing. It is a huge perennial in the same family as celery and stays green from earliest spring late into the fall. In Roman times, it was virtually ubiquitous.

2 tablespoons (30 g) unsalted butter

2 medium onions, coarsely chopped

6 cups (1.5 l) Basic Chicken Stock (page 345) or commercial chicken broth

2 pounds (900 g) firm potatoes, peeled and cut across into ¼-inch (.5-cm) slices

1 cup (30 g) loosely packed lovage leaves, cut across into narrow strips

Kosher salt, to taste

Freshly ground black pepper, to taste

IN A MEDIUM STOCKPOT, melt the butter over medium heat. Stir in the onions and lower the heat. Cook, stirring occasionally, for about 20 minutes. The onions should be very soft and nicely browned.

Stir in the stock and potatoes. Bring to a boil. Lower the heat and simmer for 20 minutes, or until the potatoes are just starting to fall apart. Stir in the lovage and simmer for 4 minutes. The soup can be made up to 3 days ahead and refrigerated.

Reheat the soup if need be. Gently whisk it with a balloon whisk so that the potato slices break up slightly and thicken the soup. Season with salt and pepper to taste.

MAKES 8 CUPS (2 L); 6 TO 8 FIRST-COURSE SERVINGS

spinach and potato soup

THIS SOUP CAN BE served in three possible ways, all of which are good: as is, puréed in a food mill or food processor, or partly puréed and part left chunky.

4 tablespoons (60 g) unsalted butter

6 medium scallions, white and 1 inch (2.5 cm) of pale green part only, cut across into thin slices

1 small clove garlic, smashed, peeled, and very finely chopped

¾ pound (360 g) spinach, stemmed, washed well, and coarsely chopped

3 cups (750 ml) Basic Chicken Stock (page 345) or commercial chicken broth

½ pound (225 g) firm potatoes, peeled and cut into 1-inch (2.5-cm) cubes

2 tablespoons fresh lemon juice

¼ teaspoon hot red pepper sauce

1 tablespoon kosher salt, or less if using commercial broth

Freshly ground black pepper, to taste

IN A MEDIUM SAUCEPAN, melt the butter over low heat. Stir in the scallions and garlic and cook for 10 minutes, stirring occasionally. Stir in the spinach and cook for 3 minutes. Stir in the remaining ingredients except for the salt and pepper and simmer for 20 minutes. Purée if desired. The soup can be made ahead to this point and refrigerated for up to 3 days. Reheat the soup if it's been refrigerated, and season with the salt and pepper to taste.

MAKES 5 CUPS (1.25 L); 4 FIRST-COURSE SERVINGS

basic potage

THESE HAVE BEEN THE basic French day-to-day and meal-to-meal soups ever since the natives took to the potato. They are not the English pottage with meat. One of my family's favorite potages is on page 15. I give many recipes. Here is a formula that permits the cook to combine, vary, and change at will: Garlic Broth (page 86) can be used instead of stock or water. The vegetables may be solid, leafy, or a combination of both. See the list below. For an entire recipe, start with about 1¼ pounds (575 g) solid vegetables, cleaned, peeled, trimmed, and cut into 1-inch (2.5-cm) cubes (to make about 3 cups; 360 to 450 g), or about 2 pounds (900 g) leafy vegetables, stemmed, washed, and cut across into wide strips (to make 5 to 8 cups; about 450 g). Or combine 1 pound (285 g) solid vegetables and 1 pound (450 g) leafy vegetables.

2 tablespoons (30 g) unsalted butter, optional

6 to 8 ounces (180 to 225 g) onion, leek, shallot, or garlic, or a mixture, cut into ½-inch (1-cm) dice

¾ pound (360 g) mashing potatoes, peeled and cut into chunks

3 to 4 cups (750 ml to 1 l) stock or water

Cut-up vegetables, per list below

Kosher salt, to taste

Freshly ground black pepper, to taste

IN A MEDIUM SAUCEPAN or a tall narrow stockpot (the taller pot is good for soups using a lot of leafy greens), melt the optional butter over medium heat. Stir in the onion, leek, shallots, and/or garlic. Cook, stirring frequently for about 10 minutes, or until translucent. Add the remaining ingredients except the seasoning and bring to a boil.

Or, if the butter is not being used, place all the ingredients except the salt and pepper in a medium saucepan or tall narrow stockpot (see above) and bring to a boil.

In either case, lower the heat and simmer until the vegetables are tender. Pass through the medium disc of a food mill, or, with more effort, a potato ricer. Or skim the solids from the cooked soup and pulse in batches in a food processor until a coarse purée is obtained. If processing, return the solids to the liquid. Season with salt and pepper.

solid vegetables: **Carrots • Peas • Celery root • Turnips • Green beans • Fennel • Broccoli • Parsnips • Cauliflower • Broccoli di rape • Celery**

leafy vegetables: **Spinach • Cabbage • Escarole • Sorrel • Kale • Chard**

MAKES ABOUT 6 CUPS (1.5 L) OF BASIC POTAGE

green potage

THIS IS A GOOD POTAGE to warm up a winter night.

    1 tablespoon (15 g) unsalted butter

    1 medium-to-large onion, thinly sliced

    1¼ pounds (600 g) mashing potatoes, peeled and cut into 1-inch
        (2.5-cm) cubes

    5 cups (1.25 l) Basic Chicken Stock (page 345) or commercial
        chicken broth

    ½ medium head broccoli, stems peeled and cut into coins,
        tops cut into florets

    ½ pound (225 g) spinach, stemmed and washed well

    4 teaspoons kosher salt, or less if using commercial broth

    Freshly ground black pepper, to taste

IN A MEDIUM SAUCEPAN, melt the butter over medium heat. Stir in the onion and cook, stirring occasionally, for 5 to 7 minutes, until wilted and translucent.

Stir in the potatoes and stock. Bring to a boil. Lower the heat and simmer, uncovered, for 10 minutes. Stir in the broccoli and spinach. Cover. Simmer until the potatoes and broccoli are completely tender, about 10 more minutes.

Strain the soup and reserve the liquid. In a food processor, purée the vegetables with a little of the reserved liquid. Whisk the purée into the remaining liquid and return to the saucepan; or pass everything through the medium disc of a food mill into the saucepan. Stir in the salt and pepper. Heat through.

MAKES 6 CUPS (1.5 L); 4 TO 5 FIRST-COURSE SERVINGS

great green soup

IF ALLOWED TO SIT in the soup, Croutons (page 429) add something special to this potage—they sort of melt into it, creating a delectable mush. Or Cubed Croutons (page 430) added at the last minute give a nice crunch for contrast.

The amount of stock called for in this recipe will not fully cover the vegetables, but not to worry, it will work. Canned stock is fine.

1 large leek, white and light green parts only, cut in half lengthwise, washed well, and cut across into thin slices

½ medium head broccoli, florets only (2 cups; 120 g) (save the stems for another use)

1 small cucumber, peeled and cut across into ¼-inch (.5-cm) slices

2¼ pounds (560 kg) peas in the pod, shelled (2 cups), or one 10-ounce (300-g) box frozen tiny peas, defrosted in a sieve under running water and drained (1⅔ cups)

1 pound (450 g) mashing potatoes, peeled and cut across into ¼-inch (.5-cm) slices

1 small bunch parsley, leaves only

1 medium bunch watercress, leaves only

½ small green cabbage, cored and shredded (about 3½ cups; 225 g)

6 cups (1.5 l) Basic Chicken Stock (page 345) or commercial chicken broth

5 teaspoons kosher salt, or less if using commercial broth

1 teaspoon white wine vinegar

20 leaves basil, washed well and cut across in narrow strips

Lots of freshly ground black pepper

IN A MEDIUM STOCKPOT, bring all the ingredients except the salt, vinegar, basil, and pepper to a boil. Lower the heat and simmer until all the vegetables are tender, about 20 minutes.

Strain the soup and reserve the liquid. In a food processor, purée the vegetables with a little of the reserved liquid and whisk the purée into the remaining liquid; or pass everything through the medium disc of a food mill. Return the soup to the pot. Season with the salt and vinegar. Allow the soup to sit for an hour or two at room temperature. The soup can be made ahead to this point and refrigerated for up to 3 days.

Stir the basil and pepper into the soup. Bring to a boil. Lower the heat and simmer for 1 minute.

MAKES 9 CUPS (2.25 L); 8 FIRST-COURSE SERVINGS

potage of turnip
AND CARROT

BOTH THE CELERY SEED and the salt should be added at the last minute, or their taste will become too pronounced.

½ pound (225 g) mashing potatoes, peeled and cut into 1-inch (2.5-cm) cubes

1 medium-to-large turnip, peeled and cut into ½-inch (1-cm) cubes

3 medium carrots, peeled and cut across into ½-inch (1-cm) slices

1 small onion, cut into ½-inch (1-cm) dice

4 medium cloves garlic, smashed and peeled

2 medium ribs celery, peeled and cut across into ½-inch (1-cm) lengths

¼ cup (19 g) coarsely chopped parsley

¼ teaspoon celery seed

1 heaping tablespoon kosher salt

1 tablespoon (15 g) unsalted butter, optional

IN A MEDIUM SAUCEPAN, bring all the vegetables—not the parsley—and 4 cups (1 l) water to a boil. Lower the heat and simmer for 10 minutes. Stir in the parsley and simmer for 10 more minutes.

Strain the soup and reserve the liquid. In a food processor, purée the vegetables with a little of the reserved liquid, then whisk the purée into the remaining liquid; or pass everything through the medium disc of a food mill. The soup can be made ahead to this point and refrigerated for up to 3 days.

Return the soup to the pan and heat through. Stir in the celery seed and salt. Remove from the heat and, if using the butter, stir it in. Serve immediately.

MAKES 6 CUPS (1.5 L); 5 TO 6 FIRST-COURSE SERVINGS

ALL OF THE PREVIOUS potages are winter soups, as is the Vegetarian Borscht (page 6), but the first-course soups that follow do particularly find their home in winter.

cabbage-dill potage

THIS IS A WINTER SOUP that turns green and fresh-tasting with a cleverly pre-pared-in-summer Zucchini Purée Soup Base. If there is none in the freezer, use the smallest zucchini in the winter market.

>   2 cups (500 ml) Zucchini Purée Soup Base (page 387) or 4 medium zucchini
>
>   1 tablespoon (15 g) unsalted butter, if using whole zucchini
>
>   ½ pound (225 g) mashing potatoes, peeled and cut in 1-inch (2.5-cm) cubes
>
>   2 large leeks, white and 1 inch (2.5 cm) of pale green parts only, washed well
>   and cut into ½-inch (1-cm) pieces
>
>   ½ small white cabbage, cored and cut into ½-inch (1-cm) dice (about 2 cups; 225 g)
>
>   5 teaspoons kosher salt
>
>   Freshly ground black pepper, to taste
>
>   2 tablespoons coarsely chopped dill
>
>   1 tablespoon olive oil, optional

IF USING WHOLE ZUCCHINI, peel, quarter them lengthwise, and then cut them across into ½-inch (1-cm) lengths. In a medium saucepan, melt the butter. Stir in the zucchini and toss to coat in butter. Cook, covered, over low heat, stirring occasionally, for 45 minutes. Pass through the medium disc of a food mill. (A food processor will yield water.) There should be 2 cups (500 ml).

In a medium saucepan, bring the potatoes, leeks, cabbage, and 4 cups (1 l) water to a boil. Lower the heat and simmer, covered, until the vegetables are soft, about 20 minutes.

Strain the soup and reserve the liquid. In a food processor, purée the vegetables with a little of the reserved liquid, then whisk into the remaining liquid; or pass everything through the medium disc of a food mill. Return the purée to the pot.

Stir the purée or base into the soup. The soup to this point can be refrigerated for up to 3 days. Heat the soup and season with salt, pepper, dill, and olive oil, if using.

MAKES 6 CUPS (1.5 L); 4 GENEROUS FIRST-COURSE SERVINGS

bourbon corn chowder

CANNED CORN turns this into a winter soup. If a thinner soup is desired, stir in a little more stock at the end.

4 tablespoons (60 g) unsalted butter

1 small onion, cut into ½-inch (1-cm) dice

2½ cups (675 ml) canned creamed corn

¼ cup (65 ml) Bourbon

¼ teaspoon freshly grated nutmeg

1 teaspoon kosher salt

Freshly ground black pepper, to taste

2 to 3 drops hot red pepper sauce

½ cup (125 ml) Basic Chicken Stock (page 345) or commercial chicken broth

½ cup (125 ml) heavy cream

IN A SMALL SAUCEPAN, melt the butter over medium heat. Stir in the onion and cook, stirring, for 5 minutes. Stir in the corn.

In a small saucepan, heat the Bourbon. Ignite it and let it flame for 1 minute.

Pour the Bourbon, still flaming, over the corn mixture. Stir in the remaining ingredients. Heat through.

MAKES ABOUT 4 CUPS (1 L); 4 FIRST-COURSE SERVINGS

acorn squash soup

ACORN SQUASH ALWAYS threaten to strangle the garden; but come winter, into which they survive with their hard skins intact, I always forgive them and welcome this brightly colored, satisfying soup.

The squash is cooked in stock, which it flavors. All of the squash is used in this soup, but there is stock left over. It can be used to make the Cream of Celery Root (page 84). I often make both and swirl one into the other to create a marbleized look. Together they make about 8 cups (2 l), 8 first-course servings.

This soup can be made with other winter squash, such as pumpkin, butternut, or calabaza; just use the same cleaned weight (about 1½ pounds; 675 g).

The squash seeds can be washed, and toasted on a baking sheet to sprinkle on top of the soup, or to salt and snack on.

2 small acorn squash, halved, peeled, seeded, and cut into 2-inch (5-cm) chunks

4 cups (1 l) Basic Chicken Stock (page 345) or commercial chicken broth

2 teaspoons vegetable oil

¼ teaspoon ground turmeric

¼ teaspoon cayenne pepper

¼ teaspoon ground mace

3 cloves garlic, smashed, peeled, and very finely chopped

1 cup (250 ml) buttermilk

2 to 3 teaspoons kosher salt, or less if using commercial broth

Freshly ground black pepper, to taste

IN A MEDIUM SAUCEPAN, bring the squash and stock to a boil. Lower the heat and simmer, covered, for 15 minutes. Strain the soup and reserve the liquid. In a food processor, purée the solids with 1 cup (250 ml) of the reserved liquid.

In a medium saucepan, warm the oil over low heat. Stir in the spices and cook, stirring, for 1 to 2 minutes, or until aromatic. Stir in the garlic and cook for 2 minutes.

Stir in the purée and 1 cup (250 ml) of the reserved cooking liquid. Bring to a boil. Lower the heat and simmer for 5 minutes. Stir in the buttermilk, salt, and pepper. (There will be about 1½ cups [375 ml] cooking liquid left over.)

MAKES ABOUT 5 CUPS (1.25 L); 4 FIRST-COURSE SERVINGS

quibebe
WINTER SQUASH SOUP

A R G E N T I N A   P R O D U C E S   A   great deal of beef, so it is logical that its squash soup uses beef stock. The soup should retain some texture and should not be completely smooth.

4 tablespoons (60 g) unsalted butter

1 medium onion, coarsely chopped

1 medium tomato, peeled, seeded, and coarsely chopped

1 very small clove garlic, smashed, peeled, and very finely chopped

½ small dried hot red pepper (pequín), crushed

2 pounds (900 g) butternut or Hubbard squash, cut into pieces, seeded, peeled, and cut into ½-inch (1-cm) dice

4 cups (1 l) Beef Stock (page 165) or, in England, imported beef or meat stock

2 teaspoons kosher salt

½ teaspoon sugar

Freshly grated Parmesan cheese, for serving

IN A MEDIUM SAUCEPAN, melt the butter over medium heat. Stir in the onion, tomato, garlic, and pepper. Cook, stirring occasionally, for 10 minutes. Stir in the squash, stock, salt, and sugar. Bring to a boil. Lower the heat and simmer, covered, for 30 minutes, or until the squash has disintegrated and thickened the soup.

Serve with Parmesan cheese.

MAKES 7 CUPS (1.75 L); 6 FIRST-COURSE SERVINGS

thick potato soup

WITH PUMPKIN

A DELICIOUS VEGETARIAN Ecuadorian soup with a lovely golden color from pumpkin and annatto, accented by the red of kidney beans and the yellow of corn.

for the refrito

> 2 tablespoons (30 g) unsalted butter
>
> 1 small red onion, finely chopped
>
> 2 teaspoons Annatto Butter (page 445)

for the soup

> 3½ pounds (1.5 kg) soup pumpkin or acorn or Hubbard squash, cut into
> 8 wedges, seeded, and peeled, each section cut across into ¼-inch (.5-cm) slices
>
> 1½ cups (375 ml) milk
>
> 2 ears fresh corn, shucked and silk removed, each cob cut across into 6 pieces
>
> 1 pound (450 g) firm potatoes, peeled and cut into ¼-inch (.5-cm) dice
>
> 1 pound (450 g) fresh kidney beans, shelled, or 1 cup (225 g) drained
> and rinsed canned kidney beans, optional
>
> 1 tablespoon kosher salt, to taste
>
> Freshly ground black pepper, to taste
>
> ¼ pound (120 g) queso blanco cheese, or mozzarella, coarsely grated, for serving

FOR THE REFRITO, in a small saucepan, melt the unsalted butter over medium heat. Stir in the onion and cook for 10 minutes, stirring occasionally. Stir in the annatto butter to melt and remove from the heat.

While the refrito cooks, in a medium stockpot, bring 6 cups (1.5 l) water and the pumpkin to a boil. Lower the heat and simmer, covered, for 25 minutes, or until the pumpkin is very soft.

In a blender, purée the refrito with ½ cup (125 ml) milk. Stir into the pumpkin, with the corn. Cook for 10 minutes. Stir in the remaining milk and the potatoes. If using the beans, add them now. Simmer, covered, over low heat for 20 minutes. The pumpkin will disintegrate, thickening the soup and turning it yellow-to-gold. Season with the salt and pepper. The soup can be made ahead to this point and refrigerated for up to 3 days.

If the soup has been refrigerated, reheat it. Stir in the cheese just before serving and allow to melt.

MAKES 10 CUPS (2.5 L); 8 FIRST-COURSE SERVINGS

repé
PLANTAIN SOUP

ANOTHER VEGETARIAN ECUADORIAN soup gets its substance from plantains, those fruits that look like bananas but need to be cooked. If the plantains are ripe, the soup will be too sweet.

> 6 small firm green plantains, peeled and cut across into ½-inch (1-cm) slices (1½ pounds [675 g] peeled)
>
> 2 cups (500 ml) milk
>
> ¼ pound (120 g) queso blanco cheese, or mozzarella, coarsely grated
>
> 1 very small onion, very finely chopped
>
> 2 tablespoons coarsely chopped parsley
>
> ½ teaspoon kosher salt
>
> ¼ teaspoon Aliño (page 444)

IN A MEDIUM SAUCEPAN OF WATER, boil the plantains for 30 minutes, or until very soft. Drain and reserve 2 cups (500 ml) of the cooking liquid.

In a food processor, purée the plantains. With the processor running, slowly pour in the milk. Process just until smooth.

In a medium saucepan, warm the reserved cooking liquid over low heat. Whisk in the purée until smooth. Stir in the remaining ingredients. Heat through.

MAKES 8 CUPS (2 L); 8 GENEROUS FIRST-COURSE SERVINGS

winter mushroom soup

THE MUSHROOM BROTH is a nice alternative to water. Porcini and cèpes and Polish mushrooms are all *Boletus,* which can be found in American woods if one knows what one is doing. Last summer, I found more than I could use and I restricted myself to *Boletus edulis,* the choicest ones. As this soup uses dried mushrooms, it can be made at any time, but it is robust and particularly welcome in winter.

12 cups (3 l) water or Mushroom Broth (page 382)

2 ounces (60 g) dried porcini mushrooms (cèpes)

2 tablespoons (30 g) unsalted butter

1 pound (450 g) fresh mushrooms, trimmed, wiped clean, and thinly sliced

1 large onion, cut into ¼-inch (.5-cm) dice

2 large leeks, white part only, cut in half lengthwise, washed well, and cut across into 1½-inch (4-cm) lengths

2 medium carrots, peeled and cut across into thin slices

½ pound (225 g) parsnips or celery root, peeled and cut into ½-inch (1-cm) dice

4 medium cloves garlic, smashed and peeled

4 bay leaves

1 cup (200 g) pearl barley, rinsed well

½ pound (225 g) firm potatoes, peeled and cut into 1-inch (2.5-cm) cubes

1 tablespoon kosher salt, or to taste

Freshly ground black pepper, to taste

½ cup (20 g) snipped dill

Sour cream, for serving, optional

IN A SMALL SAUCEPAN, bring 1½ cups water or mushroom broth just to a boil. Place the dried mushrooms in a small bowl and pour the hot water or broth over them. Soak for 15 minutes. Drain the mushrooms, reserving the liquid. Squeeze out the excess liquid and set aside. Strain the mushroom soaking liquid through a coffee filter rinsed with hot water.

In a large stockpot, melt the butter over low heat. Stir in the fresh mushrooms and cook until they soften and give off their liquid, about 10 minutes. Stir in the remaining water or broth, the soaked mushrooms and their liquid, the onion, leeks, carrots, parsnips, garlic, and bay leaves. Bring to a boil. Skim the froth as necessary. Lower the heat and simmer for 30 minutes.

Stir in the barley and simmer for 20 minutes. Stir in the potatoes. Simmer for 30 minutes, or until the barley and potatoes are tender. Discard the bay leaves. Remove from the heat. Season with the salt, pepper, and dill.

Swirl a dollop of sour cream into each serving, if desired.

MAKES 15 CUPS (3.75 L); 10 FIRST-COURSE OR 6 MAIN-COURSE SERVINGS

cabbage soup

PAPRIKA AND CARAWAY provide a hint of Hungary. Those who want more can add some sour cream to top each portion.

> 5 tablespoons (75 g) unsalted butter
>
> 4 small sweet onions, very thinly sliced
>
> 1 large white cabbage, cored and very thinly shredded (about 15 cups; 1.8 kg)
>
> 1 tablespoon sweet paprika
>
> 5 cups (1.25 l) Basic Chicken Stock (page 345) or commercial chicken broth
>
> 1 teaspoon caraway seed
>
> 1 tablespoon kosher salt, or to taste, or less if using commercial broth
>
> Freshly ground black pepper, to taste
>
> 2 tablespoons fresh lemon juice

IN A TALL NARROW STOCKPOT, melt 3 tablespoons (45 g) butter over medium heat. Stir in the onions and cook, stirring frequently, for 20 minutes. The onions should be very limp and just beginning to brown.

Stir in the remaining butter and allow it to melt. Stir in the cabbage. Raise the heat to high. Cook for 20 minutes, stirring frequently from top to bottom so that the cabbage wilts evenly.

Stir in the paprika and cook for 1 minute. Stir in the stock, caraway, and salt. Bring to a boil. Season with pepper and taste for salt. Stir in the lemon juice just before serving.

MAKES 9 TO 10 CUPS (2.25 TO 2.5 L); 8 TO 10 FIRST-COURSE SERVINGS

vegetables of substance

Much of the world has lived a great deal of the time on soup. Many of the prior recipes in this chapter have been soups out of which I would make a meal, and the book is full of more such recipes. Those in this section were conceived as meals and meant to be enjoyed that way. Some are vegetarian.

six-vegetable soup

THIS IS NOT UNRELATED TO MINESTRONE, but it has no pasta or basil and is somewhat chunkier and fresher-tasting.

  2 tablespoons (30 g) unsalted butter

  1 medium onion, cut into ¼-inch (.5-cm) dice

  1 very small clove garlic, smashed, peeled, and very finely chopped

  2 cups (500 ml) Chunky Tomato Base (page 385), drained and lightly crushed
      canned tomatoes (not plum), or sterile-pack chopped tomatoes

  8 cups (2 l) Basic Chicken Stock (page 345) or commercial chicken broth

  ¼ teaspoon dried marjoram

  ½ pound (225 g) firm potatoes, peeled and cut into ¼-inch (.5-cm) dice

  1 small carrot, peeled and cut into ¼-inch (.5-cm) dice

  ¾ pound (360 g) peas in the pod, shelled (about ⅔ cup), or 4 ounces (120 g) frozen
      peas, defrosted in a sieve under warm running water and drained (⅔ cup)

  3 medium scallions, trimmed, and thinly sliced across on the diagonal

  2 to 2½ tablespoons kosher salt, or less if using canned broth

  Freshly ground black pepper, to taste

  Cayenne pepper

  Hot red pepper sauce

IN A MEDIUM SAUCEPAN, melt the butter over medium heat. Stir in the onion and garlic and cook for 5 minutes, or until translucent. Stir in the tomatoes, stock, and marjoram. Bring to a boil. Lower the heat and simmer for 15 minutes.

Stir in the potatoes and carrot. Simmer for 5 minutes. Stir in the fresh peas, if using. Simmer for 10 more minutes.

If using frozen peas, stir them in now. Add the scallions, salt, black pepper, cayenne pepper and hot red pepper sauce and heat through.

MAKES ABOUT 10 CUPS (2.5 L); 6 MAIN-COURSE SERVINGS

cheese and potato soup

SHARING THIS ECUADORIAN vegetarian soup can be very festive, with everyone stirring in the sauces and other serving items to their own taste.

for the refrito

2 tablespoons (30 g) unsalted butter

1 small onion, finely chopped

2 teaspoons ground cumin

2 teaspoons Annatto Butter (page 445)

for the soup

3 pounds (1.4 kg) mashing potatoes, peeled and cut into 3-inch (7.5-cm) pieces

8 cups (2 l) milk

1 tablespoon chopped cilantro, including stems

1 small jalapeño pepper, seeded and cut into small dice

2 egg yolks

1½ pounds (675 g) queso blanco cheese, or mozzarella, coarsely grated

2 teaspoons kosher salt

Freshly ground black pepper, to taste

for serving

½ cup (20 g) coarsely chopped cilantro

1 avocado, seeded, peeled, and sliced

Pickled Onions (page 446)

Tamarillo Sauce (page 441) and Criolla Sauce (page 443)

FOR THE REFRITO, in a large wide pot, melt the unsalted butter over low heat. Stir in the onion and cook for 10 minutes, stirring occasionally. Stir in the cumin and cook for 1 minute, stirring to release the aroma. Stir in the annatto butter to melt.

Stir in the potatoes, the milk, reserving 2 tablespoons, 1½ cups (375 ml) water, the cilantro, and jalapeño. Bring to a boil. Lower the heat and simmer, covered, for 45 minutes. At this point, the potatoes should be cooked through. If they look too big to ladle, use a wooden spoon to break them into large chunks.

Whisk the egg yolks with the remaining milk. Temper by stirring a small amount of the hot soup into the yolks. Pour this mixture back into the soup. Stir in the cheese, salt, and pepper. Simmer, uncovered, for 5 minutes. Do not let the soup come to a boil.

Serve with the cilantro, avocado, pickled onions, tamarillo and criolla sauces.

MAKES 14 CUPS (3.5 L); 6 MAIN-COURSE SERVINGS

southwestern corn
AND TOMATO SOUP

FOR ME, this is a main course, a summer delight.

2 ounces (60 g) smoked slab bacon, cut into 1 × ½ × ½-inch (2.5 × 1 × 1-cm) matchstick strips

1 small onion, cut into ¼-inch (.5-cm) dice

1 teaspoon hot red pepper flakes

4 medium cloves garlic, smashed and peeled

⅓ cup (60 g) diced green bell pepper

⅓ cup (60 g) diced red bell pepper

1 pound (450 g) firm potatoes, peeled and cut into ½-inch (1-cm) dice

3 cups (750 ml) Plum Tomato Purée (page 386), canned Italian plum tomatoes puréed with their juice, or sterile-pack strained tomatoes

Kernels from 6 ears corn

1 tablespoon kosher salt

Freshly ground black pepper, to taste

2 tablespoons coarsely chopped cilantro

2 medium scallions, white part only, thinly sliced across

Hot red pepper sauce, to taste

IN A MEDIUM SAUCEPAN, cook the bacon over medium heat until it is crisp, about 20 minutes.

Stir in the onion, red pepper flakes, garlic, peppers, potatoes, tomato purée, and 1½ cups (375 ml) water. Bring to a boil. Lower the heat and simmer for 10 minutes. Stir in the corn and simmer for 10 minutes, or until the potatoes are tender. Season with salt and pepper. The soup can be made ahead to this point and refrigerated for up to 2 days.

If the soup has been refrigerated, reheat it. Stir in the cilantro, scallions, and hot red pepper sauce.

MAKES 8 CUPS (2 L); 4 MAIN-COURSE SERVINGS
OR 8 FIRST-COURSE SERVINGS

curried squash
AND APPLE SOUP

THIS VEGETARIAN SOUP can be a silky and succulent first course for a fall or winter evening; but I prefer to serve it as a main course with boiled rice on the side and a sprinkling of raisins and slivered almonds on top. A chutney would not be out of place.

2 medium acorn squash, cut in half lengthwise, and seeds and fibers removed

¼ cup (65 ml) vegetable oil

4 teaspoons black mustard seed

3 tablespoons curry powder

2 large Granny Smith or other tart apples, quartered, cored, cut into 1-inch (2.5-cm) cubes, and tossed with the juice of 1 lime

1 medium onion, cut into chunks

10 medium cloves garlic, smashed and peeled

1½ tablespoons very finely chopped peeled ginger

4 cups (1 l) Roasted Vegetable Broth (page 380)

Lime juice, to taste

2 teaspoons kosher salt

for serving

1 lime, sliced across into very thin rounds

¾ cup (180 g) yogurt

HEAT THE OVEN to 500°F (260°C; highest gas mark; #9 British regulo). Roast the squash cut side up in a roasting pan for 50 minutes, or until soft. Scoop the pulp from the squash.

In a medium saucepan, stir together the vegetable oil and mustard seeds over medium heat until the seeds are popping (be careful—it is very easy to burn the spices if the oil gets too hot). Stir in the curry powder and cook, stirring constantly, over medium-low heat for about 1½ minutes.

Stir in the apples, squash, onion, garlic, ginger, and stock. Bring to a boil. Lower the heat. Simmer for 20 minutes, or until the apples and onions are soft.

In a food processor, working in batches, purée the soup; or pass through the medium disc of a food mill. The soup can be made ahead to this point and refrigerated for up to 3 days.

Return the soup to the pot and heat through. Season with the lime juice and salt. Top each serving with a thin slice of lime and a dollop of yogurt.

MAKES 8 CUPS (2 L); 4 TO 6 MAIN-COURSE SERVINGS OR 8 FIRST-COURSE SERVINGS

minestrone

THERE ARE AS MANY MINESTRONES, all somewhat different, as there are regions of Italy. They are easy to confuse with the yet-larger group of *zuppe de verdura*. Zuppe de verdura are vegetable soups, without pesto, somewhat lighter in taste than minestrone, usually without pasta, and cooked for a much shorter time. In Emilia-Romagna, they use beef stock instead of water in their minestrone. In Milan, in the summer, they add cooked rice (about 2 cups [280 g]; see page 294) to the soup and eat it tepid, a variation of which I am very fond. My soup is closest to the minestrone of Liguria. According to Fred Plotkin, author of the brilliant *Recipes from Paradise: Life and Food on the Italian Riviera*, in Liguria such soups are cooked for at least an hour longer than mine, or until the vegetables are very soft.

Any Genovese will tell us that pesto must be made (pounded to a paste) in a mortar and pestle, sometimes with garlic. They say that more of the basil's perfume is released that way. In this recipe, I give an alternative method, but if tradition calls, feel free to use a mortar. It should be noted that this pesto has no cheese and no pine nuts (pignoli). It is the same kind of pesto that is used in nearby France in Soupe au Pistou (page 302).

½ cup (125 ml) plus 3 tablespoons olive oil

1 medium onion, cut into ¼-inch (.5-cm) dice

3 medium carrots, peeled and cut into ¼-inch (.5-cm) dice

2 large ribs celery, peeled and cut into ¼-inch (.5-cm) dice

½ pound (225 g) firm potatoes, peeled and cut into ¼-inch (.5-cm) dice

⅔ pound (180 g) white cabbage, cored and cut into ¼-inch (.5- cm) dice

2 medium yellow squash, trimmed and cut into ¼-inch (.5-cm) dice

½ pound (225 g) Swiss chard, leaves cut into narrow strips, stems cut
    across into slices

1 small bunch spinach, stemmed, well washed, and cut across into narrow strips

6 medium cloves garlic, smashed, peeled, and coarsely chopped

1 cup (250 ml) Chunky Tomato Base (page 385), coarsely chopped canned
    Italian plum tomatoes, or sterile-pack chopped tomatoes

Rind from a ⅔-pound (170-g) piece of Parmesan cheese

2 medium bunches basil, leaves only, well washed and dried

1 cup (120 g) cooked orzo (riso) (see page 392)

2 tablespoons kosher salt

Freshly ground black pepper, to taste

Freshly grated Parmesan cheese, for serving

continued

IN A MEDIUM STOCKPOT, cook ½ cup (125 ml) oil and the onion over medium heat, stirring occasionally, for 10 minutes. Stir in the carrots, celery, and potatoes. Cook, stirring occasionally, for 5 minutes. Stir in the cabbage and squash and cook for 5 minutes. Stir in the greens, half of the garlic, the tomatoes, 5 cups (1.25 l) water; and the cheese rind. Bring to a boil. Lower the heat and simmer for 10 to 15 minutes, until all the vegetables are tender.

Meanwhile, to make the pesto, in a food processor, coarsely purée the basil. Transfer to a blender, add the remaining garlic, and purée. With the machine running, slowly pour in the remaining oil. Continue to blend until smooth.

Remove the cheese rind from the soup. Stir in the orzo. Heat through. Stir in ¼ cup (65 ml) of the pesto. Season with the salt and pepper. The soup can be made ahead and refrigerated for up to 3 days; but do not add the orzo until reheating to serve.

If the soup has been refrigerated, reheat it, adding a little water to avoid sticking. Pass the remaining pesto and grated Parmesan cheese at the table.

MAKES 13 CUPS (3.25 L); 6 GENEROUS MAIN-COURSE SERVINGS

vegetable curry soup

THERE ARE SO MANY wonderful Indian vegetable curries that I didn't think anything would be amiss in my adding a soup version. The colors are attractive and the seasonings not too hot. If desired, add some good yogurt.

2 teaspoons ground coriander

¼ teaspoon anise seed

¼ teaspoon celery seed

¼ teaspoon yellow mustard seed

¼ teaspoon cardamom seed

¼ teaspoon ground cumin

Pinch of ground cinnamon

2 small dried hot red peppers (such as péquins)

2 tablespoons vegetable oil

1 medium onion, cut into ¼-inch (.5-cm) dice

2 medium cloves garlic, smashed, peeled, and very finely chopped

2 cups (500 ml) tomato juice

1 medium sweet potato, peeled and cut into 1-inch (2.5-cm) cubes

2 small carrots, peeled and cut across into ¼-inch (.5-cm) slices

1 small head cauliflower, cored and broken into florets (2½ cups; 180 g)

1 small head broccoli (180 g), florets only (3 cups)

3 small ribs celery, peeled and cut across into ¼-inch (.5-cm) slices

1 cup (250 ml) Tomato Purée (page 384), canned tomato purée,
    or sterile-pack strained tomatoes

¼ pound (120 g) white mushrooms, wiped clean, trimmed, and caps
    and stems cut across into ¼-inch (.5-cm) slices

1 pound (450 g) peas in the pod, shelled (scant 1 cup), or half a 10-ounce
    (300-g) package frozen peas, defrosted in a sieve under warm
    running water and drained (scant 1 cup)

1½ tablespoons fresh lime juice

2 teaspoons kosher salt, or to taste

Freshly ground black pepper, to taste

4 cups (600 g) cooked white rice (see page 294), for serving

PLACE ALL THE SPICES and the hot peppers in a spice grinder or a mortar and grind
to a powder.

In a medium saucepan, heat the oil over medium heat. Stir in the spices, onion, and
garlic and cook over medium heat, stirring, for 2 minutes, or until fragrant.

Stir in the tomato juice, 2 cups (500 ml) water, the sweet potato, and carrots. Bring
to a boil. Lower the heat and simmer for 15 minutes, or until the carrots are tender but not
mushy.

Add the cauliflower, broccoli, celery, tomato purée, and mushrooms. Return to a
boil. Lower the heat and simmer for 6 minutes. Stir in 1 cup (250 ml) water and the peas.
Return to a boil. Lower the heat and simmer for 8 minutes. Remove from the heat and stir
in the lime juice, salt, and pepper.

Place 1 cup (150 g) rice in the bottom of each bowl. Spoon the curry over the rice.

MAKES 9 CUPS (2.25 L); 4 MAIN-COURSE SERVINGS

vegetable gumbo
WITH OR WITHOUT ROUX

SOMEWHERE THERE MUST EXIST Creole vegetarians, although I have yet to meet one. If there is, this soup's for them; otherwise, it's for me. I like it so much that I have played with two versions (both in this recipe), one with a roux and one without. Try both and tel l me which is better.

I'm afraid I don't have a kale-stem soup, so the leftover stems had best be made into a vegetable dish or added, cut up, to a potage (page 99).

10 tablespoons (160 ml) vegetable oil if using roux; 6 tablespoons (100 ml) olive oil if not using roux

¾ cup (120 g) all-purpose flour, if using roux

1 large onion, cut into ¼-inch (.5-cm) dice

10 medium cloves garlic, smashed, peeled, and very finely chopped

3 medium dried hot red peppers, crumbled

2 medium bunches kale, leaves only, cut across into ½-inch (1-cm) strips

1½ pounds (670 g) fresh cranberry beans, shelled, or 2 cups (360 g) rinsed and drained canned cannellini beans

4 cups (1 l) Chunky Tomato Base (page 385), lightly crushed canned tomatoes (not plum), with their juice, or sterile-pack chopped tomatoes

1 pound (450 g) okra, stem tips removed and discarded, remaining portions cut across into ¼-inch (.5-cm) slices

Kernels from 2 ears corn

2 pounds (900 g) fava (broad) beans, shelled, blanched for 2 minutes, run under cold water, and popped out of tough outer skin, or 1 cup (6 ounces; 180 g) frozen lima beans, defrosted in a sieve under warm running water and drained

Kosher salt, to taste

½ cup (125 ml) red wine vinegar if using roux; 1 tablespoon if not using roux

Freshly ground black pepper, to taste

Hot red pepper sauce, to taste

IF USING THE ROUX, in a large wide pot, heat the vegetable oil over medium-high heat. Stir in the flour and cook, stirring continuously, for 15 minutes. At this point, the mixture should be beginning to take on a lot of color. Lower the heat to medium-low and continue to cook until the roux is a warm brown, like milk chocolate. This will take 20 to 30 minutes from the time the flour was added.

If not using the roux, in a large wide pot, heat the olive oil over medium heat. Stir in the onions and cook, stirring occasionally, for 10 minutes or until translucent.

If using the roux, stir the onions into the brown roux. Remove from the heat and continue to stir; the mixture will be hot enough to continue cooking to the point where the roux is rich chocolate brown and the onions are wilted without burning. When the onions and roux have stopped sizzling, return to medium heat.

With or without the roux, stir half of the garlic, the red peppers, and kale into the onions. Cook over medium-low heat, stirring occasionally, until the kale is wilted, about 10 minutes.

Stir in 5 cups (1.25 l) water and the fresh cranberry beans, if using. Bring to a boil. Lower the heat and simmer, partially covered, for 20 minutes.

Stir in the tomatoes, 2 cups (500 ml) water, and the okra. Return to a boil. Lower the heat and simmer for 8 minutes.

Stir in the corn, the cannellini, if using, and the fava beans. Add the remaining garlic and season with salt, vinegar, pepper, and hot red pepper sauce. Let the soup sit for at least 30 minutes or up to 1½ hours.

Reheat and serve.

MAKES 15 CUPS (3.75 L); 8 MAIN-COURSE SERVINGS

Bird soups

CHICKEN SOUPS SEEM to be the universal, international panacea, as mothering in China as in America. While I will certainly not scant them, I am as fond of turkey, duck, goose, and—when the bones are available—game bird soups.

They can be hot, clear, intense, and elegant, the start of a formal dinner on their own or with many of the delights on pages 414–420 floating in them. They can become heartier when the inhabitants are noodles—Asian or European—matzo balls, or meatballs. The clear soups can be served gelled on a hot day.

Bird soups can be robust, liquid stews, warming and comforting dinners for a cold day, and can often be made even more filling with the addition of rice, noodles, or potatoes.

Before they are cooked, chickens and other birds often need to be skinned and cut into pieces to use in soup. The skinning is a matter of preference. Cutting the bird up makes it easier to eat in soup and influences the cooking time.

To cut up a bird

Remove the giblet package from the body of the bird. Reserve the neck and gizzards for stock. Save the liver for another use. Work with strong sharp kitchen shears and a large heavy knife. The latter is especially important when cutting the bird into fourteen pieces.

To cut a bird into eight serving pieces: Cut through the skin connecting each leg/thigh to the body of the bird. Separate each leg/thigh from the carcass by pulling it away and down so that the joint becomes loose. Where the thigh meets the carcass, the joint should pop out. Cut through the place where the bone has popped out of the joint. This easily separates the thigh from the carcass.

Lay each leg/thigh piece on the counter skin side down. There will be a diagonal line of visible fat running between the leg and the thigh. Cut along this line to separate the leg from the thigh.

Using the same skin-cutting, bending-back, and popping-out method, separate each wing from the carcass, cutting the wing away through the joint. Cut the wing tips off and reserve for stock.

Tilt the carcass up so that it is propped on the neck opening. Cut down between the back and the breast, leaving the portion of the rib bones not covered by meat attached to the back portion. Cut down along either side of the breastbone to separate the breast into two pieces.

There will be eight serving pieces, plus the back, neck, and wing tips.

To cut a large bird such as a goose or duck into fourteen serving pieces: Cut the bird into eight pieces, as above.

Cut each breast crosswise in half. Do the same with each thigh. Cut through the joint between the remaining wing pieces to make two pieces. Leave the legs whole, or, if desired, cut off the knobby ends.

There will be fourteen serving pieces, plus the back, neck, and wing tips. For more manageable pieces, if the back is being used, it can be cut across into two pieces.

To skin a chicken

Cooked chicken is very easy to skin; all that needs to be done is wait until the chicken is cool enough to touch. The skin will peel off very easily. If the chicken waits longer, some of the proteins will seize up and it will be slightly more difficult to skin, but still won't be horrible. Raw chicken can be skinned whole, or in pieces.

To skin a whole chicken: Remove the wing tips. Start from the tail end of the chicken, where the legs stick out. Slip the fingers under the skin over the breast; larger chickens may have a membrane which will need to be snipped with a scissors to free the skin.

Continue to work fingers between the skin and flesh until the skin is like a balloon around the entire body of the chicken. Slip fingers into the thigh and leg and continue to loosen all the way to the ends, where the skin will be firmly attached. With a small knife, cut the skin around the tip of each leg to release it. The naked chicken can now be slipped out of its skin.

To skin chicken pieces: This is a much easier prospect. The skin on most pieces can easily be pulled off.

To poach a chicken breast: Start with boiling water. Add the split boneless, skinless chicken breasts. Return to a boil. Lower the heat and simmer for 12 to 14 minutes. A 12-ounce (360-g) chicken breast will require 5 cups (1.25 l) water. However, if the chicken is started in boiling water and enough water is used not only to cover the breast pieces but to let them swim free, the cooking time will be the same. Keep the very light stock that results and add it to the pot the next time stock is the order of the day, or reduce it by half and use it as a light Chinese stock.

The seasons of chicken soup

Chicken soup can be all things to all men, women, and children except for vegetarians. It can be a clear soup floating noodles, dumplings, or filled noodles (see From Stock to Soup, page 391), vegetables (pages 447–451), and herbs, or it can be a robust meal, such as those at the end of this chapter. If the kind of chicken soup desired is not here, don't despair. Look in the Index.

The basic Western grandmother's Chicken Soup is on page 4; but Asia (pages 128–132) and Africa (page 138) can lay claim to as many grandmother recipes as we can.

So many of the soups in this book start with chicken stock that it lives in pages 345–351 to be accessible to all. Those looking for Chinese chicken stock of the upscale kind should note the Superior Chinese Chicken Stock in Chicken Soup with Chinese Flavors (page 144). Or, for the lighter, more ubiquitous everyday stock, simply thin Basic Chicken Stock (page 345) with a third more water. These stocks can be made into soups by simply seasoning them, by following the recipes in this chapter, or by mixing and matching ingredients.

chicken soup
WITH ZING

THERE ARE DAYS on which I need a sinus-clearing soup that is easily made and good to taste. This is it. If the jalapeños are very mild, use two, or substitute two very small hot peppers, dried or fresh.

4 cups (1 l) Basic Chicken Stock (page 345) or commercial chicken broth

2 quarter-sized pieces peeled ginger

2 medium cloves garlic, peeled and thinly sliced lengthwise

1 jalapeño pepper, seeded, deribbed, and finely chopped

6 mint leaves

3 scallions, trimmed to 5 inches, white and green parts cut separately lengthwise into hair-thin strips

¼ cup (65 ml) fresh lemon juice

½ small bunch cilantro, leaves only, finely chopped

Kosher salt, to taste

Freshly ground black pepper, to taste

Cilantro leaves, for serving

IN A MEDIUM SAUCEPAN, bring the stock, ½ cup (125 ml) water, the ginger, garlic, and jalapeño to a boil. Lower the heat and simmer, partially covered, for 15 minutes.

Stir in the mint and scallion whites. Cook for 3 minutes. Stir in the scallion greens and cook just until wilted, about 1 minute. Stir in the lemon juice, chopped cilantro, salt, and pepper. Warm through.

Sprinkle each bowl with a few leaves of cilantro.

MAKES 4 CUPS (1 L); 4 FIRST-COURSE SERVINGS

chicken soup

WITH PASTINA AND GREENS

THINK OF THIS AS Italian comfort food. The recipe interests me because of a certain prissiness in it. I developed it years ago and put it in *Food for Friends.* I obviously thought whole floating cloves of garlic were unacceptable and tied them up in a cloth so that they could be removed. Today I would probably add two more cloves and let them all float, prizes for the eaters. Certainly, the cook should suit the occasion and the friends.

  2 tablespoons olive oil

  1 small onion, very finely chopped

  1 medium bunch broccoli di rape, washed, tough stems discarded, and tops and leaves cut across into 2-inch (5-cm) pieces, or

  1 head escarole [Batavia], washed in several changes of water and cut across into 2-inch (5-cm) strips

  8 cups (2 l) Basic Chicken Stock (page 345) or commercial chicken broth

  4 medium cloves garlic, unpeeled, tied in a cheesecloth bag

  Kosher salt, to taste

  Freshly ground black pepper, to taste

  ½ cup (60 g) pastina

  4 teaspoons fresh lemon juice

  Freshly grated Parmesan cheese, for serving

IN A MEDIUM SAUCEPAN, heat the oil over medium heat. Stir in the onion and cook, stirring occasionally, for 10 minutes, or until translucent. Stir in the broccoli di rape or escarole and cook for 2 minutes. Pour in the chicken stock and add the bag with the garlic cloves. Bring to a boil. Lower the heat and simmer for 30 minutes. Remove and discard the bag with the garlic cloves. Season with salt and pepper. The soup can be made ahead to this point and refrigerated for up to 2 days.

Return the soup to a boil. Stir in the pastina and simmer for 1 to 2 minutes, until just tender. Stir in the lemon juice.

Pass the Parmesan at the table.

MAKES 10 CUPS (2.5 L); 8 FIRST-COURSE SERVINGS

avgolemono

THIS IS MOTHER'S CHICKEN SOUP to a Greek. It need only be compared with the Brodo con Straciatella (page 127) to see that the difference between Greek and Italian is a matter of technique and lemon juice.

> **4 cups (1 l) Basic Chicken Stock (page 345) or commercial chicken broth**
> **6 tablespoons (90 g) Carolina or other long-grain white rice**
> **8 egg yolks**
> **¼ cup (65 ml) fresh lemon juice**
> **Kosher salt, to taste**
> **Freshly ground black pepper, to taste**

IN A MEDIUM SAUCEPAN, bring the stock to a boil. Stir in the rice and cook until tender, about 8 to 10 minutes.

Meanwhile, beat the egg yolks and lemon juice together in a large bowl.

When the rice is tender, slowly ladle half of the hot broth into the yolks to temper them, whisking constantly. Whisk the egg yolk mixture into the broth and place over low heat. Cook, stirring constantly, just long enough to thicken the soup. Do not boil. Season to taste with salt and pepper.

MAKES ABOUT 3 CUPS (750 ML); 4 FIRST-COURSE SERVINGS

brodo con straciatella

STRACIATELLA ARE LITTLE rags or strings, which is what the eggs look like when they are cooked. It is these gentle shreds that make this soup so comforting. The essentials of this soup are the stock, or brodo, the eggs, and the cheese. The spinach or other greens are variants, as is the prosciutto. Cooked peas can be used instead of the greens and if Garlic Broth (page 86) is substituted for the brodo and Serrano ham for the prosciutto, this will be a distinctly Spanish soup.

The technique in this recipe is stolen, with gratitude, from Pellegrino Artusi, a brilliant cook and gastronome who wrote *The Art of Eating Well.*

Use a pot that is large enough to hold the colander over the stock without actually touching it, so that the egg can flow freely into the soup to form the strings.

Although this soup is often found in restaurants, it is infinitely better made at home. In restaurants, the eggs seldom get to the table soft enough, as they continue to cook as they wait their way from kitchen to table.

2 eggs

4 teaspoons finely grated Parmesan cheese

A pinch of kosher salt, plus 1½ teaspoons

A pinch of freshly grated nutmeg

1 tablespoon all-purpose flour

4 cups (1 l) Extra-Rich Chicken Stock (page 349) or Beef Stock (page 165) or, in England, imported beef or meat stock

1 pound (450 g) spinach or Swiss chard, stemmed and leaves cut across into narrow strips, optional

Freshly ground black pepper, to taste

IN A SMALL BOWL, stir together the eggs, cheese, pinch of salt, the nutmeg, and flour—try not to get the eggs at all frothy.

In a medium saucepan, bring the stock to a boil. Place a colander with widely spaced holes over the boiling stock. Pour the egg mixture through the colander. Remove the colander and stir the soup once or twice. Remove from the heat or, if using the greens, lower the heat and stir them in just to heat through. Remove from the heat and season with salt and pepper. Serve immediately.

MAKES 4 CUPS (1 L) WITHOUT SPINACH, 5 CUPS (1.25 L) WITH; 4 FIRST-COURSE SERVINGS

jean-georges vongerichten's chicken soup

WITH COCONUT MILK AND LEMONGRASS

HAVING MADE SEVERAL versions of gai tom ka, I was pleased with none. Then I had lunch at Vong, one of Chef Vongerichten's marvelous restaurants, and there it was, the perfect version. He has the recipe in his book *Jean-Georges,* written with Mark Bittman. The recipe that follows is his to the letter except for my insertion of metric equivalents and the possible removal of the lime leaf.

When I made the soup, I found that the onions really needed to be very finely minced to achieve the texture I remembered so happily. I preferred the mushrooms in eighths. Soup this rich and soothing could be a meal for me, but it is a first course at the restaurant.

1 stalk lemongrass

1 tablespoon canola, rapeseed, or other neutral-flavored oil

1 medium onion, minced

1 garlic clove, minced

2 teaspoons Thai red curry paste or curry powder

Six ⅛-inch (30-mm) slices, fresh or frozen, galangal or ginger, not peeled

3 lime leaves, dried or fresh

4 cups (1 l) Jean-Georges's Chicken Stock (page 351)
   or Basic Chicken Stock (page 345)

¾ pound (360 g) boneless, skinless chicken breasts

2 cups (¼ pound; 120 g) shiitake mushrooms

One 13- to 14-ounce (375- to 415-ml) can unsweetened coconut milk

Juice of 2 limes

2 tablespoons nam pla or nuoc mam (Asian fish sauce)

3 scallions, trimmed and minced on the diagonal

¼ cup (15 g) minced cilantro

TRIM THE LEMONGRASS of its outer sheath and hard ends. Whack it in a few places with the back of a knife, then cut it into two or three pieces. In a deep skillet or medium saucepan, combine the oil, onion, and garlic and turn the heat to medium. Cook a minute, stirring, then add the lemongrass, curry paste, galangal or ginger, and lime leaves.

Cook, stirring, for 3 to 4 minutes, then add the stock. Bring to a boil, then reduce the heat to medium and cook at a moderate boil for about 15 minutes. (You may prepare the recipe in advance up to this point; refrigerate in a covered container for up to 2 days.)

While the broth cooks, cut the chicken breasts into ½- to ¾-inch (1- to 1.9-cm) cubes. Remove the stems from the shiitakes and discard or reserve for stock. Cut the caps into quarters or eighths.

Add the coconut milk, then the chicken and the mushrooms to the broth. Cook for about 5 minutes, or until the chicken is done.

Stir in the lime juice and nam pla. Taste and adjust the seasoning. Divide among four bowls, then garnish with the scallions and cilantro and serve. You may remove the galangal, lemongrass, and lime leaf before serving, or leave them in; they are delicious to gnaw on at the table.

MAKES 7½ CUPS (1.9 L); 4 LARGE FIRST-COURSE SERVINGS

vietnamese chicken soup

FAUX PHO

MAI PHAM, chef and owner of Lemon Grass Restaurant in Sacramento and the author of *The Best of Vietnamese and Thai Cooking,* kindly gave me her recipe for chicken pho. There is a recipe for the more common beef version on page 188. I have repaid her generosity by tampering with her recipe. This soup is not traditional, in that it doesn't use actual chicken pieces in the soup. But with noodles, it is substantial enough to be a main course.

In the real version, one does not start with chicken stock but instead with a chicken. I found that the chicken got overcooked and did not give enough flavor or substance to the broth.

I started again with really good chicken stock. I had prepared the seasoned broth (which can be made ahead and frozen) but was interrupted on my way to the noodles. I stuck the broth in the refrigerator. I came back to one of those happy culinary accidents. The seasoned broth had set. Unable to resist, I tasted it. It was a wonderful surprise and now it is how I usually make this soup.

The noodles and the bean sprouts can be added to make a serious hot meal. If there is a desperate sense that the meat of chicken is missing, I recommend cooking two chicken breasts as on page 123 and shredding them and adding them to the soup as it reheats.

Culantro is not a misprint for cilantro. It is a very different-looking herb, rather rubbery with oval serrated leaves. It is used in Haitian as well as Vietnamese and Thai cooking and can be found in Caribbean and Asian markets.

4 medium onions, 2 unpeeled and quartered, 2 thinly sliced

Two 4-inch (10-cm) pieces ginger, halved lengthwise

6 star anise

4 whole cloves

6 black peppercorns

5 quarts (5 l) Extra-Rich Chicken Stock (page 349), Basic Chicken Stock (page 345), or commercial chicken broth

⅓ cup (80 ml) nuoc mam (fish sauce)

5 tablespoons sugar

3 tablespoons kosher salt, or less if using commercial broth

1 large bunch cilantro, coarsely chopped

½ cup narrow strips Thai basil, holy basil, or sage

¼ cup (15 g) chopped Thai chilies or

12 leaves culantro, cut across into narrow s

8 medium scallions, trimmed and thinly sliced ac

if serving hot with noodles

2 pounds (900 g) ⅛-inch- (30-mm-) wide rice stick noodles,
     soaked for 20 minutes in warm water and drained

½ pound (225 g) mung bean or other large sprouts

for serving hot or cold

2 limes, each cut into 6 wedges

HEAT A LARGE FRYING PAN over high heat. Place the quartered onions and the ginger cut side down in the pan. Cook until beginning to blacken, about 10 minutes. Remove the ginger and reserve. Turn the onions and blacken the other cut side. Remove the pan from the heat. Rinse the onions and ginger. Wrap the star anise, cloves, and peppercorns in cheesecloth and tie with a piece of string.

In a medium stockpot, bring the stock to a boil. Add the charred onions and ginger, the spice bag, the nuoc mam, and sugar. Lower the heat. Simmer for 40 minutes.

With a slotted spoon, remove the vegetables from the stock. Remove the spice bag.

Line a sieve with a damp cloth and strain the broth. Return to the pot. Stir in the salt, ½ cup (75 g) sliced onions, ½ cup (30 g) cilantro, 3 tablespoons (7 g) basil, 2 tablespoons chilies, and, if using, the culantro. Let sit for 15 minutes. The soup can be made ahead to this point and refrigerated for up to 4 days. If homemade stock has been used, the soup can be served chilled as a gelled soup with all the accompaniments (except the noodles and sprouts) that would go with the hot soup for guests to take at will, although the soup is good without them. Add half of the scallions before chilling if serving cold.

If serving as a hot main course, in a large pot of boiling water, cook the noodles for 2 to 3 minutes. Drain. I find that if the guests are not Asian and not willing to slurp their noodles with the aid of chopsticks, it is better to break them into short pieces before using.

If the soup has been refrigerated and is to be served hot, reheat. For a first course, divide among bowls and pass the remaining chilies, cilantro, onions, scallions, and basil in bowls at the table, along with the lime wedges.

For a main course, divide the noodles evenly among six bowls. Pour about 2½ cups (625 ml) broth into each bowl. Sprinkle with the sprouts, and pass the other items as above.

MAKES 16 CUPS (4 L) BROTH; 12 TO 16 FIRST-COURSE SERVINGS, HOT OR GELLED,
WITHOUT NOODLES, OR 6 MAIN-COURSE SERVINGS WITH NOODLES

(page 124) in that it is

...m the sources of heat,

...ovides the heat, lemon-

...nd they provide an inter-

...ney can be used fresh or dry.

...ercial

..., bruised with

4 holy basil ...
1 teaspoon dried kari ...
¾ cup (15 g) cilantro leaves

IN A MEDIUM SAUCEPAN, combine all the ingredients except the cilantro. Bring to a boil. Lower the heat and simmer for 1 hour.

Correct the seasonings. Stir in the cilantro and simmer for 5 minutes.

MAKES 6 CUPS (1.5 L); 4 TO 6 FIRST-COURSE SERVINGS

Note: Those who don't want to deal with the grasses can strain the soup before adding the cilantro. This, however, is not as authentic as the original.

chicken velouté

THE FRENCH DO provide elegant first-course soups. This is a very posh one and can easily be doubled to serve a small dinner party. It is a variation of the classic sauce ivoire, which would be made with less of a richer stock. The soup can be varied with a small amount of a chopped fresh herb such as tarragon; but I like it best plain and pale.

4 tablespoons (60 g) unsalted butter

7 tablespoons (60 g) all-purpose flour

5 cups (1.25 l) Basic Chicken Stock (page 345) or commercial chicken broth

1 tablespoon kosher salt, or less if using commercial broth

Pinch of freshly grated nutmeg

3 egg yolks

¾ cup (180 ml) heavy cream

IN A SMALL HEAVY SAUCEPAN, melt the butter over low heat. Stir in the flour. Cook, stirring constantly, for 8 to 9 minutes. The mixture will be a pale golden color and will begin to thin out and become very shiny.

Pour in the stock in a slow steady stream, whisking constantly to avoid lumps. Once all the stock is incorporated, raise the heat. Slowly bring to a boil, stirring with a wooden spoon, paying special attention to the edges of the pot where the flour tends to stick. Lower the heat and cook, right below the boil, stirring constantly, for 30 minutes. Stir in the salt and nutmeg.

Whisk together the eggs and cream. Slowly add a few ladles of hot soup to the cream mixture, whisking constantly. When the cream and eggs have warmed up, stir the cream mixture into the soup. Heat, stirring, until the soup is slightly thickened and coats the back of a spoon, about 1 minute.

MAKES ABOUT 4 ½ CUPS (1.12 L); 4 FIRST-COURSE SERVINGS

Chicken meals and feasts

If chicken soup on its own is comforting, a whole meal based on chicken soup is twice as rewarding. There are a few recipes earlier in the book that make meals, such as Vietnamese Chicken Soup (Faux Pho) (page 130) and Chicken Soup (page 4).

Here are more recipes that are meals. Some of them are particularly pleasant because, as with the Faux Pho, there is a selection of things for each eater to add to the soup on an ad-lib basis—lots of passing and talking.

chicken soup meal
WITH MORELS AND TARRAGON

A HEAVENLY SOUP that is a seeming contradiction in styles because it is informal but made with luxurious, costly dried morels. When buying morels, try to choose the smallest ones. They are pleasanter to eat in this kind of soup—less cutting; their honeycomb pattern is smaller and has a pleasanter texture. The small ones tend to have a more intense flavor.

I have found most kinds of mushrooms in the wild, but never a morel. If fresh morels are a glut in the kitchen, use 3 ounces (90 g) in place of the dried morels. They do not need to be soaked. If large, they need to be cut in quarters or even eighths (bite-sized pieces). Do not soak them. Sauté them in a little butter and add to the soup at the same time as the cabbage, along with an extra cup of stock.

   1 ounce (30 g) small dried morels

   8 cups (2 l) Stock from a Whole Chicken (page 348), Basic Chicken
      Stock (page 345), or commercial chicken broth

   4 cups (750 g) shredded cooked chicken (from making stock) or 3 small
      whole skinless boneless chicken breasts

   4 small carrots, peeled and cut into ¼-inch (.5-cm) dice

   1 large leek, white and light green parts only, halved lengthwise, washed well,
      and thinly sliced across

¼ large white cabbage, dark green outer leaves removed, cored, and cut across into thin shreds, as for coleslaw (about 3 cups; 225 g)

1 bunch tarragon, leaves only

¼ pound (120 g) medium egg noodles, cooked (see page 392) and drained if making finished soup; or cook and drain while finishing soup

1 tablespoon kosher salt, or less if using commercial broth

Freshly ground black pepper, to taste

IN A SMALL SAUCEPAN, combine the morels and 2 cups (500 ml) stock and bring to a boil. Lower the heat and simmer for 5 minutes. Strain through a damp-cloth–lined sieve. Reserve the liquid and mushrooms separately.

If using the chicken breasts, in a medium saucepan, bring the remaining stock to a boil. Add the chicken and return to a boil. Lower the heat and simmer for 15 to 20 minutes, or until cooked through. Remove the chicken, leaving the stock in the pan. Allow the chicken to cool slightly before shredding.

Bring the stock left in the pan, or the remaining stock if using cooked chicken, to a boil with the carrots and leek. Lower the heat and simmer for 15 minutes, or until the carrots are easily pierced with the tip of a knife. Return to a boil and stir in the cabbage. Return to a boil. Lower the heat and simmer until the cabbage wilts, about 4 minutes. The soup can be made ahead to this point and refrigerated for up to 3 days.

If the soup has been refrigerated, reheat it. Stir in the reserved mushroom liquid and mushrooms, the chicken, tarragon, and noodles and heat through. Season with the salt and pepper and serve immediately.

MAKES 11 CUPS (2.75 L); 8 FIRST-COURSE SERVINGS OR 4 AMPLE MEALS

chicken gumbo

LOUISIANA, most particularly New Orleans and the lands that stretch west along the delta, is famous for its food. I think that its gumbos are its triumphs. The characteristic medium spiciness that still lets the other flavors, the thickening agents and the opening sauté of vegetables, shine through, to combine with the main ingredient—here chicken— is inspired and reflects French, Italian, and African influences.

The thickening can come from the roux and from filé powder. Roux in Creole or Cajun cooking is the usual combination of fat—usually butter—and flour cooked until it turns a lovely hazelnut brown. Filé is pulverized sassafras (see page 276 for using it). If filé is hard to get, the roux can be doubled and the filé omitted. Do not overcook the roux; it should be a warm chocolate color, not black. If the roux becomes overcooked, it will not thicken the soup; instead, it will separate out and float on top.

Andouille sausage can be used, if available. Cook it ahead and slice across into ¼-inch (.5-cm) slices. Or use tasso ham instead of the Virginia ham. Alternatively, the chicken can be removed from the bones after it's cooked and returned to the soup. This is good served with white rice. It's relatively spicy, so for delicate palates, the lesser amount of cayenne should be used, or a little extra liquid can be added. I like to serve this soup as a casual dish, chicken pieces or torn chicken meat, soup, and rice all passed separately so the guests can help themselves.

The roux takes some time to make. I like to make a larger amount in the microwave, which requires less stirring, and freeze it to have when the need for gumbo hits. See page 118.

7 tablespoons (115 ml) vegetable oil, plus additional if needed

Two 4-pound (1.8-kg) chickens, cut into 10 serving pieces (see page 122; breasts cut into 4 pieces)

¾ cup (100 g) all-purpose flour

1 to 2 teaspoons cayenne pepper

1 large onion, coarsely chopped

12 medium cloves garlic, smashed, peeled, and coarsely chopped

3 medium ribs celery, peeled and coarsely chopped

2 medium red bell peppers, cored, seeded, deribbed, and coarsely chopped

2 medium green bell peppers, cored, seeded, deribbed, and coarsely chopped

1 tablespoon filé powder

6 cups (1.5 l) Basic Chicken Stock (page 345) or commercial chicken broth

1 tablespoon dried thyme

1 teaspoon dried marjoram

Kosher salt, to taste

½ pound (225 g) Virginia ham, cut into ¼-inch (.5-cm) dice

1 tablespoon fresh lemon juice, or to taste

6 cups (900 g) cooked white rice (see page 294), optional

IN A LARGE heavy wide pot, heat the oil over medium-high heat. Brown the chicken, working in two batches. Remove the chicken to a bowl.

Measure the oil left in the pot—there should be ½ cup (125 ml); if there isn't enough, add additional oil to make ½ cup (125 ml). Return the oil to the pot and add the flour. Cook over medium heat, stirring aggressively to scrape up any brown bits from the bottom of the pot, for about 5 minutes. When all the bits have come up, continue to cook, stirring continuously, for 15 minutes. At this point the mixture should be beginning to take on a lot of color. Lower the heat and continue to cook until the roux is a warm brown, like milk chocolate; this should take 5 to 10 minutes more.

Stir in the cayenne pepper and onion. Remove from the heat and continue to stir; the mixture will be hot enough to continue cooking to the point where the roux is rich chocolate brown, the onions are wilted, and the cayenne aromatic, without burning. When the onions and roux have stopped sizzling, return the pot to medium heat. Stir in the garlic and celery. Cook, stirring, for 3 minutes. Stir in the peppers and cook, stirring, for 5 minutes.

Stir the filé powder into 1 cup (250 ml) of the stock. Whisk this into the rest of the stock, then whisk the stock into the vegetables and roux.

Add the browned chicken, thyme, marjoram, and salt. Stir to combine well. Bring to a boil. Lower the heat and simmer for 20 minutes. Stir in the ham and simmer for 5 minutes, or until the chicken is cooked through.

Adjust the seasoning with the lemon juice just before serving. If desired, serve over rice.

MAKES 11 CUPS (2.75 L) SOUP, PLUS CHICKEN PIECES AND RICE IF SERVING;
6 AMPLE MAIN-COURSE SERVINGS

chicken stew
WITH PEANUT BUTTER

PEANUTS WERE ONE of the great gifts of African Americans to the cooking of the United States, along with okra and talent.

In Africa, pounded peanuts are made into this dish. Peanut butter makes a quick and convenient substitute. Yams are used in Africa, but I use sweet potato for its color, rapid cooking, and flavor. I doubt that a separate chicken stock was used, and the dish can be made without it; but I prefer the added richness of the stock. The dish is very rich in any case. If desired, serve a big bowl of white rice on the side.

2 tablespoons peanut oil

1 small onion, coarsely chopped

One 3-pound (1.4-kg) chicken, cut into 8 serving pieces (see page 122; back, neck, and wing tips reserved for stock)

2½ teaspoons kosher salt

Freshly ground black pepper, to taste

⅔ cup (180 ml) crunchy Peanut Butter (page 435) or store-bought

3 cups (750 ml) Basic Chicken Stock (page 345) or commercial chicken broth

3 medium cloves garlic, smashed, peeled, and finely chopped

1 medium dried hot red pepper or ¼ teaspoon hot red pepper flakes

2 medium sweet potatoes, peeled, halved lengthwise, and each half cut across into 4 pieces

¾ pound (360 g) spinach, stemmed, washed well, and cut across into narrow strips

2 tablespoons fresh lemon juice, or to taste

Hot red pepper sauce, to taste

IN A TALL NARROW STOCKPOT, heat the oil over medium heat. Stir in the onion and cook for 10 minutes, stirring occasionally. Season the chicken with ½ teaspoon salt and pepper to taste, add to the onions, and cook, partially covered, for 8 minutes. Stir the chicken, turning the pieces over, and cook, partially covered, for 7 more minutes.

While the chicken is cooking, in a medium bowl, stir together the peanut butter and 1 cup (250 ml) stock until smooth. Stir in the remaining stock. Combine the garlic and red pepper and pound or chop as fine as possible—almost to a paste—using a mortar and pestle or a knife. Stir the garlic mixture into the stock mixture.

Stir the stock mixture into the pot. Bring to a boil, lower the heat, and simmer, partially covered, for 10 minutes.

Stir in the sweet potatoes. Poke the solids down into the pot so the potato and chicken are covered by the liquid. Bring to a boil, lower the heat, and simmer, partially covered, for 15 to 18 minutes, or until the potatoes are tender.

Stir in the spinach and cook, stirring, for 2 minutes, or until wilted. Season with the remaining salt, pepper to taste, the lemon juice, and hot red pepper sauce.

The chicken can be left on the bone, the skin on or off, or it can be skimmed out of the soup, removed from the bone and the skin discarded, torn into bite-sized pieces, and returned to the soup.

MAKES 9 CUPS (2.25 L) WITH CHICKEN ON THE BONE, 8 CUPS (2 L)
WITH CHICKEN OFF THE BONE; 4 TO 6 MAIN-COURSE SERVINGS

chicken
WITH DUMPLINGS

THIS IS FREELY ADAPTED from *Hoppin' John's Charleston, Beaufort, and Savannah Cookbook,* by John Martin Taylor. If you like it, think of him. Distaste can be attributed to me. I think it is better than chicken potpie or chicken fricassee, both of which it resembles.

> 8½ cups (1.6 l) Basic Chicken Stock (page 345) or commercial chicken broth
>
> One 3½- to 4-pound (1.6- to 1.8-kg) chicken, cut into 8 serving pieces (see page 122)
>
> 2 large ribs celery, peeled and cut across into ½-inch (1-cm) slices
>
> 3 medium carrots, peeled and cut across into ½-inch (1-cm) slices
>
> ½ pound (225 g) pearl onions, blanched for 1 minute, run under cold water, and peeled
>
> 1 large bunch parsley, 3 sprigs set aside, leaves only (from remaining sprigs), coarsely chopped
>
> 1 bay leaf
>
> 6 tablespoons (90 g) unsalted butter
>
> 6 tablespoons (50 g) all-purpose flour
>
> ¾ cup (180 ml) milk
>
> ¾ cup (180 ml) heavy cream
>
> Parsley Dumpling dough (page 418)
>
> 2 teaspoons kosher salt, or less if using commercial broth
>
> Freshly ground black pepper, to taste

IN A TALL NARROW STOCKPOT, bring the stock to a boil with the chicken, celery, carrots, and onions. Tie the parsley sprigs and bay leaf together with a piece of kitchen twine and add to the soup. Lower the heat and simmer, partially covered, for 35 to 45 minutes, or until the chicken is cooked through.

Strain through a fine-mesh sieve. Reserve the liquids and solids separately. Discard the bay leaf and parsley sprigs and allow the stock to cool.

In a wide pot, melt the butter over medium heat. Stir in the flour. Cook, stirring, for 4 to 5 minutes, or until the mixture has lost its raw flour smell.

Skim the fat from the top of the cooled stock. Combine the stock, milk, and cream. Slowly whisk into the flour mixture. Bring to a boil. Lower the heat and simmer, partially covered, stirring occasionally, for 20 minutes.

Meanwhile, remove and discard the chicken skin. Remove the meat from the bones. Discard the bones or save them for stock. Cut or tear the meat into bite-sized pieces.

Divide the dumpling dough into 12 equal pieces and form into flattish rounds.

Add the dumplings to the soup. Return to a boil, with the pot partially covered. Lower the heat and simmer for 10 minutes. Turn the dumplings and simmer for 10 minutes more, or until the dumplings are cooked through.

With a slotted spoon, carefully remove the dumplings to a plate. Stir the reserved vegetables and chicken, the chopped parsley, the salt, and pepper into the soup. Heat through. Divide the soup evenly among six bowls. Top with 2 dumplings per serving.

MAKES ABOUT 10 CUPS (2.5 L); 6 MAIN-COURSE SERVINGS

tortilla soup

ROCCOCO SOPA AZTECA

I FIRST HAD a version of this soup at the home of Shirley and Alf Collins in Seattle. We had a wonderful time sitting around their kitchen table. Shirley would get up from time to time to toast more tortillas on the electric burner. We made bowlful after bowlful, each bowl a little different depending on what we put in and how much. We drank Superior Mexican beer and had a wonderful evening.

While there is a recipe here, it's just a question of how much to allow per eater. As a rule, allow per person: 2 cups (500 ml) broth, 2 flour tortillas, ½ avocado, ⅓ cup (60 g) of shredded chicken or turkey, ⅓ medium red onion, ⅓ cup (6 g) cilantro leaves, ½ jalapeño, ½ lime, ½ small tomato, and ⅓ cup (45 g) shredded cheese.

This is more of an event than a soup. Bring the broth hot to the table and allow guests to make their own.

8 cup Basic Chicken Stock (page 345) or Roasted Turkey Stock (page 352)

Kosher salt, to taste

Freshly ground black pepper, to taste

8 flour tortillas, grilled over a burner or in a pan under a broiler until slightly crisp and mottled, and shredded

2 Hass avocados, seeded, peeled, and cut into ½-inch (1-cm) cubes

1 whole skinless boneless chicken breast, cooked and shredded

1 large red onion, coarsely chopped

1 large bunch cilantro, leaves only

2 medium jalapeño peppers, seeded and finely chopped (hotter chilies can be used for a spicier dish)

2 limes, cut into wedges

2 small tomatoes cut into ¼-inch (.5-cm) dice

1⅓ cups (120 g) shredded queso blanco, mozzarella, or rinsed mild feta cheese

IN A MEDIUM SAUCEPAN, bring the stock to a boil. Season with salt and pepper. Bring the broth to the table in a fondue pot or chafing dish to keep it hot as the diners ladle as little or as much as they desire into their bowls. Present the remaining ingredients in bowls so diners can add as many as they like.

MAKES 4 MAIN-COURSE SERVINGS

cazuela de elsa

ELSA TOBAR HAS WORKED with me for ten years. She came from Chile, and this is her recipe. It closely resembles the Ecuadorian *sancocho.* It is very beautiful; but it does require that guests not be persnickety about eating with their fingers—the corn, that is. I suppose the kernels could be removed from the cobs and added during the last few minutes of cooking, but the flavor would not be the same. To cut slices across the cob, slam the sharp blade of a heavy knife into the cob. Lift the knife and cob together and slam down on a cutting board.

2 medium carrots, peeled, halved lengthwise, and cut across into 2-inch (5-cm) lengths

1 medium yellow onion, cut into 1-inch (2.5-cm) wedges

1 medium sweet potato, peeled and cut across into ¼-inch (.5-cm) slices

One 2½- to 3-pound (1.1- to 1.4-kg) chicken, cut into 14 serving pieces (see page 122; wing tips and backs reserved for stock)

6 medium cloves garlic, smashed and peeled

4 teaspoons kosher salt, or to taste

1 large green bell pepper, cored, seeded, deribbed, and cut into 2-inch (5-cm) pieces

1 medium tomato, cored and cut in 2-inch (5-cm) chunks

2 ears corn, shucked, silk removed, and cut across into 2-inch (5-cm) rounds

¼ cup (10 g) finely chopped cilantro

Freshly ground black pepper, to taste

IN A TALL NARROW STOCKPOT, bring the carrots, onion, sweet potato, chicken, garlic, salt, and 5 cups (1.25 l) water to a boil. Lower the heat and simmer for 15 minutes. Stir in the bell pepper, tomato, and corn. Cover. Bring to a boil. Lower the heat and simmer, partially covered, for 5 minutes.

Stir in the cilantro and pepper. Simmer for 2 more minutes.

MAKES 13 CUPS (3.25 L); 6 TO 8 MAIN-COURSE SERVINGS

chicken soup

WITH CHINESE FLAVORS

THIS SOUP PRODUCES 9 cups (2.2 l) of broth and a whole chicken. The chicken can be served in the traditional Chinese mode for steamed poultry, letting the guests serve themselves from a platter with chopsticks. The broth goes in a bowl on the side. Or the meat can be removed (bones added to the reducing stock), torn into chunks, and returned to the soup along with the rest of the ingredients to be served in bowls.

The liquid from cooking the chicken, before the scallions and other ingredients are added, makes Superior Chinese Chicken Stock.

2 cups (500 ml) boiling water

½ ounce (15 g) dried wood ear mushrooms

½ ounce (15 g) dried shiitake mushrooms

One 4-pound (1.8-kg) chicken

¼ pound (120 g) Chinese smoked ham, Smithfield ham, or any hard smoked ham, cut into ½-inch (1-cm) dice

½ cup (60 g) hair-thin strips peeled ginger

10 medium scallions, white and light green parts cut across into 1-inch (2.5-cm) pieces, plus enough of the dark green thinly sliced across to make ½ cup (45 g), for serving

4 cardamom pods, seeds only

4 teaspoons kosher salt

POUR 1 CUP (250 ml) boiling water over the wood ears and 1 cup (250 ml) over the shiitakes. Allow to soak for 30 minutes.

Remove the mushrooms and squeeze out the excess liquid. Strain the liquid through a damp-cloth–lined sieve and reserve. Remove the hard stems from the shiitakes and cut the caps across into thin strips. Slice the wood ears into thin strips. Reserve the mushrooms.

In a tall narrow stockpot, bring the chicken, ham, ginger, 10 cups (2.5 l) water, and the mushroom liquid to a boil. Lower the heat and simmer for 35 minutes, skimming excess fat as necessary.

Stir in the scallion whites and light green parts, the mushrooms, cardamom, and salt. Simmer for 10 minutes.

Skim out the solids and set aside. There should be about 12 cups (3 l) liquid. Raise the heat and boil the liquid to reduce to 9 cups (2.25 l), about 25 minutes.

Meanwhile, remove the skin from the chicken. If not serving whole, tear off the meat in large chunks and return the bones to the soup as it is reducing.

If the bones were added during reduction, strain the soup and return it to the pot. Stir in the chicken meat and vegetables. Heat through.

Sprinkle the thinly sliced scallion greens over each serving just before bringing to the table.

MAKES 11 CUPS (2.75 L); 4 TO 5 MAIN-COURSE SERVINGS

a winter chicken

I DEVELOPED THIS one cold day when the vegetables around town were limited. I think the result, with the slightly bitter Belgian endive (witloof), the somewhat sweet fennel, and the aromatic celery root all making a contribution, is unusual and good. For those who don't feel fully fed with soup and bread, I serve boiled very small, firm potatoes.

4 tablespoons (60 g) unsalted butter

½ medium bulb fennel, trimmed, cored, and cut into matchstick strips

1 medium celery root, trimmed, peeled, and cut into matchstick strips

2 large Belgian endive [chicory], trimmed and cut across into ¼-inch (.5-cm) strips

1 medium onion, cut into ¼-inch (.5-cm) slices

4 cups (1 l) Basic Chicken Stock (page 345) or commercial chicken broth

1 cup (250 ml) heavy cream

2 teaspoons kosher salt, or less if using commercial broth

One 3½-pound (1.6-kg) chicken, skinned, meat removed from bones, cut into 2-inch (5-cm) squares, or 1¾ pounds (800 g) skinless boneless chicken breasts

IN A LARGE FRYING PAN, melt the butter over medium heat. Stir in the vegetables. Cook, stirring occasionally, for 5 minutes. Pour in the stock and cream. Season with the salt. Bring to a boil. Stir in the chicken. Return to a boil. Lower the heat and simmer, covered, stirring occasionally, for 20 minutes, or until the chicken is done.

MAKES 6 MAIN-COURSE SERVINGS

chicken soup
WITH LOVAGE

I LOVE LOVAGE and it goes wonderfully with chicken, as can also be seen in Lovage and Potato Soup (page 97). If necessary, replace it with tarragon and celery leaves (usually enough can be rescued from a bunch) or with dill. For the carbohydrate-hungry, boil up ½ pound (250 g) of dry medium egg noodles (page 392) and add at the end.

for the stock and chicken

> **12 cups (3.5 l) Basic Chicken Stock (page 345), commercial chicken broth, or water**
>
> **One 4- to 5-pound (1.8- to 2-kg) chicken, cut into 8 serving pieces (see page 122)**

for the soup

> **½ pound (225 g) very small white onions, blanched for 1 minute, peeled, run under cold water, and trimmed**
>
> **¾ pound (360 g) baby carrots, peeled**
>
> **½ pound (225 g) very small firm potatoes, cut in half, cooked in boiling salted water for 10 minutes, and drained**
>
> **⅓ cup (15 g) lovage leaves, cut across into narrow strips; or, if lovage isn't available, use 3 tablespoons tarragon leaves with 2 tablespoons celery leaves, or 3 tablespoons chopped dill**
>
> **Kosher salt, to taste**
>
> **Freshly ground black pepper, to taste**

FOR THE STOCK AND CHICKEN, bring the stock (or water) and chicken to a boil in a large stockpot. Lower the heat and simmer for 30 to 35 minutes. Remove the chicken. When the chicken is cool enough to handle, remove the skin and discard. Remove the meat from the bones, tear into bite-sized pieces, and reserve.

If water was used, return the bones to the pot and bring to a boil. Lower the heat and simmer for 3 hours and 30 minutes. Strain through a fine-mesh sieve.

For the soup, in a medium saucepan, bring 7 cups (1.75 l) stock (add water or reduce as necessary), the onions, and carrots to a boil. Lower the heat. Simmer, partially covered, for 10 minutes, or until the vegetables are almost done. Stir in the chicken, potatoes, lovage, salt, and pepper. Simmer for 5 minutes, or until all the vegetables are fork-tender and the chicken is hot.

MAKES 11 CUPS (2.6 L); 4 TO 5 GENEROUS MAIN-COURSE SERVINGS

On raising chickens

I AM A CITY CHILD, not a country child; but during the Second World War, we had a house in the country, and as my part in the war effort and as a sideline of a victory garden, I was assigned the job of dealing with the chickens. I collected the eggs, mucked out the henhouse, and fed the birds. I came to loathe the chickens.

No matter that I was bringing them their food, they always scattered frantically to the far end of their run in a panic when I came in. The place stank, and the eggs, far from being smooth brown beauties, were covered with feathers crusted to them with ordure.

Even worse, I came to know what a pecking order is. The flock would pick on one chicken and, if left to their own devices, peck it first naked of feathers and then to death. I would have to try to catch the benighted bird and remove it to a separate coop to recover.

I was not the one who had to take an ax to a scrawny neck to achieve chicken for cooking; but I watched in horror as the deheaded bird ran around the yard until it finally dropped. Of such realities are clichés made.

I did have to dip the bird in boiling water and then pluck out its feathers. All these experiences didn't turn me off eating chickens, but they eliminated any compassion I might have felt and made me look with deep suspicion at children's books in which chickens were charming characters or the pets of singularly adorable children.

chicken in the pot

THIS IS A RECIPE for one of what I call big or two-piece soups. The soup is generally eaten as a separate course and then the solids are served. This is a fancy French version of boiled chicken. It can be turned into a sensational feast by adding more of the accompanying vegetables, choosing for seasonality, color, and texture. Oddly enough, the quantity of any given vegetable cannot be reduced even when using many vegetables; there has to be enough of each to serve everybody.

Have saltcellars or small dishes filled with coarse salt (kosher will do if coarse sea salt is not available) for sprinkling on the cooked chicken.

> 1 black truffle, optional
> One 4- to 5-pound (1.8 to 2.25 kg) chicken
> 14 cups (3.5 l) Basic Chicken Stock (page 345) or
>   commercial chicken broth

accompanying vegetables: use three or more, 1 scant cup each

> Turnips, peeled, trimmed, and cut into ¼-inch- (.5-cm-) thick wedges
> Peas, shelled
> Whole baby carrots, peeled and trimmed
> Very tiny firm potatoes (if red, remove a thin band of skin from
>   around the middle)
> Zucchini, trimmed and cut into ½-inch (.5-cm) rounds
> Broccoli florets
> Cauliflower florets
> Radishes, trimmed
> Very young green beans, trimmed
> Thin scallions, trimmed
> Pearl onions, blanched for 1 minute, run under cold water, peeled,
>   and trimmed
> Mushroom caps
> Lemon juice, optional
> Thin asparagus spears, woody ends removed
> Small Italian artichokes, halved and chokes removed

SLICE THE TRUFFLE, if using, very thin. With fingers, carefully loosen the skin over the chicken breast, without detaching it. Spread the truffle slices evenly between the skin and breast meat of the chicken.

Open up a 2-yard length of cheesecloth and fold it in half lengthwise. Oil it so the chicken will not stick to it. Place the chicken on the cheesecloth so its length goes along the length of the cheesecloth. Bring up the two sides of the cheesecloth and pull them together. Roll them together (rolling the top edges of the paper as if wrapping a package) until they tightly meet the chicken. Knot the cheesecloth at either end as close as possible to the chicken. This way, the chicken does not have to be trussed. Knot the cheesecloth again just before each end.

In a large stockpot with two handles, bring the chicken stock to a boil. Lower the heat to a simmer and slowly, holding both ends of the cheesecloth, lower the chicken into the simmering stock. Tie the ends of the cheesecloth to the pot handles. Let the chicken simmer for 30 to 40 minutes.

While the chicken simmers, cook the accompanying vegetables separately in plenty of boiling salted water until just tender. For the mushrooms and artichokes, add some lemon juice to the water. Keep the vegetables warm. Remove the chicken from the pot, and kccp warm. Season the broth, and serve first in bowls.

Serve the poached chicken hot, surrounded by cooked vegetables in piles.

MAKES 4 SERVINGS

chicken in the pot
WITH CHINESE FLAVORS

THIS RECIPE is a variant of the Chicken Soup with Chinese Flavors (page 144), with the chicken cut into pieces and different flavorings.

8 cups (2 l) Basic Chicken Stock (page 345) or commercial chicken broth

1 ounce (30 g) dried shiitake mushrooms

Two 4-pound (1.8-kg) chickens, each cut into 8 serving pieces (see page 122) and skinned (backs, necks, and wing tips reserved for stock)

3 tablespoons hair-thin strips peeled ginger

8 medium cloves garlic, smashed and peeled

2 whole star anise or 1 heaping tablespoon star anise pieces

½ cup (125 ml) soy sauce, less if using commercial broth

2 medium bunches scallions, trimmed, white part cut into 2-inch (5-cm) lengths, enough greens cut into 2-inch (5-cm) lengths to equal 1 cup

Two 8-ounce (225-g) cans peeled and sliced water chestnuts, drained and rinsed well under cold water

½ pound (225 g) snow peas, tipped and tailed

6 cups (900 g) cooked long-grain white rice (see page 294)

BRING 2 CUPS (500 ml) of the stock to a boil. Soak the mushrooms in the stock for 15 minutes. Remove and squeeze out the liquid. Strain the soaking liquid through a damp-cloth–lined sieve or a coffee filter. Reserve the mushrooms and liquid separately.

Place the chicken, the remaining stock, the ginger, garlic, and star anise in a large wide pot. Cover and bring to a boil. Stir in the reserved mushroom liquid and the soy sauce. Return to a moderate boil. Stir in the scallion whites and the reserved mushrooms. Continue cooking at a moderate boil for 5 minutes. Stir in the water chestnuts and scallion greens. Cover and cook at a moderate boil for 5 minutes. Place the snow peas on top and return to a boil. Uncover and adjust the heat to remain at a moderate boil for 3 to 4 minutes or until the chicken is cooked through and the snow peas are cooked but still crunchy.

With tongs, remove the chicken pieces to a platter. Skim out the vegetables with a slotted spoon and scatter over the top.

Serve in large wide-rimmed bowls. Place ¾ cup (110 g) rice in the bottom of each bowl. Divide the chicken and vegetables evenly among the bowls and top each serving with about 1 cup (250 ml) of the broth.

MAKES 8 MAIN-COURSE SERVINGS

Turkey soups

Turkey is one of my very favorite soups and I can't wait until the day after Thanksgiving to have some. That hint should let you in on my thrifty pleasure of making the stock from the carcass of the roasted bird and any bones that are left on plates. (They will be boiled until sanitary.) Then the stock simmers all night (page 352).

I don't make turkey just on Thanksgiving. I often make one when I have a house full of people in the summer. They can snack off it and leave me free during the day.

Follow any recipe for roasting a turkey, or mine in *Roasting*.

turkey soup
WITH FENNEL

THIS IS A LOVELY PURÉE to serve as a first course. It is best made with a food mill to remove any strings from the fennel. However, it can be puréed in batches in a food processor and then pushed through a sieve.

> 1 large bulb fennel, trimmed (fronds chopped and reserved),
>   peeled, cored, and coarsely chopped
> 5½ cups (1.25 l) Roasted Turkey Stock (page 352), Basic Chicken
>   Stock (page 345), or commercial chicken broth
> 1 teaspoon kosher salt
> Freshly ground black pepper, to taste

IN A MEDIUM SAUCEPAN, bring the fennel and stock to a boil. Lower the heat and simmer, uncovered, for 30 minutes, or until the fennel is mushy.

Pass through the medium disc of a food mill. Return to the pot. Season with the salt and pepper and heat through.

Sprinkle each serving with some of the chopped fennel fronds.

MAKES 6 CUPS (1.5 L); 4 TO 5 FIRST-COURSE SERVINGS

turkey soup

FENNEL FIGURES in this soup as it does in the previous one; but this is not a purée, and with all the vegetables, it makes a main course. Without them, it is a hearty first course. With no turkey stock on hand, this recipe can be made with chicken stock.

> 7 cups (1.75 l) Roasted Turkey Stock (page 352), Basic Chicken Stock (page 345), or commercial chicken broth
>
> 2 medium ribs celery, peeled and coarsely chopped, including the leaves
>
> 1 medium onion, quartered
>
> 2 medium carrots, peeled and cut into chunks
>
> Stems from ½ medium bunch parsley (reserve the leaves for another use)
>
> Pinch of dried sage
>
> Pinch of dried thyme
>
> 6 ounces (180 g) medium egg noodles
>
> 2 small carrots, peeled and cut across into ¼-inch (.5-cm) slices, optional
>
> ¼ medium bulb fennel, cored and cut across into ¼-inch (.5-cm) slices, optional
>
> Kosher salt, to taste
>
> Freshly ground black pepper, to taste

IN A MEDIUM SAUCEPAN, bring the stock, celery, onion, carrots, parsley stems, sage, and thyme to a boil. Lower the heat and simmer until reduced to 5 cups (1.25 l). Strain through a fine-mesh sieve and return to the pot.

Meanwhile, cook the noodles in lightly salted boiling water until slightly under-done, about 5 minutes; drain. If using the optional vegetables, simmer them in lightly salted boiling water for 10 minutes and drain.

Season the broth with salt and pepper. Stir in the noodles, and the optional vegetables, if using them, and heat through.

MAKES 6 TO 6½ CUPS (1.5 TO 1.6 L); 4 HEARTY MAIN-COURSE SERVINGS

turkey soup meal
WITH SWISS CHARD

THIS MAKES A PERFECT post–Thanksgiving meal. Add more turkey if people are ravenous.

1 cup (90 g) bow-tie pasta

8 cups (2 l) Roasted Turkey Stock (page 352), Basic Chicken Stock (page 345),
    or commercial chicken broth

2 medium bunches Swiss chard, stems removed and cut across on the diagonal
    into ¼-inch (.5-cm) slices, greens cut across into narrow strips

10 ounces (300 g) small white boiling onions, blanched for 1 minute,
    run under cold water, and peeled

1 pound (450 g) very small firm potatoes, cut in half

3 medium ribs celery, peeled and cut diagonally across into ¼-inch (.5-cm) slices

2 tablespoons narrow strips sage

4 cups (about 450 g) bite-sized pieces cooked turkey meat

Kosher salt, to taste

Lots of freshly ground black pepper

COOK THE PASTA in lightly salted boiling water for 10 minutes. Drain and reserve.

In a medium stockpot, bring the stock to a boil. Stir in the Swiss chard stems, onions, potatoes, and celery. Return to a boil. Lower the heat and simmer for 15 minutes. Stir in the Swiss chard leaves and sage. Return to a boil. Lower the heat and simmer for 5 minutes.

Stir in the turkey and the reserved pasta. Season with salt and pepper. Heat through.

MAKES ABOUT 15 CUPS (3.75 L); 6 TO 8 MAIN-COURSE SERVINGS

Duck and goose soups

Of course, each of these birds has its own flavor; but they are both fatty and have meaty flavors, so they can be used interchangeably. Their stocks are on page 353.

duck broth

WITH NOODLES, SCALLIONS, AND RADISH

A SIMPLE AND DELICIOUS SOUP that is quickly made when the stock is on hand, which it will be if the duck is roasted my way in *Roasting.* Duck stock is easily made any time a duck has been roasted, no matter what the method.

> 4 cups (1 l) Duck Stock (page 353)
>
> 3 medium bunches scallions, trimmed, white and green parts separated, each cut across into 1-inch (2.5-cm) lengths
>
> ¼ pound (120 g) vermicelli or thin egg noodles, cooked (see page 392) and drained
>
> 1 teaspoon kosher salt
>
> 1 teaspoon freshly ground black pepper
>
> 3 medium radishes, very thinly sliced, blanched for 15 to 20 seconds in boiling water, and plunged into a bowl of ice water

IN A MEDIUM SAUCEPAN, bring the stock to a boil. Stir in the scallion whites and cook at a lively simmer for 5 minutes. Reduce the heat to medium and stir in the noodles, salt, and pepper.

Just before serving, stir in the scallion greens. Place 3 radish slices in each of six small bowls and pour in the soup.

MAKES 3 ½ CUPS (875 ML); 4 FIRST-COURSE SERVINGS

duck soup
WITH RHUBARB

REMY DOROTAN, THE CHEF-OWNER of Cendrillon, a restaurant in Manhattan, is from the Philippines. Some of his recipes are traditional, but most are inventive. I adapted this from a dish I had there. If making stock, start one day ahead.

> One 5-pound (2.25-kg) duck, skinned, meat removed from bones and
>   cut into ½-inch- (1-cm-) wide strips (bones, neck, and wing tips
>   reserved for stock); or use 5 cups (1.25 l) Duck Stock (page 353)
>   plus 1 pound (450 g) skinless boneless duck meat
>
> ¼ cup (60 g) very finely chopped peeled ginger
>
> ½ ounce (15 g) lemongrass, bulb end only, stripped to greenish heart,
>   pounded, and sliced across into thin rounds
>
> 1½ pounds (675 g) rhubarb, trimmed and cut across into 1-inch (2.5-cm) lengths
>
> 2 tablespoons sugar
>
> 2 teaspoons kosher salt
>
> 2 medium scallions, trimmed and white and green parts thinly sliced across
>   and reserved separately
>
> 4 medium radishes, sliced across into thin rounds

IF MAKING STOCK, in a tall narrow stockpot, bring the duck bones, neck, and wing tips to a boil with 8 cups (2 l) water. Bring to a boil. Lower the heat and simmer for 4 hours. If necessary, add water during simmering to keep the bones covered. Strain through a fine-mesh sieve. Refrigerate overnight.

Remove the fat from the cold stock and measure the stock: There should be at least 5 cups (1.25 l). If there is more, boil to reduce; if less, add water to make up the difference.

In a medium saucepan, bring the stock, ginger, and lemongrass to a boil. Lower the heat and simmer for 30 minutes. Strain through a fine-mesh sieve.

Return the strained stock to the saucepan and add the rhubarb. Bring to a boil. Lower the heat and simmer for 10 minutes, or until the rhubarb is very soft.

Pass through the fine disc of a food mill. Stir in the sugar and salt and return to the pan. Bring to a boil. Stir in the duck meat and return to a boil, stirring gently to ensure that the pieces don't stick together. Lower the heat and simmer for 10 minutes.

Meanwhile, bring a small saucepan of water to a boil. Blanch the scallion whites for 1 minute. Drain. Serve the soup sprinkled with the scallions and radishes.

MAKES 6 CUPS (1.5 L); 4 FIRST-COURSE SERVINGS

steamed duck

MY DEAR Barbara Tropp brought me a clever Chinese device, three-pronged tongs that open and close with a sort of plunger. It makes it possible to remove the dish in which the duck steams from the pot without spilling the liquid or burning one's hands. If one of these is unavailable, use a larger pot, making sure that there is enough room to get in to remove the pie plate on which the duck steams, and add an extra cup of stock to the pot.

I adapted this dish from a traditional Chinese recipe. It can be made in any large 3-gallon (12-l) pot. Do not use a canning or lobster pot, as they are so thin all the liquid will evaporate. A large steamer or couscous pot can be used, or an old-fashioned steamer rack opened all the way. There should be enough room for the pie plate to sit on the steamer surface and still allow some steam to come up around the pie plate.

This dish should be served as a whole duck on a platter with the vegetables and the broth in a bowl on the side. The guests can ladle some soup into their own bowls and pick the meat off the bones with chopsticks and add it to the soup. Or the meat can be removed from the bones beforehand and served in the soup.

For this recipe, a salty ham like Smithfield is best. Be careful when salting the dish if using Smithfield ham. This is a very festive dish, great for parties—and of course, stock can be made from the bones.

One 5-pound (2.25-kg) duck, wing tips removed and pricked all over with the tip of a paring knife

8 cups (2 l) Duck Stock (page 353) or water

1½ ounces (45 g) dried shiitake mushrooms

6 medium scallions, trimmed and white and green parts cut separately into 1-inch (2.5-cm) lengths

6 tablespoons (45 g) hair-thin strips peeled ginger

⅓ pound (160 g) smoked ham, cut into large matchstick strips

1 tablespoon fermented black beans

Kosher salt, to taste

IN A LARGE STOCKPOT, bring 1 gallon (4 l) water to a boil. Place the duck in the pot. Return to a boil. Cook for 5 minutes. Remove the duck to a large (11-inch; 28-cm) glass pie plate or deep heatproof platter.

Bring 3 cups (750 ml) of the stock or water to a boil. Soak the mushrooms in the stock or water for 15 minutes. Drain and strain the liquid through a fine-mesh sieve;

Bring 3 cups (750 ml) of the stock or water to a boil. Soak the mushrooms in the stock or water for 15 minutes. Drain and strain the liquid through a fine-mesh sieve; reserve. Remove and discard the mushroom stems. Cut the caps in matchstick strips.

Pour the remaining stock or water and the strained mushroom liquid into a large wide pot. Add 1 cup (250 ml) of the scallion greens, 1 tablespoon of the white part of the scallions, and 1 tablespoon ginger. Place a steamer rack in the pot. Place the plate or platter with the duck on top of the steamer rack. Stuff half of the remaining mushrooms, ginger, and scallions and half the ham into the cavity of the duck. Sprinkle the rest, along with the beans, on top of and around the duck. Cover the pot and bring to a boil. Steam will begin to escape. Lower the heat as much as possible. Do not open the pot. Cook for 1 hour and 45 minutes, or until the duck meat is tender enough to be removed from the bones with chopsticks.

When the duck is done, carefully remove the pie plate or platter from the steaming pot, taking care not to spill any of the juices accumulated in the bottom. Remove the duck and all the vegetables to a large serving platter (reserve any bones that fall off for stock). Pour the liquid from the pie plate or platter into a glass measure. Skim the fat. There will be about 1 cup (250 ml) of really rich broth; reserve it.

Strain the steaming liquid through a fine-mesh sieve into a bowl. Add the vegetables to the duck and vegetables on the platter. Skim the fat from the steaming liquid and add 1 cup (250 ml) of this liquid to the reserved duck broth, or enough to make 2 cups (500 ml) combined. If desired, season with salt. Reserve any remaining steaming liquid for stock or another use (it will be better if stock was used).

Run chopsticks along the breastbone of the duck and remove the skin. Pour ½ cup (125 ml) of broth into each eater's bowl. Invite guests to serve themselves from the platter, adding duck and vegetables to the broth with their chopsticks. More broth can be added to the bowl as it is consumed.

When dinner is over, make a stock from the bones and the reserved steaming liquid.

MAKES 1 WHOLE DUCK AND 5 CUPS (1.25 L) SOUP WHEN USING BROTH, 2 CUPS (500 ML) SOUP WHEN USING WATER; 4 MAIN-COURSE SERVINGS

duck gumbo

THIS IS ONE of my favorite gumbos. There is a fair amount of work, so I make it in large quantities for a party. I serve the rice on the side for them that wants it. I am not one of them.

Each duck needs to be cut into fourteen pieces so that they are not unwieldy in the stew and will cook quickly. If the butcher will not do it, use a cleaver to cut through the bones, or a heavy knife and a hammer. With scissors, cut away any flapping pieces of skin and fat that are not covering the meat.

Three 5-pound (2-kg) ducks, each cut into 14 pieces (see page 122)

4 medium onions, cut into ¼-inch (.5-cm) dice

¼ cup (35 g) all-purpose flour

1 head garlic, smashed, peeled, and very finely chopped

7 tablespoons plus ½ teaspoon kosher salt, or less if using commercial broth

Freshly ground black pepper, to taste

2 teaspoons cayenne pepper

1½ teaspoons hot red pepper sauce

4 cups (1 l) Chunky Tomato Base (page 385), drained and lightly crushed canned Italian plum tomatoes, or sterile-pack chopped tomatoes

12 cups (3 l) Duck Stock (page 353), Basic Chicken Stock (page 345), or commercial chicken broth

2 tablespoons fresh lemon juice

1½ pounds (675 g) okra, trimmed and thinly sliced across

5 medium carrots, cut into large matchstick strips

1¾ pounds (780 g) peas in the pod, shelled (1⅔ cups), or one 10-ounce (300 g) package frozen peas, defrosted in a sieve under warm running water and drained (1⅔ cups)

1½ pounds asparagus, woody stems snapped off, remaining portions peeled and cut across into 1-inch (2.5-cm) lengths

1 tablespoon filé powder

4 medium bunches scallions, trimmed and sliced across into ¼-inch (.5-cm) slices

3 cups (675 g) long-grain white rice

Thinly sliced scallions, for serving

HEAT A LARGE CASSEROLE over medium heat. Working in batches, add a layer of duck pieces and cook, turning as necessary, until the duck has lost its raw look and no traces of blood remain. Transfer the duck to a large sieve over a bowl to let the excess fat drain off.

Pour off the fat, leaving ¼ cup (65 ml) in the pot. (The remainder can be saved for Quick Duck Confit, page 402.) Stir in the onions and cook over medium heat for 5 minutes, or until they soften slightly. Stir in the flour and garlic. Cook for 5 to 10 minutes, stirring constantly, until the mixture is brown. Do not let it burn. Stir in 7 tablespoons salt (less if using commercial broth), black pepper to taste, 1 teaspoon cayenne pepper, and 1 teaspoon hot red pepper sauce. Cook for 1 minute.

Combine the tomatoes with the stock and whisk into the casserole. Stir in 1 tablespoon lemon juice. Bring to a boil. Lower the heat and simmer for 30 minutes.

Add all of the duck and simmer for 15 minutes, skimming the fat frequently. Reserve some of this seasoned fat for the rice.

Stir the okra and carrots into the gumbo and simmer for 20 minutes. Stir in the peas and asparagus. Simmer for 5 minutes. Stir in the filé powder and scallions. Cook until the mixture thickens slightly, about 3 minutes.

Meanwhile, to cook the rice, in a medium saucepan, bring the rice to a boil with 6 cups (1.5 l) water and the remaining salt. Cover. Lower the heat and simmer for 18 minutes, or until the rice is cooked through and all the water is absorbed. Stir in 5 tablespoons of reserved seasoned fat. Set aside and keep warm.

Season the gumbo with the remaining cayenne, hot red pepper sauce, and lemon juice. The flavor should be spicy but not overwhelming.

Sprinkle some scallions over each portion. Serve with the rice on the side for passing.

MAKES 12 AMPLE MAIN-COURSE SERVINGS

white bean soup
WITH CONFIT AND TOMATO

THIS SOUP CAN BE MADE with quick duck or goose confit or purchased confit. I use the meat from four leg and thigh pieces plus four wings of duck; the goose equivalent is two wings, two legs, and one piece of breast. Most important, the weight of the meat taken off the bone is 1¼ pounds (575 g), about 2½ cups.

> 1 tablespoon fat reserved from confit (see below) or good olive oil
>
> 1 medium onion, cut into ½-inch (1-cm) dice
>
> 6 large cloves garlic, smashed, peeled, and very finely chopped
>
> ½ pound (225 g) navy beans, soaked according to one of the methods on page 293
>
> 2 cups (500 ml) Tomato Purée (page 384), canned American tomatoes puréed with their juice, or sterile-pack strained tomatoes
>
> 4 cups (1 l) Goose Stock (page 353) or water
>
> ½ bay leaf
>
> Meat from 4 leg, 4 thigh, and 4 wing pieces of Quick Duck Confit (page 402), or purchased duck confit, or from 2 leg, 2 wing, and 1 small piece of breast from Quick Goose Confit (page 404), or purchased goose confit
>
> ¼ teaspoon Quatre Épices (page 435)
>
> 1 teaspoon celery seed
>
> 1 tablespoon kosher salt
>
> Freshly ground black pepper, to taste
>
> 1 teaspoon fresh lemon juice

IN A MEDIUM SAUCEPAN, cook the confit fat and onion over low heat for 3 minutes. Add all but 1 tablespoon of the garlic. Cook for 2 minutes, or until translucent but not browned. Stir in the beans, tomato purée, stock, and bay leaf. Bring to a boil. Lower the heat and simmer for 1 hour and 15 minutes to 1 hour and 30 minutes. The beans should be tender but not completely cooked.

Stir in the confit, quatre épices, celery seed, salt, pepper, and the remaining garlic. Simmer for 15 minutes. The soup can be made ahead to this point and refrigerated for up to 3 days.

If it has been refrigerated, reheat the soup. Stir in the lemon juice and serve immediately.

MAKES 8 CUPS (2 L); 4 MAIN-COURSE SERVINGS OR 6 TO 8 FIRST-COURSE SERVINGS

garburesque of goose

THIS AND THE STOCK recipe are from *Roasting*. This is meant to be extremely solid with solids. After finishing the soup, *faire chabrot* (spill red wine into the bowl, swish it around, and drink it). Doubled, with goose meat, it serves six as a main course.

½ cup (100 g) small white beans, soaked according to one of the
    methods on page 293

1 to 1½ tablespoons goose fat or duck fat (from confit or from
    roasting either bird)

1 small onion, coarsely chopped

3 medium cloves garlic, smashed, peeled, and very finely chopped

¼ medium head green cabbage, cored and sliced across into 1-inch (2.5-cm) pieces

3 medium carrots, peeled, halved lengthwise, and cut across into 1-inch
    (2.5-cm) lengths

1 pound (450 g) firm potatoes, peeled and cut into ¾-inch (1.8-cm) cubes

1 teaspoon chopped fresh thyme (or a pinch of dried)

1 teaspoon narrow strips fresh sage (or a pinch of dried)

3 cups (750 ml) Goose or Duck Stock (page 353) or Basic Chicken Stock (page 345)

1 small turnip, peeled, quartered, and sliced across into ⅛-inch (30-mm) pieces

1½ teaspoons kosher salt

1 cup torn meat from Quick Goose Confit (page 404) or Quick Duck
    Confit (page 402) or leftover goose or duck meat, optional

IN A SMALL SAUCEPAN, place the beans with enough water to cover by 2 inches (5 cm). Bring to a boil. Lower the heat and simmer for 45 minutes. Drain and reserve.

In a medium saucepan, melt the goose (or duck) fat over medium heat. Stir in the onion. Cook, stirring, for 5 minutes, or until translucent but not browned. Stir in the garlic. Reduce the heat to low and cook for 2 minutes. Stir in the cabbage. Cook until it wilts, about 3 minutes. Stir in the carrots and potatoes and cook, stirring, for 2 to 3 minutes.

Stir in the thyme, sage, and stock. Cover and bring to a boil. Lower the heat and simmer for 10 minutes. Stir in the turnip and season with the salt. Simmer for 3 minutes. Stir in the beans and goose or duck meat, if using it. Simmer for 5 minutes.

MAKES 6 CUPS (1.5 L); 6 FIRST-COURSE SERVINGS

The meat
of the matter

AMERICANS AND EUROPEANS love the taste of beef, along with veal, lamb, and pork. By eating them in soup, we can generally use the less-expensive cuts of meat, actually decrease our animal protein and animal fat intake, get more vegetables, and have a good time.

The exception to the idea of less meat and less expense comes with the Grand Boiled Dinners (starting on page 220), such as Bollito Misto and Pot-au-Feu.

Beef stock and dividends

It is a tragedy that in today's world, the British cannot buy beef on the bone to make stock. There, cooks will be forced to use the commercial beef or meat stock that is imported from Europe.

Beef stock is the only kind I make that requires meat for flavor. The others rely on bones. Additionally, beef bones are feeble in gelatin compared with the juvenile veal bones. It is necessary to enrich the stock by adding veal knuckle.

I use shin for the meat because it is inexpensive and I have a friend who loves marrow, but short ribs or brisket (silverside) can be used instead.

There are dividends for doing the extra work rather than using commercial stock. The meat on the beef bones can be used in the stock to make an entire meal, and if beef shin is used, the marrow can be extracted to make a savory accompanying treat when spread on toast; see page 169.

The recipe can be made into Beef in the Pot by adding as much of the meat as is desired, assorted cooked vegetables (pages 448–451), dumplings (pages 414–419) or noodles (pages 392–393); or use the recipe for Dividend Beef in the Pot (page 169).

When the stock is made, there will be 2 pounds (900 g) of boned meat (6 cups [1.5 l] torn) that can be added to soups. Extra meat can be added to Red Russian Soup (page 178) or to essentially vegetarian soups such as the bean soups on pages 298–312, or it can be used in a salad with potatoes—perhaps some beets—and a horseradish-mayonnaise dressing.

The stock is used for numerous soups in this section, as well as Beef Madrilène (page 370), Pink Bean and Radicchio Soup (page 306), and Tripe Gumbo (page 214). The beef madrilène is an exemplar of how good stock is clarified to make consommé. If that soup is eaten hot, it is an excellent consommé and can be served with any of the seemingly endless array of consommé garnitures in classic cuisine: *Petite marmite* will have small cubes of the beef and cooked cubed vegetables (pages 448–451); consommé julienne will have thin strips of carrot, turnip, heart of cabbage, onion, celery, lettuce, peas, and sorrel, and others.

beef stock

NO OTHER CHAPTER in this book except From Stock to Soup starts with stock, although stock is relevant to many of them. However, while commercial chicken stock can be used, there is really no adequate substitute for homemade beef stock. My English friends tell me, in their days of wrath, that game bird stock can be used. Game birds are cheap and readily available to them, but not to us.

Canned beef consommé or broth is, at best, unfortunate. In desperation, it is possible to use canned beef madrilène, which at least has some gelatin in it. All over Europe, even in Italy, stock (bouillon) cubes are used. In general, I don't like these compressed bits of flavoring that are heavy with salt. The beef variety is the least successful, though some cheating is possible (see Fake Beef Stock, page 168).

This recipe, with its variations for cooking in the oven (those with an Aga can use it) and in a slow-cooker, shows how important beef stock is to me. Many people may be more comfortable leaving an oven or a slow-cooker on for prolonged periods of time than their stove top.

Once all the lovely stock is made, freeze whatever is not being used immediately. It keeps virtually forever. For general notes on stock making, see pages 341–344.

Two thirds cup (180 ml) of Glace de Viande (page 355) can be stirred into either stock for added richness or to strengthen weak stock.

Please note that this is a two-stage recipe. The first is a bone broth. The way it is treated determines whether the final stock will be brown and hearty or lighter (traditionally a white stock). For the slightly lighter effect, the bones are not browned and carrots and celery are used rather than the tomatoes and garlic of the brown stock. The bone broth is always strained at the end of stage one to allow enough room for adding the beef shin in stage two.

The finished stocks made with these bone broths will gel when cold. However, that made in the slow-cooker will not gel, since it doesn't reduce or extract as much gelatin unless boiled to reduce by a cup and a half, and even then it will be a weak gel. For the oven/stove methods, if the yield after the second stage is somewhat higher than the mentioned one, once the stock has been strained, reduce to 14 cups (3.5 l) for a richer, gelling stock.

With any method, the recipe is done in stages and can be stopped after stage one and refrigerated. To continue with the recipe, bring the refrigerated broth to a boil. Simmer for 10 minutes, strain, and proceed with stage two.

To make this in a slow-cooker, the recipe must be halved, producing 8 cups (2 l).

continued

3½ pounds (1.5 kg) veal knuckle, split

3 large tomatoes, for brown stock

6 cloves garlic, for brown stock

2 medium onions, cut in half

2 medium ribs celery, for white stock

3 medium carrots, for white stock

4½ pounds (2 kg) beef shin with bone, cut across by the butcher into
    2- to 3-inch (5- to 7.5-cm) lengths

STAGE ONE (BONE BROTH)

Preroasting for a Brown Stock: Place the rack in the center of the oven and heat to 500°F (260°C; highest gas mark; #9 British regulo).

Place the veal knuckle, tomatoes, garlic, and onions (half the amounts if using a slow-cooker) in a large roasting pan. Roast for 20 minutes. Turn the vegetables and roast 25 minutes more.

Transfer the bones and vegetables to a large stockpot. Place the roasting pan on top of stove over high heat. Add 1 cup (250 ml) water. Bring to a boil, scraping all the browned bits from the bottom and sides of the pan. Remove from the heat.

On top of the stove: *For a Brown Stock,* in a large stockpot, place the preroasted solids and the liquid from the roasting pan. Add 15 cups (3.75 l) water, or enough to cover 2 inches (5 cm).

For a White Stock, place the veal knuckle, onions, celery, and carrots in a large stockpot. Add 16 cups (4 l) water, or enough to cover by 2 inches (5 cm).

For either, bring to a boil. Lower the heat to a simmer, in which gentle bubbles break the surface, and cook for 8 hours. Skim and check the level of the water every few hours; it should remain about 2 inches (5 cm) above the bones. You will need to add 6 (1.5 l) to 8 cups (2 l) water in an 8-hour cooking time unless an otoshi-buta is used (see page xii).

In the oven: Adjust the oven temperature, or heat it, to 300°F (149°C; gas mark #2; between #1 and #2 British regulo); the rack should be at the lowest possible level, with no other racks in the oven.

For a Brown Stock, in a large stockpot, combine the preroasted solids and the liquid from roasting pan. Add 15 cups (3.75 l) water, or enough to cover by 2 inches (5 cm).

For a White Stock, in a large stockpot, combine the veal knuckle, onion, celery and carrot. Add 16 cups (4 l) water, or enough to cover by 2 inches (5 cm).

For either, bring to a boil. Transfer the pot to the oven. Cook for 1 hour. Lower the heat to 250°F (121°C; gas mark #½; between #¼ and #½ British regulo) and cook for 11 hours. Check the water level every few hours; it should remain about 2 inches (5 cm) above the bones. You will need to add approximately 8 cups (2 l) in a 12-hour cooking period unless an otoshi-buta (see page xii) is used.

In a 4- to 5-quart (4- to 5-l) slow-cooker: *For a Brown Stock,* place the half-quantity of preroasted ingredients and the liquid from the roasting pan in the slow-cooker with 7 cups (1.75 l) water.

For a White Stock, place the half-quantity of veal knuckle, onion, celery, and carrots in the slow-cooker with 8 cups (2 l) water. Turn the slow cooker on to Low and cook for 12 hours.

For all methods: Strain the broth and discard the solids. Skim the fat. Add enough water to make 16 cups (4 l) for the stove-top and oven methods, 8 cups (2 l) for the slow-cooker method.

STAGE TWO (THE STOCK)

On top of the stove: Return the liquid to the stockpot, with the beef shin. Bring to a boil. Lower the heat and simmer, so bubbles are gently breaking the surface, for 2 hours and 30 minutes. The meat should be tender.

Remove the beef shin from the pot and separate the meat from the bones. Poke or scoop the marrow out of the bones and reserve. Reserve the meat and return the bones to the pot for 30 minutes.

In the oven: Return the liquid to the stockpot, with the beef shin. Bring to a boil on top of the stove. Place the pot back in the oven. Cook for 3 hours. The meat should be tender.

Remove the shin from the pot. Separate the meat from the bones and reserve the meat. Return the bones to the pot. Cook for 1 hour.

In a slow-cooker: Return the liquid to the slow-cooker, with the half-quantity of beef shin. Cook on Low for 5 hours.

Remove the shin from the pot. Separate the meat from the bones, reserve the meat, and discard the bones.

For all methods: When the meat is cool enough to handle, tear or cut it into bite-sized pieces and reserve for use in Dividend Beef in the Pot (page 169) or other soups.

Strain the liquid through a fine-mesh sieve and discard the bones, if necessary. Skim the fat. Cool to room temperature. Refrigerate for 3 hours.

Remove the fat from the top and the sediment from the bottom of the stock (see page 342). Use immediately, or refrigerate for up to 3 days or freeze.

MAKES 14 CUPS (3.5 L) ON TOP OF THE STOVE OR IN THE OVEN,
8 CUPS (2 L) IN A SLOW-COOKER

fake beef stock

ALTHOUGH THIS BEEF STOCK will gel, I would serve it on its own only if seasoned with a lot of lemon or lime juice and fresh pepper. It still has a lot of salt. It does not gel hard enough to support dilution with other ingredients.

This fake stock is meant to be used in soups. But be very careful when adding salt in any recipe in which it is used. It can easily be multiplied as needed.

Beef bouillon cubes
½ pound (225 g) lean ground beef
1 package (9 g) gelatin
½ cup water

Dissolve as many beef bouillon cubes in 4 cups (1 l) of boiling water as are called for on the package. Crumble the ground beef into the hot water and bring to a boil. Reduce the heat to a simmer and continue to cook for 30 minutes. While the beef is cooking, sprinkle the gelatin (1 tablespoon) on top of the ½ cup of water and let sit for 1 minute.

Strain the broth through a damp-cloth–lined sieve. In a small saucepan, stir the strained broth and the softened gelatin together over medium heat. Cook, stirring, at just below a simmer, for 3 minutes to dissolve the gelatin.

MAKES 4 CUPS (1 L)

dividend beef
IN THE POT

HAVING MADE BEEF STOCK, I have the makings of a beef in the pot to nourish six good friends, even more if I add, as I often do, small boiled potatoes or boiled noodles. I allow about three small new potatoes per person, or 4½ cups (about 450 g) cooked noodles, for the group.

I usually have a pot or two of mustard and some horseradish on the table.

for the soup

9 cups (2.2 l) Beef Stock (page 165) or, in England, imported beef or meat stock;
   or double recipe Fake Beef Stock (page 168) plus 3 cups (750 ml) water

3 small turnips, peeled, and each cut into 8 wedges

12 medium-to-large pearl onions, blanched for 1 minute,
   run under cold water, and peeled

2 large carrots, peeled, quartered lengthwise, and cut across into 1-inch
   (2.5-cm) lengths

4 cups (900 g) bite-sized pieces boiled beef shin (reserved from making stock)
   or 1⅔ pounds (1.75 kg) beef stew meat, cut in 1-inch (2.5 cm) pieces
   and poached in fake stock and water until tender

1½ teaspoons kosher salt

Freshly ground black pepper, to taste

for serving

⅔ pound (300 g) medium egg noodles, cooked (see page 392),
   or 18 very small firm potatoes, boiled (see page 93), optional

6 tablespoons coarsely chopped parsley

Croutons (page 429), optional

Marrow from cooking stock, optional

IN A MEDIUM STOCKPOT, bring the stock and turnips to a boil. Lower the heat and simmer, partially covered, for 10 minutes. Stir in the onions and carrots. Simmer, partially covered, for 15 minutes, or until all the vegetables are tender when pierced with the tip of a knife.

Stir in the beef and the noodles or potatoes, if using. Heat through. Season with salt and pepper. Divide among six bowls, sprinkle with parsley, and serve with croutons spread with marrow, if desired.

MAKES 12 CUPS (3 L); 6 MAIN-COURSE SERVINGS

Beef soups

beef barley soup

I LOVE BARLEY SOUPS and there are others in the book (see the Index). Rich with stock and meat and enlivened by a mere whisper of orange juice, this is a dividend soup par excellence, capable of being a meal with the addition of a salad.

8 cups (2 l) Beef Stock (page 165) or, in England, imported beef or meat stock; or double recipe Fake Beef Stock (page 168) plus 1 cup (250 ml) water

½ cup (90 g) pearl barley

2 sprigs fresh thyme (or ¼ teaspoon dried), plus 1½ teaspoons chopped fresh thyme (or ¼ teaspoon dried)

2 sprigs fresh oregano (or ⅛ teaspoon dried), plus 1½ teaspoons chopped fresh oregano (or ⅛ teaspoon dried)

1 tablespoon (15 g) unsalted butter

1 medium onion, cut into ½-inch (1-cm) dice

2 medium cloves garlic, smashed, peeled, and very finely chopped

½ pound (225 g) fresh shiitake or other mushrooms, stems discarded, wiped clean, and caps cut into 1-inch (2.5-cm) pieces

½ pound (225 g) parsley root, trimmed, peeled, and cut across into ½-inch (1-cm) slices; if unavailable, ¼ pound (120 g) parsnips

2 cups (450 g) cooked beef shin (reserved from making stock), cut into ½-inch (1-cm) pieces, or 1 pound (450 g) beef stew meat, cut into ¾-inch (1.5-cm) pieces, poached in fake stock and water until tender

2 sprigs parsley, if using parsnips

2 tablespoons kosher salt

Freshly ground black pepper, to taste

2 tablespoons fresh orange juice

IN A LARGE SAUCEPAN, bring the stock, barley, and thyme and oregano sprigs, or ¼ teaspoon dried thyme and ⅛ teaspoon dried oregano, to a boil. Lower the heat and simmer, partially covered, for 1 hour.

Meanwhile, in a small frying pan, melt the butter over medium heat. Stir in the onion and cook, stirring frequently, for 10 minutes, or until golden. Stir in the garlic and mushrooms. Continue cooking, stirring frequently, for 10 minutes. Stir in ½ cup (125 ml) water and cook until all the water has evaporated, about 5 minutes.

Remove the herb sprigs, if using, from the barley and stir in the cooked mushrooms. Simmer for 15 minutes.

Meanwhile, bring a small saucepan of salted water to a boil. Stir in the parsley root or parsnips and cook for 3 minutes. Drain.

Stir the meat and parsley root, or the parsnips and parsley sprigs, into the soup and simmer for 15 minutes. If using dried herbs, add ¼ teaspoon thyme and ⅛ teaspoon oregano after 10 minutes. Remove from the heat. The soup can be made ahead to this point and refrigerated for up to 3 days.

Reheat the soup if it has been refrigerated. Remove from the heat and stir in the remaining chopped fresh herbs, if using, and the salt and pepper. Let sit for 5 minutes, then stir in the orange juice. Serve immediately.

MAKES 9 CUPS (2.25 L); 4 MAIN-COURSE SERVINGS

oxtail soup

WITH FAVA BEANS

OXTAIL STOCK IS JUST another form of beef stock and is fabulous served as a consommé. This is another dividend soup, using the meat left from making the stock and some of the stock. Unfortunately, this wonderful soup cannot currently be made in Great Britain.

½ pound (225 g) fine egg noodles

6 cups (1.5 l) Oxtail Stock (page 356)

1 pound (450 g) baby carrots, trimmed, peeled, blanched for 2 minutes,
    and plunged into a bowl of ice water

¾ pound (360 g) pearl onions, blanched for 1 minute, run under cold water,
    and peeled

2 cups (300 g) bite-sized pieces cooked oxtail meat (reserved from making stock)

2¾ pounds (1.25 kg) fava (broad) beans, shelled, blanched for 2 minutes,
    run under cold water, and popped out of tough outer skins, or 10 ounces
    (300 g) frozen lima beans, defrosted in a sieve under warm running water
    and drained (1½ cups)

2 teaspoons kosher salt

Freshly ground black pepper, to taste

BRING A LARGE POT of salted water to a boil. Add the noodles and cook for 4 to 5 minutes. Drain and reserve.

In a medium saucepan, bring the stock to a boil. Stir in the carrots and onions. Return to a boil. Lower the heat and simmer for 8 minutes. Stir in the meat, fava or lima beans, salt, and pepper to taste. Add the noodles. Heat through and serve.

MAKES 12 CUPS (3 L); 6 MAIN-COURSE SERVINGS

much beef, no stock

Despite my espousal of beef stock, there are beef soups that do not start with a stock. Why? Because they make their own as they cook.

beef short ribs
IN A POT

I LOVE SHORT RIBS. Look for the meatiest short ribs around.

> 5 pounds (2.25 kg) beef short ribs, cut lengthwise between the ribs to make pieces approximately 3 inches (7.5 cm) square
>
> 10 ounces (300 g) pearl onions, blanched for 1 minute, run under cold water, and peeled
>
> 6 medium carrots, peeled, halved lengthwise, and cut across into thirds
>
> 18 medium mushrooms, stems discarded and wiped clean
>
> 2¼ pounds (1 kg) peas in the pod, shelled (2 cups), or one 10-ounce (300-g) package frozen peas, defrosted in a sieve under warm running water and drained (1⅔ cups)
>
> 2 tablespoons kosher salt
>
> Freshly ground black pepper, to taste
>
> 12 ounces (360 g) medium egg noodles, cooked (see page 392), for serving

IN A MEDIUM STOCKPOT, bring 12 cups (3 l) water to a boil. Add the ribs. Return to a boil. Lower the heat, cover the meat with an otoshi-buta (see page xii) or a plate to keep it submerged in the liquid, and simmer for 2 hours and 30 minutes, skimming frequently. Remove from the heat and cool to room temperature. Skim very carefully; if possible, refrigerate overnight to bring all of the fat to the surface, and lift off the fat.

Slowly return the broth to a boil. Stir in the onions and carrots. Simmer for 15 minutes. Stir in the mushroom caps and, if using, the fresh peas. Simmer for 10 minutes; if using frozen peas, stir them in after the mushrooms have simmered for 7 minutes. Season with the salt and pepper to taste. The meat will be so tender it will be falling off the bones. Remove and discard the bones if the guests are fussy or the soup plates small.

Place about a cup of cooked egg noodles in the bottom of each soup plate. Distribute the meat and vegetables evenly among the bowls and ladle the broth over everything.

MAKES 12 CUPS (3 L); 6 MAIN-COURSE SERVINGS

Bay leaves

I HAVE SMALL BAY TREES (*Laurus nobilis*) growing in both New York and Vermont. In these climates, they have to come in the house in winter. I don't mind as much with these plants, or with rosemary, when, due to a case of black thumb, they die. The dry leaves are perfectly good for culinary use.

I feel strongly about using this sweet laurel or sweet bay in cooking instead of the California "bay" leaves, which are unrelated and have a nasty resinous taste and smell. When buying bay leaves, check the label for the words "imported," "European," or "Turkish."

The pleasure of bay leaves remains undiminished by my first authorship disaster when, translating from a French book for U.S. publication, I called them laurel leaves without any modifier. Laurel leaves that grow on ornamental bushes in the garden are poisonous. I am happy to report that I know of no case of anyone's having been poisoned by following the recipe.

sour schi
STCHI

THE COLD WORLD OF Russia in winter didn't provide much in the way of fresh vegetables. Pickles of one sort or another played a large part in providing vitamins for the winter months. Sauerkraut was a widely used ingredient, as in this sauerkraut and beef soup and in the Hungarian Szekely goulash.

This meat-rich soup is an entire meal. The sauerkraut is supposed to be fresh-tasting and crunchy, not overly salty. Sometimes such sauerkraut can be found in Hungarian, German, or Polish markets. If using canned, jarred, or plastic-packed sauerkraut, drain it thoroughly in a sieve and then plunge it into boiling water for 3 minutes. Drain and place in ice water for at least 15 minutes.

Serve with good rye bread or boiled potatoes or dumplings (starting on page 414) if more substance is required.

1½ pounds (675 g) beef brisket

1 tablespoon (15 g) unsalted butter

1 large onion, coarsely chopped

1 tablespoon all-purpose flour

1 pound (450 g) good sauerkraut, drained

1 medium carrot, peeled and cut across into ¼-inch (.5-cm) slices

2 tablespoons crumbled dried porcini mushrooms (cèpes)

2 bay leaves

for serving

Sour cream

Fresh dill fronds

IN A TALL NARROW STOCKPOT, cover the brisket with 12 cups (3 l) water. Bring to a boil. Skim the scum and fat that rises to the surface. Lower the heat and simmer very gently for 2 hours and 30 minutes.

Meanwhile, in a large frying pan, melt the butter over medium heat. Stir in the onion and cook, stirring, until translucent but not browned, about 10 minutes. Sift the flour over the onions and stir to absorb. Cook, stirring, for 1 minute.

Whisk in 2 cups (500 ml) of the cooking liquid from the brisket. Cook for 2 to 3 minutes, until slightly thickened. Pour into the brisket pot and stir to combine. Stir in the remaining ingredients and simmer for 1 hour.

Remove the brisket from the soup and slice across the grain into ¼-inch (.5-cm) slices. Place two slices in each bowl. Ladle the soup over the meat. Top each portion with sour cream and fresh dill.

MAKES 10 CUPS (2.5 L), PLUS MEAT; 5 MAIN-COURSE SERVINGS

Borscht

BORSCHTS ARE WONDERFUL cold-weather soups, replete with winter vegetables, dense with flavor, and rich with aroma. They are almost paradigmatic of Russian cooking and yet the very name is confusing, covering as it does a large group of soups with slightly different names. There are Russian soups, originally from Ukraine, called *borshch* and Polish ones called *barszcz*. The Polish connection is easily understood because of the floating border between Ukraine and Poland. The Russian venue seems a clear case of adoption. Each area has a wide variety of recipes.

Most of these soups make a meal for any contemporary gourmet or peasant. They are often so full of vegetables that they seem more solid than soup. I suppose there must have been a more opulent time when they were considered one course in a banquet. Often, the hot versions were accompanied by small pastries, pirogen or piroshki, stuffed with vegetables, minced meat—often liver—or cheese.

The only constants in all this variety seem to be beets, the bright red color they provide, and a balanced sweet-and-sour flavor. There are clear barszcz, like beet consommés. There are barszcz that have a somewhat creamy consistency provided by eggs or eggs and cream. The most usual winter borscht is made with a meat base and pieces of meat and cabbage. Beef and smoked pork, such as ham hock, are the most usual meats and both may be used in one soup; but I have had a fabulous borscht with goose as the base. (Think of French garbure.) There is one somewhat unusual borscht for Passover that is made with a base called rossl, a beet-based kvass. There is even a non-red, non-beet borscht made with cabbage and the winter vegetables found in the other full-bodied borschts. There is even a tradition of borschts for fast days. These are meatless. Similar meatless barszcz are sometimes served with fried fish.

There are cold borschts for summer that are a beautiful magenta and rich with sweet and sour cream. These are usually served with a choice of garnitures; those the cook chooses are probably based on family tradition. With an ample supply of garnitures—think gazpacho—and bread, these can be a meal. I even make a gelled clear borscht topped with sour cream and caviar as an elegant opener for a summer meal.

Cabbage is almost always a component of hot borscht. It may be white or red. I particularly like the red, as it adds a wine flavor. When red cabbage is used, the amount of vinegar may need to be increased to preserve the color.

The sources of sweetness are various, ranging from the root vegetables to tomatoes or tomato concentrate (paste) to sugar. The beets themselves lend much sweetness. The acids can be vinegar, lemon juice, citric acid (vitamin C), or kvass, which, aside from in the rossl-based Passover borscht (beet kvass), seems to be a recent addition. The recipe for rossl and its derivatives can be found in Susan Friedland's *The Passover Table*.

Kvass is a fermented mildly alcoholic drink or cooking base, a sort of near beer. Most commonly it is made from stale bread, usually rye, that is covered with water and left to ferment. Sugar or yeast may be added to help the process. Elegant Moscow homes in days long past used fruit, and there is the beet-based one given on page 56—it's a sort of shortcut and does avoid fermenting in the kitchen. The rest of the year it is not used. If life is desperate, jarred boiled beets or bottled borscht can be used as a base.

Unless the borscht has meat and is being made by kosher Jews, the traditional accompaniment is a dollop of sour cream. Many, if not most, are topped with chopped dill. The dill should not be too finely chopped, or it will feel gritty in the mouth.

red russian soup

THIS IS MY LATEST VERSION of a soup I originally made for my father, who was from Slutzk, one of the disappeared shtetls near Minsk. It appears with variations in all the surrounding areas. Using red cabbage seems to be my own idea. It gives it, in combination with vinegar and beets and tomatoes, a wonderful rich red color.

In my family, we love to eat, and any leftovers are quickly snatched up by the first person in the kitchen. However, the recipe can be halved (especially as the 5½-quart [5.5-l] made does not even include the potatoes).

Coming from a long line of socialists rather than observant Jews, my favorite version includes the pork knuckle and the sour cream.

Beets vary enormously in sweetness; care must be taken to taste the soup before adding sugar and adjust accordingly. They also vary in cooking time; test for tenderness with the tip of a knife—if it easily pierces the flesh to the center of the beet, the vegetables have cooked long enough.

Remember that the soup is supposed to have a decidedly sweet-and-sour balance. After it is made, taste it, and if desired, add more sugar, vinegar, and salt in small increments until it pleases.

2½ pounds (1.15 kg) beef short ribs, separated and halved across by the butcher, or beef shin with bone, cut across into 2-inch (5-cm) slices; or 2 pounds (900 g) ham hock plus 1 pound (450 g) boneless beef chuck in one piece

2 pounds (900 g) beets, all but 2 inches (5 cm) of stems removed

4 cups (1 l) Chunky Tomato Base (page 385), lightly crushed canned tomatoes (not plum) with their juices, or sterile-pack chopped tomatoes

4 large carrots, peeled and cut across into ½-inch (1-cm) rounds

1 medium onion, coarsely chopped

1 medium red cabbage, cored and cut into 1½-inch (4-cm) squares or shredded (about 8 cups; 900 g)

8 medium cloves garlic, smashed and peeled

1 bay leaf

1 cup (250 ml) red wine vinegar

¾ cup (180 g) sugar

2 bunches dill fronds only, coarsely chopped

3 tablespoons kosher salt

⅛ teaspoon freshly ground black pepper

**10 smallish firm potatoes, boiled (see page 93), peeled, and
halved lengthwise**

About ¾ cup (180 g) sour cream

1 bunch dill, fronds only, coarsely chopped

IN A LARGE STOCKPOT, bring the short ribs, shin, or ham hock and 10 cups (2.5 l) water to a boil. Lower the heat and simmer very gently, skimming occasionally, for 1 hour and 30 minutes to 2 hours (at this point the short ribs or shin will be done). If using the ham hock, add the beef chuck and continue to simmer for 1 hour.

Remove all the meat from the liquid. Remove the meat from bones and trim off any fat. Cut the meat, including the beef chuck, if using, into ½-inch (1-cm) cubes and reserve. Skim the fat from the cooking liquid. Measure the liquid and add enough cold water to equal 7 cups (1.75 l). Return the liquid to the pot.

While the meat is cooking, in a medium stockpot, place the beets in enough water to cover. Bring to a boil. Lower the heat and simmer until the beets can be easily pierced with a knife. Trim the beets and remove the skin. Cut into large matchstick strips and set aside. Strain the cooking liquid from the beets through a coffee filter. Measure 5 cups (1.25 l) liquid; add water to make 5 cups (1.25 l) if necessary. Reserve.

Add the tomatoes, carrots, onion, cabbage, garlic, and bay leaf to the liquid reserved from cooking the meat. Bring to a boil. Lower the heat and simmer for 20 minutes, until the carrots are almost tender.

Stir in the beets and simmer for 20 minutes. Stir in the reserved beet liquid, the vinegar, sugar (see Headnote), dill, cubed meat, salt, and pepper. Remove from the heat and allow the flavors to blend for at least 1 hour, or overnight.

Reheat the soup. Place 2 boiled potato halves in each bowl. Ladle about 2 cups (500 ml) soup over the potatoes. Float 1 tablespoon (15 g) sour cream on top and sprinkle with the dill.

MAKES 5½ QUARTS (5.5 L); 10 MAIN-COURSE SERVINGS

korean beef soup

THE KOREANS ARE as nutty about beef as the British, Argentines, and Americans. They seem to be as mad over short ribs as I am. This is a traditional soup. My recipe borrows from *The Flavors of Korea,* by Marc and Kim Millon. I added the nontraditional tofu and noodles, which seem to slide in nicely.

As many Korean recipes are, this is mildly spicy. The warm aroma of the toasted sesame seeds helps the balance.

for the sauce

    2 tablespoons sesame seeds, toasted (see Note)

    6 medium cloves garlic, smashed, peeled, and finely chopped

    4 scallions, trimmed and thinly sliced across

    1 tablespoon (7 g) very finely chopped peeled ginger

    ½ cup (125 ml) soy sauce

    ¼ cup (65 ml) toasted sesame oil

    Lots of freshly ground black pepper

    3 tablespoons Basic Chicken Stock (page 345), liquid from the soup,
       or water

for the soup

    2 tablespoons sesame seeds, toasted (see Note)

    8 medium scallions, trimmed and thinly sliced across

    10 medium cloves garlic, smashed, peeled, and finely chopped

    ¼ cup (30 g) very finely chopped peeled ginger

    ¼ cup (65 ml) soy sauce

    2 tablespoons toasted sesame oil

    Lots of freshly ground black pepper

    3 pounds (1.4 kg) beef short ribs, cut across into 2-inch (5-cm) pieces
       by the butcher and scored deeply to the bone on the diagonal

    2 tablespoons vegetable oil

    Kosher salt, to taste

    ½ pound (225 g) thin rice stick noodles

    2 eggs, lightly beaten, optional

    2 teaspoons vegetable oil, optional

    Two ¼-pound (120-g) pieces firm silken tofu, cut into ¼-inch (.5-cm) cubes

FOR THE SAUCE, combine the sesame seeds with all the remaining ingredients in a small bowl and set aside.

For the soup, mix together the sesame seeds, scallions, garlic, ginger, soy sauce, sesame oil, and pepper. Toss with the meat and allow to marinate for at least 2 hours.

In a medium stockpot, heat the oil. Scrape the marinade from the meat, and reserve. Working in two batches, brown the meat on all sides. Return all the meat to the pot and add 8 cups (2 l) water and the reserved marinade. Bring to a boil. Lower the heat and simmer for 1 hour and 30 minutes to 1 hour and 45 minutes, until the beef is tender. Season with salt.

Fifteen minutes before serving, soak the rice sticks in hot water until soft. If using the eggs, heat the vegetable oil in a small nonstick frying pan and make an omelet by frying the eggs in a flat thin pancake. Slide out of the pan, allow to cool slightly, and cut into thin strips.

Just before serving the soup, stir in the tofu and heat through. Divide the noodles evenly among four bowls and top with the boiling-hot soup. Sprinkle with the omelet strips, if using. Pass the sauce on the side to be spooned over the soup or used as a dipping sauce for the meat.

MAKES 10 CUPS (2.5 L); 4 MAIN-COURSE SERVINGS

Note: To toast the sesame seeds for the sauce and the soup, in a small dry frying pan, cook the sesame seeds over medium heat, shaking the pan constantly, until lightly browned, about 2 minutes.

Small pieces of meat cook rapidly, but they don't give off enough flavor to make a rich soup. The trade-off is that with small pieces of beef, stock should be used.

goulash soup

THIS IS THE MOTHERING SOUP of Hungary. It relies on what has become a Hungarian ingredient, red peppers, dried and pulverized—that is, paprika, which comes sweet, medium, and hot. The spiciness of the dish can be adjusted by the kind(s) of paprika used. Hungarian paprika is by far the best. The American peppers traveled to Spain and from there, under the aegis of the Hapsburgs who ruled Spain, Austria, and Hungary, to Hungary. The Hungarians developed special varieties of peppers for the condiment.

Noodles and sour cream are optional additions. Adding lemon juice at the end is also optional, depending on the acidity of the tomatoes and paprika.

5 to 6 tablespoons (75 to 90 g) unsalted butter

3 pounds (1.4 kg) beef chuck, cut into 1-inch (2.5-cm) cubes

3 tablespoons all-purpose flour

6 cups (1.5 l) Beef Stock (page 165), 1½ recipes Fake Beef Stock (page 168),
 or, in England, 6 cups imported beef or meat stock

3 tablespoons medium (sweet-hot) paprika; or 3 tablespoons mild paprika
 plus ½ teaspoon cayenne pepper

1 large onion, coarsely chopped

4 cloves garlic, smashed, peeled, and coarsely chopped

2 medium red bell peppers, cored, seeded, deribbed, and cut into ½-inch
 (1-cm) dice

1½ pounds (675 g) firm potatoes, peeled and cut into ½-inch (1-cm) dice

1 teaspoon caraway seed

½ cup (125 ml) Tomato Purée (page 384), canned tomatoes (not plum)
 puréed with their juice, or sterile-pack strained tomatoes

1 tablespoon kosher salt, or more to taste

Freshly ground black pepper, to taste

2 teaspoons fresh lemon juice, optional

⅔ pound (300 g) medium egg noodles, cooked (see page 392), optional
Sour cream, optional

IN A MEDIUM STOCKPOT, melt 3 tablespoons (45 g) butter over medium heat. Toss the meat with the flour. Raise the heat to medium-high and, working in batches, brown the meat, about 2 minutes per side. As each batch is done, set it aside in a bowl. If the meat starts sticking, add 1 more tablespoon (15 g) butter. When all the meat is browned, pour 1 cup (250 ml) stock into the pan and bring to a boil, stirring and scraping the bottom to get up all the browned bits. Pour this over the meat in the bowl.

In the same pot, melt the remaining 2 tablespoons (30 g) butter over medium heat. Stir in the paprika, or paprika and cayenne, and cook for 1 minute. Add the onion and cook, stirring, for 4 minutes.

Pour in the remaining stock and scrape the bottom of the pan well. Stir in the browned meat. Bring to a boil. Lower the heat and simmer, partially covered, for 1 hour.

Stir in the garlic, peppers, and potatoes. Return to a boil. Lower the heat and simmer, partially covered, for 20 minutes.

Stir in the caraway seeds and tomato purée. Simmer for 5 minutes. Stir in the salt, pepper and, if using, the lemon juice.

Serve, if desired, with noodles and topped with a dollop of sour cream.

MAKES 13 CUPS (3.25 L); 6 MAIN-COURSE SERVINGS

½ teaspoon chili oil
2 tablespoons nuoc mam (fish sauce)
teaspoons kosher salt
hly ground black pepper, to taste
nd (360 loin, left n

beef stew

THIS IS THE EPITOME of why I prefer my stews as soups—lots of savory liquid and relatively little thickening. The confectioners' sugar may seem odd, but it caramelizes, losing its sweetness as it cooks and adding a lot of color. This makes an ample meal if served as a main course. Smoked salmon or a salad would be a good first course.

¼ cup (30 g) all-purpose flour

1 tablespoon confectioners' sugar

2 tablespoons kosher salt; 1 tablespoon plus 2 teaspoons if not using potato

2½ pounds (1.1 kg) boneless beef chuck, cut into ½-inch (1-cm) dice

¼ cup (65 ml) olive oil

⅓ pound (160 g) pearl onions, blanched for 1 minute, run under cold water, and peeled

1½ cups (375 ml) dry red wine

2 cups (500 ml) Beef Stock (page 165) or, in England, imported beef or meat stock

1 cup (250 ml) Chunky Tomato Base (page 385), lightly crushed canned tomatoes (not plum) with their juice, or sterile-pack chopped tomatoes

2 bay leaves

8 medium cloves garlic, smashed and peeled

½ bunch thyme (or 1½ teaspoons dried)

3 sprigs fresh oregano (or ¼ teaspoon dried)

½ pound (225 g) white mushrooms, stemmed, wiped clean, and quartered

1 large shiitake mushroom, stemmed, wiped clean, and cut into 1-inch (2.5-cm) pieces

2 tablespoons brandy

1 pound (450 g) firm potatoes, peeled and cut into ½-inch (1-cm) dice, optional

½ pound (225 g) small carrots, peeled, quartered lengthwise, and cut across into 1-inch (2.5-cm) lengths

2¼ pounds peas in the pod, shelled (2 cups), or one 10-ounce (300-g) package frozen baby peas, defrosted in a sieve under warm running water and drained (1⅔ cups)

Freshly ground black pepper, to taste

COMBINE THE FLOUR, confectioners' sugar, and 1 tablespoon salt in a large bowl. Add the beef and toss to coat well.

Heat 2 tablespoons oil in a large wide pot over high heat. Working in batches, brown the meat, setting each batch aside in a bowl as it is finished.

Add 1 tablespoon oil to the pot. Stir in the onions and then the wine. Bring to a boil, scraping the bottom and sides of the pan with a wooden spoon to get up the browned bits. Stir in the stock and bring to a boil. Stir in the meat, ¾ cup (180 ml) tomatoes, the bay leaves, and garlic. Bring to a boil. Lower the heat and simmer, partially covered, for 30 minutes. Stir in the thyme and oregano. Simmer for 10 more minutes.

While the meat is simmering, in a medium frying pan, heat the remaining olive oil over very high heat. Stir in the white mushrooms and cook, stirring, until they begin to brown and make a squeaking sound. Stir in the shiitake mushrooms and cook until all the liquid has been absorbed, making sure the gill side of the shiitakes is well seared. Warm the brandy in a small saucepan over very low heat. Ignite and pour it over the mushrooms. Reserve.

Bring 8 cups (2 l) water to a boil in a medium saucepan. Add the potatoes, if using, and simmer for 2 minutes. Add the carrots and simmer for 4 minutes, or until the potatoes and carrots are tender. Drain and reserve.

Stir the remaining tomatoes and, if using them, the fresh peas into the stew. Cook for 6 minutes. If using frozen peas, add them now. Stir in the carrots, potatoes, and mushrooms and warm through.

Add the remaining salt and pepper to taste, and serve.

MAKES 15 CUPS (3.75 L) WITH POTATOES; 4 TO 6 MAIN-COURSE SERVINGS;
MAKES 14 CUPS (3.5 L) WITHOUT POTATOES; 10 FIRST-COURSE SERVINGS

luxury boiled beef

ODDLY ENOUGH, the fanciest boiled beef in this book takes the least time and is not dependent on beef stock, since the lighter taste of chicken stock lets the somewhat mild taste of the filet show through. If using a well-aged piece of meat with lots of flavor, consider using the Beef Stock.

The dish is obviously a variant of boeuf à la ficelle (*ficelle* meaning "string"), the French classic in which a whole filet is poached in stock. That method, which is longer and more complicated, produces rosy slices, whereas the quicker method here does not. However, the assortment of vegetables and the tarragon make it an attractive as well as tasty dish.

Should the whole-filet method seem more attractive, wrap the filet in a double layer of cheesecloth, leaving about six inches of extra cloth at either end. Take a long sturdy string: Leaving about a dozen loose inches beyond the cloth at one end of the cheesecloth, tie it tightly to the end of the cheesecloth. Draw the string to that end of the meat and knot it tightly. Wrap the string around the meat, knotting it at intervals, along the filet. At the other end of the meat, knot the string around the cheesecloth. Pull the string to the end of the cheesecloth and make another strong knot, leaving another dozen inches of loose string.

In a 10-inch-wide two-handled pot deep enough the hold the meat covered by stock, bring the stock to a boil. Put in the wrapped meat and tie the ends of the string to the handles of the pot in such a way that the meat does not sit on the bottom of the pan. Add more stock if necessary. Return to a boil. Reduce to a simmer and cook for 10 minutes. Add the vegetables and cook for 10 minutes longer. Turn the heat off. Stir in half the tarragon and the salt and pepper.

Remove the beef from the pot to a platter by using the string handles. Remove the string and cheesecloth. Either surround the meat with the vegetables and slice it at the table, passing the noodles and broth, or proceed as in the main recipe.

5 small carrots, peeled and cut into matchstick strips

1 large leek, white and light green parts only, cut into matchstick strips and washed well

½ pound (225 g) haricots verts (small string beans), tipped and tailed

½ pound (225 g) shiitake mushrooms, stems discarded, caps wiped clean and cut across into ¼-inch- (.5-cm-) thick strips

8 cups (2 l) Basic Chicken Stock (page 345), commercial chicken broth, Beef Stock (page 165), or, in England, imported beef or meat stock

Six 1-inch- (2.5-cm-) thick slices filet mignon (about 5 ounces [150 g] each)

1 small bunch tarragon, leaves only

1 tablespoon kosher salt, or less if using commercial broth

Freshly ground black pepper, to taste

3 cups (180 g) fine egg noodles, cooked (see page 392) and drained

PLACE THE VEGETABLES in a large wide pot. Toss to combine. Pour in the stock. Bring to a boil. Lower the heat and cook at a medium boil for 5 minutes.

Add the meat in one layer on top of the vegetables. Poke the meat down into the liquid so all the pieces are covered with liquid. Cover the pot. Turn the heat up slightly to retain a moderate boil for 5 minutes. Remove the meat to a platter. (If the pieces are tied with string, cut it away.)

Stir half of the tarragon, the salt, and pepper into the soup.

Place about ½ cup cooked noodles in the bottom of each of six large wide rimmed soup bowls. Divide the meat, vegetables, and broth evenly among the bowls. Sprinkle with a few leaves of tarragon.

MAKES 6 MAIN-COURSE SERVINGS

beef soup

WITH BROAD RICE NOODLES

PHO

THE NATIONAL SOUP OF Vietnam has become a runaway success around the world. It is filling, with a lot of noodles for slurping from the bowl. If a lower noodle-to-soup ratio is desired, simply cut back on the quantity of noodles used. As little as half the amount can be used if desired.

For this soup, the tenderloin is left in the freezer for a period of about 4 hours; this causes it to become firm, and therefore easier to slice as thin as possible. It shouldn't be completely frozen, or it will not cut at all. (Maybe the butcher will do this.)

4 cups (1 l) Beef Stock (page 165) or, in England, imported
    beef or meat stock

1 small star anise, crushed with a mortar and pestle

One 1-inch (2.5-cm) piece cinnamon stick

2 teaspoons slivered peeled ginger

2 cups (500 ml) boiling water

¼ pound (120 g) broad rice noodles

½ bulb end piece of lemongrass, smashed with the back
    of a knife and minced

1 to 2 cloves garlic, smashed, peeled, and finely chopped

½ teaspoon chili oil

2 tablespoons nuoc mam (fish sauce)

1½ teaspoons kosher salt

Freshly ground black pepper, to taste

¾ pound (360 g) beef tenderloin, left in the freezer to firm for
    4 to 5 hours, then sliced as thin as possible (at least 12 slices)

1 tablespoon fresh lime juice

for serving

2 tablespoons chopped cilantro

1 medium scallion, thinly sliced across

IN A MEDIUM SAUCEPAN, bring the stock, star anise, cinnamon, and ginger to a boil. Lower the heat and cook at just below a simmer for 30 minutes. Strain through a fine-mesh sieve. Return to the pan.

Meanwhile, pour the boiling water over the noodles and allow to sit for 10 minutes. Drain and rinse under cold running water.

Stir the noodles, lemongrass, garlic, chili oil, nuoc mam, salt, and pepper into the soup. Bring to a boil. Stir in the beef and cook for 30 seconds, barely long enough for the meat to change color. The soup is hot enough that the beef will continue cooking as it is served, and the meat should not be well done. Stir in the lime juice.

Serve sprinkled with the cilantro and scallion.

MAKES 6 CUPS (1.5 L); 4 FIRST-COURSE SERVINGS

shabu-shabu

ONCE I HAD THE PLEASURE of going to Japan to judge an international culinary contest. The Japanese contestant was that great gentleman and chef, Shizuo Tsuji. While the shabu-shabu, an eater-made beef-and-vegetable meal, is my own version of this Japanese favorite, the sesame sauce is his, from *Japanese Cooking: A Simple Art*. Unfortunately, Tsuji died not long after I was in Japan.

The ponzu sauce is an adaptation of Tsuji's. Even simplified, it be made a month in advance, though will still be good if all the ingredients are simply boiled together for 10 minutes and then it is left to sit, refrigerated, overnight.

Shabu-shabu is traditionally made by each diner in the communal hot pot (also known as a Mongolian hot pot), where the kelp broth surrounds the heat-filled chimney. A chafing dish can be used. The ingredients can be arranged on one very large platter with a large bowl for the cabbage and another for the noodles. Each guest has a large bowl for the soup and two bowls for the sauce and condiments. This way of eating the dish is a party, complemented by cold Japanese beer.

Using chopsticks, the diners/cooks dip the ingredients into the broth and then dip the cooked meat into the sauces, mixing in the scallions and daikon as they go. When the tofu, cabbage, and noodles have been added, the remaining sauces are poured into the broth. A ladle is passed so that each diner can take some soup that will by now have absorbed flavors from all of the ingredients.

The version given in the recipe is useful when the table will not accommodate all the plates, platter, bowls, and hot pot. In it, everything is cooked in the kitchen and brought out in stages. Serve the meat first, then return to the kitchen to cook the vegetables and tofu. These can be served in the broth with or without noodles and with the remaining condiments and sauce poured into the soup.

If possible, have the butcher slice the meat paper-thin, which can be done by partially freezing it and using a slicer. It is almost impossible to do at home unless a slicer is available. If neither solution is possible, substitute beef fillet and slice as on page 188.

Tamari is a soy sauce of rich flavor made without any wheat. Buy it in small bottles and use it: As it is not pasteurized, it will continue to ferment when exposed to air and turn nasty after some time in a hot kitchen.

Mirin is a sweetened Japanese rice wine for cooking. It can be bought in supermarkets.

One 4-inch (10-cm) square konbu (kelp)

1 pound (450 g) boneless New York strip (shell) steak (wing rib),
    well trimmed, sliced paper-thin, and cut crosswise in half (about forty-eight
    2 × 4-inch [5 × 10-cm] pieces)

for serving

Sesame Sauce (recipe follows)

Ponzu Sauce (recipe follows)

6 medium scallions, trimmed and thinly sliced across

One 3-inch- (7.5-cm-) long 2-inch- (5-cm-) thick piece daikon
    [mouli], peeled and shredded

for the vegetables

8 medium shiitake mushrooms, stemmed, caps wiped clean and
    cut across into ½-inch (1-cm) strips

12 leaves Chinese cabbage, cut across into ½-inch
    (1-cm) strips

1 bunch edible chrysanthemum leaves or 2 small bunches
    watercress, top sprigs only, washed well

6 medium scallions, trimmed and cut across into 1-inch
    (2.5-cm) lengths

Two ¼-pound (120 g) pieces "pillow" tofu, cut into 1-inch
    (2.5-cm) squares

½ pound (225 g) soba (buckwheat) noodles, boiled for 6 minutes
    and drained, optional

IN A MEDIUM STOCKPOT, combine the konbu and 8 cups (2 l) water. Bring to a boil. Remove the konbu and discard. Lower the heat and simmer for 3 minutes.

A few pieces at a time, drop the meat into the simmering liquid for a few seconds, just until it is beginning to change color. Serve immediately, with the dipping sauces, scallions, and daikon.

Return the broth to a simmer, if necessary, and stir in the mushrooms and cabbage. Simmer for 8 minutes. Stir in the chrysanthemum or watercress. Simmer for 4 minutes. With a slotted spoon, remove the vegetables and greens to a bowl. Keep warm. Stir the scallions into the broth. Simmer for 1 minute. Stir in the tofu and simmer for 2 more minutes. Remove to the bowl with the vegetables. If this is being done at the table, the diners can eat the vegetables individually with the dipping sauces and condiments as they are done or wait until everything is done and eat at the end as a soup.

Divide the noodles, if using, evenly among the bowls and pour the broth over everything. Stir the remaining sauces and condiments into the broth.

MAKES 6 SERVINGS

sesame sauce

½ cup (90 g) white sesame seeds
¾ cup Dashi (page 366)
6 tablespoons tamari (Japanese soy sauce)
2 tablespoons mirin (sweet rice wine)
1 tablespoon sugar

IN A SMALL DRY FRYING PAN, cook the sesame seeds over medium heat, shaking the pan constantly, until lightly browned, about 2 minutes.

In a mortar and pestle, grind the still-warm seeds until flaky. Transfer to a bowl. Stir in the remaining ingredients. Ladle about ½ cup (125 ml) back to the mortar and crush to make a paste. Stir this paste back into the whole to combine.

MAKES 1½ CUPS (375 ML)

ponzu sauce

½ cup (125 ml) lemon juice
½ cup (125 ml) lime juice
Scant ½ cup (120 ml) rice wine vinegar
1 cup (250 ml) soy sauce
2 tablespoons tamari (Japanese soy sauce)
3 tablespoons mirin (sweet rice wine)
½ cup (10 g) large bonito flakes
One 2-inch (5-cm) square konbu (kelp)

IN A SMALL BOWL, combine all the ingredients. Refrigerate for 3 to 4 weeks before using; or boil and let sit at room temperature overnight. Strain through a fine-mesh sieve and discard the solids.

MAKES ABOUT 2½ CUPS (675 ML)

How I became a food writer

ONCE, A MILLION YEARS AGO, I was young with a minimal job at *Mademoiselle;* but I had an apartment, and I loved to entertain and give gifts of food. I thought of myself as a writer, although I was a copy editor. After a while, I was given the job of copyediting the work of Leo Lerman, a contributing editor and substantial, bearded man. I think they gave it to me because I had grown up with a mother who wrote chicken scrawl and I could read his writing. Moreover, I had a mind stuffed with cultural trivia, so I was liable to know what his vast array of references actually referred to.

That was about as far as my career had gotten. I was working late one night when Mr. Lerman summoned me into his office. I barely knew him. I had once brought him a pâté at Christmastime and had brief conversations about items in his copy that I needed help in tracing. I was nervous and in awe.

He asked me to sit down, and I looked into a face full of intelligence and interest. Little did I know it but I was about to become one of Leo's girls, a group that included Amy Gross, Mary Cantwell, Joan Juliet Buck, and a legion of others, a group I am proud to be part of. I also became very used to that expression of alert interest. For the many years that I enjoyed knowing him, one of his first questions was sure to be, "So, what's new?" He didn't just mean gossip about people or information about my work and family, all of which were welcome. He meant anything I had seen or heard: a new restaurant, a ballet star about to make a breakthrough, a piece of his cherished majolica seen in a shop, an art show, anything in fact that might interest me. He had an extraordinarily broad group of interests and friends and acquaintances. Dogs, volcanoes, and bugs he liked; snakes were taboo.

On that fateful evening, he said to me, "You want to write, don't you?" Like a puppy sighting a bone, I ardently said, "Oh, yes." He offered to send me to see the formidable Allene Talmey, features editor of *Vogue.* "When do I go?" "Not so fast, what are you going to tell her you write about?" "I'm a writer; I'll write about anything she wants me to write about"—the egotism of youth. "No, dear"—those were the days of "dear" and "darling" and gloves and hats in the office—"you have to tell them you write about something." Cogitation. "I'll write about art. It's the most exciting thing happening in New York and all my friends are artists." "No, dear, you will not write about art for *Vogue.*" "Why not?" "Because Allene writes about art for *Vogue.*" "Well, what should I write about?" "Write about food; you cook divinely."

And so it started. I went to see Miss Talmey (she was married—no hat). "Well, darling, if I let you write for *Vogue,* what would you write about?" "Why, Miss Talmey, I would write about food." "And, if I let you write about food for *Vogue,* what would you write about?" Now I was at a loss. I didn't know I should have had a story idea prepared. Thinking quickly, I came up with two ideas. To my shock, Miss Talmey commissioned both of them. The first was a piece on international dishes with sweet-and-sour flavoring and in it was the soup for my father on page 11.

Thank you, Leo.

okroshka

OKROSHKA, A RUSSIAN SOUP, is cold and undoubtedly has the oddest-sounding set of ingredients of all these soups, more like a salad than a soup, and yet it works wonderfully well.

The sourovetz is an actively fermenting brew. It needs to be made two weeks in advance, so think ahead if it must be authentic. It is a pain and can be replaced by light beer. Neither sourovetz nor beer should be added to the other ingredients until the soup is ready to serve as the soup is liable to turn. The best thing to do is to have all the ingredients ready and then just combine them at the last minute.

Such soups were obviously made in great houses that could be counted on to have a wonderful group of leftovers. Today, the best thing to do is to get the ingredients from a delicatessen.

> **1 pound (450 g) Russian pumpernickel or black bread plus
> 4 cups (1 l) boiling water; or 4 cups (1 l) light beer**

for the soup

> **1 hard-boiled egg**
>
> **¼ teaspoon dry mustard**
>
> **¼ cup (60 g) sour cream**
>
> **1 medium cucumber, peeled, seeded, and cut into ¼-inch (.5-cm) dice**
>
> **5 leaves Bibb lettuce, washed, center ribs cut out, and shredded**
>
> **1 medium scallion, trimmed and thinly sliced across**
>
> **½ pound (225 ml) cold roast beef, chicken, veal, and/or ham,
> cut into ½-inch (1-cm) dice**
>
> **Kosher salt, to taste**

FOR THE SOUROVETZ, cut the bread, if using, into 2-inch (5-cm) chunks. Place in a 1-gallon (4-l) glass or ceramic container with a tight-fitting lid. Cover with the boiling water. Cover the container with a double layer of cheesecloth. Allow to stand in a cool dark place for 2 weeks.

Skim any foam from the liquid. Drain the bread, reserving the liquid. Squeeze the bread to remove all liquid and discard. There should be about 6 cups (1.5 l) liquid. Refrigerate it until chilled.

For the soup, separate the yolk and white of the egg. Mince the white and reserve. With a fork, mash the yolk with mustard in a small bowl. Slowly work in the sour cream until smooth and creamy. This can be made a day ahead and refrigerated.

Pour 4 cups (1 l) of the sourovetz, or the beer, into a soup tureen. Stir in the cucumber, lettuce, scallions, and meat. Whisk in the sour cream mixture. If no ham has been used, taste for salt and adjust if necessary. Serve immediately.

MAKES ABOUT 6 CUPS (1.5 L); 6 FIRST-COURSE SERVINGS

Pork soups

Both pork and ham make wonderful soups that have an unexpected depth of flavor. Be careful when using ham. Some kinds of ham may be very salty and require using very little salt to flavor the soup. Taste first.

hot-and-sour soup

ONCE UPON A TIME, there was a fabulous restaurant in New York called Pearl's. Pearl was an attractive, witty woman born in China and married to an ex-general (of I do not know which side). At the time, it seemed to me that all the strong women who owned Chinese restaurants had been married to Chinese generals.

Pearl, herself a chorus girl, had started out at the Lotus Garden and then worked at another restaurant in the theater district, and she had made so many friends among the theater, literary, and garment-business people that they backed her in her own restaurant. Among the backers was my friend Leo Lerman. He and his friend Gray Foy went to Pearl's often. In fact, the first time I met her was at a birthday party for Leo at the prior restaurant, Canton Village. I brought a chocolate cake.

Among the many wonderful dishes that I lament after the passing of Pearl's, the first is that ultimate comfort food, steamed eggs with thin transparent noodles baked into a custard topped with a design of oyster sauce, and the second her hot-and-sour soup. I have tried to recreate it. Eating the soup not only is comforting; for me, it brings back all the splendid meals shared with friends.

4 dried shiitake mushrooms

5½ cups (1.4 l) Roasted Pork Stock (page 359)

¼ pound (120 g) boneless pork loin, or leftover roasted pork loin, cut into matchstick strips

Two ¼-pound (120-g) cakes firm silken tofu, cut into matchstick strips

3 tablespoons (24 g) cornstarch

4 to 5 tablespoons (65 to 80 ml) rice wine vinegar

1 tablespoon Chinese soy sauce

1½ teaspoons kosher salt

½ teaspoon freshly ground black pepper

One 8-ounce (225-g) can bamboo shoots, drained, blanched for
   2 minutes, and drained

2 eggs, lightly beaten

for serving

2 medium scallions, trimmed and cut across into thin slices

Toasted sesame oil

IN A SMALL BOWL, soak the mushrooms in ½ cup (125 ml) warm water for 15 minutes. Remove the mushrooms. Strain the liquid through a coffee filter and reserve. Remove and discard the mushroom stems. Slice the caps across into thin strips and reserve.

In a medium saucepan, bring the stock and mushroom soaking liquid to a boil. Stir in the mushroom strips and the raw pork, if using. Return to a boil. Lower the heat and simmer, covered, for 10 minutes. Stir in the tofu and the roast pork, if using, and simmer for 3 minutes.

In a small bowl, combine the cornstarch with ¼ cup (65 ml) water. Stir some of the hot soup into the mixture. Whisk into the soup. Stir in the vinegar, soy sauce, salt, and pepper. Simmer for 5 minutes. Stir in the bamboo shoots and heat through.

With a circular motion, pour the eggs into the soup. Stir once to break the eggs into threads.

Sprinkle each serving with scallions and a few drops of sesame oil.

MAKES 7 CUPS (1.75 L); 6 FIRST-COURSE SERVINGS

pork barley soup

FOR THOSE WHO DO NOT LIKE PORK, there are other barley soups in the book (see the Index). The pork makes a particularly hearty first-course soup.

2 teaspoons vegetable oil

1 pound (450 g) boneless pork shoulder, trimmed of excess fat and cut into 1-inch (2.5-cm) cubes

1 small onion, cut into ¼-inch (.5-cm) dice

6 cups (1.5 l) Roasted Pork Stock (page 359)

½ cup (100 g) pearl barley

1 medium rib celery, peeled and cut into ¼-inch (.5-cm) dice

20 sage leaves, cut across into narrow strips

1 large bunch flat-leaf parsley, leaves only, coarsely chopped

2½ teaspoons kosher salt

Freshly ground black pepper, to taste

IN A MEDIUM SAUCEPAN, heat the oil over high heat. Add the pork and brown on one side. Stir in the onion, turn the pork over, and brown on the other side. Pour in a little stock and scrape the bottom of the pot to get up any browned bits. Stir in the remaining stock and the barley. Bring to a boil. Lower the heat and simmer for 45 minutes.

Stir in the celery and simmer for 5 minutes. Stir in the sage and simmer for 5 minutes. Stir in the parsley and simmer for 5 more minutes. Season with the salt and pepper.

MAKES 7 CUPS (1.75 L); 5 TO 6 FIRST-COURSE SERVINGS

pork soup
WITH HERBS

THIS IS A BEAUTIFUL SOUP with a beautiful taste, a perfect start for a cool spring dinner.

I use lovage as the herb and it is wonderful. If lovage isn't available, a mixture of celery leaves and parsley can be added with the tomatoes and a little tarragon at the end as a substitute.

2 tablespoons olive oil

1 medium onion, cut into ¼-inch (.5-cm) dice

4 medium cloves garlic, smashed, peeled, and very finely chopped

¼ pound (120 g) cremini or white mushrooms, trimmed, wiped clean, and
    cut in half lengthwise, then across into ¼-inch- (.5-cm-) thick slices

6 medium tomatoes, cut into ¼-inch (.5-cm) dice

¼ cup (15 g) finely chopped parsley, if lovage is unavailable

3 to 4 tablespoons celery leaves, cut across into narrow strips,
    if lovage is unavailable

4 cups Enriched Pork Stock (page 360), Basic Chicken Stock (page 345),
    or commercial chicken broth

1 pound (450 g) pork shoulder, trimmed of excess fat and cut
    into ½-inch (1-cm) dice

½ cup (30 g) lovage leaves, cut across into narrow strips

1 teaspoon tarragon leaves, if lovage is unavailable

Kosher salt, to taste

Freshly ground black pepper, to taste

IN A MEDIUM FRYING PAN, heat the oil over medium heat. Stir in the onion and cook, stirring occasionally, for 2 minutes. Stir in the garlic and mushrooms. Cook, stirring occasionally, for 3 minutes. Stir in the tomatoes, and parsley and celery leaves, if using, and cook, stirring occasionally, for 5 minutes, or until the tomatoes have collapsed.

Meanwhile, in a medium saucepan, bring the stock and pork to a boil. Lower the heat and simmer for 15 minutes.

Stir the tomato mixture and lovage, or tarragon, into the stock. Return to a boil. Lower the heat and simmer for 2 minutes. Season with salt and pepper.

MAKES 9 CUPS (2.25 L); 8 FIRST-COURSE SERVINGS

lion's head

BARBARA TROPP

BARBARA TROPP is one of my favorite people and a wonderful cook and author of *Classic Chinese Cooking* and *The China Moon Cookbook*. I first met her when I was barely middle-aged and she was young. I was editing a magazine called *Cooking* and she wrote to us about possibly writing an article. I met with her—a tiny, elegant woman—and commissioned her first article. In that article was this soup. I have treasured it. I bring it to you in her own words:

> *This is Chinese comfort food, a deliciously soupy casserole called Lion's Head. To the lyric Chinese eye, each meatball on its bed of braised cabbage looks like the golden head of a lion surrounded by a flowing mane.*
>
> *Classic Yangchow recipes call for deep-frying the meatballs to turn them brown. You can panfry them instead or do what I do: Plunk them into the casserole nude and enjoy lighter color along with the ease.*
>
> *Lion's Head is especially fine brought to the table and served from the casserole in which it cooks. A 4- or 5-quart Chinese clay pot is the traditional and ideal vessel should you have one or wish to indulge in an inexpensive treasure from Chinese antiquity.*

for the meatballs

> **1 pound (450 g) coarsely ground pork butt**
>
> **1 thin scallion including green top, minced**
>
> **1¼ teaspoons very finely chopped peeled ginger**
>
> **1½ tablespoons soy sauce**
>
> **1 tablespoon sherry**
>
> **½ teaspoon kosher salt**
>
> **1 egg**
>
> **1 tablespoon cornstarch, dissolved in ¼ cup (65 ml) cold Basic Chicken Stock (page 345)**

for the mane

> **1 pound (450 g) Chinese (Napa) cabbage leaves, the sort with evenly broad pale green leaves wrapped tightly around a conical head**
>
> **1 tablespoon corn, peanut, or canola oil**
>
> **½ teaspoon very finely chopped peeled ginger**
>
> **½ teaspoon kosher salt**

2½ cups (675 ml) Basic Chicken Stock (page 345) or Roasted Pork Stock (page 359)

1 tablespoon cornstarch, dissolved in 2 tablespoons cold Basic Chicken Stock (page 345), to coat the meatballs

Kosher salt, to taste

FOR THE MEATBALLS: Spread the pork on a board and hand chop finely with a Chinese cleaver or chef's knife, marching up, down, and across the meat to refine its texture. Flip the ends of the meat into the middle and chop again, repeating the process five or six times, until the meat is sticky and fine. Transfer the pork to a large bowl.

Combine the remaining meatball seasonings and scrape them over the pork. With your hand, stir the meat briskly in one direction for 1 minute until well blended, then pick up the mixture in handfuls and throw it against the side of the bowl ten to fifteen times. (This classic Chinese process of "march-chopping" and "throw-mixing" gives the meat a very particular texture hallowed by Chinese eaters and otherwise inimitable.) Press plastic wrap directly on top of the meat and refrigerate it, overnight if you like.

For the mane: Cut the cabbage leaves nearly in half lengthwise (through the rib), then cut crosswise into chunky bands 2½ inches (6.25 cm) wide. Heat a wok or large heavy skillet until very hot. Lower the heat to medium, add the oil in a necklace around the pan, and swirl to glaze the bottom. Add the ginger and adjust the heat so it foams for 4 to 5 seconds. Then add the cabbage and stir-fry until the pieces are very hot and wilted, about 4 minutes. For good flavor, keep the heat high enough so the cabbage smokes and chars a bit at the edge. Sprinkle in the salt, toss to combine, and remove the pan from the heat.

Layer the cabbage in the bottom of a heavy 4- or 5-quart casserole. Add the stock and bring it slowly to a simmer.

While the stock heats, divide the meatball mixture into four portions. One by one, form each into a loose ball, cupping the meat between your palms and dipping your hands and then the finished meatball in the cornstarch mixture to generously coat the outside. As each is made, place it on top of the cabbage, equidistant in the pot so that the meatballs don't touch.

Cover the pot and simmer the casserole for 2 hours and 30 minutes. Periodically check the simmer; Chinese clay pots have a sneaky habit of climbing to a boil. Season with salt to taste.

Serve in hot shallow soup bowls, giving each guest a giant meatball surrounded by a good portion of soup and a nice bit of mane.

"SERVES 4 FOR A ONE-DISH SUPPER IN TANDEM WITH WEDGES OF PANFRIED SCALLION BREAD, CRUSTY GARLIC BREAD, OR THE LIKE"

pork and vegetable soup

I THINK OF THIS as a fall soup, for just before frost assaults my tomatoes. It is also good in winter using canned tomatoes. If in an Italian mode, pass some freshly grated Parmesan cheese.

5 cups (1.25 l) Roasted Pork Stock (page 359)

6 medium carrots, peeled and cut across into thin slices

1 medium leek, trimmed, washed well, and cut into ¼-inch (.5-cm) squares

¼ pound (120 g) bacon, cut into ¼-inch (.5-cm) dice

3 large ribs celery, peeled and cut into ¼-inch (.5-cm) dice

2 cloves garlic, smashed, peeled, and very finely chopped

2 medium tomatoes, peeled, cored, and coarsely chopped

½ pound (225 g) peas in the pod, shelled

2 cups (450 g) cooked cannellini beans (see page 293) or one 19-ounce (540 g) can cannellini beans, drained and rinsed

Kosher salt, to taste

IN A MEDIUM SAUCEPAN, bring the stock to a boil. Stir in the carrots, leek, and bacon. Return to a boil. Lower the heat and simmer for 10 minutes. Stir in the celery and garlic. Simmer until the celery is almost tender, about 10 minutes.

Stir in the tomatoes and peas. Simmer until the peas are tender, about 8 minutes. Stir in the beans. Season to taste with salt.

MAKES 8 CUPS (2 L); 6 FIRST-COURSE SERVINGS

green chili

THIS IS A VERY DIFFERENT bowl of heat from the Chili Pork Stew (page 204). It is milder and has a speckled green color that comes from the coriander and jalapeños.

Have warm flour tortillas, sour cream, extra jalapeños, and cilantro on hand for a simple warming meal.

3 pounds (1.4 kg) boneless pork shoulder, cut into 1-inch (2.5-cm) cubes

8 medium cloves garlic, smashed, peeled, and coarsely chopped

2 cups Enriched Pork Stock (page 360), Basic Chicken Stock (page 345), or commercial chicken broth

8 medium jalapeño peppers, 4 seeded and coarsely chopped, 4 just coarsely chopped

1½ pounds (675 g) tomatillos, husked, rinsed, and coarsely chopped (4 cups)

2 large bunches scallions, white part only, cut across into ¼-inch (.5-cm) slices

1 small bunch cilantro, leaves and 2 inches of stems only, coarsely chopped

Juice of 2 medium limes

1 teaspoon kosher salt, or less if using commercial broth

Freshly ground black pepper, to taste

for serving

Sour cream • Chopped jalapeños • Coarsely chopped cilantro • Warm flour tortillas

IN A MEDIUM SAUCEPAN, working in batches, brown the meat over high heat. As each batch is finished, set it aside. Lower the heat to medium. Return all the meat to the pan, add half of the garlic, and cook, stirring, for 1 minute, without browning. Stir in the stock. Bring to a boil. Lower the heat, partially cover, and simmer, stirring occasionally, for 45 minutes.

Stir in the jalapeños, tomatillos, and scallions. Simmer for 10 minutes. Stir in the rest of the garlic and the cilantro. Simmer for 5 minutes. Season with the lime juice, salt, and pepper.

Pass sour cream, jalapeños, and cilantro with the soup, and serve warm flour tortillas on the side.

MAKES 10 CUPS (2.5 L); 4 TO 5 MAIN-COURSE SERVINGS

chili pork stew

AN ECCENTRIC but deliciously soupy stew, with a substantial spiciness that, if there are spice-sensitive eaters involved, can be cut down by a third.

The heat comes from a powder that is made only from chilies and has no cumin, oregano, or other seasonings. In the United Kingdom, that will be chili powder. In the United States, one has to be careful to look for pure chili powder—otherwise it may be mixed. If pure chili powder is unavailable, cut down on the cumin in the recipe.

The meat can be cut into slices to lay in the bottom of each bowl, or it can be shredded and stirred into the soup. A large spoon of sour cream or rice can be added to each serving.

2¾ pound (1.2 kg) boneless pork shoulder, at room temperature

1 medium onion, cut into ¼-inch (.5-cm) dice

4 medium cloves garlic, smashed, peeled, and finely chopped

2 tablespoons crushed dried hot red peppers

2¼ teaspoons ground cumin

2¼ teaspoons ground coriander

4 teaspoons pure chili powder

¾ teaspoon dried oregano

¾ teaspoon dried marjoram

½ teaspoon cayenne pepper

2 cups (500 ml) Chunky Tomato Base (page 385), lightly crushed canned tomatoes (not plum) with their juice, or sterile-pack chopped tomatoes

3 cups (750 ml) Roasted Pork Stock (page 359), Basic Chicken Stock (page 345), or commercial chicken broth

4 cups (900 g) cooked kidney beans (see page 293) or two 19-ounce (530-g) cans kidney beans, drained and rinsed

Kosher salt, to taste

for serving

6 cups (900 g) cooked white rice (see page 294), optional

6 tablespoons (90 g) sour cream, optional

IN A TALL NARROW STOCKPOT, brown the pork on all sides over high heat. Remove the pork and set aside. Stir in the onion, garlic, spices, and herbs. Lower the heat and cook until the spices are aromatic, about 2 minutes.

Return the meat to the pot. Stir in the tomatoes and stock. Bring to a boil. Lower the heat and simmer, covered, for 2 hours and 15 minutes. Turn the meat every 30 minutes. Remove the meat from the soup and allow the meat to cool slightly.

Skim as much fat from the top of the soup as possible. Stir in the beans and salt. Slice the meat across the grain into thin slices (they will not be regular in size).

Return the meat to the pot and heat through. If desired, serve over white rice, topped with sour cream.

MAKES 10 CUPS (2.5 L), PLUS MEAT; 6 OR MORE MAIN-COURSE SERVINGS

Lamb soups

Lamb is not America's favorite meat; but I love it. Perhaps I can help us to catch up with the New Zealanders, the Australians, and the British by offering this selection of lamb soup recipes.

lamb and sorrel soup

LAMB AND SORREL are at their best in the spring. They make a delightful combination, the acidity of the sorrel cutting the somewhat heavy taste of the lamb.

> 1 pound (450 g) lamb shoulder, trimmed of excess fat and cut into
> ¾-inch (1.5-cm) cubes, or 2 cups cubed leftover cooked lamb
>
> 6 cups (1.5 l) Lamb Stock (page 361)
>
> 1 pound (450 g) firm potatoes, peeled and cut into ½-inch
> (1-cm) dice
>
> 4 tablespoons (60 g) unsalted butter
>
> 9 ounces (270 g) sorrel leaves (about 2 bunches, stemmed),
> cut across into narrow strips (about 6 cups)
>
> 1 tablespoon kosher salt
>
> Freshly ground black pepper, to taste

IN A MEDIUM SAUCEPAN, bring the raw lamb, if using, and the stock to a boil. Lower the heat and simmer for 15 minutes. Stir in the potatoes. Return to a boil. Lower the heat, stir in the cooked lamb, if using, and simmer for 15 minutes.

Meanwhile, in a medium frying pan, melt the butter. Stir in the sorrel and cook over medium heat, stirring, until the sorrel has wilted and changed color, about 2 minutes.

Stir the sorrel into the soup. Season with the salt and pepper.

MAKES 10 CUPS (2.5 L); 8 TO 9 FIRST-COURSE SERVINGS OR
4 TO 5 MAIN-COURSE SERVINGS

Pot and acid

DESPITE THE PROVOCATIVE TITLE, this is about ordinary cooking. One of the most frequent mistakes in cooking is preparing acidic foods in aluminum or cast iron.

Dramatic instances of the flaw have been provided by readers who have made my Sorrel Soup (page 55) and called or written to complain about the nasty black color and the unpleasant taste. Invariably they have ignored my instructions to cook in a nonreactive pot. Sorrel is extremely high in acid.

There are many other acidic ingredients that will suffer in such pots. Tomatoes, white wine, and vinegar are only a few. If buying pots, stick to stainless steel with a diffusing base of another metal or well-lined copper.

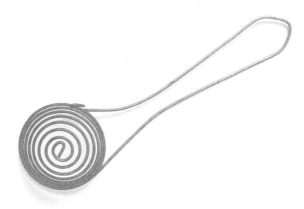

lamb soup
IRISH STYLE

DRIVING DOWN THE ROAD in Ireland, my progress has often been impeded by a slowly meandering flock of sheep. If they are just crossing the road, it is only a fifteen-minute delay; but if they are going from here to there, it is a good idea to have a book and resign oneself to the wait. The sight of them from the rear is extraordinary. So the farmers can identify the members of a flock should one stray, their wool is painted with bright splashes of color. It being Ireland, the preferred colors are orange and green. Some sheep are just one or the other; sometimes they are both; and the arrangement of the stripes can vary as well. Imagine it.

> **6 cups (1.5 l) Lamb Stock (page 361)**
>
> **1 pound (450 g) boneless lamb shoulder, trimmed of excess fat and cut into ½-inch (1-cm) dice (2 cups), or an equal amount of leftover cooked lamb**
>
> **½ pound (225 g) pearl onions, blanched for 1 minute, run under cold water, peeled, and cut in half**
>
> **1 large turnip, peeled and cut into ¼-inch (.5-cm) cubes**
>
> **½ pound (225 g) firm potatoes, peeled and cut into ¼-inch (.5-cm) cubes**
>
> **1½ tablespoons cornstarch**
>
> **1 tablespoon kosher salt**
>
> **Several grinds of black pepper**
>
> **1 bunch flat-leaf parsley, leaves only, coarsely chopped**

IN A MEDIUM SAUCEPAN, bring the stock and lamb (if not using cooked) to a boil. Lower the heat and simmer very gently for 15 minutes. Stir in the vegetables and the cooked lamb, if using, and return to a boil. Lower the heat and simmer for 15 minutes.

In a small bowl, combine the cornstarch with a few tablespoons of the broth to make a smooth paste. Stir in ¼ cup (65 ml) more of the broth. Return the soup to a boil and whisk in the cornstarch mixture. Simmer vigorously for 3 to 4 minutes, or until the soup thickens slightly. Season with the salt and pepper and stir in the parsley.

MAKES 9 CUPS (2.25 L); 8 FIRST-COURSE SERVINGS

lamb and chick pea soup

CHORBA

CHICK PEAS ARE CALLED *garbanzos* in Spanish, *ceci* in Italian. I often cheat and buy them canned, as after cooking they sometimes have a papery skin that has to be removed, which is boring. When I use canned, I make sure to drain them and rinse them very well in cold water.

The flavors of this soup are vaguely Moroccan—may Paula Wolfert forgive me. She is the one who told me that *chorba* means "soup" in Arabic. Harissa is a spicy sauce used by Moroccans and Tunisians. It can be bought in tubes.

1 tablespoon lamb fat (skimmed from chilled lamb stock) or olive oil

¾ pound (360 g) boneless lamb shoulder, trimmed of excess fat and
    cut into ¼-inch (.5-cm) dice

1 small onion, cut into ¼-inch (.5-cm) dice

4 medium cloves garlic, smashed, peeled, and very finely chopped

1¼ teaspoons ground cumin

5 cups (1.25 l) Lamb Stock (page 361), Basic Chicken Stock (page 345),
    or commercial chicken broth

2 cups (550 g) cooked chick peas (see page 294) or one 19-ounce (540 g)
    can chick peas, drained and rinsed

1 tablespoon kosher salt, or less if using commercial broth and/or canned chick peas

1 medium bunch flat-leaf spinach, stemmed, washed well, and coarsely chopped

2 tablespoons fresh lemon juice

1 tablespoon coarsely chopped mint

Freshly ground black pepper, to taste

Harissa, to taste, optional

MELT THE LAMB FAT in a medium stockpot over medium heat and let the fat sizzle until its liquid has evaporated; or heat the olive oil. Stir in the lamb and onion. Cook, stirring occasionally, until the lamb changes color and most of the liquid has evaporated, about 7 minutes. Stir in half the garlic and the cumin. Cook, stirring, for 2 minutes, or until the lamb begins to brown.

Stir in the stock, chick peas, and salt. Bring to a boil. Lower the heat and simmer, uncovered, for 10 minutes. Stir in the spinach, lemon juice, mint, and the remaining garlic. Simmer for 1 minute. Season with pepper, harissa to taste, and, if necessary, salt.

MAKES 6 CUPS (1.5 L); 6 FIRST-COURSE SERVINGS

curried squash
AND LAMB SOUP

THIS SOUP CAN CHEER any late fall or winter day. It is made with acorn squash, which will be available then. A double serving and a salad makes a family dinner with some good bread to sop up the last drops.

This soup, as so many are, is a user of leftovers. As I often roast a leg of lamb, I often have them available. Sometimes I have the lamb stock—so quickly made—but the leftover lamb has been long eaten. I just substitute raw lamb for cooked.

> Bones from 1 leg of lamb, about 1½ pounds (675 g), jointed and cut up if possible (remove any shards), or 8 cups (2 l) Lamb Stock (page 361)
>
> 2 medium acorn squash, cut in half, seeded, peeled, and cut into 2-inch (5-cm) cubes
>
> 2½ tablespoons vegetable oil
>
> 2 medium carrots, peeled and cut into ¼-inch (.5-cm) dice
>
> 1 medium onion, cut into ¼-inch (.5-cm) dice
>
> 2 tablespoons curry powder (East Indian preferred)
>
> 2 teaspoons coarsely chopped fresh thyme (or 1 teaspoon dried)
>
> 1 clove garlic, smashed, peeled, and coarsely chopped
>
> 1½ cups ½-inch (1-cm) cubes (¾ pound; 360 g) cooked or raw lamb
>
> 1 tablespoon kosher salt

IF NOT USING STOCK, in a tall narrow stockpot, bring the lamb bones and 8 cups (2 l) water to a boil. Lower the heat and simmer for 45 minutes. Stir in the squash and simmer for 45 minutes longer. If using stock, in a tall narrow stockpot, bring the stock to a boil. Stir in the squash and simmer for 45 minutes.

Meanwhile, in a medium saucepan, heat the oil over low heat. Stir in the carrots, onion, curry powder, thyme, and garlic. Cook, stirring occasionally, for 8 minutes. Stir in the lamb cubes and cook for 2 more minutes.

When the squash has simmered for 45 minutes, remove the lamb bones, if using. Mash the squash with a potato masher or the back of a wooden spoon. Stir in the vegetables and lamb. Return to a boil. Lower the heat and simmer for 20 minutes, or until the lamb is tender but not dry. Season with the salt.

MAKES 8 CUPS (2 L); 8 FIRST-COURSE SERVINGS

lamb mulligatawny soup

THIS EXCELLENT SOUP is one of those recipes adapted by the British from Indian food during their stay under the Raj. As with most things British, it is only very mildly spicy.

5 medium cloves garlic, smashed and peeled

4 teaspoons very finely chopped peeled ginger

2 tablespoons (30 g) unsalted butter

1 medium onion, cut into ¼-inch (.5-cm) dice

1 tablespoon curry powder (East Indian preferred)

1 teaspoon ground cumin

⅛ teaspoon cayenne pepper

½ pound (225 g) boneless lamb shoulder, trimmed of excess fat and
    cut into ½-inch (1-cm) dice

6 cups (1.5 l) Lamb Stock (page 361)

2 medium carrots, peeled and cut into ¼-inch (.5-cm) dice

1 medium rib celery, peeled and cut into ¼-inch (.5-cm) dice

1½ cups (330 g) red lentils

1 tablespoon kosher salt

1 tablespoon fresh lemon juice

Freshly ground black pepper, to taste

IN A BLENDER, purée the garlic, ginger, and ¼ cup (65 ml) water.

In a medium saucepan, melt the butter over medium heat. Stir in the onion and cook for 5 minutes, or until translucent. Stir in the spices and cook, stirring, for 1 minute to release the aromas. Stir in the lamb. Raise the heat and cook, stirring, until the lamb begins to brown. Be careful not to burn the spices.

Stir in the stock, garlic/ginger mixture, and the vegetables. Bring to a boil. Lower the heat and simmer for 10 minutes. Stir in the lentils and simmer for 8 minutes, or until the lentils and lamb are tender.

Season with the salt, lemon juice, and pepper.

MAKES 9 CUPS (2.25 1); 8 FIRST-COURSE SERVINGS

Other meat soups

In the following pages live the soups made with innards. Those who find these traditional ingredients repulsive should beware. Consider giving them a chance. They taste good. And don't forget my veal soup on page 27.

rossolnik

THIS RUSSIAN SOUP MAY SEEM unappealing, as its primary ingredient is lamb kidneys and it is flavored with pickles and pickle juice, but I really suggest trying it. It is surprisingly delicious and rich-tasting without requiring a stock first. It is also pleasantly inexpensive.

1 pound (450 g) lamb kidneys

1 medium carrot, peeled and cut across into ¼-inch (.5-cm) slices

⅓ pound (160 g) parsley root or celery root, peeled, quartered, and cut across into ¼-inch (.5-cm) slices

1 large onion, halved and cut across into ⅛-inch (.25-cm) slices

¼ pound (120 g) white mushrooms, trimmed, wiped clean, and cut across into ¼-inch (.5-cm) slices, optional

10 ounces (300 g) mashing potatoes, peeled and cut into ½-inch (1-cm) dice

1 bay leaf

2 tablespoons coarsely chopped parsley

1½ cups (300 g) cooked barley (see page 294); reduce to 1 cup (200 g) if not serving immediately

2 half-sour pickles, cut into ½-inch (1-cm) chunks

¼ cup (10 g) coarsely chopped dill

⅓ cup (80 ml), more or less, pickle juice (this must be to taste, as no two pickle juices will ever be the same)

1 teaspoon kosher salt, or to taste

Freshly ground black pepper, to taste

TRIM THE KIDNEYS of all fat. Holding each kidney upright with the rounded edge resting on the cutting board, slice in half lengthwise top to bottom to create two kidney-shaped pieces half as thick as before. There will be a small bit of fat in the dimple of the kidney. Holding this firmly, scrape along the veins with a small knife so that you remove veins and fat at one time. Cut the kidneys across into ¼-inch (.5-cm) slices.

In a medium saucepan, cover the kidneys, vegetables, and potatoes with 5 cups (1.25 l) cold water. Add the bay leaf and chopped parsley. Bring to a boil. Skim, lower the heat, and simmer for 10 minutes. Stir in the barley. Remove from the heat and let sit for 15 minutes.

Stir in the pickles, dill, pickle juice, salt, and pepper. Bring the soup to a boil. Lower the heat and simmer for 5 minutes. Adjust the seasoning as necessary. Serve immediately.

MAKES ABOUT 8 CUPS (2 L); 4 MAIN-COURSE SERVINGS

tripe gumbo

JAMES BEARD MADE San Francisco's Stanford Court his second home. He always stayed there when he was in town. Toward the end of his life, he was virtually living there a great part of the time. When I went out to teach with him, I stayed there as well, in a little room that adjoined his suite. It was fun. James Nassikas, then the owner of the hotel, was a fabulous host. There was only one down side to the stay: James Beard was a very early riser and every morning he would knock on my door about six to see if I was awake. Reminding myself that it was nine, New York time, I would struggle bleary-eyed to my feet and into a robe for breakfast. All and all, I wouldn't have missed it.

Many years ago, Jim Beard had a fabulous birthday party given by Jimmy Nassikas. It was a charity event, the first of those events at which a group of famous chefs got together to cook for a worthwhile cause. I was asked to be one of the cooks. Since Jim loved innards (our first night in town was always spent at Le Central eating blood sausage), I made up this tripe gumbo.

It was a success. I hope some readers will try it. While boiled rice would be the normal add-in starch, I have also used an eccentric half of a boiled potato in the middle of each bowl.

3½ tablespoons kosher salt

5 pounds (2.2 kg) honeycomb tripe, cut into 1-inch (2.5-cm) pieces

12 cups (3 l) Basic Chicken Stock (page 345) or commercial chicken broth, or more if needed

¼ cup (65 ml) rendered veal kidney fat, vegetable oil, or butter

2 large onions, very finely chopped

1 head garlic, smashed, peeled, and very finely chopped

3 tablespoons all-purpose flour

2 teaspoons cayenne pepper

1½ teaspoons hot red pepper sauce

3 cups (750 ml) Chunky Tomato Base (page 385), lightly crushed canned tomatoes (not plum) with their juice, or sterile-pack chopped tomatoes

About 1 to 2 cups (250 to 500 ml) Beef Stock (page 165) or, in England, imported beef or meat stock

2 bunches scallions, green part only, thinly sliced across

¼ pound (120 g) baby okra, cut across into ¼-inch (.5-cm) slices

¼ cup (65 ml) fresh lemon juice

Freshly ground black pepper, to taste

3 to 4 medium firm potatoes, boiled, peeled, and halved (see page 93), or 5 cups (750 g) cooked white rice (see page 294), optional

IN A LARGE STOCKPOT, bring 4 quarts (4 l) water to a boil. Add 2 tablespoons salt and the tripe and blanch for 5 minutes, stirring once. Drain. Rinse the stockpot.

Return the tripe to the stockpot and add the chicken stock along with 1 tablespoon salt. Bring to a boil. Lower the heat and simmer for 3 hours and 30 minutes. Drain the tripe and reserve the stock. At this point there should be about 10 cups (2.5 l) of stock. If necessary, add more chicken stock, or reduce, so that there is a total of 10 cups (2.5 l) stock.

Heat the kidney fat, oil, or butter in the stockpot. Stir in the onions and all but ¼ teaspoon of the garlic. Cook over medium heat until the onions are soft but not brown. Stir in the flour and cook, stirring constantly, over medium-low heat until the mixture is deep brown, about 25 minutes.

Stir in the cayenne and the hot red pepper sauce. Cook for 1 minute. Whisk in the reserved stock. Bring to a boil. Stir in the tripe, the tomatoes, and 1 cup (250 ml) beef stock. Lower the heat and simmer for 30 to 45 minutes, or until the tripe is very tender. There should be 10 cups (2.5 l) soup. Add beef stock if needed or reduce the broth if more than 10 cups (2.5 l) in volume. The soup can be made ahead to this point and refrigerated for up to 2 days.

If it has been refrigerated, reheat the soup. Stir in the scallions, okra, lemon juice, the remaining salt and garlic, and black pepper to taste. Simmer for 2 minutes. Serve with the rice or potatoes, if desired.

MAKES 10 CUPS (2.5 L); 6 TO 8 MAIN-COURSE SERVINGS

red menudo

MENUDO IS A TYPICAL New Year's Day dish in Mexico. It is a great hang-over remedy.

I love Rick Bayless and his food. With his blessing, I have adapted this recipe for red menudo from one of his. I hope he likes it.

Dark flat dried New Mexico chilies are used for this menudo. The chilies are maroon in color, rather large, shiny, and mild in flavor.

There is also a white menudo that I do not like as much. The best recipe is in Diana Kennedy's *The Art of Mexican Cooking*. When I made it, I cleaned the tripe in Rick's fashion and added extra lime juice at the end.

 2 pounds (900 g) honeycomb tripe
 1 tablespoon fresh lime juice
 1 tablespoon kosher salt
 3 medium cloves garlic, smashed, peeled, and coarsely chopped
 1 small onion, coarsely chopped
 2 teaspoons dried oregano

for the chili purée

 6 New Mexico chilies (1½ ounces; 45 g), stemmed, seeded, and
    torn into large pieces
 1½ teaspoons kosher salt
 ½ teaspoon ground cumin

 2 tablespoons fresh lime juice
 1 tablespoon kosher salt

IN A LARGE BOWL, soak the tripe in water to cover for 1 to 2 hours, changing the water three times. Drain.

Rub the lime juice and salt vigorously into the tripe. Let sit for 30 minutes. Cover with cold water again and soak for 1 to 2 more hours, changing the water three times. Drain the tripe and cut it into 1-inch (2.5-cm) pieces.

Place the tripe and 6 cups (1.5 l) water in a tall narrow stockpot. Bring to a boil. Lower the heat and simmer, partially covered, for 1 hour and 30 minutes. Stir in the garlic, onion, and oregano. Simmer for 1 hour and 30 minutes.

For the chili purée, place a small frying pan over medium heat. Fry the pepper pieces a few seconds on each side, until they are beginning to bubble and color slightly. Remove, place in a bowl, and cover with hot water. Soak, weighted down with a jar of water, for 30 minutes. Drain.

Squeeze out the excess liquid from the peppers. In a blender, purée with the salt and cumin.

When the tripe is done, stir in the chili purée, lime juice, and salt.

MAKES 6 CUPS (1.5 L); 6 FIRST-COURSE SERVINGS

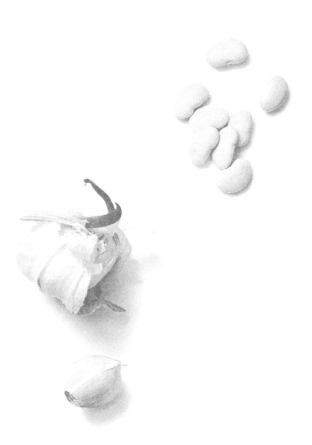

goat soup

WITH HARICOTS VERTS

NOW, I KNOW MOST people don't cook goat. However, those who are blessed with Hispanic butchers may be able to find it.

If goat stock is to be used, it must be made ahead. The soup can be made ahead—say there is goat left from a barbecue—and the beans cooked and added at the last minute. A bowl of Creamy Polenta (page 431), passed among the guests, would be welcome.

2¾ pounds (1.25 kg) boneless goat meat, cut into 1-inch (2.5-cm) pieces,
    or an equal amount of veal stew meat, from the shoulder

1½ tablespoons olive oil, plus additional if necessary

1 medium onion, cut into thin slices

1 tablespoon all-purpose flour

¾ cup (180 ml) red wine, such as a Côtes du Rhone

4½ cups (1.12 l) Goat Stock (page 361), Basic Chicken Stock (page 345),
    or commercial chicken broth if using goat; or Beef Stock (page 165)
    or, in England, imported beef or meat stock if using veal

½ pound (225 g) haricots verts or very young string beans,
    tipped and tailed

2 sage leaves

½ bay leaf

1 teaspoon kosher salt, or less if using commercial broth

2 teaspoons fresh lemon juice

PLACE A RACK in the center of the oven. Heat to 500°F (260°C; highest gas mark; #9 British regulo).

Rub the meat with the olive oil and place in a medium roasting pan. Roast for 15 minutes. Pour the juices that have accumulated in the bottom of the pan into a measuring cup. Turn the pieces of meat. Roast for 15 minutes. Pour the additional pan juices into the cup. Skim the fat from the liquid and reserve it separately from the juices. Don't soak the roasting pan yet.

In a medium saucepan, cook the onion in 3 tablespoons of the reserved fat over medium heat, stirring frequently, for 15 minutes, or until brown. (Keep the remaining fat.) Stir the meat into the onions. Add the flour and toss to coat. Pour in the reserved juices.

Place the roasting pan on top of the stove over high heat. Pour in the wine and bring to a boil, scraping up any browned bits from the bottom and sides of the pan with a wooden spoon. Boil to reduce by half. Pour over the meat, along with 3½ cups (875 ml) stock. Bring to a boil. Lower the heat and simmer, partially covered, for 2 hours, or until the meat is tender when pierced with the tip of a knife.

Skim the fat from the top of the soup. The soup can be made ahead to this point and refrigerated for up to 3 days.

Place 2 tablespoons of the remaining fat in a small saucepan over medium heat; if the veal hasn't provided enough fat, use olive oil. (Any leftover fat can be discarded.) Stir in the haricots verts, sage, and bay leaf, and toss to coat with fat. Pour in the remaining stock. Bring to a boil. Lower the heat and simmer for 5 minutes, or until the beans are tender.

If the soup has been refrigerated, reheat it. Stir in the haricot verts. Season with the salt and lemon juice.

MAKES 8 CUPS (2 L); 4 MAIN-COURSE SERVINGS

grand boiled dinners

POT-AU-FEU, BOLLITO MISTO, COCIDO, AND BOILED DINNER

THESE ARE WHAT I CALL "two-piece soups," the extravaganzas of the carnivore world, soups that are destined to be eaten in two or more courses. There is a first course, soup, followed by a main course of the meats and vegetables that have been cooked to make the soup. According to the country by which the dish is inspired, there will be condiments too.

As these are rather free-form, one's own version can be made using the cooking times starting on page 222.

They are feasts, eaten at home or in restaurants—where the Bollito Misto even has its own, very grand, serving wagon. Meats are taken out of the broth and sliced and served. These soups are made for a group. The quantity is increased by adding more cuts of meat rather than by increasing the size of the cut, unless the group to be served is huge.

Stock is not necessary, although it can be used. The various meats will provide the broth. However, if marrow bones are used, they may be cooked first and the bone broth skimmed and used for cooking the other meats.

Some traditional recipes call for cooking all the meats chosen in the same pot, adding them according to the length of time they need to cook, starting with the longest-cooking ones. This can be a heroic undertaking requiring a gargantuan pot if lots of meats are chosen. Consider cooking them in a few pots at the same time, or sequentially, taking one out when it is done and then adding another.

Many Italian recipes call for cooking a calf's head as one of the meats. Five heads later, I conclude that I will omit this option. It may just be that the heads I had available were too large.

I find that it is better to cook the vegetables separately. Otherwise, there is the risk of a murky broth and overcooked vegetables. See the vegetable timings on pages 448–451. Generally, larger vegetables are used in these soups. They can be cooked toward the end of the meat cooking time, using some of the broth from the meat.

For the difference between meats started in cold or in boiling liquid, see page 222. For all meats starting in cold liquid, bring liquid to cover to a boil. Lower the heat and start timing when the liquid is at a slow simmer. For meats starting in boiling liquid, add the meat to the boiling liquid and allow the liquid to return to a boil. Lower the heat and begin timing when the liquid is at a slow simmer. The liquid should remain at a constant very slow simmer through the entire process.

BOLLITO MISTO

Bollito misto is common to several regions of Italy: Emilia-Romagna, Lombardy, Piemonte, and the Veneto. Each region has its own variations using different cuts of meat. Piemonte uses breast of veal, shoulder roast of beef, rump roast of beef, beef ribs (I use beef short ribs), veal tail (I use oxtail), a hen (or capon), veal head, veal tongue, and veal sausage. Lombardy's is simpler, using head and tongue of veal, cotechino, capon, rump roast of beef, veal breast, and sometimes breast of veal. That of Emilia-Romagna is the simplest, using pork, under-muscle of ribs, head and tongue of veal, pig's foot, and rump roast of beef. That of the Veneto (Verona in particular) is not markedly different from that of other regions, aside from the use of a sauce that is a sort of bread, marrow, and broth pap heavily peppered (*peanà*), which I didn't like, and horseradish.

Because of the size of the meats, bollito misto is generally made in a few pots: one for the beef, veal, and turkey; one for the head and tongue; and one for the sausage (always cook the sausage separately).

The liquid for bollito misto is usually water—just enough to cover the meats—flavored by one or more onions (stuck with a clove), celery, carrot, peppercorns, and parsley. The liquid can be further enriched with the addition of thyme, bay leaf, leek, orange zest (no white pith), and even garlic.

The vegetables for bollito misto are simple: carrots (peeled), celery (peeled), very small firm potatoes (well scrubbed), tomatoes, and perhaps red pepper (strips).

POT-AU-FEU

Pot-au-feu is the very essence of mythical French home cooking and may include chicken and beef—no veal. It is traditionally served with three or more of a wide variety of vegetables, including turnips (peeled and halved if small, quartered if large), carrots (peeled), escarole or Batavia (whole head), cabbage (wedges), celery root (peeled and quartered), fennel bulb (halved if large, whole if small), celery (peeled), string beans (tipped and tailed), very small firm potatoes (well scrubbed), and leeks (whole, well cleaned). If cabbage is used, it is cooked separately so the soup isn't too cabbagey.

The addition of sea snails and an aïoli sauce turns this into the grand aïoli of Provence at Christmas.

Frequently in traditional recipes, the vegetables were added to the simmering meat very close to the beginning of the cooking time, or at least an hour before the end of cooking. The vegetables would simmer from one to three hours and were very soft. I prefer to follow the timings on pages 448–451.

COCIDO

Cocido is virtually the Spanish national dish, a big boiled meal that varies from region to region and even has a Jewish version without the pork. It is characterized by chick peas (the Catalan version uses potatoes and noodles instead) and sometimes even has dried beans. It uses the same vegetables as bollito misto. In addition to the beef and chicken, it normally includes some ham, some bacon, a ham hock, and a cooking—not dry—sausage. Some regions throw in a few simple meatballs at the end, made with eggs, ground beef, parsley, paprika, and garlic. In Madrid, they seem to use corned beef; but I seldom find that this improves the taste of broth even if the meat is boiled first to remove excess salt. (Chick pea cooking times are on page 294.)

BOILED DINNER

The boiled dinner seems to be typically New England and uses corned beef, vegetables as above, and possibly tongue. Again, I find the broth unpalatable.

THE CONDIMENTS

Bollito misto: Enriched Vinaigrette (page 436) in Lombardy, Bagnèt Verd (page 437) and Bagnèt Ross (page 438), in Piemonte, the Veneto, and, sometimes, Lombardy

Pot-au-feu: Croutons (page 429), grated Swiss cheese, gherkins, mustards, pickled onions, coarse salt, Fresh Horseradish Condiment (page 440), and Aïoli (page 432)

COOKING TIMES FOR MEATS

Beef brisket: 2 to 4 pounds (900 g to 1.8 kg): Starting in *cold liquid,* brought to a boil, and then simmered: 3 to 4 hours. Starting in *boiling liquid* and then simmered: 3 to 4 hours.

Beef rump roast: 3 pounds (1.4 kg): Starting in *cold liquid,* brought to a boil, and then simmered: 3 hours. Starting in *boiling liquid* and then simmered: 3 hours to 3 hours and 30 minutes.

Beef shoulder roast: 3 pounds (1.4 kg): Starting in *cold liquid,* brought to a boil, and then simmered: 2 to 3 hours. Starting in *boiling liquid* and then simmered: 2 hours and 30 minutes to 3 hours and 30 minutes.

Beef shin with bone: 2 to 4 pounds (900 g to 1.8 kg), cut across into 2-inch (5-cm) pieces: Starting in *cold liquid,* brought to a boil, and then simmered: 1 hour and 30 minutes to 2 hours. Starting in *boiling liquid* and then simmered: 1 hour and 30 minutes to 2 hours and 15 minutes.

Oxtail (or veal tail if available): ¼ pound (120 g) pieces, about 1 inch (2.5 cm) long: Starting in *cold liquid,* brought to a boil, and then simmered: 1 hour and 45 minutes to 2 hours and 15 minutes. Starting with *boiling liquid* and then simmered: 2 hours and 15 minutes to 2 hours and 30 minutes.

Beef short ribs (or regular beef rib): 3 to 5 pounds (1.4 to 2.25 kg): Starting in *cold liquid,* brought to a boil, and then simmered: 1 hour 30 minutes to 2 hours. Starting in *boiling liquid* and then simmered: 2 hours and 30 minutes to 3 hours.

Beef tongue: 3 pounds (1.4 kg): Starting in *boiling liquid* and then simmered: 1 hour, removed and skin removed, returned to liquid, and simmered for 2 hours and 30 minutes to 2 hours and 45 minutes.

Marrow bones: The marrow bones should be placed in a pot just large enough to hold them standing upright, so that the cooking time will not change; the amount of water will change in direct ratio to how many bones there are and the size of the pot. The bones should first be soaked in water and salt (½ cup [145 g] salt to 8 cups [2 l] water) for about 30 minutes. Starting in *cold liquid:* 10 minutes at just under a simmer, allowed to cool slightly in the water and then removed with a pair of tongs

Veal breast: 3 pounds (1.4 kg): Starting in *cold liquid,* brought to a boil, and then simmered: 2 hours and 15 minutes to 2 hours and 45 minutes. Starting in *boiling liquid* and then simmered: 2 hours and 30 minutes to 3 hours

Veal shank: 1½-inch- (4-cm-) thick slices across the bone: Starting in *cold liquid,* brought to a boil, and then simmered: 1 hour and 30 minutes to 2 hours. Starting in *boiling liquid* and then simmered: 1 hour and 45 minutes to 2 hours and 15 minutes

Veal tongue: 1 pound (450 g) each: Starting in *cold liquid,* brought to a boil, and then simmered: 1 hour and 45 minutes to 2 hours. Starting in *simmering liquid* and then simmered: 2 hours.

Ham hock or pig's foot: Starting in *cold liquid,* brought to a boil, and then simmered: 2 hours and 30 minutes to 3 hours. Starting in *simmering liquid* and then simmered: about 3 hours.

Whole chicken, unstuffed or stuffed: 3 to 4 pounds (1.4 to 1.8 kg): Starting in *cold liquid,* brought to a boil, and then simmered: 40 minutes to 1 hour, or 1 hour 30 minutes if stuffed. Starting in *boiling liquid* and then simmered: 1 hour, or 1 hour 45 minutes if stuffed.

Cotechino sausage (or other Italian spicy pepper or garlic sausage) and French, Italian, Spanish, or Hungarian sausages: 3 pounds (1.4 kg): Starting in *cold water,* brought to a boil, and then simmered: 2 hours to 2 hours and 30 minutes; for some sausages, a presoak is recommended—check with the butcher.

Swimmers
in soup

THIS IS NOT that old joke about a fly doing the backstroke in your soup. This is about all the wonderful things in the sea and rivers and lakes that can very easily be turned into soups to start and soups that make a meal. By and large, such soups were developed by fishermen and their wives and are thrifty, using bones and a little bit of this and that—not always the finest species—to make savory dishes.

Cooks should feel free to use what is readily available, substituting where need be for the fish and shellfish and cephalopods that inhabit the recipes. One has to be sensible. If one is substituting catfish for carp in Freshwater Fish and Summer Vegetable Soup (page 256), for example, it is important to realize that catfish will cook more quickly and should be added later in the recipe.

Some soups are more elegant. Shrimp Bisque (page 228) is a restaurant soup, and oysters have become so expensive that Creamy Oyster Soup (page 247) is meant for occasions.

It is handy to know your fish seller well enough to get the fish filleted when desired. Always get the bones or the shrimp shells. They have been paid for and are good for making stocks. Remember that even if a good filleting job has been done on the fish, it will need to have some pin bones removed. Running one's fingers against the grain of the fish, one should be able to feel the tips of these tiny bones, which can then be removed with needle-nosed pliers or strong tweezers. Any time I cook a whole fish—I, of course, recommend roasting—I save the head and bones and thrust them into the stockpot. See pages 362–363 for recipes.

When making these soups, taste before adding salt. The amount needed will vary greatly depending on the seafood used. The season of the year, as well as where the seafood is from, has a great effect on the salinity of the seafood.

Normally, I use kosher salt, which is coarse and therefore less salt is actually used than would be if I were using the same volume measure of table salt. Gros sel, or coarse sea salt, can be substituted. Generally, sea salt is expensive and I don't use it; but it certainly makes sense in fish and seafood dishes, even if the taste of each sea and ocean is different. (Remember licking your lips after coming out from a swim?)

Soups containing fish are generally shaken in the pot to blend the flavors rather than being stirred. This prevents shredding the fish. It is usually easier to do this with the pot covered. If the blending doesn't seem to be going well, or the pot is too large to shake, a wooden spoon handle can be thrust into the soup at three or four points and wiggled.

For openers

Although there are many recipes in this book for large soups of fish and seafood that make meals, I am particularly partial to such soups, both hot and cold, that are meant to open a meal.

shellfish soups

Often shellfish will give off, when cooked, enough liquid to provide a stock on their own and require nothing else. Shrimp soups generally require a shrimp stock made from the shells or chicken stock.

It is hard to say how many cups a recipe will make when the seafood is served in the shell. The safest thing is to follow the guidelines for number of servings. If finicky friends are being served, the seafood can be taken out of the shell and briefly reheated in the soup. The number of servings will stay the same. However, if the seafood is served in the shell, large bowls will be needed, as well as an extra bowl for discarded shells.

shrimp bisque

THIS ELEGANT, lightly creamy, and deep-tasting soup is the kind found in formal French restaurants. Bisques are more appropriate to restaurants than to homes. Professional kitchens tend to have lots of shellfish shells hanging around, and so it costs them very little to make bisques, and they have large machines for crushing the shells and lots of help, which makes it easy.

As a home cook, I don't have those things; this is the only bisque recipe in the book. Shrimp shells are soft and easy to work with. They are plentiful and inexpensive. I either save shrimp shells when I cook other dishes and pop them in a freezer bag until I have enough to make stock, or I talk to the fish man and buy—usually for a nominal price—as many shrimp shells as he has on hand or can get over a day or so.

2 pounds (900 g) shrimp shells

2 cups (500 ml) dry white wine

12 large shrimp in the shell

5 tablespoons (79 g) unsalted butter

2 tablespoons olive oil

1 small onion, coarsely chopped

1 small carrot, peeled and coarsely chopped

1 small rib celery, coarsely chopped

1 medium clove garlic, smashed and peeled

2 whole cloves

1 sprig thyme

⅓ cup (80 ml) Cognac or brandy

6 small ripe tomatoes (1 pound; 450 g), cored and coarsely chopped

2 teaspoons tomato paste

1 sprig tarragon

6 tablespoons (50 g) all-purpose flour

2 tablespoons mild paprika

1 cup (250 ml) heavy cream

5 teaspoons kosher salt

Hot red pepper sauce, to taste

Fresh lemon juice, to taste

IN A MEDIUM SAUCEPAN, bring 1 pound (450 g) shrimp shells, 5 cups (1.25 l) water, and 1 cup (250 ml) wine to a boil. Lower the heat and simmer for 15 minutes. Add 2 cups (500 ml) water and return to a boil. Stir in the shrimp, pushing the shrimp down into the liquid. Return to a boil. Cover, remove from the heat, and let sit for 5 minutes.

Remove the whole shrimp from the pan. Peel and quarter the shrimp. Discard the shells and refrigerate the shrimp. Strain the liquid through a fine-mesh sieve, pushing down firmly to extract as much liquid as possible. Discard the used shells and reserve the liquid. Measure 6 cups (1.5 l); reserve any additional for another use.

In a medium stockpot, heat 2 tablespoons butter and the oil over high heat. When the fat is very hot, add the remaining shrimp shells and cook, stirring, for 8 to 10 minutes, until the shells take on quite a bit of color.

Stir in the onion, carrot, celery, garlic, cloves, and thyme. Lower the heat to the lowest possible level and cook, stirring occasionally, for 10 minutes.

Pour in the remaining wine and the brandy. Raise the heat. Bring just to a boil. Pour in the reserved cooking liquid. Bring to a boil. Stir in the tomatoes. Dilute the tomato paste with a little of the liquid and stir into the pot. Bring to a boil. Lower the heat and simmer, covered, for 25 minutes. Add the tarragon and simmer for 3 minutes more.

Strain the broth first through a colander to remove the large pieces and then through a damp-cloth–lined sieve. There should be 6 cups (1.5 l). Reserve.

In a medium saucepan, melt the remaining butter over very low heat. Stir in the flour and paprika to make a roux. Cook, alternately stirring and mashing the scanty roux down in the pan, for 5 minutes.

Whisk 1 cup (250 ml) of the reserved liquid into the pan until smooth. Slowly whisk in the remaining liquid. Bring to a boil, whisking frequently, to ensure a smooth soup. Lower the heat and simmer, stirring with a wooden spoon, especially around the edges of the pan, for 10 minutes. The soup can be made ahead up to this point and refrigerated.

To serve, reheat the soup if it has been refrigerated. Stir in the cream, salt, hot red pepper sauce, lemon juice, and reserved shrimp and heat through.

MAKES 6 CUPS (1.5 L); 6 FIRST-COURSE SERVINGS

Shrimp

SHRIMP MAY BE THE WORLD'S most popular seafood and throwing a shrimp on the barbie may by now be proverbial; but it is far from the only way to cook shrimp. We have only to think of cocktail parties to get some idea of how much shrimp is consumed. Shrimp can be boiled, steamed, grilled, broiled, roasted, sautéed, and braised in soups and stews. It makes wonderful soups that are quickly cooked (aside from the gumbo on page 276). It is versatile and goes well with a wide variety of seasonings. It is happy in dishes from almost every ethnic group, as it is a favorite all over the world and grows or is farmed in both salt and fresh water.

Shrimp is delicious cold, turning up in chilled soups and salads. And, as a boon to the hot and frazzled cook, it can be bought already cooked and cleaned.

Shrimp shells can make stock for other seafood dishes or be used in shrimp sauces and bisques.

Shrimp come in a wide variety of sizes and colors. We eat those ranging in size from that of a thumbnail to ten to twelve inches long with their heads on. Europeans tend to call the larger shrimp prawns; Americans do not. There are even smaller, microscopic, shrimp in lakes and rivers that cannot be eaten by us but are the food that turn trout pink.

Even though they may appear to be fresh, much of the shelled shrimp we buy has been frozen and then defrosted and laid out on ice. When using frozen shrimp—ask the fish seller—it is better to cook it straight from the frozen state. A whole package may be large. To use just what is needed, unwrap the package. Hold the block of frozen shrimp in a cloth and whack it smartly on the edge of a counter at the point where the block should be split. The needed amount of shrimp will break off and the rest can be tightly wrapped and replaced in the freezer for another time. Add two minutes to the cooking time when using frozen instead of fresh or defrosted shrimp.

Whether fresh or frozen, almost all the shrimp we buy have had their heads removed. Leaving the heads on quickly turns them mushy, particularly the spot shrimp from the Pacific Northwest and tiger shrimp from Southeast Asia. This is unfortunate, as the heads can add a great deal of flavor. When we see a recipe using the heads, it has usually been developed in France, where the gray shrimp, like lobster, can stay alive out of the water for some time.

On the East Coast of the United States, fresh shrimp are usually white or pink shrimp from Florida. Sometimes there will also be brown shrimp, but they are an iffy buy, as they tend to have a strong iodine taste. Some white shrimp come in from Mexico, but they are frozen. All Asian shrimp have been frozen. On the West Coast of the United States, fresh shrimp are generally "spot prawns." The Hawaiian blue prawns that are available with their heads on and live also have claws and are not a true shrimp. The giant Spanish big reds used to be available, but they have not been in the market recently.

In California and Washington, "bay" shrimp, tiny sweet shrimp with red shells, used to come into the market and were a critical part of a Cobb salad. Today, these shrimp are shelled mechanically on the fishing boats, using huge amounts of water, which renders them virtually tasteless. They are known to the restaurant trade as TT shrimp. Some also come from northern European waters.

The Japanese and Chinese pay a huge premium for live shrimp, usually freshwater shrimp that will stay alive in water. We almost never see them in markets. If we are very lucky, in winter or the very early part of spring, we may find in the best markets Santa Barbara or Monterey shrimp with the orangey roe still in place. They should be briefly sautéed and eaten as a delicacy.

Although really fresh, good shrimp have a discrete flavor, they mysteriously retain enough flavor when cooked to stand up to the powerful seasonings of gumbo and curry; but they do not overwhelm the more delicate herbal seasonings. They have a great affinity for citrus flavors.

I have some guilt at recommending what is an already overfished resource. Farmed shrimp are no alternative, as the farmers, mostly in Southeast Asia, have been busily polluting the coastal waters, rendering them unusable for anything.

I doubt that I have enough virtue to really give up cooking or eating shrimp. At least, a few of them go a much longer way in soup than in a red-bathed shrimp cocktail.

sour prawn soup

TOM YAM GUNG

THIS IS A CLASSIC Thai soup. The best recipe I have found is in *The Essential Thai Cookbook* by Vatcharin Bhumichitr. He has graciously allowed me to use it. I have borrowed it with only minor changes, primarily to the sauce.

> 4 cups (1 l) Basic Chicken Stock (page 345) or commercial chicken broth
>
> 2 tablespoons Tom Yam Sauce (recipe follows)
>
> 4 kaffir lime leaves
>
> Two 2-inch (5-cm) pieces bulb end of lemongrass, smashed with the back of a knife and cut across into narrow strips
>
> 6 tablespoons (80 ml) nuoc mam (fish sauce)
>
> 4 small hot red chilies, finely chopped
>
> 1 teaspoon sugar
>
> 16 straw mushrooms, cut in half
>
> 1 pound (450 g) medium shrimp, peeled and deveined
>
> 6 tablespoons (80 ml) fresh lemon juice

IN A MEDIUM SAUCEPAN, bring the stock and tom yam sauce to a boil. Stir in the lime leaves, lemongrass, fish sauce, chilies, and sugar. Return to a boil. Lower the heat and simmer for 2 minutes.

Stir in the mushrooms and simmer for 1 minute. Stir in the shrimp and simmer for 1 minute, or until just opaque. Stir in the lemon juice.

MAKES 6½ CUPS (1.6 L); 4 TO 5 FIRST-COURSE SERVINGS

tom yam sauce

1 cup (250 ml) vegetable oil

1 large head garlic, smashed, peeled, and very finely chopped

2 small shallots, very finely chopped

4 dried guajillo chilies and 2 dried cascabel chilies, broken into small pieces, or ¾ cup (60 g) coarsely chopped medium-hot dried chilies

¼ cup (10 g) dried shrimp (available at Asian markets)

2 tablespoons sugar

2 teaspoons kosher salt

2 teaspoons tamarind pulp

HEAT ½ CUP (125 ML) oil in a medium saucepan over medium heat. Add the garlic and fry for about 5 minutes, or until golden brown. Strain the oil through a fine sieve; reserve the garlic.

Return the oil to the saucepan and reheat. Add the shallots and fry until golden brown and crispy, about 5 minutes. Strain the oil through a fine sieve; reserve the shallots.

Return the oil to the saucepan and lower the heat slightly. Add the chili peppers and fry until just beginning to darken, about 2 minutes. Add the garlic, shallots, shrimp, sugar, and salt to the saucepan. Cook, stirring, over medium heat until the sugar dissolves, 2 to 3 minutes. Remove from the heat.

Place the tamarind pulp in a small bowl with 2 tablespoons very hot water for about 5 minutes. Squeeze and knead the tamarind well with your fingers to dissolve everything that can be dissolved. Discard the seeds and fibers.

Place the chili pepper mixture in a blender with the rest of the oil and the tamarind. Purée until a thick oily sauce is achieved.

MAKES 1½ CUPS (375 ML)

shrimp broth

THIS SOUP CAN BE started the day before it is to be served by making the broth and the shrimp ball mixture. Then it's a matter of minutes to finish it. The soup is a light starter before a heavy main course.

Throwing out food offends me. I save my shrimp shells and use them to make broth.

The shells of the shrimp used in this recipe do not make enough broth for the soup. However, they make just enough broth to make up the shortfall in the shrimp broth recipe. Cover the shells with 1½ cups (375 ml) water, bring to a boil, lower the heat, and simmer for 20 minutes; strain. This should make about 1½ cups (375 ml), which can be added to already prepared broth.

for the shrimp balls

¾ pound (360 g) medium shrimp, peeled and deveined, shells reserved

2 ounces (60 g) raw unsalted pork fat, coarsely chopped

3 large scallions, trimmed, white part chopped, green part cut across into thin slices, and kept separate

2½ tablespoons cornstarch

1 teaspoon kosher salt

2 eggs, lightly beaten

1½ teaspoons Chinese chili paste with garlic

2 tablespoons sesame seeds

for the soup

7 cups (1.75 l) Shrimp Broth (page 365)

1 small carrot, peeled and cut into hair-thin strips

2 medium scallions, trimmed and cut into hair-thin strips

2 tablespoons soy sauce

1½ teaspoons kosher salt

FOR THE SHRIMP BALLS, bring 5 cups (1.25 l) water to a boil in a medium saucepan. Stir in the shrimp. Return to a boil and remove from the heat. Allow the shrimp to sit in the hot water for 5 minutes; drain and set aside to cool.

234   SOUP *a way of life*

When the shrimp are cool, place them with the pork fat, the white part of the scallions, 1½ teaspoons cornstarch, the salt, and eggs in a food processor. Process until very smooth, stopping to scrape down the sides of the bowl.

Scrape the mixture into a small bowl. Stir in the chili paste, scallion greens, and sesame seeds. Refrigerate for 2 hours, or until cold.

Mix the remaining cornstarch with ¼ cup (65 ml) water. Form the shrimp paste into 16 balls (use 1 rounded tablespoon per ball) and coat in the cornstarch mixture.

For the soup, bring the shrimp broth to a boil in a medium saucepan. Stir in the carrot. Lower the heat and simmer, covered, for 3 minutes. Return to a boil and carefully place the shrimp balls in the broth. Lower the heat and simmer, covered, for 1 minute. Stir in the scallion strips and simmer, covered, for 4 minutes. Remove from the heat and season with the soy sauce and salt.

MAKES 7 CUPS (1.75 L); 6 FIRST-COURSE SERVINGS

y doing the ...ckstroke in your soup. This is abou...

onderful things in the sea and rivers and lakes that c...

ery easily ... ...ed into soups to start and ...

dashi with shrimp

THIS VERY ECLECTIC soup borrows from several Asian cuisines.

2 cups (500 ml) boiling water

½ ounce (15 g) dried shiitake mushrooms

1½ pounds (675 g) medium shrimp, peeled and deveined, shells reserved

2½ cups (625 ml) Dashi (page 366) or instant dashi

3 tablespoons fermented black beans

2 tablespoons hair-thin strips peeled ginger

4 medium scallions, trimmed to 8 inches (20 cm), whites cut across into
   2 pieces each and then in half lengthwise, greens cut across into thin slices

4 ribs bok choy (very little of the green leaf), cut across into narrow strips

½ pound (225 g) button mushrooms, trimmed and wiped clean

Two 1.7-ounce (50-g) packages rice sticks or bean vermicelli cooked in
   1½ quarts (1.5 l) boiling water for 3 minutes, drained, and tossed
   with 2 teaspoons vegetable oil

Kosher salt, to taste

1 cup (20 g) cilantro leaves, for serving

POUR THE BOILING WATER over the dried mushrooms. Soak for 30 minutes.

Meanwhile, place the shrimp shells and 2½ cups (625 ml) water in a small saucepan. Bring to a boil. Lower the heat and simmer, covered, for 20 minutes. Strain through a fine-mesh sieve (there should be about 2 cups [500 ml]). Combine with the dashi in a medium saucepan.

In a small saucepan, bring ¾ cup (180 ml) water to a boil. Stir in the fermented black beans. Boil for 1 minute. Stir into the dashi.

When the mushrooms have softened, remove from the liquid. Strain the liquid through a coffee filter (there should be 1½ cups [375 ml]) and add to the dashi. Discard the mushroom stems and cut the caps across into ¼-inch- (.5-cm-) thick slices.

Stir the ginger, reconstituted mushrooms, and scallion whites into the dashi broth. Bring to a boil. Lower the heat and simmer for 5 minutes. Stir in the bok choy and button mushrooms. Simmer, covered, for 10 minutes.

Stir in the shrimp, scallion greens, and noodles. Simmer until the shrimp is opaque, about 2 minutes. Season with salt. Pass the cilantro at the table.

MAKES 12 CUPS (3 L); 4 MAIN-COURSE SERVINGS OR 8 FIRST-COURSE SERVINGS

236   SOUP *a way of life*

cold pea and mint purée

WITH SHRIMP

THIS IS NOT STRICTLY a seafood soup. The beautiful green is the frame for the pink shrimp.

**4 cups (1 l) Basic Chicken Stock (page 345)
or commercial chicken broth**

3 cups (90 g) packed mint leaves, coarsely chopped

5 pounds (2.25 kg) peas in the pod, shelled (4½ cups)

1 tablespoon fresh lemon juice

1 teaspoon kosher salt, or less if using commercial broth

6 to 8 drops hot red pepper sauce

for serving

4 large shrimp
Small mint leaves

IN A MEDIUM SAUCEPAN, bring the stock to a boil. Lower the heat. Stir in the chopped mint and simmer for 15 minutes. Stir in the peas and simmer for 8 to 10 minutes, until tender. Remove from the heat and drain in a fine-mesh sieve, reserving both the solids and the liquid.

In a food processor, purée the peas and mint, scraping down the sides as necessary. Add 1½ to 2 tablespoons of the reserved liquid to the work bowl as necessary to help smooth the purée. Press the purée through a fine-mesh sieve. Discard the pea skins left in the sieve. Thin the purée with the remaining liquid to the desired consistency. Season with the lemon juice, salt, and hot red pepper sauce. Chill.

Prepare the shrimp by removing all the shell except for that of the tail tip from each one. Cut the shrimp in half from head end to tail end, through the vein. Holding the tail with a pair of chopsticks, immerse each shrimp in boiling salted water just until it turns pink. Do not overcook. The shrimp will curl to look like a scorpion.

Pour some purée into each bowl and top with a curled shrimp and a small mint leaf.

MAKES 4 CUPS (1 ML); 4 FIRST-COURSE SERVINGS

mussels, clams, and shrimp

IN PARSLEY BROTH

MOVING FROM JUST SHRIMP to shrimp and...brings us to this light and quickly prepared, simple mixed seafood soup. Try it before a grilled meat, a roast chicken, or, in summer, a large salad with vegetables. If the eaters won't use their hands, shell the shrimp and take the mussels and clams out of their shells after cooking.

> 12 small clams, well scrubbed
>
> 16 mussels, well scrubbed and debearded
>
> 8 large shrimp in the shell
>
> 1 small dried hot red pepper
>
> 3 medium bunches parsley, leaves only, finely chopped
>
> 2 medium cloves garlic, smashed, peeled,
>   and chopped with the parsley

IN A MEDIUM SAUCEPAN, bring the clams and 1 cup (250 ml) water to a boil. Boil for 5 minutes. Stir in the mussels, shrimp, red pepper, parsley/garlic mixture, and ½ cup (125 ml) water. Cover. Cook for 5 minutes, or until the mussels have opened and the shrimp are pink.

Remove everything to a large bowl. Add 1 cup (250 ml) water to the pot. Bring to a boil. Swirl the liquid around in the pot to catch any pieces of parsley that may be clinging to the sides. Pour into the rest of the soup.

Divide the shellfish evenly among four serving bowls. Pour the broth over. Serve immediately.

MAKES 4 FIRST-COURSE SERVINGS

quarter-hour soup

CLAMS TEND TO BE an American taste; in England, cockles, or *palourdes,* in France, can be substituted.

Chris Styler had a dish called quarter-hour soup about twenty years ago in Rhode Island. He has never seen a recipe for it since. Based on his description, I came up with this. It is quick, easy, and fresh-tasting.

2½ cups (625 ml) Basic Chicken Stock (page 345) or commercial
    chicken broth

1 medium bunch parsley, leaves only, finely chopped

5 medium scallions, white part only, thinly sliced across

1 tablespoon finely ground fresh black pepper

30 littleneck clams, well scrubbed

Juice of 3 limes (⅓ cup; 80 ml)

1 teaspoon kosher salt, or less if using commercial broth

IN A MEDIUM SAUCEPAN, bring the stock to a boil. Stir in the parsley, scallions, and pepper. Cook at a low boil for 5 minutes. Stir in the clams and cover. Return to a boil and cook for about 5 minutes, or until all the clams are open. Stir in the lime juice and salt.

Serve immediately, or remove the clams from the shells and return to the broth before serving.

MAKES 4 CUPS (1 L) WITH THE CLAMS OUT OF THE SHELL; 4 FIRST-COURSE SERVINGS

Mussels

WHEN I WAS MUCH YOUNGER and the Riviera in summer was already cheek to jowl with burning people in bikinis who were so slim they made me self-conscious, there were still areas of the shore unbuilt with large luxurious houses. My friend Jeanette Leroy's boyfriend of the era was an *ancien combatant de guerre* (veteran). He had been injured in World War II. The government offered him as recompense the boon of a holiday stay in a government property. He chose a tiny lighthouse at the end of the point of land that juts into the sea between Cannes and Nice, the Cap d'Antibes.

The keeper of this small protective beam was another *ancien combatant de guerre*. His pet was a coatimundi that scampered up outer walls and rested in window niches.

We used to gather in the morning on the rocky outcropping to pick mussels. Come lunchtime, we had a large pot with a little seawater or white wine boiling over an outdoor fire; if we had been to market, some shallots—the large red Provençal kind—or garlic as well. There would be ripe tomatoes, basil, and local olive oil for salad, a large loaf of bread, and more bottles of white wine dangling on strings in the sea to chill.

The mussels went into the pot. The lid was put on. Soon after, the mussels opened. They were tumbled into a large bowl that we set on top of the rough planks and sawhorses that formed our table. We feasted, using an empty shell as tweezers to extract the next slightly nutty, briny bit of meat and throwing the shells into a large metal bucket.

These small mussels with their highly esteemed, lightly coral meat are *Mytillus galloprovincialis* (the province of Gaul, according to the Romans), or Mediterranean mussels. Imagine my surprise when Jon Rowley, a seafood expert from Seattle, sent me some locally caught mussels to see if I could help identify them. There they were, my old friends, presumably immigrants from Europe on a ship's hull.

Other summers, I harvested the North American blue mussels, really almost black, off Bar Harbor, Maine, and cooked them.

Both these mussels are splendid in soup, as is the similar-tasting brown-shelled *dattere di mare,* or *datte de mer,* although it is of another species altogether. I do not like New Zealand green-lipped mussels in soup.

Before choosing a recipe, be sure to check the Billi Bi on page 11. Also, be sure to ask for farmed mussels when buying them from a store. They will be cleaner. Self-picked mussels will need to be scrubbed with a stiff brush or a synthetic scouring pad—never use a metal scouring pad—and debearded. This last means to give a good hard tug at any projecting black bits sticking out of the shell or to scrape them off with a small sharp knife.

mussel and tomato soup

THIS IS NOT UNLIKE the mussels marinara in many Italian restaurants, but I think it is lighter and better. It does require friends who are willing to get their hands dirty. Serve lots of bread for dunking as well as a large spoon and an oyster fork each, if they are available. The recipe is easily doubled, but then the mussels may take a little longer to open.

3 tablespoons olive oil

3 medium cloves garlic, smashed, peeled, and very finely chopped

1 teaspoon dried oregano

1 pound (450 g) ripe tomatoes, peeled and chopped;
    or 2 cups (500 ml) Chunky Tomato Base (page 385),
    drained and lightly crushed canned tomatoes (not plum),
    or sterile-pack chopped tomatoes

1½ cups (375 ml) dry white wine

2 pounds (900 g) mussels, scrubbed and debearded

2 tablespoons coarsely chopped parsley

Kosher salt, to taste

Freshly ground black pepper, to taste

IN A MEDIUM SAUCEPAN, warm the oil over medium heat. Stir in the garlic and oregano. Cook, stirring, for about 1 minute, until the garlic becomes soft but does not brown. Stir in the tomatoes and cook, stirring occasionally, for about 2 minutes. Stir in the wine and bring to a boil. Lower the heat and simmer for about 5 minutes.

Stir in the mussels, cover, and cook, shaking the pan occasionally, for about 3 minutes, or until the mussels have opened.

Remove from the heat, stir in the parsley, and season to taste with salt and pepper.

MAKES 4 FIRST-COURSE SERVINGS

ginger-scallop soup

PALE AND SENSATIONAL, flecked with green if the leeks are used, this soup can start the most festive of meals. The recipe can be doubled. The broth can be made ahead and the leeks blanched; but I have to excuse myself from the table for about five minutes to cook the scallops and whisk in the butter—much like making a beurre blanc.

½ pound (225 g) ginger, unpeeled, thinly sliced across

1 leek, green part only, washed well and cut into
  hair-thin strips, optional

1 pound (450 g) bay scallops

8 tablespoons (120 g) cold unsalted butter,
  cut into ½-inch (1-cm) pieces

⅛ teaspoon cayenne pepper

1 tablespoon fresh lemon juice

1½ teaspoons kosher salt, or to taste

¼ cup (35 g) cooked long-grain white rice (see page 294),
  optional

IN A SMALL SAUCEPAN, bring 5 cups (1.25 l) water and the ginger to a boil. Lower the heat and simmer for 20 to 30 minutes, or until the liquid has reduced to 3 cups (750 ml). Strain through a fine-mesh sieve. Reserve the liquid and discard the ginger.

Meanwhile, if using the leek, bring a small saucepan of salted water to a boil. Stir in the leek. Lower the heat and simmer for 15 minutes. Drain and reserve.

In a medium saucepan, return the ginger liquid to a gentle simmer. Stir in the scallops. Simmer for 1½ to 2 minutes, or until they become opaque. Do not overcook, or they will become rubbery.

With a slotted spoon, remove the scallops and set aside. Over low heat, whisk the butter into the liquid, a few pieces at a time. While whisking, add the cayenne, lemon juice, and salt to taste. Remove from the heat and stir in the scallops and, if using, the leek. For a slightly heartier soup, add the rice along with the scallops.

MAKES 5 CUPS (1.25 L); 4 FIRST-COURSE SERVINGS

scallop and endive soup

IF I DO SAY SO MYSELF, this is spectacularly good. The slight bitterness of the endive balances the sweetness of the scallops. The tarragon provides a top note to the base of the cream.

> 2 pounds (900 g) sea scallops, small connective muscles removed and reserved
>
> 3 medium shallots, coarsely chopped
>
> 1 cup (250 ml) dry white wine
>
> 3 large Belgian endive [chicory], trimmed and cut across into ½-inch (1-cm) pieces
>
> ¼ cup (4 g) tarragon leaves
>
> 1 cup (250 ml) heavy cream
>
> 1 tablespoon cornstarch
>
> 2 teaspoons kosher salt
>
> Freshly ground black pepper, to taste

PLACE THE CONNECTIVE MUSCLES from the scallops, the shallots, the wine, and 3 cups (750 ml) water in a small saucepan. Bring to a boil. Lower the heat and simmer for 15 minutes. Strain through a fine-mesh sieve into a medium saucepan and discard the solids.

Bring the liquid to a boil. Stir in the endive. Return to a boil. Add the scallops and tarragon, stirring once to separate the scallops. Return barely to a simmer, without stirring again.

Stir in ½ cup (125 ml) heavy cream. Dissolve the cornstarch in the remaining cream. Ladle a few spoonfuls of the hot soup into the cornstarch mixture. Pour the cornstarch mixture back into the soup, stirring gently to incorporate. Cover and return to a boil. As soon the soup returns to a boil, uncover the pot, or it will overflow. Lower the heat and simmer, uncovered, for 3 minutes. Season with the salt and pepper.

MAKES 9 CUPS (1.75 L); 8 FIRST-COURSE SERVINGS

Oysters

OYSTERS SEEM TO COME with as many names as wine, and the names refer to many different things: Some refer to the place where the oysters are grown; some to the species, of which there are only six; and some are made up and are no help at all.

Brought up in New York, I started young with oysters named after their port of origin, namely Blue Point ("bloo pernts," as A. J. Leibling would have pointed out) from nearby Long Island. A period of living in Boston introduced me to Cape Cod's. Little did I know then that these slowest-growing (five years to maturity) and best of East Coast oysters would be subdivided into naming by town: Wellfleet, Chatham, and Wareham.

My first trip to Paris offered blissful instruction on the meaningful distinction between genera rather than places: *huîtres plates,* the true or flat-shelled oysters, and the *huîtres creuses,* with their deep oval shells resembling most the North American Eastern Seaboard oysters. They were often called Portugaise in those days, because the original spat, or seed, came from Portugal in 1868. In the 1970s, they were nearly wiped out by disease. Today, ninety percent of the creuses are actually a related but different species.

Further confusion arises as the French call many plates Belon after a particularly prestigious bit of Brittany. Some huîtres creuses are called *fines de claire,* having been raised in special flat ocean basins, previously salt basins, such as those at Marennes. However, I found, if an oyster was actually called a Marennes, it probably had a hint of iodine in the flavor and a slight green hue.

Moreover, I had to learn that these Europeans came in sizes from 000 to 4 for the flat oysters and 1 to 4 for the Portugaise. The lower the number, the bigger and more expensive. I was very proud of my knowledge, which was certified and rewarded with a midnight pig-out on a New Year's Eve.

Years later, a particularly nasty London winter with the last of the pea soup fogs—I couldn't find my car for three days—was ameliorated by my discovery of British oysters. I ate them when I could afford them, which was, sadly, seldom. These oysters were round and flat like my French loves and were named after the towns from which they came. My favorites were the Colchesters. I didn't yet know that there was a greater snobbery in appreciating the Colchesters called Pyefleets, from the Pyefleet Creek. There are other native British oysters, such as the Royal Whitstables, and then there are those grown from Brittany seed oysters.

Jim Beard introduced me to the tiny Olympias, the only American true oyster, no bigger than a thumbnail. They came from his native Oregon; but I had much to learn about other West Coast oysters. Deep oval and frilly, they were grown, originally, from Japanese seed, up and down the West Coast, from Hog Island on Tomales Bay in California and up through Yaguina Bay in Oregon, to, in Washington, Wescott Bay on San Juan Island, Shoalwater Bay in Willapa, and Quilcene and Hama Hama in the Hood Canal, and all the way up to Lasqueti Island in British Columbia. Then there is another Japanese oyster, known as kumamoto, with a small, almost conical shell.

From the Atlantic shores come Absecon (a spot near Atlantic City), oysters big enough to eat with a knife and fork; the Apalachicolas (Florida's western coast); the Chincoteagues (Virginia); Cotuits (Massachusetts); and Malpeques (Prince Edward Island).

European flat oysters are grown on both U.S. coasts, often under the misleading place name of Belon. Worse complications may yet be in the wings as we begin to get a separate species of true oysters from Chile.

One summer, I confronted Ireland's wide diversity of excellent oysters, flat and oval species from Kinsale to Galway. Another year I enjoyed the excellent Sydney rock oysters on a trip to Australia.

Some gourmets more discerning than I may be able to keep in mind the identity of a taste to go with each of the oyster species and locations. For the purposes of soup, it is best to buy shucked oysters by the pint and not worry about nomenclature. They certainly won't be flat oysters or Olympias.

Cooking cannot sanitize oysters. They will turn bouncing-ball-rubber-hard before they reach a high-enough temperature. However, I will continue to enjoy all sorts of oysters in cold months, asking only that they come from clean water. Oysters are one of the few foods for which I am willing to risk my health.

oysters rockefeller soup

FRANKLY, I WAS VERY SKEPTICAL when Adele Adato, a lovely New Orleans lady, offered me this recipe for the book I told her that I was writing. I had had oysters Rockefeller a few times in New Orleans and been less than overwhelmed. However, I knew Adele was a fine cook, so I tried it. I loved it.

> 1 pound (450 g) spinach, stemmed, blanched for 1 minute, drained, and squeezed dry, or one 10-ounce (300-g) box frozen spinach, thawed and squeezed dry
>
> 1 small onion, coarsely chopped
>
> 1 large rib celery with leaves, coarsely chopped
>
> ½ medium bunch parsley, stemmed and coarsely chopped
>
> 3 medium scallions, white and light green parts only, thinly sliced across
>
> ¼ cup (15 g) coarsely chopped iceberg lettuce
>
> 4 tablespoons (60 g) unsalted butter
>
> 2 tablespoons anchovy paste
>
> 1 teaspoon kosher salt, or less, if using commercial stock
>
> ½ teaspoon freshly ground black pepper
>
> 2 to 3 tablespoons fresh lemon juice, or to taste
>
> 3 tablespoons all-purpose flour
>
> 3 dozen oysters, shucked, with their liquid
>
> 1¼ cups (320 ml) Basic Chicken Stock (page 345) or commercial chicken broth
>
> 2 teaspoons Worcestershire sauce
>
> 2 cups (500 ml) half-and-half or light cream
>
> 2 tablespoons freshly grated Parmesan cheese
>
> 2 tablespoons Italian-seasoned bread crumbs; or plain toasted bread crumbs plus a tiny pinch each of dried oregano and thyme
>
> 1 tablespoon anise-flavored liquor (not liqueur; page 247), optional

IN A FOOD PROCESSOR, purée the spinach, onion, celery, parsley, scallions, and lettuce.

In a medium saucepan, melt the butter over medium heat. Stir in the puréed vegetables and cook, stirring frequently, for 8 minutes. Stir in the anchovy paste, salt, pepper, lemon juice, and flour.

Stir in the oysters with their liquid. Bring just to a simmer and cook for 3 minutes. Stir in the stock and Worcestershire sauce. Bring to a boil. Lower the heat and simmer for 2 minutes. Stir in the half-and-half, Parmesan cheese, and bread crumbs. Heat through. Just before serving, stir in the liquor, if desired.

MAKES 7 CUPS (1.75 L); 6 FIRST-COURSE SERVINGS

Anise

THERE SEEMS TO BE no happier marriage of flavors than seafood and anise. There are lots of ways that an anise flavor is added to soup. It can be added as a primary ingredient like bulb fennel, as a seasoning like anise or fennel seeds, or chopped fronds of herb fennel, or as anise-flavored liquors such as Pastis or Pernod (these are not sweet liqueurs). Raki or ouzo can be substituted.

creamy oyster soup

THIS IS A RICH and substantial soup for a winter night. Those who don't like a creamy oyster soup can try the oyster soup on page 20. A double portion of this would make a delightful dinner.

   3 dozen oysters, shucked, with their liquid
   4 cups (1 l) Basic Fish Stock (page 362)
   1¼ pounds (575 g) mashing potatoes, peeled and
      cut into ¼-inch (.5-cm) dice
   1 cup (250 ml) heavy cream
   3 generous pinches saffron threads
   1 medium bunch scallions, trimmed and thinly sliced across
   2 teaspoons kosher salt

PLACE THE OYSTERS in a strainer set over a large bowl to catch the liquid.

In a medium saucepan, bring the stock and potatoes to a boil. Lower the heat and simmer for 8 minutes. Stir in the oyster liquid, cream, and saffron. Return to a boil. Lower the heat and simmer for 8 minutes.

Cut each oyster in half with kitchen scissors. Stir the oysters into the soup with the scallions and salt. Cook for 1 to 2 minutes, or until the oysters begin to curl at the edges. Remove from the heat. Let sit for a few minutes to mellow the flavors, and serve.

MAKES 8 CUPS (2 L); 8 FIRST-COURSE SERVINGS

clam chowder

WHILE I USE CLAMS in the shell, it is possible to use shucked, or even canned, chopped clams; but it means using clam juice. Be careful when salting; clam juice is already salty. As a part-time New Englander, I would put a halved ship's biscuit in the bottom of each bowl. I normally would use bacon lardons and the fat that results from making them in the chowder. To try this, cut a quarter pound of slab bacon into small cubes. Fry them in a small pan until crisp. Remove with a slotted spoon; drain on paper towels and sprinkle on at the end. Use 2 tablespoons of the fat instead of butter to make the soup.

36 medium little-neck clams, well scrubbed; or 1¼ cups chopped clam meat, from 9 quahogs or other clams, plus 3 cups (750 ml) clam juice

1 tablespoon (15 g) unsalted butter

1½ tablespoons all-purpose flour

½ teaspoon ground mace

A pinch of cayenne pepper

1 large onion, finely chopped

1 pound (450 g) firm potatoes, peeled and cut into ¼-inch (.5-cm) dice

1 cup (250 ml) heavy cream

Kosher salt, to taste

Freshly ground black pepper, to taste

IF USING CLAMS IN THE SHELL, in a medium stockpot, bring 2 cups (500 ml) water to a boil. Add the clams, cover, and lower the heat slightly. Cook at a low boil until all the clams have opened, 5 to 7 minutes. Remove the clams. Strain the liquid through a coffee filter and reserve. There should be 3 cups (750 ml). Coarsely chop the clams.

In a medium saucepan, melt the butter. Stir in the flour, mace, and cayenne pepper. Cook over low heat for 2 minutes, stirring. Stir in the onion and cook, stirring and scraping the flour from the sides of the pan frequently, for 10 minutes, or until the onion is translucent.

Whisk 1 cup (250 ml) of the clam broth or juice into the pot until the mixture is smooth. Slowly whisk in the remaining clam broth or juice. Stir in the potatoes. There should be enough liquid to cover the potatoes; if there isn't, add additional water to barely cover. Bring to a boil, stirring frequently to ensure a smooth soup. Lower the heat and simmer for 12 minutes, or until the potatoes are almost done.

Stir in the clams and cream. Heat through. Season with salt if needed and pepper.

MAKES 6 CUPS (1.5 L); 6 FIRST-COURSE SERVINGS

OXTAIL SOUP WITH
FAVA BEANS, *page 172*

FACING PAGE

CHICKEN SOUP MEAL WITH
MORELS AND TARRAGON, *page 134*

ABOVE

MATZOH BALLS, *page 13*
IN SEASONED CHICKEN BROTH

BELOW

THE PISTOU, *page 302*

FACING PAGE

SOUPE AU PISTOU, *page 302*

FACING PAGE

VEGETARIAN BORSCHT, *page 6*

ABOVE

DUCK BROTH WITH NOODLES,
SCALLIONS, AND RADISH, *page 154*

BELOW

CAZUELA DE ELSA, *page 143*

FACING PAGE

CORN CHOWDER, *page 74*

FACING PAGE

TORTILLA SOUP, *page 142*

ABOVE

TWO GAZPACHOS,
LEFT: RED, *page 25;* RIGHT: GREEN, *page 32*

BELOW

BROWN BEEF STOCK:
STAGE ONE, *page 165*

FACING PAGE

GARLIC SOUP WITH A
POACHED EGG, *page 87*

FACING PAGE

THREE PURÉED CURRIED SOUPS,
CLOCKWISE FROM LEFT: TOMATO, *page 72;*
ONION, *page 77;* CARROT, *page 82*

ABOVE

VEGETABLE CURRY SOUP, *page 116*

CIOPPINO, *page 266*

seafood chowder

NOT ALL BRINY CHOWDERS are clam. Some of my favorites work on the same principal but have an assortment of sea denizens.

16 medium littleneck clams, well scrubbed; or ½ cup (90 g) chopped clam
    meat, from 4 quahogs or other clams, plus 2 cups (500 ml) clam juice

2 tablespoons (30 g) unsalted butter

1 tablespoon all-purpose flour

¼ teaspoon ground mace

⅛ teaspoon cayenne pepper

1 large yellow onion, finely chopped

1 cup (250 ml) skim milk

1½ pounds (675 g) firm potatoes, peeled and cut into ¼-inch (.5-cm) dice

½ pound (225 g) flounder fillets, cut into 1½-inch (4-cm) pieces

1 pound large shrimp, peeled and deveined

½ cup (125 ml) heavy cream

Kosher salt, to taste

Freshly ground black pepper, to taste

IF USING CLAMS IN THE SHELL, in a medium stockpot, bring 2 cups (500 ml) water to a boil. Add the clams, cover, and lower the heat slightly. Cook at a low boil until all the clams have opened, 5 to 7 minutes. Remove the clams. Strain the liquid through coffee filter and reserve. There should be about 2 cups (500 ml). Coarsely chop the clams.

In a medium saucepan, melt the butter. Stir in the flour, mace, and cayenne pepper. Cook over low heat for 2 minutes, stirring. Stir in the onion and cook, stirring and scraping the flour from the sides of the pan frequently, for 10 minutes, or until the onion is translucent.

Whisk 1 cup (250 ml) of the clam broth or juice into the pot until the mixture is smooth. Slowly whisk in the remaining clam broth or juice. Whisk in the skim milk and stir in the potatoes. There should be enough liquid to cover the potatoes; if there isn't, add additional water to barely cover. Bring to a boil, stirring frequently to ensure a smooth soup. Lower the heat and simmer for 10 to 12 minutes, or until the potatoes are almost done.

Stir in the flounder and shrimp. Return to a boil, lower the heat, and simmer for 2 minutes. Stir in the clams and cream. Heat through. Season if needed.

MAKES 8 CUPS (2 L); 8 FIRST-COURSE SERVINGS

Fish stock can be easily turned into fish soup with a handful of vegetables (see pages 448–451 for cooking times), some herbs and seasoning, and even another handful of thin egg noodles. Gelled Fish Soup (page 372) can easily be used as a hot fish soup. The liquid left from making Fish Soup Caribbean Style (page 262) makes a delicious opener soup.

Light fish soups are good starters before meat meals. More substantial ones can precede a salad or a pasta.

ceviche soup

I AM INCORRIGIBLE IN thinking constantly about soup. Thanks to my good friend and culinary buddy Irene Sax, I went to a very good Peruvian restaurant in Brooklyn, Coco Roco. There we had an extraordinarily good and unusual ceviche. It was rather soupy, and I immediately thought how foolish it was of me not to have imagined turning the many marvelous ceviches into soups. The next morning I did just that.

The soup is rather intense in flavor, especially if made with less water and served in the hollowed-out papaya shells. I think that most people will find that a half cup is enough for a first course. If the large amount of water is added, the soup must be chilled for at least four hours. It will thicken and give more servings.

I prefer this soup at a cool room temperature; but if serving it chilled—unless using the larger amount of water—which means that it will have been sitting at least an hour in the refrigerator, reduce the jalapeño slightly as the bite increases as the soup sits.

10 ounces (300 g) flounder fillets

3 medium ripe papayas (about 14 ounces [420 g] each)

Juice of 4 medium limes (½ cup)

2 teaspoons kosher salt

1½ teaspoons peeled grated ginger

1 small red onion, finely chopped

1 medium jalapeño pepper, seeded and finely chopped

½ medium bunch cilantro, leaves only, chopped medium-fine

LAY THE FISH OUT ON the counter. Separate the fillets along the natural division, removing the membrane along with any remaining bones. Cut the fillets lengthwise into strips 1 to 1¼ inches (2.5 to 3 cm) wide. Slice across into strips about ¼ inch (.5 cm) wide. Place the fish in a glass or ceramic bowl.

Cut the papayas in half lengthwise. Scrape out the seeds. Carefully scoop out the flesh, leaving the skins intact; there should be about 3 cups (450 g). In a food processor, purée all but ½ cup (120 g) of the papaya; there should be 1½ cups (375 ml) of purée. Cut the remaining papaya into ¼-inch (.5-cm) dice and refrigerate.

Stir the lime juice, salt, and ginger into the fish; let sit for 5 minutes. Stir in the onion and let sit for 10 minutes. Stir in the papaya purée, jalapeño, and cilantro. Let the mixture sit for 7 minutes. Stir in ¼ to 2 cups (65 to 500 ml) water.

Serve at room temperature or chilled (if serving chilled, leave in the refrigerator for at least 1 hour but not more than 8 hours) in the scooped-out papaya skins and sprinkled with a few teaspoons of diced papaya.

MAKES 4 TO 6 CUPS (1 TO 1.5 L); 4 TO 8 FIRST-COURSE SERVINGS

fish soup

THIS IS A SOUP that can go two ways. It can be a clear soup, in which case the lemon juice may be omitted, as it can cloud the broth. Or it can be a fish and vegetable soup. In either case, a cup of cooked instant couscous can be stirred in at the end.

> **8 cups (2 l) Basic Fish Stock (page 362)**
>
> **½ medium leek, trimmed, washed well, and cut across into 1-inch (2.5-cm) chunks *or* cut across into 1-inch (2.5-cm) lengths and then lengthwise into very thin strips**
>
> **1 medium carrot, peeled and cut into chunks *or* cut across into 1-inch (2.5-cm) lengths and then lengthwise into very thin strips**
>
> **1 rib celery, peeled and cut across into 1-inch (2.5-cm) chunks *or* cut across into 1-inch (2.5-cm) lengths and then lengthwise into very thin strips**
>
> **6 sprigs parsley, left whole *or* coarsely chopped**
>
> **1 bay leaf**
>
> **Pinch of fresh thyme leaves**
>
> **1 medium clove garlic, smashed and peeled *or* smashed, peeled, and chopped**
>
> **½ cinnamon stick**
>
> **½ teaspoon cumin seed**
>
> **1 whole clove**
>
> **Pinch of anise seed**
>
> **½ teaspoon lightly crushed peppercorns *or* freshly ground black pepper, to taste**
>
> **Kosher salt, to taste**
>
> **Hot red pepper sauce**
>
> **Fresh lemon juice, to taste, optional**

FOR A CLEAR SOUP, bring the stock, the chunks of leek, carrot, and celery, the parsley sprigs, bay leaf, thyme, the whole garlic clove, the cinnamon stick, cumin seed, clove, anise seed, and crushed peppercorns to a boil. Lower the heat and simmer, uncovered, until reduced by half. Strain through a damp-cloth–lined sieve. Season as desired.

To make a soup with vegetables, in a tall narrow stockpot, bring the stock to a boil. Wrap the bay leaf, thyme, cinnamon stick, cumin seed, clove, and anise seed in cheesecloth and tie with kitchen string. Add this to the stock. Simmer, uncovered, for 15 minutes.

Add the thinly sliced leek, carrot, and celery and the chopped garlic. Simmer for 10 minutes. Remove the cheesecloth bag. Stir in the parsley. Season as desired.

MAKES 4 CUPS (1 L) AS A CLEAR SOUP, 6 CUPS (1.5 L)
WITH THE VEGETABLES; 4 FIRST-COURSE SERVINGS

salmon

ALTHOUGH NOT A SOUP in the usual sense of the word, this delicious combination of spring flavors has too much sauce to be served any other way than in a bowl with a spoon. It is a good first course for a festive dinner, or a light main course at lunch.

The recipe can be easily doubled if there is extra salmon stock on hand. A stock is made in the first step of this recipe, but if Salmon Stock (page 364) is on hand, use that instead. Be sure to cut the sorrel across the leaves, not along the grain, so that the rib is cut into small pieces. Avoid reactive pots, such as aluminum, like the plague.

One 18-ounce (510-g) salmon head, cut into 4 or 5 pieces

1 small onion, cut into quarters

2 medium cloves garlic, smashed and peeled

**One 1-pound (450-g) piece salmon fillet (about 1 inch [2.5 cm] thick),
 any pin bones removed with a pair of pliers**

1½ ounces (45 g) sorrel, stemmed and cut across into narrow strips (¾ cup)

1 teaspoon kosher salt

Freshly ground black pepper, to taste

½ cup (125 ml) heavy cream

PLACE THE FISH HEAD and 6 cups (1.5 l) water in a medium saucepan. Bring to a boil. Lower the heat and simmer for 1 hour.

Add the onion and garlic and simmer for 50 minutes, or until the fish head is falling apart.

Place the salmon fillet, flesh side down, in the stock. Gently press the fillet down into the pot so the fish is almost covered with liquid. Cover and simmer for 8 to 10 minutes, or until the fish is medium-rare. Cook longer for well-done. Using a flat spatula so as to keep the fish whole, remove it to a plate. Allow to cool for a few minutes and remove the skin. Cut the fish across into 4 pieces.

Strain the stock through a fine-mesh sieve; there should be 2 cups (500 ml). Return the stock to the pan, along with the sorrel and salt. Bring to a boil. Lower the heat and simmer for 5 minutes. Stir in the pepper and cream. Simmer for 2 minutes.

Place a piece of fish in the bottom of each bowl and pour about ½ cup (125 ml) sauce over each piece.

MAKES ABOUT 2 CUPS (500 ML) SAUCE, PLUS FISH; 4 FIRST-COURSE SERVINGS

ciarla's fish soup

ALBERTO CIARLA IS THE CHEF-PROPRIETOR of an extraordinary fish restaurant in Rome's Trastevere. He has done lots of research on old Roman recipes and is a connoisseur of Italian wine. While there is a jazzy dining room, I much prefer one of the tiny tables set behind some shrubs on the street.

At Ciarla's, the soup is much richer and more elegant, containing as it does a rock lobster; but this is still good eating. It is so good that I recommend an ample serving as a first course before a light meal. At Ciarla's, that would be a simply prepared fish.

¼ pound (120 g) slab bacon, cut into ¼ × ¼ × ½-inch (.5 × .5 × 1-cm) lardons

1 tablespoon olive oil

1 tablespoon medium-hot paprika; or 1 tablespoon sweet paprika plus
⅛ teaspoon cayenne pepper

1 medium onion, coarsely chopped

3 cloves garlic, smashed and peeled

½ cup (125 ml) dry white wine

2 cups (500 ml) Basic Fish Stock (page 362)

3 dry lasagna noodles, broken across into 1-inch (2.5-cm) pieces

8 littleneck clams, well scrubbed

½ cup (125 ml) Tomato Purée (page 384), canned tomato purée,
or sterile-pack strained tomatoes

4 mussels, scrubbed and debearded

1 cup (225 g) cooked pink or white beans (see page 293)
or drained and rinsed canned beans

½ pound (225 g) cleaned squid, bodies sliced across into ¼-inch (.5-cm)
rings and tentacles quartered; or ½ pound (225 g) bay scallops

Pinch of dried sage

Pinch of dried thyme

1 teaspoon kosher salt

Pinch of freshly ground black pepper

IN A MEDIUM SAUCEPAN, cook the bacon over medium heat, stirring occasionally, for 20 minutes, or until crisp. With a slotted spoon, remove the bacon from the pan and drain on paper towels.

Pour off all but 1 tablespoon bacon fat from the pan and lower the heat to medium-low. Add the oil and paprika, or paprika and cayenne, and cook, stirring, for 1 minute. Stir in the onion and garlic. Cook, stirring, for 10 minutes.

Pour in the wine and bring to a boil. Boil for 1 minute. Pour in the stock and return to a boil. Stir in the noodles and simmer for 6 minutes. Add the clams, cover, and simmer for 3 to 4 minutes, until they are just beginning to open. Stir in the tomato purée and mussels. Cover and simmer for 2 minutes. Stir in the beans, squid or scallops, sage, and thyme. Simmer for 2 minutes, or until the squid or scallops are opaque and the beans are hot. Season with the salt and pepper to taste.

Divide the solids evenly among four bowls, pour the broth over and sprinkle each serving with about 1 tablespoon crisp bacon.

MAKES 6 CUPS (1.5 L); 4 FIRST-COURSE SERVINGS

freshwater fish
AND SUMMER VEGETABLE SOUP

THE WHOLE WORLD does not have a seacoast. Inland countries make their fish soups with freshwater fish or fish that swim up streams to spawn. Many of these soups are excellent although, oddly enough, many freshwater fish are bony and need to be thoroughly filleted before cooking (except for eel—pages 286–289—which cannot be). Originally, I made this with carp, which does have a voluptuous feel in the mouth, but I hesitate to recommend it as it has a plethora of tiny bones. There are many other good freshwater fish that are easier to use.

6 cups (1.5 l) Basic Fish Stock (page 362)

1 small beet, scrubbed and cut into matchstick strips

2 small carrots, peeled and cut into matchstick strips

1 medium zucchini, trimmed, halved lengthwise, seeds scooped
    out with a spoon, and cut into matchstick strips

1 medium yellow summer squash, trimmed, halved lengthwise,
    seeds scooped out with a spoon, and cut into matchstick strips

1 pound (450 g) peas in the pod, shelled (1 scant cup), or half
    of a 10-ounce (300-g) package frozen peas, defrosted in a
    sieve under warm running water and drained (⅔ cup)

1½ pounds (675 g) freshwater fish fillets, such as carp,
    perch, pike, or trout, all bones carefully removed
    and cut into 1-inch (2.5-cm) squares

1 medium bunch dill, fronds only, coarsely chopped

1 tablespoon kosher salt

Freshly ground black pepper, to taste

1 cup (225 g) sour cream, for serving

IN A MEDIUM SAUCEPAN, bring the stock to a boil. Stir in the beet and carrots. Return to a boil. Lower the heat and simmer for 5 minutes. Stir in the zucchini and squash and simmer for 10 minutes. Stir in the peas and simmer for 3 minutes. Add the fish and simmer for 2 minutes. Stir in the dill, salt, and pepper.

Pass the sour cream at the table.

MAKES 7 CUPS (1.75 L); 6 FIRST-COURSE SERVINGS OR 4 MAIN-COURSE SERVINGS

fall fish stew

THIS PRETTY SOUP—with the green of the lima beans, the deep orange-gold of the sweet potatoes, and the lighter, brighter gold of the rouille—is quickly made if fish stock is on hand. The rouille lets me slide smoothly into the next topic, Mediterranean fish soups (page 258).

1 tablespoon plus 1 teaspoon kosher salt

2 small sweet potatoes, peeled and thinly sliced

One 10-ounce (300-g) package frozen baby lima beans, defrosted in a sieve under warm running water and drained, or 3 pounds (1.35 kg) fresh fava beans, shelled, blanched for 2 minutes, run under cold water, and popped out of tough outer skins

2 cups (500 ml) Basic Fish Stock (page 362)

1 pound (450 g) cod fillets, cut into 1½-inch (4-cm) pieces

⅔ cup (160 ml) Rouille (page 433)

Freshly ground black pepper, to taste

Lemon juice, to taste

PLACE 3 QUARTS (1 l) water, 1 tablespoon salt, and the potatoes in a medium saucepan. Bring to a boil. Lower the heat and simmer until the potatoes are tender but not fully cooked, about 10 minutes. Drain.

In a medium saucepan, bring the potatoes, beans, and stock to a boil. Lower the heat to a simmer. Add the fish and simmer for 2 minutes.

In a small bowl, whisk 1 cup (250 ml) of the broth into the rouille. Stir the rouille mixture into the soup. Reduce the heat to low and cook, stirring carefully so as not to break up fish too much, for 2 minutes, or until the fish is cooked through and the soup is thickened. Season with the 1 teaspoon salt, pepper, and lemon juice.

MAKES 6 CUPS (1.5 L); 6 FIRST-COURSE SERVINGS

Mediterranean fish soups

THE LONG OVAL OF SHORE that surrounds the Mediterranean and its offshoots, the Aegean and Adriatic, seems to have as many fish and seafood soups as peoples. Naturally, these peoples have depended on the sea for their livelihood. The fishermen would make their soups from the cheap fish that were hard to sell and ingredients such as wine that they could carry with them. Over the years, these soups have developed, many of them into full-blown feasts.

Probably the earliest version of a Mediterranean fish soup was similar to that version of *kakavia*, the prototypic Greek fish soup, described by Diane Kochilas in her book *The Food and Wine of Greece*. It is little more than fish and seafood with seawater, olive oil, and lemon juice. Today's kakavia is much like the other seafood soups of the region.

Characteristic of these soups is an ample use of garlic, whether directly in the cooked part of the soup or as a major ingredient of accompanying sauces, such as aïoli (ali-oli in Catalan). Olive oil is basic. Tomatoes are very frequent, as are peppers and one variety or another of anise flavoring (page 247).

I have a bad habit of thinking of these as Provençal soups since I have spent so much time in the South of France; but right down the coast, the Genovese have their own traditional versions, including *ciuppin*. Fred Plotkin, in his brilliant *Recipes from Paradise,* contends that the recipe traveled along with pesto and many others from Italy to France. I tend to think that the region provided its own impetus from ingredients and that there was a prior influence from the Greek colonization of much of Provence. Many of these soups start with a refrito or soffrito, chopped vegetables cooked in olive oil.

As with many other soups, there has been a tendency to use increasingly expensive fish and seafood and to make the base more and more refined; but these did start as soups using leftovers and what is often thrown out in the United States as trash fish. The soups may have chunks of fish or whole fish in them or may be puréed. They can be first courses or main courses.

These soups often are served with stale bread or croutons in them, sauces such as aïoli or rouille on the side, and grated cheese, boiled potatoes, or noodles. Whole peeled cloves of garlic are sometimes passed to rub on the croutons before they go into the soup.

fish soup provençal

WITH PASTA

THIS IS A SIMPLE FIRST-COURSE puréed soup with noodles. I make the recipe with red snapper, but a less-expensive fish can be substituted. Or, use 8 cups (2 l) of fish stock and a 1-pound (450-g) piece of fillet.

One 2-pound (900-g) red snapper

¼ cup (65 ml) olive oil

1 large onion, finely chopped

6 medium tomatoes, peeled and cut into ¼-inch (.5-cm) dice

2 ounces (60 g) vermicelli (fine noodles), broken into 2-inch (5-cm) lengths

1 vial (.25 g) saffron threads

1½ tablespoons kosher salt

Freshly ground black pepper, to taste

2 ounces (60 g) Swiss cheese, grated, for serving

CLEAN AND WASH THE FISH. Remove the head and tail and place them in a tall narrow stockpot with 8 cups (2 l) water. Bring to a boil. Lower the heat and simmer for 15 minutes. Add the body of the fish. Return to a boil. Lower the heat and simmer for 20 minutes.

With a slotted spoon, remove the fish to a platter. Allow the broth to cool slightly. Strain through a fine-mesh sieve. Discard the head and tail.

Scrape the skin off the fish. Remove the upper fillet, going down the center and pushing in either direction. Lift out the backbone and free the second fillet. In a food processor, purée the fish.

In a medium stockpot, heat the oil over medium heat. Stir in the onion and cook, stirring occasionally, until soft but not brown, about 7 minutes. Stir in the tomatoes and cook for 5 minutes. Stir in the broth. Bring to a boil. Stir in the vermicelli and saffron. Boil for 6 to 10 minutes or until the vermicelli is done.

Stir in the fish purée, breaking it up with a wooden spoon to distribute it evenly in the broth. Season with the salt and pepper.

Pass the cheese at the table.

MAKES ABOUT 12 CUPS (3 L); 8 TO 10 FIRST-COURSE SERVINGS

bourride

OF MONKFISH

THE NITTY-GRITTY of the argument between the proponents of Liguria (Fred Plotkin and Colman Andrews) and the Francophiles such as myself could be said to crystallize around bourride and buridda. They are totally different animals. Bourride is a magnificent invention, a fish soup that may be made with one or more kinds of fish and that is thickened and flavored with an aïoli that miraculously doesn't separate as it cooks, and lends a creamy, garlicky texture. Buridda, on the other hand, is a slow-cooking fish and seafood (no shellfish, but shrimp, cuttlefish, and octopus) stew like a thicker version of a bouillabaisse.

A monkfish bourride is traditional. I particularly like it because the fish doesn't tend to overcook. Other fish may be substituted, but should not be cooked as long.

5 cups (1.25 l) Basic Fish Stock (page 362)

2 medium onions, halved

6 sprigs thyme, tied together with kitchen twine

6 strips orange zest (about 2 × ½ inch; 5 × 1 cm)

2 bay leaves

1 medium bulb fennel, trimmed, quartered, cored, and cut lengthwise into thin strips

3 pounds (1.4 kg) monkfish fillets, cut into 2½ inch (6-cm) chunks

6 egg yolks

1 cup (240 ml) Aïoli (page 432)

Kosher salt, to taste

for serving

Croutons (page 429)

Aïoli (page 432)

IN A MEDIUM SAUCEPAN, combine the stock, onions, thyme, orange zest, and bay leaves. Bring to a boil. Lower the heat and simmer, covered, for 10 minutes. Stir in the fennel and simmer for 10 more minutes, or until the vegetables are very soft. Stir in the fish. Return to a boil. Lower the heat and simmer for 15 minutes, or until the fish is cooked through.

With a slotted spoon, remove the solids, and reserve the broth in the saucepan. Discard the onions and thyme, reserving the fish, fennel, and orange zest.

In a small bowl, whisk together the egg yolks and 1 cup aïoli. Gradually whisk in 2 cups (500 ml) of the reserved broth. Whisk the mixture back into the remaining broth. Cook over medium-low heat, whisking constantly, at just below a simmer, until the soup thickens.

The soup can be made ahead to this point and the solids and soup reserved separately. If necessary, gently reheat the soup. Gently stir in the reserved solids and heat through. Season with salt.

Serve the croutons and the additional aïoli on the side.

MAKES 11 CUPS (2.75 L); 10 FIRST-COURSE SERVINGS OR 4 MAIN-COURSE SERVINGS

fish soup

CARIBBEAN STYLE

THE FRENCH ISLANDS of the Caribbean, not oddly, have fish soups strongly influenced by French fish soups. People who live there have combined these influences with local ingredients to make a filling soup that is part purée and part cooked fish.

The kind of hot pepper used should suit the tastes of the eaters—any kind from a jalapeño to a Scotch bonnet. The liquid left from cooking the fish will be about 2½ cups (625 ml). It is not added to the soup, but it is delicious in its own right. It can be saved and eaten the next day.

bain antillais

> **Juice of 2 lemons**
>
> **½ cup (125 ml) dry white wine**
>
> **½ teaspoon kosher salt**
>
> **½ fresh hot pepper, seeded, deveined, and very finely chopped**
>
> **2 cloves garlic, smashed, peeled, and very finely chopped**

for the soup

> **1½ pounds (675 g) small whole fish—red snapper, butterfish, etc.—cut into 3-inch (7.5-cm) chunks, with heads and tails**
>
> **2 pounds (900 g) small white fish fillets, skinned and cut into 2-inch (5-cm) chunks (if possible, get all the bones, heads, and tails)**
>
> **2 tablespoons olive oil**
>
> **1 large carrot, peeled and cut into ½-inch (1-cm) dice**
>
> **4 medium leeks, trimmed, well washed, and cut across into ½-inch (1-cm) lengths**
>
> **One 1-pound (450-g) chunk of calabaza or butternut squash, peeled, seeded, and cut into 1-inch (2.5-cm) cubes**
>
> **¼ pound (120 g) white yam or mashing potato, peeled and cut into ½-inch (1-cm) dice**
>
> **1 medium turnip, peeled and cut into ½-inch (1-cm) dice**
>
> **1 large tomato, cut into 1-inch (2.5-cm) cubes**
>
> **8 medium scallions, trimmed and thinly sliced across**
>
> **¼ teaspoon crumbled dried thyme**
>
> **2 cloves garlic, smashed and peeled**
>
> **1 bay leaf**

2 small jalapeño peppers, seeded, deveined, and very finely chopped

¼ cup (60 ml) Chunky Tomato Base (page 385), lightly crushed canned tomatoes (not plum) with their juice, or sterile-pack chopped tomatoes

½ cup (125 ml) dry white wine

1 tablespoon kosher salt

Freshly ground black pepper, to taste

¼ teaspoon hot red pepper sauce

FOR THE BAIN ANTILLAIS, combine all the ingredients in a glass bowl.

Wash the whole fish well to remove any traces of blood. Place the fish and fillets in the bain Antillais and allow to marinate for 1 to 2 hours.

Heat the oil in a medium stockpot over medium-to-high heat. Add the whole fish and all the bones, heads, and tails (leave the fillets in the marinade until the end of the recipe), and cook, stirring, for 2 minutes. Stir in the carrot, leeks, calabaza (or butternut), yam (or potato), turnip, and tomato. Stir to coat with oil. Stir in 2 cups (500 ml) water, the scallions, thyme, garlic, bay leaf, and jalapeño peppers. Bring to a boil. Lower the heat and simmer for 45 minutes, or until the fish is falling off the bones and the vegetables are very soft.

Strain through a fine-mesh sieve, reserving the solids. Remove the heads and large bones. Pass the vegetables and fish through a food mill fitted with the fine disc, or purée in a food processor. There should be about 3 cups (750 ml) liquid and 3 cups (750 ml) purée. Stir 1 cup (250 ml) of the liquid into the purée. Stir in the tomatoes and the white wine. Season with the salt, pepper, and hot red pepper sauce.

Pour the remaining liquid into a small saucepan. Bring quickly to a boil. Remove from the heat and add the reserved fish fillets. Cover and allow to steep for 5 minutes.

Meanwhile, heat the purée and ladle into bowls. Remove the now-cooked fish from the liquid with a slotted spoon and add to the soup. Serve immediately.

MAKES 7 CUPS (1.75 L); 6 FIRST-COURSE SERVINGS

brandade soup

BRANDADE IS A DELICIOUS spread made with salt cod, normally served with fried croutons or poached eggs. From an ample supply of leftovers resulting from a large party, I made a soup. It was good enough that I made a recipe so it could be made on purpose. It can be made with stockfish, but I find the taste stronger and less pleasant.

This soup is quite rich. It is nice served with garlic-rubbed croutons floating on top.

> 1 pound (450 g) mashing potatoes, peeled and
> quartered lengthwise
>
> 1 pound (450 g) salt cod, desalinated (see Note)
> and cut into 1-inch (2.5-cm) chunks
>
> 2 medium cloves garlic, smashed and peeled
>
> 6 tablespoons (90 ml) heavy cream
>
> 6 tablespoons (90 ml) olive oil
>
> Freshly ground black pepper, to taste
>
> Croutons (page 429), rubbed with a garlic clove,
> for serving, optional

IN A SMALL SAUCEPAN, cover the potatoes with water. Bring to a boil. Lower the heat and simmer for 20 minutes, or until the potatoes are tender. Drain and peel the potatoes. Pass through the medium disc of a food mill while they are still warm.

In a food processor, finely chop the cod and garlic. Add the potatoes and 2 tablespoons cream. Pulse to combine. With the machine running, slowly pour in the remaining heavy cream and the olive oil. Scrape down the sides of the bowl and process until smooth.

Scrape the mixture into a medium saucepan and stir in 3 cups (750 ml) water. Slowly, stirring frequently, heat the soup to just below simmering. Season with pepper. Pass the croutons.

Note: To desalinate salt cod, choose one of the methods below.

Conventional: Rinse salt cod under cold running water for 2 minutes. Place in a large bowl and cover with cold water. Cover and refrigerate for 24 hours, changing the water at least three times.

Microwave: Rinse salt cod under cold running water for 2 minutes. Place in a 14 × 9 × 2-inch (35 × 22.5 × 5-cm) oval dish with 6 cups (1.5 l) cold water. Cover tightly with microwave plastic wrap. Cook at 100% power in a high-wattage oven for 6 minutes. Prick the plastic to release the steam. Remove from the oven and uncover. Drain and rinse with cold water. Repeat the process two more times.

MAKES 6 CUPS (1.5 L); 6 FIRST-COURSE SERVINGS

Hearty meals

Here is a selection of substantial recipes for fish and seafood soups, Mediterranean and other, that require only wine, bread, and salad to be a meal.

family fish soup
WITH ORZO—A MEAL

A QUICKLY MADE MEAL that can be served with Croutons (page 429) and Rouille (page 433) or Aïoli (page 432) if desired. The orzo adds a Greek touch.

¼ cup (65 ml) olive oil

6 to 7 large cloves garlic, smashed, peeled, and coarsely chopped

½ cup (125 ml) dry white wine

1 teaspoon anise seed; 2 teaspoons if using chicken stock

5 teaspoons kosher salt, or less if using commercial broth

4 cups (1 l) Chunky Tomato Base (page 385), lightly crushed canned tomatoes (not plum) with their juice, or sterile-pack chopped tomatoes

4½ cups (1.25 l) Roasted Fish Stock (page 363), Basic Fish Stock (page 362), Basic Chicken Stock (page 345), or commercial chicken broth

½ cup (90 g) orzo (riso)

Freshly ground black pepper, to taste

2 cups (360 g) bite-sized pieces leftover cooked fish or 1½ pounds (675 g) fresh white fish fillets, cut into large chunks

¾ pound (360 g) very small firm potatoes, boiled (see page 93), cooled, and cut across into ¼-inch (.5-cm) slices

IN A TALL NARROW STOCKPOT, heat the oil over medium heat. Stir in the garlic and cook for 5 minutes. Pour in the wine. Bring to a boil. Stir in the anise seed, 1 tablespoon salt, the tomatoes, and stock. Bring to a boil. Boil for 5 minutes. The soup can be made ahead to this point and refrigerated for up to 3 days.

If the soup has been refrigerated, return it to a boil. Stir in the orzo. Lower the heat and simmer for 8 minutes. Season with pepper. Stir in the fish and potatoes and heat through, only about 2 minutes (even if using the fresh fish). Add the remaining salt. Serve immediately.

MAKES 12 CUPS (3 L); 8 FIRST-COURSE SERVINGS OR 4 AMPLE MEALS

cioppino

WHILE IT IS USUALLY CLAIMED that this is a San Francisco invention, it would seem obvious that it is the happy adaptation by a displaced Genovese of a native ciuppin to American ingredients.

2½ pounds (1.14 kg) swordfish, skinned and skin reserved,
    meat cut into 1-inch (2.5-cm) chunks

1 pound (450 g) medium shrimp, peeled and deveined,
    shells reserved

½ cup (125 ml) olive oil

1 large onion, cut into ¼-inch (.5-cm) dice

4 medium cloves garlic, smashed, peeled, and coarsely chopped

1 medium green bell pepper, cored, seeded, deribbed,
    and coarsely chopped

½ pound (225 g) white mushrooms, stemmed, wiped clean,
    and coarsely chopped

1 medium bunch parsley, leaves only, coarsely chopped

⅓ cup (85 ml) tomato paste

6 medium tomatoes, cored and cut into ½-inch (1-cm) dice

3 cups (750 ml) dry red wine

24 littleneck clams, scrubbed well

½ teaspoon dried oregano

60 small mussels (about 2 pounds; 900 g), scrubbed and debearded

One 2-pound (900-g) lobster, cut through the shell into pieces about
    3 inches (7.5 cm) long; if possible, have the fishmonger
    do this (see Notes)

3 tablespoons kosher salt, or to taste

Freshly ground black pepper, to taste

IN A SMALL SAUCEPAN, cover the swordfish skin and shrimp shells with water. Bring to a boil. Lower the heat and simmer while the seafood is cooking, to make a broth. When the seafood is done, strain the liquid and reserve 1 cup (250 ml).

In the largest wide pot available, place the oil, onion, garlic, green pepper, mushrooms, and half the parsley. Toss the vegetables to coat with oil. Cook over medium heat, stirring occasionally, for 10 minutes, or until the vegetables are limp. Raise the heat slightly, stir in the tomato paste, and cook for 1 minute. Stir in the tomatoes and cook, covered, until the tomatoes collapse, about 10 minutes.

Stir in 2 cups (500 ml) red wine. Bring to a boil. Add the clams and oregano and cook, covered, until the clams begin to open, about 5 minutes. Add the swordfish, shrimp, mussels, and lobster. Cook, covered, for 5 more minutes, or until all the seafood is just cooked through.

Skim out the solids and reserve. Stir in the remaining red wine, the 1 cup (250 ml) of shrimp shell/swordfish skin broth, the salt and pepper.

Stir in the remaining parsley and heat through. Divide the seafood evenly among the bowls and top with the broth.

MAKES 8 MAIN-COURSE SERVINGS

Notes: If the guests do not like shells, the seafood can be steamed separately in a small amount of water or stock and shelled; strain the liquid and add to the broth.

On the West Coast, a king crab can be used instead of the lobster; on the East Coast, 3 Maryland blue crabs can be substituted.

bouillabaisse

BOUILLABAISSE IS PRACTICALLY a religion from Marseilles all along the French coast of the Mediterranean to the Italian border. This is a version that is makeable away from those hallowed precincts. The bony and ugly fish such as chapon and rascasse that provide the binding gelatin are usually unavailable in the United States. To replace them, I suggest using a good fish stock. It is the vigorous boiling of the stock with the acid of the wine and the tomatoes that binds in the oil. Use a good one. Good tomatoes are also essential. (No fisherman ever peeled a tomato, but I do.) If they are unavailable—this should be a summer dish—use the base that has providently been made ahead.

Moreover, most of my guests are uncomfortable with bones in their soup, so I substitute fillets for whole fish. Bouillabaisse is not a seafood dish; it is all fish. However, I give a variation for adding seafood for those who like it.

The perfume and color of saffron are essential. I use twice as much when I am feeling lavish.

I love the potatoes boiled in the soup that are often served alongside the bouillabaisse. Choose. In addition to the platter of fish and the soup, it is also customary to serve oil-baked croutons to be rubbed with peeled cloves of garlic, along with the rouille. Grated Gruyère can be passed. This is a mix-and-match event. Usually the festivities start with a bowl of soup floating croutons with rouille spread on top. Then the mixing and matching begins. For a massive event, double the recipe. I have even committed the heresy of steaming lobsters to replace the traditional langoustes, halving them, and serving them on an extra platter.

½ cup (125 ml) olive oil

1 tablespoon chili powder containing cumin; or 2 teaspoons pure
    chili powder plus 1 teaspoon ground cumin

A pinch of cayenne pepper

2 medium onions, finely chopped

½ bunch flat-leaf parsley, leaves only, coarsely chopped

1 pound (450 g) cod fillets, pin bones removed and cut into 2 × 4-inch
    (5 × 10-cm) pieces

1 pound (450 g) mackerel, hake, or whiting fillets, or a mixture,
    pin bones removed and cut into 2 × 4-inch (5 × 10-cm) pieces

1½ vials (.25 g) saffron threads

½ cup (125 ml) dry white wine

6 tablespoons (100 ml) dry anise-flavored liquor (not liqueur; page 247)

4 large tomatoes, peeled and coarsely chopped, or 4 cups (1 l) Chunky Tomato Base (page 385) or sterile-pack chopped tomatoes; or 5 tomatoes or 5 cups (1.25 l) Chunky Tomato Base if using potatoes

4 cups (1 l) Basic Fish Stock (page 362); or 5 cups (1.25 l) if using potatoes

4 large cloves garlic, smashed, peeled, and coarsely chopped

1 tablespoon kosher salt, or to taste

2 tablespoons finely chopped fennel greens, if available

2 pounds (900 g) red snapper or striped bass fillets, pin bones removed and cut into large pieces

15 medium hard-shelled clams, scrubbed, optional

15 mussels, scrubbed and debearded, optional

15 medium shrimp, peeled and deveined, optional

3 medium firm potatoes, peeled and cut across into ⅛-inch (30-mm) slices, optional

for serving

Rouille (page 433)

Croutons (page 429)

A clove of peeled garlic per guest

IN A LARGE BRAISING POT, heat ¼ cup (65 ml) olive oil over medium heat. Stir in the chili powder and cayenne pepper. Cook, stirring, for 1 minute. Lower the heat and stir in the onions. Cook, stirring, until the onions are soft but not brown, about 10 minutes. Stir in the parsley, cod, and the 1 pound (450 g) assorted fish.

Meanwhile, dissolve the saffron in the wine.

In a small saucepan, heat the anise-flavored liquor over low heat. Carefully set a match to it to ignite. Pour the flaming liquid over the fish. Add the tomatoes, fish stock, the saffron and wine, the garlic, salt, fennel greens, and the remaining olive oil.

If using the shellfish, remove 1 cup (250 ml) of the liquid to a medium saucepan. If using the potatoes, remove 3 cups (750 ml) of the liquid to another medium saucepan.

Cover the braising pot, and bring to a boil. (In the meantime, cook the shellfish and potatoes, if using, as below.) Boil for 7 minutes. Add the red snapper or striped bass in one layer, cover, and continue to boil for 1 minute. With a slotted spoon, remove the red snapper or bass to a large platter and keep warm. Most of the cod and other fish will have disintegrated to thicken the broth.

Meanwhile, if using the shellfish, add the clams to the medium saucepan containing 1 cup (250 ml) of liquid. Cover and bring to a boil. Boil for 3 minutes. Add the mussels and the shrimp. Cover the pot again and cook until the mussels open and the shrimp are just opaque. With a slotted spoon, remove the shellfish to the platter of fish and keep warm. Add the liquid in the pan to the braising pot.

If using the potatoes, stir them into the pan containing 3 cups (750 ml) of liquid and add enough water to cover them. Bring to a boil. Lower the heat and simmer for about 10 minutes, or until the potatoes are tender. With a slotted spoon, remove the potatoes to a bowl and keep warm. Add the liquid remaining in the pan to the braising pot.

Bring the combined liquids to a boil. Continue to boil until amalgamated.

If desired, stir 3 tablespoons of the soup into the rouille.

Spread 2 croutons per person with a little rouille. Place 2 croutons in the bottom of each huge soup bowl. Strain the broth and spoon over the bread. Serve the fish and shellfish, bowls of rouille, garlic, the potatoes, if using, and additional croutons on the side.

MAKES 8 MAIN-COURSE SERVINGS WITHOUT SHELLFISH, 10 TO 12 WITH SHELLFISH

no-tomato fish soup

IT SEEMS HARD TO BELIEVE, but one fall day I had eaten enough tomatoes and even enough tomato-accented fish soup. However, when I went to the market—in landlocked Vermont—there was a rare offering of various fish that the manager had gone down early in the morning to Boston Harbor to get. I felt it would be scouting fortune to ignore the offerings. I concocted this tomato-free soup that all the eaters seemed to like. I used steamers, and their juice needs to be filtered and the black covering of the spout removed.

1¾ pounds (780 g) steamers or small clams, such as cherrystones, scrubbed

¾ cup (160 g) orzo (riso)

½ cup (125 ml) olive oil

1½ pounds (675 g) monkfish fillets, cut into 2-inch (5-cm) chunks

1½ cups (375 ml) dry white wine (not too acidic)

2 pounds (900 g) white fish fillets (striped bass, grouper, or red snapper), skin on, pin bones removed and cut into 4-inch (10-cm) squares

1½ pounds (675 g) sea scallops

2 teaspoons kosher salt, plus additional to taste

1 cup (45 g) loosely packed tarragon leaves

⅓ cup (7 g) minced chives

Freshly ground black pepper, to taste

2 pounds (900 g) small mussels, scrubbed and debearded

IN A LARGE WIDE POT, bring 3 cups (750 ml) water to a boil. Add the clams. Cover and cook for 5 to 10 minutes, until the clams open. Remove from the pot. Strain the broth through a damp-cloth–lined sieve or a coffee filter rinsed with hot water and reserve. Remove the clams from their shells, rinse the meat, and, if using steamers, pull off the black encircling tissue and spout covering.

Bring 4 cups (1 l) lightly salted water to a boil in a small saucepan. Add the orzo and cook until almost done, about 8 minutes. Drain and run under cold water to stop the cooking. Cover with a little cold water and reserve.

Heat the oil in the large pot. Add the monkfish and cook until opaque on all sides. Add the reserved clam broth and wine. Bring to a boil. Lower the heat and cook at low boil for 5 minutes. Raise the heat and add the bass or other fillets, skin side down. Cover and cook over medium heat for 5 minutes. Add the scallops and salt. Cover and cook for 2 minutes.

Add the herbs and season liberally with pepper. Cover and raise the heat. When the liquid begins to boil, add the mussels. Cook, covered, for 4 minutes, or until the mussels open. Remove the solids and divide evenly among serving bowls.

Drain the orzo and add it, along with the reserved clams, to the broth. Bring to a boil. Correct the seasoning with salt and pepper. Ladle into the bowls with the fish and shellfish.

MAKES 6 TO 8 GENEROUS MAIN-COURSE SERVINGS

kale and clam
STEW

AMERICA IS FULL OF PEOPLE who have come here to escape persecution or simply to make a living. The descendants of many Portuguese sailors and fishermen still live in Provincetown, Massachusetts, and make foods based on Portuguese originals. This hearty soup is a delicious example.

Fortunately, both kale and clams are at their best in cold weather, just when I am tempted to cook pork. I originally made this version after I had baked a ham. I generally start a ham by gently poaching it in water before glazing it in the oven; thus I had ham stock as well as leftover meat. This is a freestanding version using pork stock and bacon to add some of the ham's smokiness. A typical Portuguese addition would be the sausage.

For me this soup is a meal, and I would serve it to only four or six as a main course.

¾ **pound (360 g) kale, stemmed and leaves cut across into 1-inch (2.5-cm) strips**

5 **cups (1.25 l) Roasted Pork Stock (page 359)**

¼ **pound (120 g) bacon, cut into ¼-inch (.5-cm) dice**

2 **cloves garlic, smashed and peeled**

1 **pound (450 g) firm potatoes, peeled, halved lengthwise, and cut across into ¼-inch (.5-cm) slices**

18 **small clams, well scrubbed**

Freshly ground black pepper, to taste

18 **slices firm linguiça sausage, optional**

PLACE THE KALE, with the washing water that clings to it, in a tall narrow stockpot over low heat. Cook, stirring frequently, just until wilted. Stir in the stock, bacon, and garlic. Bring to a boil. Lower the heat and simmer until the kale is almost tender, about 20 minutes.

Stir in the potatoes and simmer until almost tender, about 20 minutes longer.

Add the clams, hinge side down. Cover, return to a boil, and cook until the clams open, 5 to 10 minutes. Unless the clams are very small, shuck them and return them to the soup; if not shucking, remove the clams from the pot.

Stir in the pepper and the linguiça, if using. Ladle the soup into serving bowls. Divide the clams, if they are unshucked, among the bowls.

MAKES 10 CUPS (2.5 L); 4 TO 6 MAIN-COURSE SERVINGS

mussels with sauerkraut
AND RIESLING

I WILL ADMIT that this was one of my stranger ideas—combining Alsatian wine and sauerkraut with seaside mussels—as if Alsace stretched to the ocean. I think it turned out very well.

1 medium onion, cut across into ¼-inch (.5-cm) slices

1 cup (250 ml) Riesling

1½ pounds (675 g) sauerkraut, rinsed

3 dozen small mussels (about 1½ pounds; 675 ml), well scrubbed and debearded

1 cup (250 ml) half-and-half

2 teaspoons caraway seed

Kosher salt, to taste

Freshly ground black pepper, to taste

IN A MEDIUM STOCKPOT, bring the onion and wine to a boil. Lower the heat and simmer for 5 minutes. Stir in the sauerkraut and mussels. Cover. Return to a boil. Lower the heat and simmer for 3 minutes. Stir in the half-and-half, 1 cup (250 ml) water, and the caraway seeds. Return to a simmer. Remove from the heat and season with salt and pepper.

Strain through a fine-mesh sieve. Divide the solids and liquid equally among four bowls.

MAKES 8 CUPS (2 L); 4 MAIN-COURSE SERVINGS

red vinegar seafood

THIS IS A SORT OF bastardized buridda with mussels and scallops added for non-Mediterranean cooks and replacing wine with vinegar. The fish are used to make a stock; they can be replaced by 2 cups (500 l) of Basic Fish Stock (page 362), with only a slight loss of texture.

⅓ cup (80 ml) olive oil

1 small onion, cut into ¼-inch (.5-cm) dice

1 medium carrot, peeled and cut into ¼-inch (.5-cm) dice

1 large rib celery, peeled and cut into ¼-inch (.5-cm) dice

4 medium cloves garlic, smashed, peeled, and very finely chopped

5 anchovy fillets, chopped

¼ cup (21 g) chopped basil

¼ cup (30 g) chopped parsley

¼ cup (7.5 g) dried porcini mushrooms (cèpes)

½ to ¾ cup (125 to 180 ml) red wine vinegar

2 pounds (900 g) assorted white fish, such as red snapper, cod, and/or bass, on or off the bone

1 or 2 cleaned squid, body and tentacles, cut into 1-inch (2.5-cm) pieces

6 clams, scrubbed

24 mussels, scrubbed and debearded

½ pound (225 g) scallops

½ pound (225 g) medium shrimp, peeled and deveined

Kosher salt, to taste

Freshly ground black pepper, to taste

Croutons (page 429) or thick slices of stale bread, for serving

IN A LARGE STOCKPOT, heat the oil over medium heat. Stir in the onion and cook, stirring frequently, until browned, about 10 minutes. Stir in the carrot, celery, garlic, anchovies, basil, and parsley. Reduce the heat and cook until the carrot and celery are just tender, about 10 minutes.

Meanwhile, soak the mushrooms in ½ cup (125 ml) hot water for 15 minutes. Drain. Strain the liquid and reserve.

Stir ½ cup (125 ml) red wine vinegar, the mushrooms and their soaking liquid, and 1½ cups (375 ml) water into the pot. Bring to a boil. Stir in the fish and squid. Cover the pot and cook for 5 minutes. Add the clams, cover, and cook for 5 minutes. Add the mussels, scallops, and shrimp. Cover the pot and shake to stir the mixture. Cook for another 3 to 5 minutes, or until the clams and mussels have opened and the shrimp and scallops are just cooked. Remove from the heat.

Transfer the shellfish to a bowl. Strain the liquid through a fine-mesh sieve, pressing on the solids to extract all the liquid. Discard all the fish and vegetables. Return the liquid to the pan and stir in vinegar, salt, and pepper to taste. Bring to a boil.

Return the shellfish to the soup and reheat carefully. Serve in soup plates over the croutons.

MAKES 6 MAIN-COURSE SERVINGS

shrimp gumbo

HERE IS A SHRIMP GUMBO that is relatively tame as to spice. There are more eccentric versions such as Duck Gumbo (page 158) and Tripe Gumbo (page 214), as well as the standard Chicken Gumbo (page 136). For those who want a jolt, simply double the pepper quantities.

I have had my method of adding the filé powder before the end of the cooking queried by those afraid of mucilaginous strands in the soup. I prefer to add it this way, whisking well, because the other method can leave a raw taste of filé. Equally important is just cutting off the caps of the okra pods without exposing the tubules inside, which also contain a gluey substance. Use the smallest pods available. Filé is sassafras; gumbo is okra.

2 pounds (900 g) medium shrimp, peeled and deveined, shells reserved

6 cups (1.5) Basic Chicken Stock (page 345), Shrimp Broth (page 365), or commercial chicken broth

4 tablespoons (60 g) butter

¼ cup (30 g) all-purpose flour

1 large yellow onion, cut across into ¼-inch (.5-cm) slices

3 medium ribs celery, trimmed, leaves reserved, peeled, and cut across into ¼-inch (.5-cm) slices

½ cup (15 g) coarsely chopped reserved celery leaves

10 medium cloves garlic, smashed and peeled

2 teaspoons dried thyme

½ teaspoon cayenne pepper

2 teaspoons filé powder

½ pound (225 g) fresh okra, caps trimmed, leaving pods intact

1 tablespoon kosher salt

2 tablespoons fresh lemon juice

Freshly ground black pepper, to taste

¼ teaspoon hot red pepper sauce

4 cups (600 g) cooked white rice (see page 294), optional

IN A MEDIUM SAUCEPAN, bring the shrimp shells and stock to a boil. Lower the heat and simmer, partially covered, for 30 minutes. Strain through a fine-mesh sieve.

To make the roux, in a medium saucepan, melt the butter over medium heat. Stir in the flour and cook, stirring constantly, until it becomes golden brown. Turn the heat to low and continue cooking, stirring constantly, until the mixture is a medium chocolate color; this will take about 20 to 25 minutes from when the flour was added.

Stir the onion, celery, celery leaves, garlic, thyme, and cayenne pepper into the roux. Cook, stirring, over medium heat for 8 minutes. Stir in the filé powder and okra. Slowly whisk in the shrimp stock. Scrape down the sides of the pot so the spices don't scorch. Bring to a boil, whisking frequently to ensure a smooth soup. Lower the heat and simmer for 6 minutes. The soup can be made ahead to this point and refrigerated for 1 day.

If the soup has been refrigerated, return to a boil. Lower the heat and simmer for 6 minutes. Stir in the shrimp. Return to a boil. The shrimp should be just cooked through at this point. If they are not quite done, lower the heat and simmer for 1 to 2 minutes. Remove from the heat and stir in the salt, lemon juice, pepper, and hot red pepper sauce. Serve over rice, if desired.

MAKES ABOUT 8 CUPS (2 L); 8 FIRST-COURSE SERVINGS OR
5 MAIN-COURSE SERVINGS WITH RICE

Note: To make brown roux in a microwave, melt the butter in a 1-quart (1-l) soufflé dish, uncovered, at 100% power for 3 minutes. Remove from the oven and whisk in the flour. Cook, uncovered, at 100% power for 8 minutes, stirring twice.

cod soup

WITH FRESH CRANBERRY BEANS

THIS IS ONE OF MY ODDITIES, an end-of-summer cod soup that is quickly made using either cranberry beans or cucumber. It does require fish stock. Run to the freezer.

5 cups (1.25 l) Basic Fish Stock (page 362)

1 cup (250 ml) dry white wine

1 pound (450 g) very small firm potatoes, cut in half

2 medium shallots, very finely chopped

1¾ pounds (790 g) fresh cranberry beans, shelled; or 1 medium hothouse cucumber, peeled and cut across into ½-inch (1-cm) slices

½ pound (225 g) peas in the pod, shelled (scant ½ cup)

Four 7-ounce (210-g) cod fillets, pin bones removed

1 small bunch dill, fronds only, finely chopped

Kosher salt, to taste

IN A MEDIUM SAUCEPAN, bring the stock and wine to a boil. Stir in the potatoes, shallots, and, if using, the beans. Return to a boil. Lower the heat and simmer for 8 minutes. If using the cucumber, stir it in now. Simmer for 5 minutes. Stir in the peas and simmer for 2 minutes.

Add the fish. Return to a boil. Lower the heat and simmer for 6 minutes, or until just cooked. Stir in the dill and season with salt.

MAKES 10 CUPS (2.5 L); 5 TO 6 MAIN-COURSE SERVINGS

portuguese cod soup

IT ALWAYS SEEMED STRANGE to me that coastal lands along the Atlantic, the Adriatic, and Mediterranean are rich in recipes for salt cod, a product imported from northern waters. I suspect it is in response to the danger inherent in fishing during inclement cold water that is responsible. Salt cod must be desalinated—have some of its salt leached out with water—before use.

This soup can be made substituting white beans for potatoes and kale for the spinach and coriander. Fresh mackerel may be used instead of salt cod, in which case, sauté the fish along with the potatoes.

¼ cup (65 ml) olive oil

1 pound (450 g) firm potatoes, peeled and thinly sliced

2 medium cloves garlic, smashed, peeled, and thinly sliced

1 bunch cilantro, leaves only

1 pound (450 g) spinach, stemmed, washed well, and cut across
   into 1-inch (2.5-cm) strips

1 pound (900 g) salt cod, desalinated (see Note on page 264) and
   cut into 2-inch (5-cm) squares

½ cup (125 ml) dry white wine

Kosher salt, to taste

Freshly ground black pepper, to taste

IN A MEDIUM SAUCEPAN, cook the oil and potatoes over medium heat, shaking occasionally, until the potatoes are imbued with the oil, about 1 minute. Stir in the garlic, cilantro, spinach, cod, wine, and 4 cups (1 l) water. Bring to a boil. Lower the heat, cover, and simmer, shaking the pan occasionally, for 20 minutes, or until the potatoes are thoroughly cooked.

Season with salt and pepper.

MAKES 8 CUPS (2 L); 4 MAIN-COURSE SERVINGS;
6 TO 8 FIRST-COURSE SERVINGS

green stew of fish

THE MOST FAMOUS fish soup-stew is bouillabaisse. It takes lots of ingredients and it's good. Other people as well as I have written many recipes for it; but there are recipes just as good that are simpler. This fresh-tasting, green soup is delicious.

3 tablespoons (45 g) unsalted butter

1 medium onion, thinly sliced

6 cups (1.5 l) Basic Fish Stock (page 362)

1 pound (450 g) firm potatoes, peeled and cut into ¾-inch (2-cm) cubes

1 medium head escarole [Batavia], trimmed, washed, and torn into 2-inch (5-cm) pieces

36 mussels, well scrubbed and debearded

1 large bunch spinach, stemmed, washed well, and leaves cut across into 1-inch (2.5-cm) strips

4 bunches flat-leaf parsley, leaves only, coarsely chopped

2 pounds (900 g) white fish fillets, cut into 2-inch (5-cm) chunks

Kosher salt, to taste

Freshly ground black pepper, to taste

2 tablespoons fresh lemon juice, or to taste

IN A LARGE STOCKPOT, melt the butter over medium-low heat. Stir in the onion and cook, stirring occasionally, for 10 minutes, or until limp and transparent.

Pour in the stock and bring to a boil. Stir in the potatoes and lower the heat. Simmer for 10 minutes.

Stir in the escarole and cook for 3 minutes. Add the mussels and cook for 2 minutes. Stir in the spinach, parsley, and fish and cook for 1 minute, or until the fish is opaque, the mussels have opened, and the potatoes are tender.

Season with salt, pepper, and the lemon juice and simmer for 1 minute to allow the flavors to meld.

MAKES 6 HEARTY MAIN-COURSE SERVINGS

chupa de pescado

THERE IS A STRONG Hispanic, Central and South American, tradition of seafood soups.

¼ cup (65 ml) olive oil

1 small onion, finely chopped

1 small rib celery, peeled and finely chopped

1 large clove garlic, smashed, peeled, and very thinly sliced

¼ teaspoon hot red pepper flakes

½ teaspoon ground cumin

½ medium red bell pepper, cored, seeded, deribbed, and diced

½ medium green bell pepper, cored, seeded, deribbed, and diced

6 cups (1.5 l) Basic Fish Stock (page 362); or 3 cups (375 ml)
    Basic Fish Stock plus 3 cups (375 ml) strained clam juice

½ cup (125 ml) dry white wine

12 littleneck clams, scrubbed

¾ pound (360 g) mixed fish fillets—red snapper, halibut, tilefish, etc.—
    cut into 1½-inch (3.75-cm) chunks

½ pound (225 g) large shrimp, peeled and deveined

1 small tomato, peeled, seeded, and cut into ¼-inch (.5-cm) dice

½ cup (10 g) loosely packed cilantro sprigs

¼ cup (65 ml) fresh lime juice

2 teaspoons kosher salt

Freshly ground black pepper, to taste

IN A MEDIUM STOCKPOT, heat the olive oil over medium heat. Stir in the onion, celery, garlic, pepper flakes, cumin, and red and green peppers. Cook, stirring, for 5 minutes.

Pour in the stock and wine. Bring to a boil. Add the clams, cover, and cook until the clams just begin to open, about 5 minutes. Add the fish, shrimp, and tomato. Cook, covered, for about 3 minutes, or until the fish is just opaque.

Remove from the stove and stir in the cilantro, lime juice, salt, and pepper.

MAKES 8 CUPS (2 L); 4 TO 6 MAIN-COURSE SERVINGS

solianka

ODDLY, THIS Russian soup can be made with meat as well as fish; but the very finest version is made with sturgeon, fish that when fresh does not disintegrate with prolonged cooking. The finest solianka of the tsars was made with sterlet sturgeon, also used in the clear soup called *ouhka*. Sterlet sturgeon is not available any longer, an ecological tragedy.

What may seem like a particularly unlikely group of seasonings, including as it does pickles and olives, makes for a beautiful and unexpected treat, especially as both sturgeon and salmon make delightfully tinted stocks. This amount of salmon is good as a main course for eight or a first course for sixteen. If the quantities are halved, it makes a first course for eight. As sturgeon is a denser fish, there is less volume to the pound and the slices will be smaller. For ample main-course servings, increase the weight to 4½ pounds (2 kg).

The first step in this recipe is to make a stock; if Salmon Stock (page 364) is on hand, use 10 cups (2.5 1) to replace the stock made in this recipe. If making sturgeon stock, discard the bones after straining the stock, unless you want to bother to poke the spinal marrow out of the bones. This is the *vesiga* so esteemed by the Russians. It can be cut into small pieces and added to the soup or dried and used in a coulibiac. It is not necessary.

for the stock

> **4 pounds (1.8 kg) salmon or sturgeon bones and head, well washed
> to remove any blood**

for the soup

> **4 tablespoons (60 g) unsalted butter**
>
> **1 large onion, finely chopped**
>
> **4 medium shallots, thinly sliced**
>
> **½ pound (225 ml) mushrooms, trimmed, wiped clean, and thinly sliced**
>
> **1 ounce (60 g) dried porcini mushrooms (cèpes), optional**
>
> **3 medium carrots, peeled and cut across into ¼-inch (.5-cm) rounds**
>
> **3 large ribs celery, peeled and cut across on the diagonal into ¼-inch
> (.5-cm) slices**
>
> **3 medium leeks, white and light green parts only, washed well
> and cut across into very thin slices**

2 medium parsnips, peeled and cut into ¼-inch (.5-cm) dice

2 tablespoons tomato paste

4 pounds (1.8 kg) sturgeon or salmon fillet, skinned, pin bones removed, and cut into 10 equal pieces

2 tablespoons capers, rinsed

3 tablespoons pitted and chopped Kalamata olives

7 sour pickles, chopped (2 cups; 375 g)

Kosher salt, to taste

Freshly ground black pepper, to taste

FOR THE STOCK, in a large nonaluminum stockpot, bring the fish bones and 3 quarts (3 l) water to a boil over low heat. Skim off any froth, but not the fat. Lower the heat and simmer for 5 hours. Add cold water from time to time to keep the level even.

Strain the broth through a fine-mesh sieve. The broth will be a beautiful golden (sturgeon) or apricot (salmon) color. There will be about 10 cups (2.5 l).

For the soup, in a large wide pot, melt the butter. Stir in the onion, shallots, and fresh mushrooms. Cook, stirring, over low heat until almost soft, about 15 minutes.

Meanwhile, if using the dried mushrooms, simmer them in 1 cup (250 ml) of the broth for 4 minutes. Drain, strain the liquid through a coffee filter, and add it to the rest of the broth.

Add the rest of the vegetables and the reconstituted mushrooms to the onion mixture. Whisk the tomato paste into the broth and stir into the vegetables. Bring to a boil. Lower the heat and simmer for 20 minutes.

Add the fish and simmer for about 4 minutes for salmon, about 8 minutes for sturgeon.

Stir in the remaining ingredients. Heat through and serve.

MAKES 14 CUPS (3.5 L) BROTH AND VEGETABLES; 8 MAIN-COURSE SERVINGS OR 16 FIRST-COURSE SERVINGS

sicilian salt cod stew

YES, EVEN IN Sicily they use salt cod.

½ cup (125 ml) olive oil

10 cloves garlic, smashed, peeled, and very finely chopped

2 pounds (900 g) firm potatoes, peeled, halved lengthwise, and cut across
    into ¼-inch (½-cm) slices

7 cups (1.75 l) Chunky Tomato Base (page 385), canned Italian plum tomatoes,
    coarsely chopped, with their juice, or sterile-pack chopped tomatoes

2 pounds (900 g) salt cod, desalinated (see Note on page 264)

1½ cups (310 g) oil-cured black olives, pitted and roughly chopped

1 cup (250 ml) dry white wine

2 bay leaves

2 sprigs fresh thyme or ¼ teaspoon dried

Pinch of sugar

Freshly ground black pepper, to taste

⅔ cup (100 g) golden raisins

¼ cup (40 g) pine nuts

IN A LARGE STOCKPOT, heat the oil over medium heat. Stir in the garlic and cook until soft, about 5 minutes. Stir in the potatoes and tomatoes. Bring to a boil. Lower the heat and simmer for 10 minutes.

Add the remaining ingredients except the raisins and pine nuts. Return to a boil. Lower the heat and simmer, covered, for about 30 minutes, or until the potatoes and fish are cooked through. Do not stir, or the fish and potatoes will break up and dissolve. If it is necessary to move the ingredients around or to remove anything stuck to the bottom of the pot, stick a wooden spoon in the center and move it around.

Add the raisins and pine nuts and cook for 2 more minutes.

MAKES 16 CUPS (4 L); 8 MAIN-COURSE SERVINGS

belgian fish stew

T H E   R E M O V A L   O F   B O N E S from carp is a tedious process. It's easy to see why this fish is used, almost exclusively, ground up for gefilte fish. Once all the bones are removed, the fish is in many pieces, which is not so great for broiling or grilling, but perfectly suitable for soups. Monkfish, which is a good substitute, doesn't usually come with the bones, but if using it, see if the fishmonger will send some along; or use 1½ cups (375 ml) fish stock and only 1 bottle of beer.

¾ pound (360 g) carp or monkfish bones and heads, washed and
    cut into 2-inch (5-cm) pieces

Two 12-ounce (375-ml) bottles Belgian beer or other dark beer

1 tablespoon (15 g) unsalted butter

4 medium shallots, thinly sliced

½ pound (225 g) mushrooms, trimmed, wiped clean,
    and thinly sliced

2 large ribs celery, peeled and cut into matchstick strips

1 tablespoon chopped parsley

1½ pounds (675 g) carp fillets or 1 pound (450 g) monkfish fillets,
    all bones carefully removed and cut into 1-inch (2.5-cm) squares

2 egg yolks

1 cup (250 ml) heavy cream

2 teaspoons kosher salt

Freshly ground black pepper, to taste

I N   A   M E D I U M   S A U C E P A N , bring the fish bones and beer to a boil. Lower the heat and simmer for 20 minutes. Strain through a fine-mesh sieve; there should be 3 cups (750 ml).

In a medium saucepan, melt the butter over medium heat. Stir in the shallots. Cook, stirring, for 2 minutes. Stir in the mushrooms and celery. Cook, stirring occasionally, for 8 minutes. Pour in the beer-stock mixture and bring to a boil. Stir in the parsley and fish. Return to a boil. Lower the heat and simmer for 2 minutes.

In a small bowl, beat the egg yolks and cream together. Slowly ladle in some of the hot soup, whisking constantly, until you have added about one third of the soup and raised the temperature of the egg yolks. Whisk the mixture back into the pot. Slowly return to a boil, stirring carefully, to keep the fish in chunks. Season with the salt and pepper.

MAKES 8 CUPS (2 L); 4 TO 6 MAIN-COURSE SERVINGS

Eel

MANY YEARS AGO, when I was about fourteen, I worked at a summer camp that was connected with a settlement house. The counselors were a group of high-minded, undertrained kids from a variety of backgrounds. One day, we were startled when a lovely young thing came back from a sortie to the stream that ran through one of the fields to proudly show off her catch, a gaggle of live eels. Knowing little, like the others, I refused to share the treat that she cooked up. Those of the readers who feel as I did then can stop reading this chapter here.

While Italian, Chinese, Catalan, Spanish, Portuguese, northern German, and French eaters are delighted by the idea of eel and the English will gladly consume smoked and jellied eel, Americans shy away. The result is classic economics: Lack of demand produces lack of supply. Midwinter, it is possible to get a fish market to order eel and, if there is a good Chinatown in the area, a visit will probably garner a store with live eels. I have gone to the docks in Provincetown when the catch was coming in and bought eels that otherwise would have been thrown away.

No matter where eels are bought, it is imperative to get them skinned and cleaned and cut into two-inch lengths. This is not a job for the amateur.

Originally, I had about ten eel recipes for this book; but despite the most understanding and supportive of editors and publishers, I decided that was overkill and omitted most of them. Hamburg's famous eel soup was one of the victims. While all of the recipes can easily be doubled or tripled, I have kept them small. It may be hard to find a seasoned group of eaters who will happily spit out the small bones of the eel.

A modest hint: Once when an eel aficionado was coming to dinner, my stove mysteriously refused to work. I put the matelote (page 288) on an electric hot tray, where it cooked for hours. A slow cooker could be tried.

All eel soups do well with boiled potatoes or fried Cubed Croutons (page 430).

stewed eels
COMACCHIO STYLE

COMACCHIO IS A REGION of Italy famous for its eels. I here follow the recipe of Pellegrino Artusi, a marvelous gastronome. It is to be noted that, unlike most recipes for eel, it does not start by sautéing the eel. In Comacchio, they quite rightly believe that eel has enough fat on its own.

2 large onions, cut into chunks

1 large carrot, peeled and cut into chunks

1 medium rib celery, peeled and cut into chunks

1 medium bunch parsley, leaves only

Peel of ½ lemon, white pith scraped off

3 tablespoons kosher salt

Freshly ground black pepper, to taste

2 pounds (900 g) cleaned and skinned eel, cut across into
    2-inch (5-cm) lengths

2 tablespoons red wine vinegar

¼ cup Tomato Purée (65 ml) (page 384), canned tomato purée,
    or sterile-pack strained tomatoes

HEAT THE OVEN to 275°F (135°C; gas mark #½; #½ British regulo).

In a food processor, pulse the onions, carrot, celery, and parsley until coarsely chopped.

Place the lemon peel and the chopped vegetables in a medium saucepan. Pour in 6 cups (1.5 l) water. Stir in the salt and bring to a boil. Lower the heat and simmer for 25 minutes. Discard the lemon peel. Season with lots of black pepper.

Arrange the eel in one layer in a medium (about 8 inches [20 cm] in diameter) ovenproof casserole, preferably earthenware. Carefully pour the simmered vegetables over the eel. Cover, place in the oven, and cook for 25 to 30 minutes, depending on the diameter of the eel.

Combine the vinegar and tomato purée with 1 cup (250 ml) of the cooking liquid. Carefully pour into the soup and shake the pot to mix; do not touch the eel, which would fall apart. Cover and return to the oven for 10 minutes.

To serve, place two to three pieces of eel in the bottom of each bowl. Divide the cooking liquid evenly among the bowls.

MAKES 10 CUPS (2.5 l); 4 MAIN-COURSE SERVINGS

matelote

TRADITIONALLY, THE WINE with which matelote is made depends on the region of France through which the river or stream in which they are found runs. Along the Loire, white wine is used and the eel is sometimes replaced by river fish, such as pike (if substituting, cook only 15 minutes). My strange combination of wines comes from what was open in my kitchen the day I developed this recipe. I liked the sweetness from some of the wine—it reinforced the sweetness of the onions. However, red wine alone can be used, or a dry white wine. The basic country rule for matelote is an equal weight of onions and eel.

2 tablespoons olive oil

3 large onions, quartered and thinly sliced

½ pound (225 g) white mushrooms, trimmed, wiped clean, and thinly sliced

4 cups (1 l) dry red wine

1 cup (250 ml) sweetish white wine, such as Riesling or Vouvray

8 large cloves garlic, unpeeled

1 bay leaf

2 pounds (900 g) cleaned and skinned eel, cut across into 2-inch (5-cm) pieces

4 tablespoons (60 g) unsalted butter, at room temperature, cut into pieces

¼ cup (25 g) all-purpose flour

1 tablespoon kosher salt

Freshly ground black pepper, to taste

IN A MEDIUM STOCKPOT, heat the olive oil over high heat. Stir in the onions and cook, stirring, for 12 minutes, or until golden brown. Stir in the mushrooms and cook, stirring, for 2 minutes.

Stir in 1 cup (250 ml) red wine and bring to a boil, scraping up any browned bits at the bottom of the pot with a wooden spoon. Stir in the remaining red wine, the white wine, garlic, and bay leaf. Bring to a boil. Add the eel in one layer. Return just to a simmer. Lower the heat as much as possible and barely simmer for 1 hour and 25 minutes.

In a small bowl, work the butter and flour together with a wooden spoon to make a smooth paste. Pour one ladle of soup into the butter paste and stir to thin slightly and smooth out any lumps. Pour this into the soup. Distribute the mixture through the soup without breaking up the pieces of eel, by wiggling the spoon back and forth in the pot without actually stirring or touching the eel. Bring to a boil and boil for 2 minutes, until the soup has thickened. Season with the salt and pepper.

MAKES 11 CUPS (2.75 L); 4 MAIN-COURSE SERVINGS

catalan eel soup

I AM A NEW CONVERT to Catalonia and its food. The slight heat of this recipe is very appealing. It cuts the fat in much the same way that the vinegar or wine does in other recipes. I adapted it from *Traditional Catalan Cooking* by Jaume Fábrega. Serve this soup only to people who don't mind spitting out bones.

½ cup (125 ml) olive oil

6 large cloves garlic, smashed and peeled

1 tablespoon mild paprika

2 small dried hot red peppers, such as pequín, crumbled

2 pounds (900 g) skinned and cleaned eel, with heads left on,
    cut across into 2-inch (5-cm) lengths

1 pound (450 g) firm potatoes, peeled and cut across into ¼-inch
    (.5-cm) slices

Kosher salt, to taste

2 tablespoons red wine vinegar

IN A MEDIUM STOCKPOT, heat the oil over medium-high heat for 2 minutes. Stir in the garlic and cook, stirring, for about 2 minutes, or until the garlic is turning a toasty brown. Stir in the paprika and cook, stirring, until it turns slightly brown, about 30 seconds.

Pour in 8 cups (2 l) water. Stir in the chili peppers and cover the pot. Bring to a boil. Add the eel, cover, and return to a boil. Stir in the potatoes, cover, and return to a boil. Lower the heat and simmer for 20 minutes.

Remove and discard the eel heads. Strain the soup. Reserve the solids and return the liquid to the pot. Bring the liquid to a boil. Continue to boil until reduced to 5 cups (1.25 l), 20 to 30 minutes. Skim most of the fat, but not all, as it contains a great deal of flavor.

Stir the solids into the reduced liquid. Heat through and season with salt to taste and the vinegar

MAKES 8 CUPS (2 L); 8 FIRST-COURSE SERVINGS OR 4 MAIN-COURSE SERVINGS

"Oats, peas, beans, and barley grow..."

ANYONE WANTING TO KNOW how Esau's birthright was bought has only to look in this chapter; he sold it for a mess of potage and that was lentil soup. There are several lentil soup recipes in this chapter, along with others for the homely staple foods, the bean, grain, and legume soups, that sustained our ancestors and still give us pleasure today. I had wanted to include soups from seeds as well, but when I tested them, I found that I wasn't happy with any of them. Chestnut soup was cloying on the tongue. Hungarian caraway soup was distressing. Worst of all, almond soup tasted like glue.

Those wanting such recipes will have to look in other books, although there are good cold almond soups on pages 35 and 37. I was particularly distressed by the results with the hot almond soups, as I had learned from the late Rudolf Grewe, a culinary scholar and linguist, that the earliest written recipe was an Arabic one for a medicinal soup of almonds. Such soups often had chicken. Later, the chicken was dropped and, with sweetening, the soup developed into blancmange. I had hoped to extend this tradition, but a soup I don't like has no place in this book.

Many soups from the ingredients that I do like, such as those from Ecuador (page 319), are vegetarian and others can be made so using the stocks on pages 380–383 or Garlic Broth (page 86).

The modern world did not invent the idea of combining such foods to make complete proteins. Some of the combinations may have been fortuitous outcomes of combinations that arose from availability and the common human desire for variation.

A look at the repertoire of Italian soups shows that Italians have combined almost every bean and legume and grain available to them with savory results. I have not tried to include them all. There is a representative selection and it is possible to make infinite variations by changing the combinations and, where pasta is used, changing the variety. They further increase the grain selection by sometimes serving grilled polenta on the side, and there is always bread.

While these recipes are self-contained, soups such as these are great users of leftovers—not only the stray carrot or piece of onion left from a prior recipe, but if desired, actual leftovers. A little ratatouille, some tomatoes Provençale, a spoonful of Southern greens, last night's carrots or peas, even soggy salad can all go in bean soups along with or instead of the opening sauté.

The cooking of many of these starches is time-consuming. I have often used the contents of cans as a starting point. This works least well in the simplest soups, such as Pasta e Fagioli (page 310) or Doug Rodriguez's Black Bean Soup (page 305), that rely on the savory liquid created by the beans as they cook.

It used to be that all recipes for these ingredients warned us to pick them over looking for pebbles and other detritus. Today, I find that this is generally not necessary.

There are many more soups using these ingredients in other parts of the book. Check the Index.

THREE GOOD WAYS TO SOAK BEANS

The cold soak: Place the beans in a pot. Add water to cover by 2 inches (5 cm). Refrigerate overnight. When it is time to cook, drain the beans and cover with fresh water.

The hot soak: Place the beans in a pot. Add water to cover by 2 inches (5 cm). Bring to a boil. Remove from the heat and let sit for 1 hour. When it is time to cook, drain and cover with fresh water.

The microwave: For 2 cups (410 g) dried beans or legumes: Place in a 5-quart (5-l) casserole with a tightly fitting lid with 2 cups (500 ml) water. Cook at 100% power for 15 minutes in a 650- to 700-watt oven. Remove from the oven and let stand, covered, for 5 minutes. Uncover and add 2 cups (500 ml) very hot tap water. Re-cover and let stand for 1 hour. Drain. Cover with fresh water to cook.

TO COOK THE BEANS

Either start with unsoaked beans or drain soaked beans. Rinse the beans and place in an appropriately sized pot. Add fresh water to cover by 2 inches (5 cm), or the amount called for in the specific recipe. Bring to a boil. Lower the heat and simmer for 1 to 3 hours, depending on the type and age of the bean, until the beans are soft but not bursting.

YIELDS AND COOKING TIMES FOR BEANS AND GRAINS

Large dried beans: black-eyed peas, cannellini, red and black kidney beans, pink beans, pinto beans

Small dried beans: flageolets, white haricot beans, black turtle beans

Legumes: broad (fava) beans, chick peas, lentils, split peas

> 1 cup (180 g) large dried beans = 2 cups soaked, 2½ cups cooked (425 g)
> 1 cup (205 g) small beans = 2½ cups soaked, 3 scant cups cooked (500 to 600 g)
> 1 cup drained canned beans = 6 to 8 ounces (180 to 225 g)

Spelt, farro, dinkel, wheat berries (hard winter): These grains can be used in basically the same manner. Slightly different cooking times and methods. Spelt: 1 cup (180 g) spelt to 4 cups (1 l) water. Bring to a boil. Lower the heat and simmer for 1 hour and 10 minutes. It will retain its crunch. This will yield about 3 cups (360 g). The spelt can also be soaked overnight in cold water to cover by ¾-inch (2 cm). Drain. Cover with water in a 1 : 1 ratio and simmer until done. It will take about 25 minutes. The result is basically the same. Spelt has a longer grain and takes a slightly shorter time to cook than farro but the grains are basically interchangeable. Wheat berries can also be soaked and cooked this way, with the same yield.

Barley: ½ pound (225 g) = 1 cup raw = 5 cups (900 g) cooked. Simmer for 1 hour to 1 hour and 15 minutes.

Chick peas: ¼ pound (120 g) = ½ cup dried = 1¼ to 1½ cups (225 to 270 g) cooked = 1 cup purée. Simmer for 1 hour and 30 minutes to 3 hours, depending on age of chick peas.

Lentils: 1 cup (180 g) dry = 2¼ cups cooked. Simmer for 30 to 40 minutes.

YIELDS AND COOKING TIMES FOR RICE

1 cup (225 g) raw long-grain white rice cooked in 2 cups (500 ml) water for 15 minutes = 2½ cups (375 g), enough for 5 soup servings

1 cup (225 g) basmati rice soaked for 20 minutes in 1¾ cups (425 ml) water, then simmered for 15 minutes = 3 cups (420 g)

Fresh bean soups

fresh cranberry bean soup
WITH TOMATO

FRESH SHELLING BEANS in the pod and the last of the tomatoes usually are plentiful at the same time. If the beans are available and good tomatoes not, use the tomato base. When done, the cranberry beans or other fresh beans are creamy without being floury. Top with a drizzle of very good olive oil.

> 3 tablespoons olive oil
>
> 1 medium onion, cut into ½-inch (1-cm) dice
>
> 5 cups (1.25 l) Chunky Tomato Base (page 385) or sterile-pack chopped tomatoes;
>   or 2½ pounds (1.1 kg) ripe tomatoes, cored and cut into 1-inch (2.5-cm) cubes
>
> 1 pound (450 g) fresh cranberry beans, shelled
>
> 4 leaves holy basil or Italian basil, minced
>
> 2 leaves fresh sage, minced, or a pinch of dried
>
> 1 teaspoon minced fresh oregano or ¼ teaspoon dried
>
> 1 teaspoon minced lemon thyme
>
> 1½ teaspoons kosher salt
>
> Very good olive oil, for serving
>
> Freshly ground black pepper, to taste, for serving

IN A MEDIUM SAUCEPAN, warm the olive oil over low heat. Stir in the onion. Cook, stirring occasionally, for about 12 minutes or until translucent.

Raise the heat and stir in the fresh tomatoes. Bring to a boil. Lower the heat and simmer, stirring occasionally, for 20 minutes, or until the tomatoes are soft and liquid. Or stir base or sterile-pack tomatoes into the cooked onions and bring to a boil.

Stir in the beans and 1¾ cups (450 ml) water. Bring to a boil. Lower the heat and simmer for 10 minutes. If using dried herbs, stir them in now. In either case, simmer for another 10 minutes.

If using fresh herbs, stir them in now. Simmer for 1 minute. Season with the salt. Remove from the heat and let rest for at least 30 minutes before serving.

Serve drizzled with good olive oil and a grind of black pepper.

MAKES 6 CUPS (1.5 L); 4 GENEROUS FIRST-COURSE SERVINGS

thick potato soup

THIS IS THE FIRST of the wonderful meatless soups of Ecuador in this chapter. To learn more about the potatoes, see pages 92–93. For other ingredients and add-ins that are served on the side and may be unfamiliar, see pages 441–446. If there is refrito on hand, use it and omit the first three ingredients.

for the refrito

> **2 tablespoons (30 g) unsalted butter**
>
> **1 medium onion, minced**
>
> **2 teaspoons Annatto Butter (page 445)**

for the soup

> **1 pound (450 g) mashing potatoes, peeled and cut across into ⅛-inch (30-mm) slices**
>
> **1 pound (450 g) firm potatoes, peeled and cut into 1-inch (2.5-cm) cubes**
>
> **1½ cups (375 ml) milk**
>
> **2½ teaspoons kosher salt**
>
> **Freshly ground black pepper, to taste**
>
> **3¾ pounds (1.7 kg) fava (broad) beans, shelled, blanched for 2 minutes, run under cold water, and popped out of tough outer skins, or one 10-ounce (300-g) package frozen baby lima beans, defrosted in a sieve under warm running water and drained**
>
> **3 sprigs cilantro, optional**

for serving

> **3 avocados, seeded, peeled, and sliced**
>
> **3 hard-boiled eggs, peeled and cut across in half**
>
> **½ cup (20 g) coarsely chopped cilantro**
>
> **2 large heads Bibb lettuce, cored and cut across into shreds**
>
> **Tamarillo Sauce (page 441)**
>
> **Pickled Onions (page 446)**

FOR THE REFRITO (this can be replaced with a single recipe of Refrito, page 446), in a medium saucepan, melt the unsalted butter over medium heat. Stir in the onion and cook, stirring, until soft and translucent, about 10 minutes. Stir in the annatto butter and allow to melt.

Stir in the potatoes. Cook, stirring constantly, for 10 minutes, or until the potatoes are beginning to look translucent. Pour in the milk and 6 cups (1.5 l) water. Bring to a boil. Lower the heat and simmer for 30 minutes, or until the mashing potatoes begin to fall apart and thicken the soup. Season with the salt and pepper.

In a blender, purée ¾ cup (115 g) of the favas or limas with 1 cup (250 ml) of the broth (do not purée any of the cubed potatoes). Scrape the purée into the soup. Stir in the remaining beans. The soup can be made ahead up to this point and refrigerated for up to 3 days.

To serve, reheat the soup and stir in the sprigs of cilantro, if using. Divide the avocado and boiled eggs among six soup bowls. Ladle the soup into the bowls. Pass bowls of the cilantro, lettuce, tamarillo sauce, and pickled onions at the table.

MAKES 8 CUPS (2 L); 6 FIRST-COURSE SERVINGS

Dried bean soups

Dried beans are endlessly useful staples. They come in a broad variety of colors and sizes. In addition to being used in the soups as given, one kind can replace another and a handful of cooked beans can be added to many soups. Look at pages 293–294 for timings and how much of the cooked beans will result from a quantity of dried beans.

nappei-jiru
JAPANESE VEGETABLE SOUP

I OFTEN FORGET THAT TOFU, or bean curd, is actually made from soybeans. When I first made this soup, adzuki beans were virtually unobtainable. I substituted kidney beans, which are the same color and have a similar flavor. While I use chicken broth, it would be more authentic—and vegetarian—to use konbu dashi.

for the flavored bean curd

¾ cup (180 ml) Basic Chicken Stock (page 345) or commercial chicken broth

¼ cup (65 ml) soy sauce

4 teaspoons sugar

Two ¼-pound (120-g) pieces firm silken tofu

for the soup

8 large or 12 small dried shiitake mushrooms

6 cups (1.5 l) Basic Chicken Stock (page 345), commercial chicken broth, or Konbo Dashi (page 383)

1 medium carrot, peeled and cut into ¼-inch (.5-cm) dice

½ cup (60 g) peeled, diced turnip

1 cup (225 g) cooked adzuki beans or red kidney beans (see page 293), or drained and rinsed canned beans

¼ pound (120 g) daikon [mouli], peeled and cut into ¼-inch (.5-cm) dice

2 tablespoons light soy sauce

1 teaspoon kosher salt, or less if using commercial broth

2 tablespoons cornstarch

3 medium scallions, white and light green parts only, thinly sliced across on the diagonal

FOR THE TOFU, in a small saucepan, bring the stock, soy sauce, and sugar to a boil. Add the tofu. Lower the heat and simmer for 10 minutes. Drain. Cut the tofu into 1-inch (2.5-cm) cubes and reserve.

For the soup, soak the mushrooms in 2 cups (500 ml) warm water for 20 minutes. Drain; strain and reserve the liquid. Discard the mushroom stems and slice the mushroom caps across into thin strips.

In a medium saucepan, bring the stock or dashi to a boil. Stir in the carrot and turnip. Return to a boil. Lower the heat and simmer for 15 minutes. Stir in the beans, tofu, mushrooms, daikon, soy sauce, and salt.

Dissolve the cornstarch in the reserved mushroom soaking liquid. Stir into the soup and return to a boil. Sprinkle the scallions over the soup just before serving.

MAKES 8 CUPS (2 L); 6 FIRST-COURSE SERVINGS

Man or machine

pesto or pistou

ONE OF THE MOST PLEASING shapes that I know is the mortar's, curving solidly and plumply upward. I have always had a selection of mortars, from the rosy stone one such as the one the Troisgros brothers used to use to serve butter to a Roman bronze apothecary mortar, rough Japanese earthenware mortars, and semismooth ordinary ones. There was still one missing to make me happy. Jim Beard had in his kitchen a mammoth mortar carved from an enormous block of white stone. From time to time, I would see such a mortar in a French antique shop; but, somehow, the task of getting it crated and shipped seemed overwhelming. When James Beard died, I had thought I would buy his mortar and, perhaps, some of his copper molds. At the last minute, I found that I could not bring myself to go to the auction: It would be too hard to see all those well-remembered things dispersed.

Much to my surprise, the following Christmas, a loving friend presented me with the mortar and its solid pestle. As I am not as tall as Jim, I have had to have a special low table made so that I can pound properly. I can remember Jim making aïoli in it using only garlic, salt, and olive oil. Now, I make pesto.

Any Genovese or Niçoise will ardently advocate not the need but the necessity of a mortar and pestle to make a true pesto or pistou. They claim that the obligatory smoothness and the ultimate release of the marvelous smells and flavors can only be achieved by the strenuous plying of the pestle. I agree that the result using a mortar and lots of arm power is superior. The recommended procedure is to grind the basil, garlic, and the nuts, if using, to a smooth pomade, always rotating the pestle in the same direction—much as, in my premixer childhood, one was instructed to always beat the cake batter in one direction.

However, I am often lazy and still want my pesto. Then I will use a food processor or a blender. The result is very good.

Sometimes in winter, I will start with basil put up at the end of summer. My method is to melt the basil (reducing the quantity) by heating it in some olive oil and then purée it in a food processor. I pack it into ice cube trays, and when the cubes are frozen, pop them into a plastic bag to use during the winter. One or two in a soup or stew brightens everything up.

Despite common belief, Ligurian or Genovese pesto for soup often is made without pine nuts. French pistou never has nuts or cheese; it may have tomatoes and other herbs. When I want an intensely green sauce, I use one third parsley.

simple white bean
AND PESTO SOUP

I AM NOT ALWAYS the purest of the pure; no Lochinvar I. Often I just want a good result in a hurry. This is a terrific soup for such an occasion, with all sorts of optional shortcuts. I probably would make the pesto—no nuts.

2 cups (500 ml) Basic Chicken Stock (page 345) or commercial chicken broth

4 cups (800 g) cooked small white beans (see page 293) or two 19-ounce (540-g) cans small white beans, drained and rinsed

2 tablespoons Pesto Sauce (page 434) or store-bought

2 tablespoons freshly grated Parmesan cheese

Freshly ground black pepper, to taste

IN A MEDIUM SAUCEPAN, bring the chicken stock and beans to a boil. Lower the heat. Stir in the remaining ingredients. Simmer for 1 minute.

MAKES 4 CUPS (1 L); 4 FIRST-COURSE SERVINGS

Basil

WHILE THERE IS MUCH DISCUSSION in the culinary literature on pesto method, there is less on the kind of basil to use. Given that there are myriad varieties, each with its own flavor, this is a real question. There is a variety called *Ocimum basilicum,* or Genovese, that is a specially developed large leaf basil for pesto. Sweet basil is the best substitute. The dwarf or bush basils, *Ocimum basilicum minimum,* have small leaves, which are more pungent and tougher. They are better suited to adding whole to stews. *Ocimum sanctum*—biblical, holy, or sacred basil—is the variety of India, while *Ocimum sp* is the true Thai basil, a milder version of anise basil. If possible, it should be used in Thai and Vietnamese dishes.

All of the basils can easily be grown in pots. Plants seem to flourish in every Greek doorway in sawn-off olive oil cans.

soupe au pistou

THE FRENCH MAKE ANY NUMBER of soups with a nutless version of pesto called *pistou.* Feel free to use a mortar and pestle. This is a particularly nice and somewhat unusual version, worth noting and using. The cup of pistou can be a pasta sauce, or to stir red into other soups. The French also have soups of the same name. This one is related to Minestrone (page 115).

> ¾ cup (180 g) white beans, soaked according to one of the methods
> on page 293 and drained

for the pistou

> 3 sprigs parsley
>
> 3 sprigs thyme
>
> 2 sage leaves
>
> 2 bay leaves
>
> 5 teaspoons kosher salt
>
> ¼ teaspoon dried oregano
>
> 1 medium tomato, cored and a cross cut in the flower end
>
> 1 medium bunch basil, leaves only, washed well

3 medium cloves garlic, smashed, peeled, and coarsely chopped

½ cup (45 g) freshly grated Parmesan cheese

2 tablespoons olive oil

½ teaspoon kosher salt

Freshly ground black pepper, to taste

for the soup

3 medium carrots, peeled and cut into ¼-inch (.5-cm) dice

1 medium onion, cut into ¼-inch (.5-cm) dice

½ pound (225 g) firm potatoes, peeled and cut into ¼-inch (.5-cm) dice

2 medium zucchini, trimmed and cut into ¼-inch (.5-cm) dice

⅔ pound (180 g) flat yellow or green beans, tipped and tailed

1 cup (90 g) elbow macaroni

2 tablespoons tomato paste, optional (winter addition, if tomatoes have no flavor)

Kosher salt, to taste

Freshly ground black pepper, to taste

TO COOK THE BEANS, in a medium saucepan, place the beans and 8 cups (2 l) water. Bring to a boil. Lower the heat and simmer for 1 hour, or until the beans are tender. Drain, reserving 5 cups (1.25 l) of the liquid; add water if needed.

For the pistou, tie the parsley, thyme, sage, and bay leaves together into a bouquet with kitchen twine. In a medium saucepan, bring the bean cooking liquid, salt, herb bouquet, and oregano to a boil. Drop the tomato into the liquid and cook for 15 seconds, turning the tomato over halfway through the cooking time. Remove the tomato with a slotted spoon and plunge into cold water to cool. Peel, seed, and coarsely chop the tomato. Reserve the liquid and herbs for the soup.

In a food processor, pulse the basil, tomato, and garlic ten times. Stop and scrape down the sides of the bowl. Pulse ten more times. Add the cheese, olive oil, salt, and pepper; pulse to incorporate. The mixture shouldn't be too fine.

For the soup, return the bean cooking liquid to a boil. Stir in the carrots, onion, potatoes, and half of the zucchini. Return to a boil. Lower the heat and simmer for 10 minutes. Remove the herb bouquet. Stir in the beans and mush everything up a bit with a wooden spoon. The soup can be made ahead to this point and refrigerated for up to 2 days.

If it has been refrigerated, return the soup to a boil. Stir in the remaining zucchini, the flat beans, and the macaroni. Return to a boil. Lower the heat and simmer, stirring occasionally so nothing sticks, for 6 minutes. Stir in the tomato paste, if using, then stir in the pistou. Season with salt and pepper to taste.

MAKES 10 CUPS (2.5 L); 8 FIRST-COURSE SERVINGS; 1 CUP (90 G) PISTOU

black bean

THIS INCREDIBLY SIMPLE SOUP is a great pleasure on a cold night in the fall. The pistou is nutless and cheeseless. It can be replaced with one recipe of Pesto (page 434), or store-bought (when in a hurry and using canned beans).

> 1 pound (450 g) black beans, soaked according to any of the methods on page 293 and drained, or 6 cups (1 kg) rinsed and drained canned beans
>
> 2 large bunches basil, leaves only, washed well
>
> 6 medium cloves garlic, smashed and peeled
>
> ½ cup (125 ml) olive oil
>
> 3½ cups (875 ml) Vegetable Broth (page 380), Basic Chicken Stock (page 345), or water, if using canned beans
>
> 1 tablespoon kosher salt
>
> ¼ cup (15 g) coarsely chopped basil, for serving

IF USING DRIED BEANS, in a medium saucepan, combine the beans with water to cover by 2 inches (5 cm). Bring to a boil. Lower the heat and simmer, partially covered, for 1 hour, or until the beans are very soft and beginning to burst. Remove from the heat.

In a blender, purée the basil, garlic, and ¼ cup (65 ml) olive oil.

In a food processor, working in batches if necessary, purée the cooked beans with their liquid (about 3 cups [875 ml]); or, if using canned beans, purée with the 3½ cups (875 ml) broth, stock, or water. Scrape back into the saucepan (or scrape the canned bean purée into a medium saucepan) and stir in the pesto and salt. Heat through.

Swirl in the remaining olive oil. Top each serving with a little chopped basil.

MAKES ABOUT 7 CUPS (1.75 L); 6 FIRST-COURSE SERVINGS

doug rodriguez's
BLACK BEAN SOUP

WHEN I TASTED THIS SOUP, Doug was chef at a Miami restaurant. He told me the recipe was his mother's. He moved to New York and published the recipe in his first book, *Nuevo Latino*. I love the savory and light vegetarian flavor. It is generous of him to share it since he has a book of soups, *Latin Ladles*. The beans are not soaked first, which is typical of many Cuban black bean soups. In this way, the soups get all of the bean flavor.

1 pound (450 g) black beans

2 bay laurel leaves (see page 174)

1 cup (250 ml) extra virgin olive oil

2 large red bell peppers, cored, seeded, deribbed, and cut into ¼-inch (.5-cm) dice

2 medium shallots, coarsely chopped

2 medium onions, coarsely chopped

8 medium cloves garlic, smashed, peeled, and coarsely chopped

1 tablespoon ground cumin

2 tablespoons dried oregano

2 tablespoons chopped oregano

1½ tablespoons sugar, or to taste

2 tablespoons kosher salt, or to taste

for serving

1 medium red onion, thinly sliced

1 cup (225 g) sour cream, optional

IN A MEDIUM STOCKPOT, bring the beans, 12 cups (3 l) water, and the bay leaves to a boil. Lower the heat and simmer, stirring frequently, for 2 hours and 30 minutes to 3 hours, until tender. Add more water if necessary to keep the beans covered.

Meanwhile, in a medium frying pan, heat the oil over medium heat. Stir in the peppers, shallots, and onions. Cook, stirring frequently, for 8 minutes, or until the onions are translucent. Stir in the garlic, cumin, and the dried and fresh oregano and cook for 2 minutes. Remove from the heat and allow to cool slightly. Purée in a blender.

When the beans are almost done, stir in the purée, sugar, and salt. Continue to simmer until the beans are tender, another 20 to 30 minutes. Adjust the seasonings.

Serve with the sliced red onion and sour cream, if desired, on the side.

MAKES 10 CUPS (2.5 L); 8 TO 10 FIRST-COURSE SERVINGS

pink bean
AND RADICCHIO SOUP

THIS IS A MADE-UP SOUP, but I think very good. Imagine it as the result of a thrifty Italian's having leftover braised radicchio, which is what actually happened to this thrifty non-Italian. A larger batch can be made by making more radicchio.

We are used to seeing the round red chicory balls for salad, which have a dangerous similarity to red cabbage, called radicchio. Actually, there are many kinds of these forced heads of cut-back chicory. Most are meant to be cooked. Endive (witloof, chicory) can be substituted and the beans changed to cannellini or white navy beans.

for the radicchio

4 medium heads Treviso or Chioggia radicchio, stalks trimmed to
   ½ inch (1 cm) and split in half lengthwise

4 tablespoons (60 g) unsalted butter, cut into ¼-inch (.5-cm) dice

Kosher salt, to taste

Freshly ground black pepper, to taste

About 6 cups (1.5 l) Basic Beef Stock (page 165) or, in England, imported beef or
   meat stock, Basic Chicken Stock (page 345), or commercial chicken broth

for the soup

½ pound (225 g) pink beans (Spanish habichuelas rosadas), soaked according
   to one of the methods on page 293 and drained

1 pound (450 g) firm potatoes, peeled and cut into ½-inch (1-cm) cubes

Kosher salt, to taste

Freshly ground black pepper, to taste

2 teaspoons shredded basil

2 teaspoons olive oil

Freshly grated Parmesan cheese, for serving

TO BAKE THE RADICCHIO, heat the oven to 300°F (150°C; gas mark #2; #1 British regulo). Place the radicchio cut side up in a baking dish just large enough to hold it. Tuck the butter between the leaves of each half. Sprinkle with salt and pepper. Pour in stock to cover by 1½ inches (4 cm), about 5½ cups (1.4 l).

Cover tightly with aluminum foil and bake for 20 minutes. Carefully—because of the steam—uncover and turn the radicchio. Re-cover and bake for an additional 20 to 30 minutes, or until a skewer easily pierces the stalk end.

Drain the radicchio, reserving 5 cups (1.25 l) of the broth; add water or stock if need be. Cut the radicchio crosswise into ½-inch (1-cm) strips.

For the soup, in a medium saucepan, bring the beans and radicchio liquid to a boil. Lower the heat and simmer, partially covered, for 1 hour to 1 hour and 30 minutes, or until tender.

Meanwhile, in a small saucepan, cover the potatoes with water and bring to a boil. Lower the heat and simmer for 10 minutes. Drain and reserve.

Stir the potatoes, radicchio, salt, pepper, basil, and olive oil into the beans and return to a boil. Lower the heat and simmer for 3 minutes.

Pass Parmesan cheese at the table.

MAKES ABOUT 6 CUPS (1.5 L); 6 FIRST-COURSE SERVINGS

bean and swiss chard soup

ZUPPA DI FAGIOLO E BIETE

CLEARLY THIS IS AN Italian soup. *Biete* is Swiss chard, usually green, although I have a fondness for the drama and beefy taste of the red-stemmed kind.

½ pound (225 g) Swiss chard or kale, trimmed

1 teaspoon kosher salt, plus additional to taste

2 flat anchovy fillets

¼ teaspoon fresh rosemary leaves or dried

⅓ cup (80 ml) olive oil

2 medium garlic cloves, smashed and peeled

1 cup (225 g) cooked small white beans (see page 293) or drained and rinsed canned beans

4 cups (1 l) Basic Chicken Stock (page 345) or commercial chicken broth

Freshly ground black pepper, to taste

½ cup (60 g) small shell macaroni

Freshly grated Parmesan cheese, for serving

IN A MEDIUM SAUCEPAN, cook the chard with ½ cup (125 ml) water and the salt over medium heat until tender. Drain the chard, reserving any liquid that remains. Coarsely chop the chard.

Very finely chop anchovies together with the rosemary.

In a medium saucepan, stir together the oil and garlic over medium-high heat. Cook, stirring frequently, until the garlic is pale gold, about 10 minutes. Stir in the anchovies and rosemary. Cook, stirring, for 1 minute. Discard the garlic. Stir in the chard and cook for 2 to 3 minutes, stirring to thoroughly coat it with the oil. Stir in the beans. Cook for 3 minutes.

Stir in the reserved cooking liquid and the stock. Season with salt and pepper. Bring to a boil and stir in the macaroni. Boil for 6 minutes, or until the pasta is tender. Adjust the seasoning, if necessary.

Pass Parmesan cheese at the table.

MAKES ABOUT 5 CUPS (1.25 L); 4 FIRST-COURSE SERVINGS

white bean, chorizo,

IF MY FRIENDS ARE SQUEAMISH about whole cloves of garlic, I mash the cloves against the side of the pot just before serving. They will flavor and thicken the soup. This is the kind of soup my grandmother would have made if she had been a good cook—it can always be thinned with a little water to serve a larger crowd.

1 tablespoon olive oil

2 medium heads garlic, smashed and peeled

8 cups (2 l) Enriched Pork Stock (page 360), Basic Chicken Stock (page 345), or commercial chicken broth

1 pound (450 g) small white beans or dried baby lima beans, soaked according to one of the methods on page 293 and drained

2 links (150 g) chorizo, cut across into thin slices

2 medium bunches broccoli di rape, stems cut off, yellow and wilted leaves discarded, tops and leaves only, and cut across into ½ inch (1-cm) pieces

Kosher salt, to taste

Freshly ground black pepper, to taste

IN A MEDIUM STOCKPOT, warm the oil over low heat. Stir in the garlic and cook, stirring frequently, until it turns translucent and soft but not brown, about 10 minutes. Stir in the stock and beans. Bring to a boil. Lower the heat and simmer, covered, until the beans are tender, about 1 hour.

Meanwhile, in a large frying pan, cook the chorizo over medium heat, stirring, until it changes color and begins to render its fat, about 3 minutes. Stir in the broccoli di rape a handful at a time and cook until wilted. Continue cooking and stirring until all the rape is bright green, about 4 minutes.

Stir the rape mixture into the beans and return to a boil. Lower the heat and simmer for 5 minutes. Season with salt and pepper.

MAKES 8 CUPS (2 L); 6 FIRST-COURSE SERVINGS

pasta e fagioli

THIS IS PROBABLY the best known of the hearty bean and pasta soups from Italy, more specifically, Sicily.

It is virtually a solid. Some people may desire a more soupy soup. In that case, reserve the extra bean cooking liquid and add more liquid as desired. If the soup is made ahead, the beans and pasta may absorb a lot of liquid—especially the pasta, which can take over the whole soup. It is better to cook the soup just until the point when the pasta is added. Cook the pasta just before the soup is served. The soup is typically served warm rather than hot.

1½ cups (300 g) small white beans, soaked according to one of the
    methods on page 293 and drained

¼ cup (65 ml) olive oil

1 medium clove garlic, smashed and peeled, plus, if desired, 4 medium
    cloves garlic, smashed, peeled, and very finely chopped

2 medium ribs celery, peeled and coarsely chopped

4 medium plum tomatoes, cored, peeled, and cut into ¼-inch (.5-cm) dice,
    or 2 cups (500 ml) Chunky Tomato Base (page 385), lightly crushed
    canned Italian plum tomatoes with their juice, or sterile-pack
    chopped tomatoes

½ small dried hot red pepper, crumbled

1 teaspoon tomato paste

4 teaspoons kosher salt

1 cup (150 g) ditalini or tubetti

¼ teaspoon dried oregano

2 tablespoons finely chopped Italian parsley, optional

Freshly ground black pepper, to taste

Great olive oil, for serving

IN A MEDIUM STOCKPOT, bring the beans to a boil with 10 cups (2.5 l) fresh water. Lower the heat and simmer, partially covered, for 1 hour, or until the beans are tender.

While the beans are cooking, in a medium frying pan, heat the oil over medium heat. Add the smashed garlic clove and cook until it turns golden. Remove the garlic and discard it. Stir in the celery and cook, stirring occasionally, for 3 minutes. Stir in the tomatoes and hot red pepper. Dissolve the tomato paste in ½ cup (125 ml) water. Stir into the tomatoes and add 1 teaspoon salt. Bring to a boil. Lower the heat and simmer for 15 minutes. Remove from the heat.

When the beans are done, drain, reserving the liquid. In a food processor, purée half of the beans with 1 cup (250 ml) of the bean cooking liquid.

In a medium saucepan, stir the puréed beans into the remaining whole beans, along with 2½ cups (625 ml) of the reserved bean cooking liquid. Scrape the cooked tomatoes into the pot. The soup can be made ahead to this point and refrigerated for up to 2 days.

Bring the soup to a boil. Stir in the pasta and oregano. Return to a boil. Lower the heat slightly and cook at a low boil, stirring frequently to avoid scorching, for 9 minutes. If using, stir in the chopped garlic and parsley and cook for 1 more minute. Season with the remaining salt and pepper to taste.

Serve topped with a drizzle of great olive oil.

MAKES 7 CUPS (1.75 L); 6 FIRST-COURSE SERVINGS

navy bean purée

THIS IS NOT THE Senate's famous bean soup. Instead, it takes its inspiration from the goose and bean dishes of southwestern France. It is a good dish made after roasting a goose. If there is some goose meat left, add it, cut into smallish pieces.

   1 pound (450 g) navy beans soaked according to one of the methods
      described on page 293 and drained
   1 medium head garlic, smashed and peeled
   ½ small bunch flat-leaf parsley, leaves only, very finely chopped
   4 teaspoons kosher salt, or less if using commercial broth
   1 teaspoon freshly ground black pepper
   ¼ cup (65 ml) olive oil
   3 cups (750 ml) Goose Stock (page 353), Basic Chicken Stock (page 345),
      or commercial chicken broth
   Goose cracklings (see page 404), optional, for serving

IN A MEDIUM SAUCEPAN, bring the beans and 6 cups (1.5 l) fresh water to a boil. Lower the heat and simmer for 1 hour.

Stir in the garlic and simmer for 30 minutes.

Stir the parsley, salt, pepper, and oil into the beans. In a food processor, working in batches, purée to form a smooth paste. Return to the pot and stir in the stock. Heat through.

Sprinkle goose cracklings over each serving, if desired.

MAKES 8 CUPS (2 L); 8 FIRST-COURSE SERVINGS

Soups with legumes

Legumes are another great group of starches. Lentils find their home here. As true beans did not get to Europe or Asia until after the discovery of the Americas, these were the staples of those kitchens early on.

cold peanut soup

PEANUTS, OR GROUNDNUTS, are not nuts. They are legumes that grow in pods like peas. They grow under the ground and have to be dug like potatoes. Made into peanut butter, they are an easily stored protein-rich soup base. It is possible to make one's own peanut butter from unsalted peanuts. Grind them in a food processor or blender, adding a little peanut oil (see the recipe on page 435).

Delicious but not wildly attractive, the soup can be dressed up with the sweetness of red bell peppers to make an elegant starter on a hot day.

¼ pound (120 g) shelled unsalted peanuts
2 small jalapeño peppers, seeded
2 tablespoons curry powder
2 cups (500 ml) Basic Chicken Stock (page 345) or commercial chicken broth
1⅓ cups (320 ml) low-fat milk
Juice of 1 lemon
1½ teaspoons kosher salt, or less if using commercial broth
10 to 15 slivers red bell pepper, optional

IN A BLENDER, purée the peanuts, jalapeños, curry powder, and 1 cup (250 ml) stock. Scrape down the sides of the jar. With the machine running, slowly pour in the remaining stock. Scrape the mixture into a metal bowl. Stir in the milk, 1 cup (250 ml) water, the lemon juice, and salt. Refrigerate for several hours, or overnight.

Top each serving with a few slivers of red pepper, if desired.

MAKES 5 CUPS (1.25 L); 4 TO 5 FIRST-COURSE SERVINGS

spicy peanut butter soup

HOT OR COLD

THIS SPICIER VERSION of the previous soup is extremely comforting hot, although it can be served cold.

> 1 tablespoon (15 g) unsalted butter
>
> 1 small onion, very finely chopped
>
> 1 tablespoon chili powder
>
> 2½ cups (625 ml) Basic Chicken Stock (page 345) or commercial chicken broth (plus 1 cup [250 ml] if serving cold)
>
> 1 cup (250 ml) Peanut Butter (page 435) or store-bought
>
> 1 cup (250 ml) milk, light cream, or half-and-half
>
> 3 tablespoons fresh lemon juice
>
> Kosher salt, to taste
>
> 1 teaspoon freshly ground black pepper
>
> 8 drops hot red pepper sauce

IN A SMALL SAUCEPAN, melt the butter over medium heat. Stir in the onion and chili powder and cook, stirring, until the onion is soft and wilted, about 10 minutes.

Stir in the stock and bring to a boil. Lower the heat and simmer for 15 minutes. Whisk in the peanut butter. Continue whisking until the mixture is smooth. Add the remaining ingredients and whisk until smooth. Simmer for 5 minutes.

Serve immediately, or refrigerate for 2 hours, or overnight. If chilling, thin with 1 cup (250 ml) additional cold stock just before serving.

MAKES 4 CUPS (1 L); 4 FIRST-COURSE SERVINGS

lentils

Lentils come in several colors: brown, green, orange, and red. The brown take slightly longer to cook than the others. Lentils have a rich meaty flavor that makes even the vegetarian soups using them feel substantial.

lentil soup

BACON RIND CAN BE omitted and Roasted Vegetable Broth (page 380) or Mushroom Broth (page 382) substituted for the beef stock to make a vegetarian soup.

Bacon rind (skin) can be gotten from a butcher who slices his own bacon from a slab. It adds gelatin and flavor to soups and stews. It is the French "couenne" often put at the bottom of a pot of stew to prevent sticking.

> **1 tablespoon olive oil**
> **½ pound (225 g) bacon rind, cut across into thick strips**
> **3 large ribs celery, peeled and cut into ¼-inch (.5-cm) dice**
> **3 medium carrots, peeled and cut into ¼-inch (.5-cm) dice**
> **1 small yellow onion, cut into ¼-inch (.5-cm) dice**
> **3 cloves garlic, smashed, peeled, and minced**
> **1 tablespoon ground cumin**
> **1½ teaspoons chili powder**
> **3 cups (750 ml) Beef Stock (page 165) or, in England, imported beef or meat stock**
> **1 cup (180 g) brown lentils**
> **½ cup (30 g) coarsely chopped parsley**
> **2 teaspoons fresh lemon juice**
> **Freshly ground black pepper, to taste**

IN A MEDIUM SAUCEPAN, heat the olive oil and bacon rind over medium heat. Stir in the celery, carrots, onion, garlic, cumin, and chili powder. Cook for about 5 minutes, or until the vegetables have softened.

Stir in the stock, 3 cups (750 ml) water, and the lentils. Bring to a boil. Lower the heat and simmer for 40 minutes, or until the lentils are very soft, stirring occasionally.

Remove from the heat. Remove the pieces of bacon rind. In a food processor, purée about half of the lentils. Stir the purée back into the pan, with the parsley, lemon juice, and black pepper. Heat through.

MAKES 6 CUPS (1.5 L); 6 FIRST-COURSE SERVINGS

chard and lentil soup

SWISS CHARD IS mostly available in the fall—that is its peak time—but in some areas, it can be found all year. There are two kinds, white-stemmed green-leafed chard and the stronger-flavored red or ruby chard, also known as rhubarb chard, with its red-veined leaves and licorice-thin stems. There is a pronounced difference in the taste. The red is very beet-y. If you don't like beets, you won't like it. The white is milder.

I have used the milder green leaves in this soup, but the earthy red-veined leaves would work well too. This is a very substantial soup that can be thinned with a little extra water or stock, another cup or two. With a salad and thick-crusted bread, this is a good, hearty meal. If the bunches of chard are larger than those called for, throw them in—the amount is flexible. The stems can go in a potage (see page 99).

¼ cup (65 ml) olive oil

1 teaspoon sweet paprika

1 teaspoon ground cumin

2 medium bunches scallions, trimmed, white part cut across into ¼-inch (.5-cm) pieces, enough green part cut across to make ½ cup (15 g)

1 pound (450 g) brown lentils

5½ to 6 cups (1.2 to 1.5 l) Basic Chicken Stock (page 345) or commercial chicken broth

3 small cloves garlic, smashed and peeled

1⅓ pounds (580 g) green Swiss chard, stemmed (stems reserved for another use), leaves roughly chopped

1 medium bunch cilantro, coarsely chopped

1 tablespoon fresh lemon juice

Kosher salt, to taste

Freshly ground black pepper, to taste

IN A MEDIUM SAUCEPAN, heat the olive oil, paprika, and cumin over low heat, stirring, until the spices are aromatic, 2 to 4 minutes. Stir in the scallion whites. Cook until wilted, about 5 minutes.

Stir in the lentils, stock, and garlic. Bring to a boil. Lower the heat and simmer for 20 to 30 minutes, or until the lentils are almost done.

Stir in the scallion greens, chard, cilantro, and lemon juice. Simmer for 5 to 10 minutes, until the chard is cooked through and the lentils are soft. Season with salt, if necessary, and pepper.

MAKES 8 CUPS (2 L); 8 FIRST-COURSE SERVINGS OR 4 MAIN-COURSE SERVINGS

clove-scented
LENTIL PURÉE

PURÉED AND WITH orange flecks of carrot and the somewhat unexpected addition of cloves, this is about as elegant as lentils get.

The pork belly can be ordered through a butcher, if unavailable at the supermarket. The puréeing of the soup may take a little longer than expected—probably a few minutes—the lentils should be really smooth.

½ pound (225 g) pork belly (uncured bacon), skin (rind) removed
and reserved, meat cut into ¼-inch (.5-cm) dice

2 medium onions, coarsely chopped

4 medium cloves garlic, smashed and peeled

1 pound (450 g) brown lentils

3 sprigs thyme

1 bay leaf

2 small carrots, peeled and cut in half lengthwise, then across
into ¼-inch (.5-cm) slices

⅛ teaspoon ground cloves

4 teaspoons kosher salt, or to taste

1 tablespoon good olive oil

PLACE THE SKIN OF THE PORK BELLY in a medium saucepan. Add the onions, garlic, lentils, and 9 cups (2.25 l) water. Tie the thyme and bay leaf together and add to the pan. Bring to a boil. Lower the heat and simmer for 40 minutes.

While the lentils are cooking, in a medium saucepan, cook the pork belly cubes over medium heat, stirring occasionally, until the fat has rendered and the pork pieces are brown and crisp, 20 to 30 minutes. With a slotted spoon, remove the pork and drain on paper towels.

Stir the carrots into the fat. Lower the heat and cook, stirring occasionally, for 15 minutes, or until the carrots are tender.

When the lentils are done, drain them in a sieve; reserve the liquid. Discard the pork belly skin. In a food processor, purée the lentils, with a little of the cooking liquid. Whisk the purée into the remaining cooking liquid.

Stir the soup into the carrots and return to a boil. Lower the heat. Stir in the cloves and salt. Remove from the heat and stir in the olive oil and the crisp pork pieces.

MAKES 9 CUPS (2.25 L); 8 FIRST-COURSE SERVINGS

lentil soup

FROM ECUADOR

A ROBUST SOUP for a winter's night.

½ cup (90 g) brown lentils
2 teaspoons very finely chopped onion
1 medium clove garlic, smashed, peeled, and minced
¾ teaspoon Annatto Butter (page 445)
1 small tomato, peeled and cut into ½-inch (1-cm) cubes
⅛ teaspoon dried oregano
⅛ teaspoon ground cumin
½ pound (225 g) firm potatoes, peeled and cut into ½-inch (1-cm) cubes
2 green cabbage leaves, cut into 1½-inch (4-cm) squares
2 teaspoons chopped cilantro
½ teaspoon Aliño (page 444), plus additional, if desired, to pass with soup
1 teaspoon kosher salt
Freshly ground black pepper, to taste

IN A MEDIUM SAUCEPAN, stir together the lentils, 3 cups (750 ml) water, the onion, garlic, annatto butter, tomato, oregano, and cumin. Bring to a boil. Lower the heat and simmer, covered, for 25 minutes, or until the lentils are tender.

Stir in the remaining ingredients. Cover. Simmer until the potatoes are tender, about 20 minutes.

If desired, pass additional aliño on the side.

MAKES 4 CUPS (1 L); 4 FIRST-COURSE SERVINGS

Ecuadorian soups

EACH REGION OF ECUADOR has its own soups, ample and wonderfully varied. They are often accompanied by a wide assortment of sauces and vegetables, raw and cooked, to mix in at will. These soups are the national dishes of Ecuador and at the heart of almost every meal, as a main course, as a substantial opener to be followed by the simplest of dishes, or as the whole meal. These soups are the nostalgia of every Ecuadorian away from home, the hallmark of mother's cooking, the carriers of past tradition, local custom, and flavors and steam-wafted aromas of foods locally grown. Flavorings are discreet. This is not the home of the palate-numbing blast of hot pepper or the soup green with coriander.

My favorite Ecuadorian soups come from the gorgeous volcano-cone-accented highlands that stretch north from Quito into the Andes. They are the inventions of Inca peoples, although influenced by techniques and ingredients introduced by the Spanish. I tasted them and acquired the basic recipes in homes, restaurants, inns, and, best of all in local open-air markets offering potatoes (see page 92). These potatoes are among the starches—beans, corn, and grains—that form the base of the soups. Along the coast, soups are often seafood-based.

Inland, as people have become richer, so have many of the soups, coming to include meat stocks, lard, and bits of meats. Even so, these soup meals are a healthier, less-expensive way of eating than basing the bulk of the meal on meat. I find a chicken or pork stock base unnecessary and prefer the more old-fashioned, healthful versions that allow the incredible variety of starch and vegetable flavors to sing through.

In the open-air market, stalls are made with planks and hold great pots of simmering soup. The plank tables are set with an array of condiments and a selection of things to add to one's bowl of soup: sliced peeled avocados, thinly sliced lettuce, cilantro, boiled eggs, sauces (pages 441–443), white cheese, and even whole boiled potatoes and shredded chicken.

The soups are served in pretty much the same way in restaurants and homes. Sometimes the soups will come with the added ingredients already in the individual bowls, and sometimes these will be in the middle of the table, along with bowls of salsas, and perhaps, aliño.

The cheese and milk are a post-Spanish addition to simple Incan soups, but I use them, as they make for a balanced meal. It is possible to substitute soft mozzarella for the fresh white cheese used in Ecuador. Almost all of the remaining ingredients are indigenous to the Andes.

The starting point for almost all of the soups is a *refrito*—a recipe element of chopped and sautéed vegetables common in Spain and Italy. The refrito can vary not only from country to country and region to region, but from one cook to another as well. Annatto (achiote) seeds are sautéed in fat to give a mellow background flavor and a pronounced orange-red color. Then onions and various other aromatic herbs or vegetables are added and cooked slowly to make a splendid base for the recipe. The color is soft, the flavor rich but integral to the dish.

The usual fat, of which little is used, mainly for sautéing the annatto, is lard. I replace it with butter, which seems to make almost no difference in the flavor and extracts a more intense color. Use land if desired; or use canola oil in a search for greater healthfulness, but the color will be less intense. The sautéed annatto will keep indefinitely in the refrigerator, as will the other soup condiments: criolla sauce, a spicy red sauce added individually at the table to bean, lentil, and cheese soups and also served with boiled meats, empanadas, and tamales and sopped on bread; pickled onions, served alongside potato and chicken soups, as well as with fried fish, chicken, and plantain dishes; aliño, a black-pepper-and-garlic-based seasoning also used in meat fillings for empanadas and as a dry marinade on meat and fish; and tamarillo sauce, a divine purplish-red, mildly spicy concoction that I can happily eat on vegetables and can even imagine it on hamburgers. A few sprigs of fresh coriander—stems (which have a separate musky flavor) and leaves—are added to many soups at the end of the cooking—again, not to assert their presence, but to lend a unifying perfume.

Quinoa has only become readily available in our markets in recent years. Even today, you may have to look in health food stores to find this extremely healthful Andes native. The quinoa we can buy is, however, cleaner than that found in Ecuadorian markets and doesn't have to be picked over for pebbles. It is washed at home not because it is dirty, but because the grains are coated in a bitter soapy substance, saponin. Nature provides it as a protection for the grain.

The pumpkin used in the Andes is a winter squash with bright orange flesh that gives the soups a fabulous color. I use the French pumpkin that has deep lobes and is flattish, the kind shown being changed into a coach in illustrations of *Cinderella*. A West Indian calabaza or Hubbard or crookneck can be used. The soup made with pumpkin, incidentally, is beautiful and one of my showpieces. Lupine beans, called *chochos* (the famous Roman *lupinas*), are widely used, but hard to find in North

America. I substitute favas (broad) or lima beans, as do most Ecuadorians away from the Andes. Epazote, sometimes called wormseed, is also used as a seasoning. I, unlike the local children, do not like it.

Hominy, lentils, and plantains are other starchy vegetables that vary these soups. Don't be afraid that the soups will be bland. They have rich, intriguing flavors, a variety of textures, and a warm and wonderful hominess. Some, such as the Thick Potato Soup with Pumpkin (page 107) and the locra, Thick Potato Soup with Favas (page 296), are brilliantly colored. They, as well as the Cheese and Potato Soup (page 112), with its numerous additions for serving, would work splendidly at a buffet party. Serve the soup from the pot in large bowls. Add nothing to the meal other than extra condiments, bread, salad, fruit for dessert, and beer or Chilean red wine (which is widely available in Ecuador). The soups made with slices of cooked corncob may be served by fishing them out and putting them on a separate dish for more squeamish friends who don't want to fish with their fingers. Do cook them in the soup, however, as they add sweetness and flavor as well as color and drama.

Tamarillos may be unfamiliar. They are becoming available and are used in the cooking of the U.S. Southwest. In Ecuador, where they were cultivated by the Incas, they are called *tomate de árbol* and are made into a divine concoction that I have enjoyed not only stirred into these soups, but also with vegetables, meats, and fish. Today, they are farmed in India, Indonesia, and New Zealand. They grow thickly in bunches on low trees and can be red or yellow (both taste the same), but I almost always saw red ones in Ecuador. I prefer the red because of the beautiful color they give to the sauces. The flavor is a marvelous bittersweet mix of tart and sweet, with an appetite-awakening perfume. The fruit is egg-shaped, glossy, and roughly three inches long. The flesh is yellow. Cooking tamarillos gives them an intense purplish-red color. Putting them through a food mill removes the seeds and any hard bits of skin. Ecuadorians sieve them. Ecuadorians also use these plum-like fruits for juice, in dessert, and for marmalade. Since their season is limited, Tomato Plum Sauce (page 442) can be used instead.

These soups are advantageous in that they can be made ahead. Slightly undercook the ones with potatoes-meant-to-stay-firm so that they don't get soggy with reheating.

chick pea soup

THIS RECIPE IS A VARIATION on a southern Spanish theme. Chick peas are extremely nourishing and can be substituted for beans or pasta in many soups. They would be particularly good in Chicken Soup with Pastina and Greens (page 125).

If cooking the chick peas from scratch, save the liquid and use it to replace the water in the recipe.

1 medium onion, cut into chunks

12 medium cloves garlic, smashed and peeled

½ medium bunch parsley, leaves and about 1 inch (2.5 cm) of stems only

¼ cup (65 ml) olive oil

1 tablespoon paprika

1 medium-to-large very ripe tomato, peeled and coarsely chopped; or ¾ cup (180 ml) Chunky Tomato Base (page 385), drained and coarsely chopped canned tomatoes (not plum), or sterile-pack chopped tomatoes

Two ¼ × 2-inch (1 × 5-cm) strips of lemon zest

Two ¼ × 2-inch (1×5-cm) strips of orange zest

2 bay leaves

2 cups (360 g) cooked chick peas (see page 294) or drained and rinsed canned chick peas

2 teaspoons fennel seed

2 teaspoons kosher salt

Freshly ground black pepper, to taste

IN A FOOD PROCESSOR, pulse the onion, garlic, and parsley until chopped medium-fine.

In a medium stockpot, heat the oil over medium-high heat until it is shimmering. Stir in the onion mixture. Cook, stirring, for 5 minutes. Stir in the paprika and cook for 1 more minute.

Stir in 2 cups (500 ml) water, the tomato, lemon and orange zest, and the bay leaves. Bring to a boil. Lower the heat and simmer for 5 minutes. Stir in the chick peas. Bring to a boil, lower the heat, and simmer for 30 minutes.

Stir in the fennel seed and simmer for 5 minutes. Season with the salt and pepper. Stir in enough water to make 5½ cups (1.4 l), about 3 cups (750 ml). Heat through before serving.

MAKES 5½ CUPS (1.4 L); 4 FIRST-COURSE SERVINGS

Tamarind

THIS LARGE TREE, probably native to Africa but much cultivated in India, bears large brown leguminous seed pods that contain a sticky pulp surrounding large seeds. The pulp, with seeds, is sold in Indian and Pakistani shops. To get at the pulp, it is necessary to soak it in hot water and then put it through a sieve, extracting as much juice and pulp as possible and leaving the seeds behind.

The pulpy liquid is acidic. This acid does not break down with prolonged cooking and is thus very suitable for typically long-cooking Indian dishes that complement their complex spice flavorings with acid.

namita panjabi's rasam
CORIANDER SOUP

UNTIL RECENTLY, I had never had rasam, a spicy soup that became addictive as I sipped it. It is a favorite in India. I tasted it at the venerable Veerswami Restaurant in London, which has recently been taken over and refurbished—visually, culinarily, and spiritually—by Namita Panjabi, who kindly sent the recipe.

When I first made it, I got scared when I got to the part of the recipe that Namita calls "tempering." The soup seemed too hot to need anything more. However, I have great faith in her and I plunged ahead. To my surprise the soup got rounder rather than hotter.

The spiciness of the soup can be increased or decreased by the chili peppers used. I used two small green Thai chilies (very hot) and two medium-sized green chilies of medium hotness. Reserve the cooked dal for Dal Soup (page 326).

The asafetida ("foetid [nasty] smell") acts the way ambergris does in perfume, as a stabilizer and blender of aromas and flavors. It is an essential element of Indian cooking.

1⅓ cups (300 g) dried toor dal (small yellow split peas) or 8 cups (2 l) dal cooking liquid reserved from Dal Soup (page 326)

1 tablespoon black peppercorns

2 teaspoons cumin seed

2 teaspoons coriander seed

2 teaspoons crumbled dried hot red pepper

½ teaspoon fenugreek seed

8 medium cloves garlic, smashed and peeled

One 6-inch (15-cm) piece ginger (about 4 ounces; 120 g), peeled and cut into 20 quarter-sized pieces

10 fresh curry (kari) leaves; or 10 dried curry leaves, simmered for 1 minute in water and drained

8 fresh green chilies, stemmed and seeded if desired, for less heat

2 medium bunches cilantro, leaves and stems, coarsely chopped

¼ cup (65 ml) tamarind pulp

¼ cup (65 ml) vegetable or canola oil

4 medium tomatoes, cored and quartered

½ teaspoon turmeric

A large pinch of asafetida

4 teaspoons kosher salt

2 teaspoons sugar

    1 tablespoon cumin seed

    1 tablespoon mustard seed

    4 small dried hot red peppers, crumbled

    2 tablespoons coriander seed

    2 tablespoons vegetable or canola oil

About ½ cup (20 g) coarsely chopped cilantro, for serving

IF STARTING WITH DRIED DAL, in a medium stockpot, bring the dal to a boil with 4 quarts (4 l) water. Skim any foam that rises to the surface. Lower the heat and simmer for 30 minutes, or until soft. Remove from the heat and let sit for 15 minutes. Drain in a sieve. Reserve 8 cups (2 l) of the liquid for this soup, and the cooked dal, about 3 cups (750 ml), for Dal Soup (page 326).

In a spice mill, coarsely grind the peppercorns, cumin seed, coriander seed, crumbled hot red pepper, and fenugreek. Set aside.

In a food processor, coarsely chop the garlic, ginger, curry leaves, and fresh green chilies. Add the cilantro and continue to process, stopping a few times to scrape down the sides of the bowl, until puréed.

Pour ¾ cup (180 ml) plus 2 tablespoons very hot water over the tamarind and let sit for 15 minutes. Mash the pulp with fingers. Pour the liquid through a strainer, pressing down on the solids to squeeze out as much juice as possible. Discard the seeds and skin. There should be about 5 tablespoons juice. Set aside.

In a medium saucepan, heat the oil over medium heat. Stir in the dried spice mix and cook until sizzling, about 20 seconds. Stir in the cilantro purée and cook, stirring, for 3 minutes. Stir in the tomatoes and cook, stirring, especially at the beginning, for 10 minutes; enough liquid should have come out of the tomatoes at this point to prevent sticking. Cover the pot and cook for 5 more minutes, until the tomatoes have completely collapsed. Stir in the turmeric and cook for 30 seconds. Stir in the tamarind juice and the asafetida.

Stir the 8 cups (2 l) dal cooking liquid into the tomato mixture. Bring to a boil. Lower the heat and simmer for 10 minutes. Strain the soup through a very fine sieve or a cheesecloth-lined sieve and add enough water to make 8 cups (2 l); discard the solids. Stir in the salt and sugar. The soup can be made ahead to this point and refrigerated for 3 days.

For the tempering mixture, in a spice mill, grind the cumin seed, mustard seed, hot red peppers, and coriander seed until fine. In a small saucepan, heat the oil over medium heat. Stir in the spice mix. Cook, stirring, for 2 minutes.

When it's time to serve the soup, bring to a boil. Remove from the heat and stir in the tempering ingredients and the cilantro.

MAKES 8 CUPS (2 L); 8 FIRST-COURSE SERVING

dal soup

DAL, COOKED AND SEMIPURÉED PULSES, such as lentils, split peas, and the like, are a part of most Indian meals, serving as condiments or soothers, depending on their spicing. In combination with rice, they make for substantial nutrition.

I thought that dal would make a very good soup. I decided to use toor dal, a sort of small yellow split pea, to make the soup, as I had just gotten Namita Panjabi's recipe for the rasam (page 324) I had had at her restaurant. In that recipe, the dal are cooked and only the liquid used. I suspect that the rasam soup originated as a way of using up the savory liquid from cooking the pulses.

If not making the rasam, use some of the cooking liquid to replace the water in this recipe. If desired, this recipe can be halved. The degree of spice is decided by the choice of green chilies. The curry leaves and mustard seeds, which are mild and aromatic, can be found in Asian markets.

1⅓ cups (300 g) dried toor dal (small yellow split peas) or 3 cups cooked dal,
    reserved from making Namita Panjabi's Rasam (page 324)

4 tablespoons tamarind pulp

2 tablespoons (30 g) unsalted butter

4 medium onions, thinly sliced

2 medium cloves garlic, smashed and peeled

½ teaspoon turmeric

14 medium tomatoes, cored and cut into ¾-inch (1.9-cm) cubes

6 small green chilies, stemmed

1 tablespoon kosher salt

2 tablespoons vegetable or canola oil

2 teaspoons black mustard seeds

4 small dried hot red peppers, crumbled

10 dried curry (kari) leaves

IF STARTING WITH DRIED DAL, in a medium stockpot, bring the dal to a boil with 4 quarts (4 l) water. Skim any foam that rises to the surface. Lower the heat and simmer for 30 minutes, or until soft. Remove from the heat and let sit for 15 minutes. Drain in a sieve. Reserve all the cooking liquid, about 8 cups (2 l), for Namita Panjabi's Rasam (page 324); or reserve 3 cups (750 ml) of the liquid for this recipe and discard the rest. Reserve the cooked dal separately.

Meanwhile, in a small bowl, pour ¾ cup (180 ml) very hot water over the tamarind and let sit for 15 minutes. Mash the pulp with fingers. Pour the liquid through a strainer, pressing down on the solids to squeeze out as much juice as possible. Discard the seeds and skin. There should be about ¼ cup juice. Set aside.

In a medium stockpot, melt the butter over medium heat. Stir in the onions, garlic, and turmeric. Cook, stirring, for 6 minutes. Stir in the tomatoes, fresh chilies, 3 cups (750 ml) water or reserved dal cooking liquid, the salt, and 3 tablespoons tamarind juice. Bring to a boil. Lower the heat and simmer, stirring occasionally, for 25 minutes, or until the tomatoes have collapsed.

Stir the cooked dal into the tomatoes. Pass through the fine disc of a food mill; or, in a food processor, working in batches, purée the soup and pass through a fine sieve, pressing down to extract as much of the liquid and solids as possible while removing the tomato skins. Return to the pan.

In a small frying pan, heat the oil over medium heat. Add the mustard seeds and cook until they start to turn gray. Stir in the dried chilies and curry leaves. Cook, stirring, for 30 seconds. Remove from the heat and carefully—there will probably be some splattering when the soup hits the hot pan—stir a little of the soup into the pan. Stir this mixture into the rest of the soup. Bring to a boil. Lower the heat and let simmer for 5 minutes. Remove from the heat and let sit for 15 minutes to allow the flavors to blend.

Return the soup to the stove and heat through. If desired, stir in the remaining tamarind juice.

MAKES 12 CUPS (3 L); 12 FIRST-COURSE SERVINGS

Grain soups

We tend to think of grains as the staples of life: in black, white, gold, and yellow breads, flat and round; in bowls of rice, brown and white; as mamaliga and polenta and as breakfast cereal. Gruels and paps, the Roman soldier's polenta made from millet or spelt, and Scotch oatmeal are basic and sustaining at the beginning and end of life and all through it.

Soups are thinner gruels but with oomph and flavor. Grains are often a major component of them as well.

shredded chicken and ginger congee

NATHAN FONG'S MOTHER'S

NATHAN FONG, a delightful man from Vancouver, is a cook, food stylist, and television personality. Unlike many other food people, such as myself, he was fortunate in having a mother who is a wonderful cook. When I explained to him that I was looking for a truly sensational congee, like the good son and friend that he is, he said his mother's was the best and offered it to me.

As a Cantonese, she is a user of dried fish and seafood. The dried scallops (available in Chinatowns) give a very special flavor. The fresh scallops are less pungent and original, but quite satisfactory.

Although congee recipes usually start with raw rice, as does this one, congee—a breakfast soup that is relatively bland and comforting—seems to me to be the Chinese equivalent of hash. Instead of using up leftover potatoes, they use up leftover rice, which dinner will almost always provide. Oddly enough, using leftover rice does not decisively shorten the cooking time.

¾ cup (150 g) raw long-grain white rice, or 1½ cups (225 g) left over from dinner
1 tablespoon plus ½ teaspoon kosher salt
½ cup (125 ml) plus 2 tablespoons vegetable oil

10 cups (2.5 l) Basic Chicken Stock (page 345) or commercial chicken broth

1 medium skinless boneless chicken breast

1 tablespoon hair-thin strips peeled ginger plus 3 tablespoons very finely chopped peeled ginger

4 large dried scallops (1 ounce; 30 g) or 8 large sea scallops (½ pound; 225 g)

½ ounce (15 g) dried shiitake mushrooms

3 medium scallions, thinly sliced across

½ teaspoon hot red pepper flakes, optional

for serving

½ cup (90 g) dry-roasted peanuts, coarsely chopped

12 cilantro sprigs

Soy sauce

Toasted sesame oil

Freshly ground white pepper

IN A SMALL BOWL, cover the rice with cold water. Add 1 tablespoon salt and 2 tablespoons vegetable oil. Allow to sit at room temperature for 8 hours, or overnight.

In a medium saucepan, bring the stock to a boil with the chicken breast, ginger strips, and the dried scallops, if using. Lower the heat and simmer for 10 minutes, or until the chicken is cooked through. Remove the chicken and allow to cool slightly. If using the dried scallops, continue cooking for 30 minutes, or until the scallops are soft.

If using the fresh scallops, add them to the stock now and simmer for 5 minutes. Remove the scallops.

Add the soaked rice, with its liquid, to the broth and bring to a boil. Lower the heat and simmer very gently, covered and stirring frequently, for 4 hours, or until the rice is very soft and falling apart, almost like a purée.

Meanwhile, soak the dried mushrooms in 1 cup (250 ml) hot water for 15 minutes. Drain. Remove the mushroom stems and cut the caps across into thin strips.

Stir the shredded chicken, the scallops, and mushrooms into the congee. Cover and simmer, stirring occasionally, for 30 more minutes.

Meanwhile, in a food processor or blender, purée the very finely chopped ginger, the scallions, the remaining salt, and oil, and the red pepper flakes.

Ladle the congee into bowls and drizzle with the purée. Top with the chopped peanuts and cilantro. Season with soy sauce, sesame oil, and white pepper.

MAKES ABOUT 8 CUPS (2 L); 8 FIRST-COURSE SERVINGS

spelt and lentil soup

PIERO SELVAGGIO has a fabulous restaurant in Los Angeles called Valentino. I try to get there when I am out west. One night, I was there on Mother's Day. In the next room, a private one, was a party that turned out to be made up of Piero and his wife, their children, and his mother, as well as the same complement for Wolfgang Puck. Their happiness was the best memory of the evening. The next best was the following soup. Piero kindly sent me the recipe, with his comments:

This is Roman poverty cooking at its plainest. Use the smallest lentils you can find; keep both lentils and farro warm at all times (if they get cool, they get starchy); and if you need to add more water to the soup, make sure it is boiling before you add it. Farro, or spelt, is available at better Italian groceries, but if you can't find it you can get much the same effect with wheat berries from the health food store.

Lentilles vertes de Puys are the best quality of lentils available. Spelt is available half-peeled as well as integral (whole). The half-peeled will look striped and take less time to cook. If using it or wheat berries or farro, see page 293. This soup can be made only a short while ahead and must be kept warm. See Piero's comments.

4 teaspoons kosher salt

1 cup (210 g) spelt, wheat berries, or farro

1 small carrot, peeled and cut across into 2 pieces

1 large rib celery, cut across into 2 pieces

1 small bay leaf

1⅓ cups (360 g) small green or brown lentils, rinsed and drained

3 tablespoons olive oil

1 medium shallot, cut into ¼-inch (.5-cm) dice

2 small garlic cloves, smashed and peeled

3 medium plum tomatoes, peeled and cut into ¼-inch (.5-cm) dice

¼ teaspoon hot red pepper flakes

Freshly ground black pepper, to taste

Coarsely ground black pepper, to taste, for serving

Very good olive oil, for serving

IN A MEDIUM SAUCEPAN, bring 4 cups (1 l) water and ¼ teaspoon salt to a boil. Stir in the spelt. Return to a boil. Lower the heat and simmer, partially covered, for 40 minutes to 1 hour, or until the spelt is almost done but retains some crunch. Most of the liquid will have been absorbed. Set aside and keep warm.

Meanwhile, in a medium saucepan, bring the carrot, celery, bay leaf, and 5½ cups (1.3 l) water to a boil. Stir in the lentils and ¼ teaspoon salt. Return to a boil. Lower the heat and simmer, partially covered, for about 15 minutes, or until the lentils are beginning to soften. Set aside and cover to keep warm, so they don't become gummy.

While the spelt and lentils are cooking, in a medium stockpot, cook the oil, shallot, garlic, tomatoes, and red pepper flakes over medium heat for about 5 minutes, or until the tomatoes begin to soften.

Remove the carrot, celery, and bay leaf from the lentils and discard them. Stir the lentils and their liquid into the tomato mixture. Bring to a boil. Lower the heat and cook, stirring frequently, for 5 minutes. Stir in the spelt and any remaining liquid and simmer for 10 minutes. Remove the garlic cloves. Season with the remaining salt and pepper.

Ladle into soup plates and sprinkle with coarsely ground black pepper to taste. Top each with a thin stream of very good olive oil.

MAKES 10 CUPS (2.5 L); 8 TO 10 FIRST-COURSE SERVINGS

winter wheat soup

A SECOND VEGETARIAN WHEAT SOUP, this is well worth try-ing. The recipe calls for winter wheat berries, but it could just as easily be made with spelt. The cooking time difference is minimal. If cooked wheat berries or spelt are on hand, sim-ply add 9 cups (2.25 l) water to 2¾ cups (360 g) cooked berries and continue from there.

1 cup (210 g) wheat berries or spelt

1 large carrot, peeled, halved lengthwise, and cut across into thin slices

2 medium parsnips, peeled, cut in half lengthwise and then across into ¼-inch (.5-cm) slices

1 medium turnip, peeled and cut into thin wedges

2 large leeks, white part only, split in half lengthwise, washed well, and cut across into thin slices

1 medium sweet potato, peeled and cut into ½-inch (1-cm) cubes

3 medium ribs celery, peeled and cut across into thin slices

½ cup (40 g) celery leaves, coarsely chopped

2 tablespoons kosher salt

½ cup (10 g) cilantro leaves

Freshly ground black pepper, to taste

IN A MEDIUM STOCKPOT, bring the wheat berries and 13 cups (3.25 l) water to a boil. Lower the heat and simmer, partially covered, for 50 minutes, or until the wheat berries are almost cooked through, but not mushy.

Stir in the carrot, parsnips, turnip, and leeks. Return to a boil. Lower the heat and simmer, uncovered, for 10 minutes. Stir in the sweet potato and celery. Simmer for 10 more minutes.

Stir in the celery leaves and salt. Simmer for 1 minute. Add the cilantro and simmer for 1 minute. Season with pepper.

MAKES 13 CUPS (3.2 L); 6 MAIN-COURSE SERVINGS

mushroom barley soup

BARLEY IS AN ANCIENT GRAIN. This is a vegetarian barley soup—
no stock. Barley swells a lot as it sits. If not using the soup right away, use a third less barley.
For a richer soup, use mushroom broth to replace the water in this recipe.

> 8 cups (2 l) water or Mushroom Broth (page 383)
>
> ½ ounce (15 g) dried porcini mushrooms (cèpes)
>
> 1 cup (225 g) pearl barley
>
> 1 medium carrot, peeled and cut into ¼-inch (.5-cm) dice
>
> 2 small ribs celery, peeled and cut into ¼-inch (.5-cm) dice
>
> 1 tablespoon (15 g) unsalted butter
>
> 1 small onion, minced
>
> ¼ pound (120 g) white mushrooms, trimmed, wiped clean, and thinly sliced
>
> 3 medium cloves garlic, smashed, peeled, and minced
>
> 1 tablespoon coarsely chopped celery leaves
>
> ¼ cup (15 g) coarsely chopped dill
>
> 4 teaspoons kosher salt
>
> Freshly ground black pepper, to taste

IN A SMALL SAUCEPAN, bring 1 cup (250 ml) water or mushroom broth to a boil.
Pour it over the dried mushrooms. Soak for 15 minutes. Remove the mushrooms from the
water and squeeze out the excess liquid. Strain the soaking liquid through a fine-mesh
sieve. Reserve the mushrooms and liquid separately.

In a medium saucepan, bring the barley, carrot, celery, rehydrated mushrooms, and
remaining water or mushroom broth to a boil. Lower the heat and simmer, covered, for
30 minutes.

Meanwhile, in a medium frying pan, melt the butter over medium heat. Stir in the
onion. Cook, stirring occasionally, for 8 minutes, or until soft. Stir in the fresh mushrooms
and cook for 5 minutes. Remove the mushroom/onion mixture to a bowl.

Return the frying pan to the burner, pour the mushroom soaking liquid into the
pan, and raise the heat. Bring the liquid to a boil, stirring and scraping the bottom of the
pan with a wooden spoon to release any brown bits stuck there. Add with the mush-
room/onion mixture to the soup. Return to a boil. Lower the heat and simmer, covered,
for 10 minutes. Stir in the garlic. Simmer, covered, for 5 minutes. Remove from the heat,
stir in the remaining ingredients, and serve.

MAKES 8 CUPS (2 L); 6 FIRST-COURSE SERVINGS

quinoa soup

TO ME THIS IS the mother soup of Ecuador, extremely simple and surprisingly good.

for the refrito

2 tablespoons (30 g) unsalted butter

2 large onions, very finely chopped

5 large garlic cloves, smashed, peeled, and finely chopped

1 tablespoon Annatto Butter (page 445)

for the soup

1⅓ cups (240 g) quinoa, rinsed well in a sieve

1½ pounds (675 g) firm potatoes, peeled and cut into 1-inch (2.5-cm) cubes, optional

¾ pound (360 g) fried pork rinds, optional

2 cups (500 ml) milk

3 sprigs cilantro

2½ teaspoons kosher salt

Freshly ground black pepper, to taste

Ground Roasted Peanuts, optional (recipe follows)

FOR THE REFRITO, in a medium stockpot, melt the unsalted butter over low heat. Stir in the onions and garlic. Cook, stirring, for 10 minutes, or until the onions are soft and translucent. Stir in the annatto butter and allow to melt.

Stir in the quinoa, 8 cups (2 l) water, and, if using, the potatoes (if using the potatoes add an additional 2 cups [500 ml] water). Bring to a boil. Lower the heat and simmer for 30 minutes. If using the pork rinds, add them now. Either way, continue to simmer for another 30 minutes.

Stir in the milk, cilantro, salt, and pepper. If using the ground peanuts, add them now. Further reduce the heat and simmer, very gently, for 15 minutes.

MAKES ABOUT 14 CUPS (3.5 L); 8 TO 10 FIRST-COURSE SERVINGS
OR 4 TO 5 MAIN-COURSE SERVINGS

ground roasted peanuts

1 cup (120 g) shelled roasted peanuts, skins rubbed off

HEAT THE OVEN TO 375°F (190°C; gas mark #5; #5 British regulo).

In a shallow baking dish, toast the peanuts in the middle of the oven for 5 to 10 minutes, or until a shade darker, being careful not to burn them. Cool the peanuts completely.

In a food processor, pulse the peanuts until ground fine (do not grind to the point at which oil is released). Ground peanuts keep, covered tightly, for 3 weeks.

MAKES 1 CUP (250 ML)

oatmeal soup

WHEN I TOOK THE LINE from an old children's song as the title of this chapter, it occurred to me that I didn't have an oatmeal soup. I was sure that the Scots, with their love of oatmeal, must have one. I looked in Elizabeth Craig's *Hotch Potch*. I tinkered with the recipe a great deal, so blame it on me if you do not like what I find to be a very comforting soup. If making it ahead of time, slightly undercook the oats so they will be perfect when the soup is reheated.

1 tablespoon (15 g) unsalted butter

3 small carrots, peeled and finely chopped

1 medium leek, white part only, washed well and finely chopped

⅓ cup (60 g) steel-cut oats

3 cups (750 ml) Lamb Stock (page 361)

1 bay leaf

1 cup (250 ml) milk

2 teaspoons kosher salt

Freshly ground black pepper, to taste

3 tablespoons finely chopped parsley

IN A MEDIUM SAUCEPAN, melt the butter over medium heat. Stir in the carrots and leek. Cook, stirring, for 3 minutes. Stir in the oats. Cook, stirring, for 3 minutes.

Pour in the stock. Add the bay leaf and bring to a boil. Lower the heat and simmer very gently, covered, for 30 to 35 minutes, until the oats are very soft.

Stir in the milk, salt, pepper, and parsley. Return to a boil. Remove from the heat and let sit for 15 minutes to allow the flavors to mellow.

MAKES 5 CUPS (1.25 L); 4 FIRST-COURSE SERVINGS

hominy soup

HOMINY IS DRIED AND PROCESSED corn kernels. It is extensively used in posole in the American Southwest; it appears here in a final Ecuadorian soup.

3 tablespoons (45 g) unsalted butter

1 medium-to-large yellow onion, minced

12 cloves garlic, smashed, peeled, and coarsely chopped

1 teaspoon ground cumin

1 small red onion, minced

Two 30-ounce (850-g) cans hominy, drained and rinsed

1½ pounds (680 g) fresh cranberry beans, shelled

One 10-ounce (300 g) package frozen baby lima beans, defrosted in a sieve under cold running water and drained

Kernels from 6 ears corn

2 red bell peppers, cored, seeded, deribbed, and cut into ¼-inch (.5-cm) dice

2 tablespoons kosher salt

Freshly ground black pepper, to taste

6 sprigs cilantro

for serving

½ cup (20 g) coarsely chopped cilantro

Pickled Onions (page 446)

Tamarillo Sauce (page 441)

IN A TALL STOCKPOT, melt the butter over low heat. Stir in the yellow onions, garlic, and cumin. Cook, stirring, over low heat for 5 minutes, or until all the liquid has been absorbed.

Stir in the red onion, 5 cups (1.25 l) water, the hominy, and cranberry beans. Bring to a boil. Lower the heat and simmer, covered, for 20 minutes, or until the beans are cooked.

Stir in the lima beans, corn, bell peppers, salt, pepper, and the sprigs of cilantro. Simmer for 5 minutes.

Serve with bowls of the chopped cilantro, pickled onions, and tamarillo sauce.

MAKES 14 CUPS (3.5 L); 10 TO 12 FIRST-COURSE SERVINGS

The soul
of soup

THE HUMOR OF SOUP is essentially aqueous. This is the oldest idea of a humor, before blood, choler, phlegm, and melancholy and certainly before my preference, laughter. The soul of soup is liquid, water in some form. It may be actual water, stock, wine, milk, or the juice of fruit or vegetables or vegetable bases (pages 384–389). Those that need to be made before the soup is started are in this chapter. Having them stored in the freezer puts me in a good humor.

The chapter also has a lovely group of Gelled Gems, soups that, by and large, use the stocks and bases. They are on pages 367–379.

Whenever bones are available, they should be turned into stock or frozen to make stock at a later time. The stock can be frozen in usable quantities or into ice cubes, to be the base for soup or to drop into a stew or other dish.

When vegetables are in season, there is likely—think of zucchini—to be a surplus, or they will be cheaply available. This is the time to make the soup bases to be frozen and later add a taste of summer to winter soups and sauces.

Stocks

I LOVE THE *Oxford English Dictionary.* Its erudition and information are a never-ending source of comfort to me. The first set of it I ever had was given to me, on the occasion of my marriage, by a much older European gentleman who believed that I had the makings of a poet. That set was damaged in a flood. My current set was the gift of the man who loves me even though I am not a poet.

All this introduces my finding that *stock* is a wonderful word whose history implies the organization of clear liquids made from bone and flesh. *Stock* originally meant the trunk of a tree deprived of its branches and leaves. That is a culinary stock. *Stock* took on many derivative meanings: the root stock of vine plantings; the family line, as in "he came of fine stock."

Stock is not a soup. To be a soup, it requires seasoning and, perhaps, the addition of vegetables as a seasoning that is strained out or as an addition to be eaten. My stocks are made without vegetables so that they will not turn sour. Soup may call for a starch: noodles, dumplings, or rice. Stock is a base that makes the finished dish possible. My stocks are strong and nude of any ingredients other than bones and sometimes, as in Beef Stock (page 165), meat. They improve my soups and cooking in general.

A stock made with vegetables, flesh, herbs, and seasonings is a broth, a bouillon, a brühe, or a brodo—all the same word. The most ancient of these is the broth of the chicken or beef in the pot, the pot-au-feu, the bollito misto.

A consommé (which word also has the meaning in French of the English "consummate"—best) goes a step beyond these (not in virtue but in technique) because it is clarified. Finally, there is the double or triple consommé, what the French call the *consommé fort* and the Austrians and Germans *kraftbrühe.* For this, the original consommé or stock is used as the liquid in which fresh meat and bones and vegetables are cooked before the clarification. If the clarification uses meat as well as egg whites, we arrive at the triple consommé. This the most elegant of all the clear soups.

The same result cannot be achieved by simply doubling the amount of solids in the original amount of liquid. There will not be room in the pot unless the liquid is increased, which defeats the purpose.

I love consommé, but it seems to be disappearing. It used to be offered at any self-respecting formal dinner as the alternative to a cream soup. Chefs or Viennese housewives were judged by the quality of their consommé. A whole galaxy of things to put in clear soup evolved; for more of which, see page 391. All consommés will gel and can be served cold.

The basics of stock

Aside from Beef Stock (page 165), no meat is required to make these stocks, only bones. The bones may be purchased—usually cheaply—or may come from meat, poultry, or fish that has been previously cooked for a meal. Stock made from previously cooked foods will have a darker color and deeper flavor.

Extra bones of a sort different from the dominant may be added to increase the amount of gelatin in the stock. It is gelatin that gives much of the smooth silkiness on the tongue. Today, calf's knuckle is generally used. The calf's foot used in the past seems to me to give an unpleasantly strong taste of its own. If available, chicken or duck feet may be used for their respective stocks. Pig's foot or knuckle can also be used in meat stocks. In strongly flavored meat stocks, the skin (rind) of pork or cured pork such as bacon can be added.

When meat such as beef or chicken is used, the meat will be better if the liquid is boiling before it is added. The stock will be stronger if the meat is added to cold liquid.

Meat is generally added when it is desired for its own sake as part of the dish or as part of a meal, or for leftovers.

The process: A proper pot is important. See page xiv for a description of materials and sizes. Stockpots are generally about twice as tall as they are wide. This shape constantly forces the cooking liquid through and over the bones to get maximum extraction. The liquid should cover the solids by at least two inches. Better a pot that is taller than need be than one that is too small.

Temperature and timing: The liquid or the liquid and the bones (sometimes with meat) must come to a full boil. Unless the liquid has been seen to boil, it is almost impossible to know that it is at a high enough temperature. The heat should be reduced as indicated in the recipe so that the liquid just simmers—burps a bubble from time to time—or to an even lower heat so that the surface of the liquid shimmers and moves slightly.

After the liquid has boiled, there will often be a nasty scum, particularly when meat is being used, that rises to the top. It should be skimmed off. I use a slotted spoon.

My stocks cook for much longer than most people's, although it should be said that in large restaurant kitchens, stocks often cook all night. For those who are uncomfortable leaving the stove top on when they are out of the house or asleep, there are instructions for cooking the stock in the oven (also in an Aga from retained heat) after it has come to the boil or in a slow-cooker. (Slow-cookers do not have a very large capacity.)

Some stocks are cooked uncovered. This makes it easier to be sure that they do not come back to a boil. However, there will be more evaporation, and more water may need to be added from time to time. A lid can be left slightly askew so that there is less heat buildup and evaporation, or that invaluable Japanese utensil, the round wooden otoshi-buta with a handle, can float on the liquid, leaving enough of a margin around it so that the heat doesn't build up and the liquid doesn't evaporate.

There is a reason why it is so important that the liquid doesn't continue to boil. One of the main things that is happening as stock is made is that lots of gelatin is being extracted from the bones. If the liquid boils, the gelatin will bind—hold forever—in fat and solid, making a mess.

One of the ways to tell if the stock has cooked long enough—other than following the timing in a recipe—is to note when the bones come loose from each other. A chicken neck will separate into the smaller bones. Larger joints will come loose as well.

Browning: Bones, meat, and vegetables may be browned before being added to the stockpot. This is generally done in the oven. Browned ingredients add color and flavor to the finished stock. The ingredients should not be browned if a light-colored stock is desired.

Adding the vegetables: When vegetables are to be added depends somewhat on their purpose. If they are meant to be eaten as part of a soup meal, then they should not be cooked longer than will make them palatable. This, however, has nothing to do with the somewhat odd fad for crunchy vegetables that has sprung up in the last decades. Vegetables cooked in the stock will not only lend it their flavor, but will also absorb succulence from the stock. They should be added just to give them somewhat more than normal time to cook. Look at Minestrone (page 115) for an indication. Vegetables that are meant only to provide flavor but not to be eaten can cook for as much as an hour. They should not be added so early that they will cook long enough to give a grassy flavor to the stock. It is often better simply to simmer the vegetables as needed once the stock is made. That way the larger stock amount stays neutral in flavor and there is no risk of the stock's turning—fermenting—sour. Follow the recipes.

Vegetables that are purely an add-in should be cooked separately according to the information starting on page 448.

Skimming: While stock does not have to be skimmed continuously after the first skimming when it has come to a boil, occasional skimming is an aid to clear stock. Also, in cases where the fat is very strongly flavored (lamb, for instance), skimming will prevent that strong flavor from getting into the stock. After the stock has finished cooking, it should be allowed to sit for around twenty minutes, when a final skimming can take place.

If it is all possible, the stock should be refrigerated overnight. The fat will rise to the surface and harden, making it easier to remove. The sediment will settle to the bottom of the stock. It can be removed as well. I don't bother if I am using the stock for an earthy bean soup, but I do if I am making an elegant consommé. To separate the sediment from the bottom of liquid stock, spoon the clear stock from the top, leaving the sediment behind. If the stock has gelled, turn it out of its bowl and scrape off the sediment-laden layer. I tend to eat it. Clarification may remove it, but it is iffy.

Clarifying: Not all stock needs to be clarified, especially if it has simmered gently. For clear soups and consommés, it must be.

There are two ways to clarify stock. To clarify 1 quart, use ¼ pound (120 g) of ground meat, 3 egg whites and shells, and 1 small tomato, chopped. Stock can also be clarified without meat, using only the egg whites and shells and the tomato. The tomato provides a little bit of acid, which aids the clarification.

The liquid should be cool. Mix the meat, egg white and crushed shells, and tomato together. Whisk into the cool stock. Or add the egg whites, slightly whipped along with the tomato, to the cool stock.

Bring to a boil over medium heat, stirring frequently. As the liquid heats, the proteins will begin to coagulate and rise to the top, trapping the impurities that cloud the stock. A solid-looking mass, known as the raft, will begin to form on top of the liquid; when this happens, stop stirring.

When the liquid reaches a boil, it will foam up around the edges of the raft, which will begin to fold over. As soon as this happens, turn the heat way down.

At this point, the liquid should be almost clear. Poke a hole in center of the raft so the liquid is visible. The heat should be so low that the liquid is barely moving.

When the meat/egg white/tomato way is being used, the stock can simmer for up to 45 minutes, but I usually simmer it for about 20 minutes, allowing the flavor from the ground meat to infuse the stock. When just egg whites and tomato are used to clarify—if the stock is allowed to simmer too long—the egg whites will begin to leach out some of the flavor from the broth. Simmer long enough to clarify, but not so long that flavor is lost, 5 to 10 minutes.

Any particles that were still floating around in the soup when it came to a boil will become attached to the raft and the soup beneath will be crystal-clear.

Aromatics such as pepper, thyme, garlic, or minced carrot and celery can be added to the ground meat/egg white/tomato mixture. This will impart additional flavor. Do not add pepper after clarifying, or there will be nasty specks in the beauty.

When the liquid has finished simmering, carefully ladle the soup out of the pot and strain through a damp-cloth–lined sieve, leaving the solids behind. If there are particles floating in the soup, strain again, through a coffee filter rinsed in hot water.

Season with kosher salt.

There is another method that I don't use, but which was brought to my attention by Michael Batterberry. The method, which uses egg whites only, appears in *Northern Italian Cooking* by Francesco Ghedini. His book certainly shows that Italian brodo is as good as French bouillon.

Use 4 egg whites for 2 quarts (2 l) of stock. With a wire whisk, beat 1½ cups (375 ml) of the broth with the egg whites in a very clean large bowl. Bring the rest of the stock to a boil in a medium saucepan. Then, continually whisking the egg white mixture, gradually pour the boiling broth into it in a very thin stream. Return the mixture to the saucepan and set over moderate heat until it barely reaches a simmer, continually stirring it slowly with the wire whisk so that egg whites constantly circulate. As soon as the liquid begins to simmer, stop stirring. The egg whites will mount to the surface. Reduce the heat even further, so that the liquid no longer simmers, and cook for another 10 minutes. Strain as above.

Storing stock: Stock should always be refrigerated. It is a perfect growing medium for bacteria and should not be left at room temperature for any period of time. Stocks made with vegetables can sour quickly, particularly in summer. They should be refrigerated as soon as possible.

Stock can be refrigerated for up to three days. To keep it for a longer time, it should be frozen, tightly covered, for up to six months. Be sure to label stock that is frozen. One will look much like another, and a disaster can take place if fish stock is added to a chicken soup. Freeze in small amounts so it is easy to make soup as desired.

Bird stocks

For many people the world over, these are what make possible what is meant by soup.

basic chicken stock

ONE OF THE SAD REALITIES of contemporary life is the almost total unavailability of fowls, aged birds of substantial size that are tough but full of flavor and lots of enriching gelatin in the bones. Today's birds are slaughtered young, before they start producing thin-shelled eggs with double yolks. Those of us who are women can sympathize—osteoporosis and lessened fertility.

The live-poultry markets of the past are disappearing. However, Asian markets will often sell chicken feet that can be added to the other bones to enrich the stock. There is very little point in using (wasting) chicken meat to make stock unless the chicken is wanted for the soup or another purpose such as salad. See Stock from a Whole Chicken (page 348). Many supermarkets sell backs and necks, or chicken wings can be used—see Jean-Georges's Chicken Stock (page 351). I keep a plastic bag in the freezer and throw in odds and ends of unused chicken parts—necks and wing tips—until I have enough to make stock. Hearts and gizzards can be used; livers cannot.

As I roast chicken frequently, I break up the carcass after everyone has eaten and add it, along with any gizzards, hearts, and bones from the plates to my bag or to my pot. Stock made with bones from a roast will have a somewhat darker, deeper flavor; I don't bother to roast fresh parts or bones when I get them. I simply cover them with water and proceed as in this recipe.

Extra-Rich Chicken Stock (page 340) is just that, and it is also more gelatinous. It is the stock that should be used for gelled soups (pages 367–379) unless gelatin is to be added to the stock. Light or Chinese-style chicken stock can be found on page 144, or use Jean-Georges's.

For Roasted Chicken Stock, use the bones left over from roasting a chicken, cover with water, and simmer until the bones fall apart. The bones from one 5-pound (2.25-kg) chicken will make about 6 cups (1.5 l) stock. Even though the stocks made in the oven and in the slow-cooker cook for more than twice as long as stock made on the stove, the gelling quality and flavor are the same. This is due to the gentle cooking methods, which extract flavor and gelatin at a slower rate.

Any of these stocks needs only seasoning and the vegetable(s) of choice, a starch such as rice or noodles, or an herb—dill is always good with chicken—to be a soup. Look at pages 390–431 for these add-ins, as well as dumplings such as matzo balls and filled pastas, wontons included. If using a slow-cooker, use only half the quantities listed.

5 pounds (2.25 kg) chicken backs and necks
12 cups (3 l) water

TO MAKE THE STOCK on top of the stove, in a tall narrow stockpot, bring the bones and water to a boil. Skim the fat. Lower the heat and simmer gently, so bubbles are barely breaking the surface of the liquid, for at least 4 hours and up to 12; add water as needed to keep the bones covered. Skim as necessary to remove as much fat as possible. If the pot is covered with an otoshi-buta (page xii) or a lid slightly ajar, there will be less evaporation.

To make the stock in the oven, place a rack on the lowest level of the oven and heat the oven to 250°F (121°C; gas mark #½; #½ British regulo).

In a tall narrow stockpot, bring the bones and water to a boil. Skim the fat. Place in the oven for 4 hours; add water if needed. Remove and skim the fat. Return to the oven for at least 5 hours and up to 8.

To make the stock in a slow-cooker, start with 2½ pounds (1.1 kg) bones and 6 cups (1.5 l) water for a 4-quart (4-l) cooker. Place the bones in the slow-cooker and pour the water over. Cover and turn the heat on low. Cook for 11 to 12 hours.

In all methods, the bones will be falling apart when the stock is done.

Strain the stock through a fine-mesh sieve. Skim fat. Cool to room temperature. Refrigerate for 3 hours.

Remove the fat from the top of the stock and the sediment from the bottom (see page 342). Use immediately, or refrigerate for up to 3 days or freeze.

MAKES 10 CUPS (2.5 L) ON TOP OF THE STOVE, 8 CUPS (2 L) IN THE OVEN,
6 CUPS (1.5 L) IN A SLOW-COOKER

fake chicken stock

THERE ARE TIMES when I want a stock, don't have any on hand, and don't have time to make a real one, but have a little time to do something a bit better than just open a can or dissolve a stock cube in water. This is better.

1 large can (6 cups; 1.5 l) commercial chicken broth or 6 cups (1.5 l) water with the appropriate number of stock cubes

1 pound (450 g) chicken bones, backs, necks, or wings, or a combination

1 large yellow onion, skin on, quartered

2 packages (18 g) gelatin

IN A MEDIUM SAUCEPAN, bring the broth, bones, and onion to a boil. Lower the heat slightly. Cook at a low boil for 30 minutes.

Strain through a fine-mesh sieve, pressing down on the solids to extract as much liquid as possible. Skim the fat. Return the broth to the saucepan.

Sprinkle the gelatin over ½ cup (125 ml) cold water and let sit for 2 minutes. With a rubber spatula, scrape the gelatin into the broth. Heat the broth over medium heat, stirring, until the gelatin is completely dissolved.

MAKES 5 CUPS (1.25 L)

stock

SOMETIMES POACHED CHICKEN is desired, either for soup or for salad or another dish. The chicken can be cooked whole or in pieces. The skin can be removed if desired.

The chicken or fowl will yield about 1¾ pounds (780 g) meat. This is about 3 cups torn white meat and 4 cups torn dark meat—7 cups in all. This recipe can be used to make stock from the carcass of a whole chicken, left over from dinner. Use the same amount of water, but simmer for 12 hours, or overnight, or at least 5 hours.

One 5-pound (2.25-kg) chicken or fowl
8 cups (2 l) water

IN A TALL NARROW STOCKPOT, bring the chicken or fowl and water to a boil. Lower the heat and simmer for 30 minutes if using a chicken, 2 hours if using a fowl. Remove the chicken or fowl and allow to cool slightly. Leave the stock at a simmer.

Remove and discard the poultry skin. Remove the meat and reserve for another use. Break up the carcass and return to the pot; simmer for at least 4 hours and 30 minutes for a chicken, 4 hours for a fowl, and up to 12 hours for either. Add water as necessary to keep the bones covered. Partially covering the pot with a lid or using an otoshi-buta (page xii) will mean less evaporation.

Strain through a fine-mesh sieve. Skim the fat. Cool to room temperature. Refrigerate for 3 hours.

Remove the fat from the top of the stock and the sediment from the bottom (see page 342). Use immediately, or refrigerate for up to 3 days or freeze.

MAKES 6 CUPS (1.5 L)

extra-rich

THIS RECIPE PRODUCES a very strong gelatinous stock. Don't use it for most cold soups, as they will turn solid; but it is perfect for aspics or gelled soups.

> **6 pounds (2.7 kg) chicken backs and necks**
> **17 cups (4.3 l) water**

IN A TALL NARROW STOCKPOT, bring the bones and water to a boil. Skim the fat. Lower the heat and simmer gently, so that bubbles are barely breaking on the surface, for 12 hours, skimming the fat as necessary. Partially covering the pot with a lid or using an otoshi-buta (page xii) will mean less evaporation.

Strain through a fine-mesh sieve. Skim the fat. Cool to room temperature. Refrigerate for 3 hours.

Remove the fat from the top of the stock and the sediment from the bottom (see page 342). Use immediately, or refrigerate for up to 3 days or freeze.

MAKES 8 CUPS (2 L)

chicken consommé

THE ESSENCE OF CHICKEN, a clear, golden yellow ambrosia that slips down the throat pleasurably, either hot or cold. It really is perfect on its own, but if a need is felt to add things, anything other than an herb should be cooked separately, so as not to cloud the consommé (see page 391). Tarragon or dill would be the herb of choice.

for the stock

> 7½ cups (1.9 l) Extra-Rich Chicken Stock (page 349)
> 1 medium onion, cut in half
> 1 medium carrot, peeled and cut into 2-inch (5-cm) lengths
> 1 medium rib celery, cut into 2-inch (5-cm) lengths
> 4 sprigs flat-leaf parsley

for the consommé

> ½ cup (5 ounces; 150 g) ground chicken
> 4 egg whites, plus shells from 4 eggs
> ½ medium tomato, chopped
> 3 cracked black peppercorns, optional
> 2½ teaspoons kosher salt, or to taste

FOR THE STOCK, in a medium saucepan, bring the stock to a boil with the onion, carrot, celery, and parsley. Lower the heat and simmer, partially covered, for 30 minutes. Place a medium-sized stainless steel bowl inside a larger bowl that is filled with ice and a little bit of water. Strain the stock through a fine-mesh sieve into the stainless steel bowl. Stir until no longer hot to the touch.

For the consommé, return the stock to the medium saucepan. Mash together the chicken, egg whites and shells, tomato, and, if using, the peppercorns. Whisk into the stock. Bring to a boil over medium heat, stirring frequently. As the liquid heats, the proteins will begin to coagulate and rise to the top, trapping the impurities that cloud the stock. A solid-looking mass, the "raft," will begin to form on top of the liquid; when this happens, stop stirring. When the liquid returns to a boil, it will foam up around the edges of the raft, which will begin to fold over. Immediately turn the heat way down.

At this point, the liquid should be almost clear. Poke a hole in the center of the raft so you can see the liquid. The heat should be so low that the liquid is barely moving. Cook at this level for 20 minutes. Any particles that were still floating around in the soup when it came to a boil will become attached to the raft, and the soup should be crystal-clear.

Remove from the heat. Ladle the soup from the pot, leaving the raft behind by tilting the pan and pushing the raft to one side. Strain the soup through a damp-cloth–lined sieve. Do not press down on any solids in the sieve, as small particles can get through and cloud the liquid. If any particles remain, strain again, this time through a coffee filter rinsed in hot water. Season with the kosher salt.

MAKES 5 CUPS (1.25 L); 5 FIRST-COURSE SERVINGS

jean-georges's
CHICKEN STOCK

USE THIS STOCK, as he gives it in his book, for Jean-Georges Vongerichten's Chicken Soup with Coconut and Lemongrass (page 128)

1 medium onion, peeled

6 whole cloves

3 garlic cloves, cut in half

2 pounds (900 g) chicken wings

1 carrot, peeled

1 stalk celery

3 or 4 thyme sprigs

1 leek, trimmed and washed

STUD THE ONION with the cloves, then combine all the ingredients in a large saucepan or small stockpot with 10 cups (2.5 l) water. Turn the heat to medium-high and bring to a boil. As soon as bubbles start coming to the surface, adjust the heat so that the mixture cooks at a steady simmer, but not a rapid boil.

Cook for about 1½ hours, stirring occasionally. Cool slightly, then strain, pressing lightly on the solids to extract some of their liquid (don't press too hard, or you will cloud the mixture unnecessarily). Use immediately, or refrigerate for up to 3 days or freeze for up to 3 months.

MAKES 8 CUPS (2 L)

roasted turkey stock

TURKEY SOUP is the best part of the turkey, a luscious home for good egg noodles, cooked rice, or, if you are sadly alone, a poached egg.

Although turkey stock is good made using just water, it will be richer and fuller if started with chicken stock. After one successful bout of stock making, try starting with the carcass and part of a previous batch of stock and water if needed.

Season this broth with salt and pepper and serve with Albóndigas (page 420), 8 per person in 1½ cups (375 ml) of broth, as a savory first course. Also see the soups on pages 151–153.

I suppose that turkey stock could be made with a whole turkey, but I never do. I roast and serve the turkey and then snatch back all the bones in pleasant anticipation of a wonderful meal.

> **Carcass of a roasted 8- to 15-pound (3.6- to 6.8-kg) turkey, broken or cut into pieces, plus the gizzard, heart, and neck**
>
> **12 cups (3 l) Basic Chicken Stock (page 345), commercial chicken broth, or water**

BRING THE CARCASS, gizzard, heart, neck, and liquid to a boil in a large stockpot. Skim the fat. Lower the heat. Simmer for 6 hours or longer (I sometimes leave it for 12 hours or longer), skimming from time to time. Partially covering the pot with a lid or using an otoshi-buta (page xii) will mean less evaporation. Otherwise, more water may need to be added for the longer cooking times.

Strain the stock through a fine-mesh sieve. The stock can be refrigerated at this point and continued another day.

Skim off the fat from the stock. Return to the pot and boil to reduce the liquid to 10 cups (2.5 l). Cool to room temperature. Refrigerate for 3 hours.

Remove the fat from the top of the stock and the sediment from the bottom (see page 342). Use immediately, or refrigerate for up to 3 days or freeze.

MAKES 10 CUPS (2.5 L)

duck or goose stock

MY WAY OF ROASTING a duck (see *Roasting: A Simple Art*) always yields a dividend of duck broth. After the duck is eaten, the bones go back in the broth for more cooking. No matter how the duck is cooked, duck stock is one of those marvelous bonuses from roasting a duck dinner. After the guests have enjoyed all the delicious meat, the remaining bare bones will provide a glistening amber broth to enjoy as is or to use in a more complex soup or sauce. Don't be timid about snatching back the bones from guests' plates; remember they will boil. If there aren't enough bones to make stock right away, freeze what is available and make the stock after another party.

> **Carcasses and bones from 1 to 3 roasted ducks or one 12-pound
> (5.4-kg) goose, plus uncooked necks and wing tips,
> all broken into small pieces**
>
> **3 to 5 quarts (3 to 5 l) water for duck stock, about 4 quarts
> (4 l) water for goose stock**

IN A STOCKPOT large enough to hold the bones covered by at least 2 inches (5 cm) of water and leaving as much headroom, place the carcasses and bones. Add water to cover by 1 inch (2.5 cm). Bring to a boil. Skim any scum that rises to the surface.

If making goose stock, partially cover, using an otoshi-buta (page xii) or a lid. For either stock, lower the heat to a simmer, skimming as necessary, for 9 hours for the goose stock, or 6 to 12 hours, depending on the strength desired, for the duck. Add water as necessary to keep the bones covered by 1 inch (2.5 cm).

Strain through a fine-mesh sieve. Skim the fat. Cool to room temperature. Refrigerate for 3 hours.

Remove the fat from the top of the stock and the sediment from the bottom (see page 342). Use immediately, or refrigerate for up to 3 days or freeze.

MAKES 7 TO 10 CUPS (1.75 TO 2.5 L) DUCK STOCK, 10 CUPS (2.5 L) GOOSE STOCK

Meat stocks

Come winter, much as I love chicken and vegetable soups, I develop a craving for substantial, robustly flavored meat soups. For that, I need stocks. The soups live mainly on pages 169–192. Beef Stock is on page 165; other meat stocks follow.

beef consommé

THIS IS A SIMPLE clarified consommé. The beef stock it starts with is intense in flavor. Beef consommé welcomes thyme, sage, or star anise. If using dried herbs or spices, add them to the cool liquid before clarifying.

5 cups (1.25 l) cool Beef Stock (page 165) or, in England, imported beef or meat stock

4½ ounces (130 g) lean ground beef

3 egg whites, whipped until slightly frothy, plus shells from 3 eggs

1 small tomato, chopped

Kosher salt, to taste

PLACE THE STOCK in a small saucepan. Mash together the meat, egg whites and shells, and tomato. Whisk into the stock. Bring to a boil over medium heat, stirring frequently. As the liquid heats, the proteins will begin to coagulate and rise to the top, trapping the impurities that would cloud the stock. A solid-looking mass, the "raft," will begin to form on top of the liquid; when this happens, stop stirring. When the liquid reaches a boil, it will foam up around the edges of the raft, which will begin to fold over. As soon as this happens, turn the heat way down.

At this point, the liquid should be almost clear. Poke a hole in the center of the raft so the liquid is visible. The heat should be so low that the liquid is barely moving. Cook at this level for 20 minutes. Any particles that were still floating around in the soup when it came to a boil will become attached to the raft, and the soup should be crystal-clear.

Remove from the heat. Pushing the raft to one side, ladle the soup from the pot, leaving the raft behind, and strain it through a damp-cloth–lined sieve. Do not press down on any solids in the sieve, as small particles can get through and cloud the liquid. If any particles remain, strain again, this time through a coffee filter rinsed with hot water.

Season with kosher salt.

MAKES 4 CUPS (1 L); 4 FIRST-COURSE SERVINGS

glace de viande
MEAT GLAZE

REGULAR BEEF STOCK is on page 165. Glace de viande is a very concentrated stock, a secret of classic cuisine. Some people, particularly in Great Britain, will need to start with imported beef or meat stock; or, possibly, they can buy prepared glace de viande. Small amounts of it can be added to a stock or soup that is not as intense as one might like, or it can be used in sauces, braises, and stews.

6 pounds (2.7 kg) beef for stock or stew, cut into 1-inch (2.5-cm) cubes

6 pounds (2.7 kg) beef bones, cut across into 2-inch (5-cm) pieces

4 pounds (1.8 kg) cracked veal knuckles or veal bones

2 medium ribs celery, each cut across into 3 or 4 pieces

2 medium carrots, peeled and each cut across into 3 or 4 pieces

2 medium onions, each cut into 3 or 4 pieces

4 bay leaves, broken

4 garlic cloves, unpeeled

6 quarts (6 l) water, or to cover

HEAT THE OVEN to 500°F (260°C; highest gas mark; #9 British regulo). Place the beef and bones in large roasting pans and roast until brown, about 40 minutes.

Place the browned beef and bones in a large stockpot with the remaining ingredients. Add the water and bring to a boil. Lower the heat and simmer for 6 to 8 hours, skimming the fat as necessary. Strain through a fine-mesh sieve. Skim the fat thoroughly.

Return the stock to the pot. Bring to a boil. Lower the heat to medium and allow it to boil slowly until reduced to 4 cups (1 l). Transfer to a small saucepan and continue to reduce over medium heat. When the stock has reduced to about 1½ cups (375 ml), lower the heat to low. Continue to reduce it, stirring and watching carefully to avoid burning, until a thick, dark, syrupy glaze is obtained.

MAKES ABOUT ⅔ CUP (180 ML)

oxtail stock

OXTAIL STOCK, Triple Oxtail Consommé (page 357), and oxtail soups are some of the great delights of the table, with an intense flavor all their own. This stock will produce 1¾ pounds (790 g), or 5 cups, torn meat for use, along with the stock, in Oxtail Soup with Fava Beans (page 172) and other soups. This stock can substitute for Beef Stock (page 165).

6 pounds (2.7 kg) oxtails, cut into pieces about 1 inch (2.5-cm) long
16 cups (4 l) water

PLACE ONE RACK in the center of the oven and one in the bottom third. Heat to 500°F (260°C; highest gas mark; #9 British regulo).

Place the oxtails in two medium roasting pans. Place one pan on each rack. Roast for 15 minutes. Turn the pieces over and switch the pan positions in the oven. Roast for 15 more minutes. Remove the pans from the oven and transfer the oxtails to a tall narrow stockpot.

Pour or spoon off the excess fat from the roasting pans. Put one pan on top of the stove over high heat. Add 1 cup (250 ml) water and bring to a boil, scraping up any browned bits on the bottom and sides of the pan with a wooden spoon. Let reduce by half. Pour this liquid over the oxtails in the stockpot. Repeat with the second pan.

Pour 10 cups (2.5 l) water over the bones. Bring to a boil. Lower the heat and simmer very gently, skimming as necessary, for 2 hours and 45 minutes.

Remove the oxtails. As soon as they are cool enough to handle, remove the meat from bones and reserve. Return the bones to pot. Add the remaining water. Return to a boil, lower the heat, and simmer for 8 hours, skimming as necessary. Add additional water as necessary to keep the bones covered.

Strain through a fine-mesh sieve, discarding the bones. Skim the fat. Cool to room temperature, and refrigerate for 3 hours.

Remove the fat from the top of the stock and the sediment from the bottom (see page 342). Use immediately, or refrigerate for up to 3 days or freeze.

MAKES 10 CUPS (2.5 L)

triple oxtail consommé

THE *SUMMUM BONUM* of consommé is a rich golden liquid or jelly. I would never play around with it except for tasting for salt or floating something in it. For example, the meat from the oxtail could be substituted in the Duck or Goose Confit Ravioli (page 400); the ravioli should be poached in lightly salted water before adding to the consommé.

This will give an extra dividend of oxtail meat as in the preceding recipe. It is actually a triple consommé, as ground meat is added in the clarification.

for the double consommé

> 3 pounds (1.8 kg) oxtails, cut across into 1-inch (2.5-cm) pieces
>
> 1 cup (250 ml) water
>
> 8 cups (2 l) Oxtail Stock (page 356)
>
> 1 medium onion, cut in half
>
> 1 medium carrot, peeled and cut across into 2-inch (5-cm) lengths
>
> 1 medium rib celery, cut across into 2-inch (5-cm) lengths
>
> 1 medium tomato
>
> ½ (split lengthwise) medium leek, white and light green parts only, well washed
>
> 1 bay leaf
>
> 6 sprigs flat-leaf parsley

for the triple consommé

> ½ cup (150 g) lean ground beef
>
> 4 egg whites, plus shells from 4 eggs
>
> ½ medium tomato, chopped
>
> 3 cracked black peppercorns, optional
>
> 1½ teaspoons kosher salt, or to taste

FOR THE STOCK, place a rack in the center of the oven and heat to 500°F (260°C; highest gas mark; #9 British regulo).

Place the oxtails in a small roasting pan and roast for 15 minutes. With a pair of tongs, turn each piece over. Roast for 15 more minutes. Remove the oxtails from the pan and place in a tall narrow stockpot.

Pour the fat out of the pan and place the roasting pan on top of stove over high heat. Add the water and bring to a boil, scraping all the browned bits from the bottom and sides of the pan. Pour this liquid over the oxtails.

continued

Add the stock. Bring to a boil. Lower the heat and simmer for 1 hour and 30 minutes. At this point, check the oxtails for doneness. If they are tender, remove from the pot and allow to cool slightly. Remove and reserve the meat, discard the fat, and return the bones to the pot. Simmer for 30 minutes more. If the oxtails aren't done at 1 hour and 30 minutes, continue to cook until they are. Then remove from the pot and treat as above, returning the bones to the pot for another 30 minutes.

Add the vegetables and herbs to the stock and return to a boil. Lower the heat and simmer for 30 minutes. Strain through a fine-mesh sieve. The vegetables can be kept for munching, if desired. Discard the bones. There should be 6 cups (1.5 l) stock. Refrigerate overnight; lift or scrape the fat from the top.

For the consommé, in a medium saucepan, over medium-low heat, liquefy the stock about two thirds of the way. Remove from the heat and allow the rest to liquefy in the warm liquid. This will allow the stock to liquefy while staying relatively cool.

Mash together the meat, egg whites and shells, tomato, and, if using, the peppercorns. Whisk into the stock. Bring to a boil over medium heat, stirring frequently. As the liquid heats, the proteins will begin to coagulate and rise to the top, trapping the impurities that cloud the stock. A solid-looking mass, the "raft," will begin to form on top of the liquid; when this happens, stop stirring. When the liquid reaches a boil, it will foam up around the edges of the raft, which will begin to fold over. As soon as this happens, turn the heat way down.

At this point the liquid should be almost clear. Poke a hole in the center of the raft so the liquid is visible. The heat should be so low that the liquid is barely moving. Cook at this level for 20 minutes. Any particles that were still floating around in the soup when it came to a boil will become attached to the raft, and the soup should be crystal-clear.

Remove from the heat. Pushing the raft to one side, ladle the soup from the pot, leaving the raft behind, and strain through a damp-cloth–lined sieve. Do not press down on any solids in the sieve, as small particles can get through and cloud the liquid. If any particles remain, strain again, this time through a coffee filter rinsed in hot water.

Season with the kosher salt.

MAKES 5 CUPS (1.25 L); 5 FIRST-COURSE SERVINGS

roasted pork stock

PORK MAKES A DEEP and savory stock. The roasting of the bones gives color and flavor. Use for Pork Barley Soup (page 198) and Hot-and-Sour Soup (page 196).

Bones and scraps from roast rack of pork
½ cup (125 ml) red wine or water
10 cups (2.5 l) water, or to cover

PLACE A RACK in the center of the oven. Heat oven to 500°F (260°C; highest gas mark; #9 British regulo).

Put all the bones in a small roasting pan. Roast for 10 minutes. Turn the bones. Roast for 10 minutes more. This extra roasting gives the stock an even richer flavor.

Transfer the bones and any pork scraps to a medium saucepan. Pour any fat from the roasting pan. Place the pan on top of the stove over high heat. Pour in the wine or water. Bring to a boil, scraping up the browned bits from the bottom and sides of the pan with a wooden spoon. Let the liquid reduce by half. Pour the liquid over the bones.

Add the water, to just cover the bones. Bring to a boil. Lower the heat and simmer, skimming the fat and scum as necessary for at least 8 hours; 12 is even better. Check the water level every 2 hours, keeping the bones covered by at least 1 inch (2.5 cm).

Strain through a fine-mesh sieve. Skim the fat. Add enough water to make 6 cups (1.5 l). Let cool to room temperature. Refrigerate for 3 hours.

Remove the fat from top of the stock and the sediment from the bottom (see page 342). Use immediately, or refrigerate for up to 3 days or freeze.

MAKES 6 CUPS (1.5 L)

enriched pork stock

WHILE THE PRECEDING PORK STOCK is excellent, it is not gelatin-rich. When I want a denser stock for soups such as Green Chili (page 203), White Bean, Chorizo, and Broccoli di Rape Soup (page 309), and Pork Soup with Herbs (page 199), I use this one.

1 pork shoulder bone
1 pig's foot, split
14 cups (3.5 l) water or Roasted Pork Stock (page 359)

IN A TALL NARROW STOCKPOT, combine the shoulder bone, pig's foot, and water or stock. Bring to a boil. Lower the heat and simmer, skimming the fat as necessary, for 6 hours.

Strain through a fine-mesh sieve. Skim the fat. Let cool to room temperature. Refrigerate for 3 hours.

Remove the fat from the top of the stock and the sediment from the bottom (see page 342). Use immediately, or refrigerate for up to 3 days or freeze.

MAKES 11 CUPS (2.75 L)

lamb or goat stock

LAMB STOCK has a marvelously rich flavor, as does goat stock made by substituting goat bones and scraps for lamb.

Use the lamb stock in Lamb and Sorrel Soup (page 206), Lamb Soup Irish Style (page 208), Lamb and Chick Pea Soup (page 209), or Lamb Mulligatawny Soup (page 211).

Bones and scraps from saddle, rack, or leg of lamb, raw or roasted
Cold water to cover by 2 inches

BREAK UP THE BONES of the lamb saddle, or separate the bones to fit in a medium stockpot. Cover with water by 2 inches (5 cm). Bring to a boil. Skim the fat and scum. Lower the heat and simmer, partially covered, or covered with an otoshi-buta (see page xii), for 8 hours, adding water as necessary to keep bones covered.

Strain through a fine-mesh sieve. Skim the fat. Cool to room temperature. Refrigerate for 3 hours.

Remove the fat from the top of the stock and the sediment from the bottom (see page 342). Use immediately, or refrigerate for up to 3 days or freeze.

YIELD DEPENDS ON AMOUNT OF BONES USED

Sea stocks

The world is full of fabulous fish and shellfish soups. Most of them are improved by, or require, a good stock. The Mediterranean fish soups that depend on lots of little bony fish that are hard to find away from the coast can successfully be emulated only by making a stock.

basic fish stock

THERE IS A MYTH that comes from French cooking that fish stock must not be cooked for more than twenty to forty minutes. As an ignorant young cook, for many years, I cooked my fish stocks for long hours, just as I did my other stocks. As I learned more, I persisted in my very satisfactory habit.

It was not until years later, when I began to work with restaurants, that I understood the shibboleth. French restaurant chefs use the frames of flatfish, flounder and sole, for their stock. These bones do give a bitter stock if cooked longer than twenty minutes, or forty at the outside. But if no flatfish bones are used, the stock can cook for four to six hours, extracting all the gelatin to make a wonderfully rich stock. (I would have thought that any country that invented bouillabaisse, dependent on the gelatin to bind the ingredients together, would have figured this out.)

I use fish bones, heads, and cod collars, if available. These are free or very cheap. When I order fish fillets, I always ask for the heads and bones, since I have paid for them. It is better not to use the heads and bones from oily fish such as mackerel and bluefish or salmon, which make heavy stock, unless the soup is an unusual one like fish solianka. Bones and heads of white-fleshed fish such as snapper, bass, and cod, including the cod collar, can be used, as can the bones and head from previously cooked fish. The stock can be strained and frozen to use as wanted.

All gills should be cut out of the heads and the bones thoroughly rinsed to remove any blood, which can make the stock bitter.

In general, unless it is required in the dependent recipe, it is better not to use wine or to season the stock when making it. Such elements can always be added later. A neutral stock provides more flexibility. It can be the base for an endless variety of quickly made soups. It can be the base—with a roux and a little bit of cream—for elegant fish sauces to which fresh herbs and seafood can be added. Or a small amount of a fish glaze made by reducing the stock can be added to a tomato, curry, or other sauce to marry it to the fish with which it will be served. Rice to accompany a fish dish can have some of the water for cooking replaced by an equal amount of stock. If the fish flavor of the stock is too strong, replace some of it with white wine for balance.

As a cook for my family of fish-soup aficionados, I like to know that with an intense fish stock on hand I can quickly make a Provençal fish soup. Those who want can throw in a handful or two of broken-up thin egg noodles or orzo pasta. Croutons (page 429), raw cloves of garlic with which to rub them, and Rouille (page 433) or Aïoli (page 432) or grated Parmesan can be put on the table for people to use as they will.

This stock is used for Chupa de Pescado (page 281), Bouillabaisse (page 268), Oyster Soup with Broth (page 20), Creamy Oyster Soup (page 247), Bourride of Monkfish (page 260), Fall Fish Stew (page 257), Ciarla's Fish Soup (page 254), and Green Stew of Fish (page 280).

5 pounds (2.25 kg) nonoily fish heads and bones, such as cod, red snapper, grouper, and/or bass

11 cups (2.75 l) water

1 cup (250 ml) white wine, optional

WASH THE FISH HEADS and bones very well to eliminate all traces of blood. Cut out the oil-rich gills with scissors. Put the fish heads and bones in a medium stockpot and cover with the water and, if using, the white wine. Bring to a boil. Skim off the scum that rises to the top. Lower the heat and simmer the stock, skimming as necessary, for 4 hours.

Strain through a fine-mesh sieve. Use immediately, or cool to room temperature and refrigerate for up to 3 days or freeze.

MAKES 8 CUPS (2 L)

Roasted Fish Stock: Replace the uncooked bones with bones left from roasted fish. Use the same ratio of water to bones.

Double-Rich Fish Stock: Simmer the stock for an additional 2 to 4 hours, or until reduced to 4 cups (1 l), and strain; or starting with the unreduced stock, simmer 8 cups (2 l) with a fresh 3 pounds (1.4 kg) of nonoily fish bones and heads until reduced to 4 cups (1 l) about 4 hours. Makes 4 cups.

salmon stock

ALTHOUGH SALMON IS AN OILY FISH and a stock made from its bones cannot be used in everything, it is special in Solianka (page 282) and Salmon with Sorrel Soup (page 253). A sturgeon stock can be made the same way and will have a lovely golden color rather than the pale peach color of salmon stock.

Frame, head, skin, and small bones from a roasted
    4-pound (1.8-kg) salmon
½ cup (125 ml) dry white wine
4 cups (1 l) water

PUT ALL THE FISH REMNANTS in a large saucepan. Add the wine and 3½ cups (875 ml) water. Bring to a boil. Lower the heat and simmer for 1 hour and 30 minutes. Skim the froth off the top with metal spoon every 30 or 45 minutes.

Add the remaining water to the stock. Simmer for 30 minutes.

Strain through a fine-mesh sieve. Use immediately, or cool to room temperature and refrigerate for up to 3 days or freeze.

MAKES 2 ¼ CUPS (560 ML)

shrimp broth

NOT ONLY DOES THIS appeal to my thrifty soul—making stock from something that is regularly thrown out—it is also rapid. Shrimp shells can often be gotten free or for a nominal amount from fish stores. Whenever I shell shrimp, I throw the shells in a plastic bag in the freezer and add more as available until I have enough for stock.

Use for Shrimp Broth with Shrimp Balls (page 234) and Shrimp Gumbo (page 276), or cook some Shrimp and Pork Wontons (page 412) in the stock and add some chopped scallion greens as well.

Shells from 4 pounds (1.8 k) shrimp
8 cups (2 l) water

IN A MEDIUM SAUCEPAN, bring the shells and water to a boil. Lower the heat. Simmer for 30 minutes.

Strain through a fine-mesh sieve. Use immediately, or cool to room temperature and refrigerate for up to 3 days or freeze.

MAKES ABOUT 6 CUPS (750 ML)

dashi

THIS MAKES A VERY light stock without the mirin, soy, and salt. There are a few kinds of commercially available instant dashi. One I tried contained dried bonito, salt, and glucose. It is strong, dark, and salty-sweet.

One 8-inch (20-cm) length konbu (kelp)
4 cups (1 l) water
½ cup (20 g) loosely packed large shavings dried bonito flakes
2 teaspoons dark soy sauce
2 teaspoons mirin (sweet rice wine)
1 teaspoon kosher salt

PLACE THE KONBU in a small saucepan with the water. Bring to a boil. Remove the konbu and reserve for another use.

Remove from the heat, stir in the bonito flakes, and allow them to settle to the bottom of the broth.

Strain through a damp-cloth–lined sieve; gather up the cloth and squeeze out the excess liquid. Discard the bonito flakes. Stir in the soy sauce, mirin, and salt.

MAKES ABOUT 3½ CUPS (875 ML)

Note: For instant dashi, 4 teaspoons instant dashi powder mixed with 1 cup (250 ml) hot water makes a very strong broth.

Gelled gems

Not all gelled soups require a strong gelling stock, but many do. It seemed appropriate to put these soups here.

chicken soup

WITH DILL, GELLED OR HOT

THIS IS A LOVELY way to start a summer meal, perhaps before a whole poached or roasted fish, a big salad, and fresh berries with sorbet. This is also delightful hot.

4 cups (1 l) Extra-Rich Chicken Stock (page 349) or Basic Chicken Stock (page 345)

1 tablespoon gelatin, if using Basic Chicken Stock

1 small onion, quartered

1 small carrot, peeled and coarsely chopped

Freshly ground black pepper, to taste

2 tablespoons fresh lemon juice

¾ teaspoon kosher salt

2 tablespoons coarsely chopped dill

4 sprigs dill, for serving

4 lemon wedges, for serving

Sour cream, if serving gelled

IN A MEDIUM SAUCEPAN, bring the stock (reserve ½ cup [125 m] if using gelatin), onion, carrot, and pepper to a boil. Lower the heat and simmer for 20 minutes.

If using the gelatin, sprinkle it over the reserved ½ cup (125 ml) stock. Let sit for 2 minutes to soften. Stir it into the soup and cook over medium heat, stirring constantly, until the gelatin is dissolved.

For either version, pour the stock through a damp-cloth-lined sieve and discard the solids. Season with the lemon juice and salt.

Refrigerate until cool and slightly thickened, then stir in the chopped dill. If serving gelled, divide among four soup bowls and chill until set.

Top each portion with a dill sprig and serve a wedge of lemon. Serve with sour cream on the side if serving gelled.

MAKES 4 CUPS (1 L); 4 FIRST-COURSE SERVINGS

The elegance of clarity

WHEN I WAS A LITTLE GIRL, I loved Jell-O. I didn't love the taste, but I loved the way it shone and wiggled and the slippery smoothness when it went down my throat. Even then, I realized that the luster was greater in a clear bowl that permitted the light to get through. The glass custard cups of then are replaced by crystal today—I use the finger bowls I no longer use for fingers—so the light can bounce through the soups. They can be left smooth, roiled with the tines of a fork, or cut into rough cubes.

Now that I am grown up, I can have all that fun and wonderful flavors as well. I eat and make gelled soups. The best known is probably madrilène (page 370). However, it is possible to have all sorts of gelled essences; the flavors must be intense, or they will fade away when cold.

Any strong stock can be clarified, seasoned, and set to chill. Do not try these recipes with ordinary weak stocks that do not have all the gelatin extracted from the bones. Before or after clarification, the stock can be infused with an herb or some spices. Think of duck stock with star anise, turkey with tarragon or lovage, beef with orange zest, or fish with lemongrass and curry leaves. Don't add citrus juices until serving. They will cloud these beauties.

Now is the time to admit to a weakness for a summer diet snack of a well-chilled can of beef or chicken madrilène (although not as good as the gelled soups that I make), liberally sprinkled with lemon or lime juice and fresh ground pepper.

Not all gelled soups are clear and gem-like, but often their silky texture is a special reward.

Meat- and fish-based stocks gel on their own when properly made. Fruit and vegetable essences do not. It is possible to use either gelatin, which is an animal product, or agar-agar (see page 374), which is made from a seaweed and is therefore vegetarian. Agar-agar has the added property of holding its shape at room temperature. Even though agar-agar will set at room temperature, it is not a wonderful idea to leave things, even if totally vegetarian, made with it out of the refrigerator for a long time. In laboratories, it is used as a culture medium. However, this ability is useful on a hot summer night.

lemongrass ginger

CONSOMMÉ

HERE IS A JAZZIER VERSION of gelled chicken stock, given bite and energy with Asian seasonings. Look also at Vietnamese Chicken Soup (page 130).

Sixteen ½-inch (1-cm), cubes peeled ginger (5 ounces; 150 g)

Three 2-inch (5-cm) pieces bulb end of lemongrass (from 3 stalks) and three 2-inch (5-cm) pieces from greener end, cut across into thin strips

3 serrano chili peppers, cut across into ¼-inch (.5-cm) slices

Grated zest of 4 limes

12 cups (3 l) Extra-Rich Chicken Stock (page 349)

1½ tablespoons kosher salt

8 egg whites, lightly beaten, plus shells from 8 eggs, crushed

1 pound (450 g) ground chicken

1 large tomato cut into ¼-inch (.5-cm) dice

for serving

2 tablespoons coarsely chopped cilantro

2 limes, each cut into 3 wedges and seeded

IN A TALL NARROW STOCKPOT, bring the ginger, lemongrass, chilies, lime zest, and stock to a boil. Lower the heat and simmer for 10 minutes. Remove from the heat and cool. Season with the salt.

Mash the egg whites and shells, the ground meat, and the tomato together. Whisk this into the cooled broth. Slowly bring the mixture to a boil, stirring frequently with a wooden spoon. As the liquid comes to a boil, the solids will come to the top of the broth, forming a "raft." This will draw the impurities out of the stock to leave a clear broth. When the soup has come to a boil, immediately lower the heat. Poke a hole in the raft and simmer, very slowly, for 15 minutes. The resulting broth should be crystal clear.

Disturbing the soup as little as possible, ladle the soup through a sieve lined with a coffee filter rinsed in hot water or a doubled paper towel. Do not press down on the solids. Chill overnight.

Sprinkle each serving with 1 teaspoon of chopped cilantro. Pass the lime wedges separately.

MAKES 7 CUPS (1.75 L); 6 FIRST-COURSE SERVINGS

beef madrilène

THIS IS THE GREAT CLASSIC and a great reward for making really good stock. It is also good hot. To leave a maximum of flavor, I use only six egg whites instead of the more usual nine. This means the clarification (see page 343) is fragile. Go carefully.

12 cups (3 l) Beef Stock (page 165)
6 medium tomatoes, cored and cut into 1-inch (2.5-cm) cubes
6 egg whites, beaten until slightly frothy
1 teaspoon kosher salt

IN A MEDIUM SAUCEPAN, bring the stock and tomatoes to a boil. Lower the heat and simmer for 20 minutes, or until the tomatoes are very soft. Strain through a damp-cloth–lined sieve. Return to the pan and allow to cool.

Whisk in the egg whites. Bring the liquid slowly to a boil, stirring frequently. As the liquid heats, the egg white will begin to coagulate and rise to the top. Continue stirring until the liquid begins to simmer and a solid mass, or "raft," starts to form on top of the soup. When the liquid comes to a boil, the edges of the mass will fold over. Immediately lower the heat and poke a hole in the center of the mass. Simmer over very low heat until all the egg white has coagulated at the top and the liquid is very clear, about 10 minutes.

Remove from the heat. Carefully ladle the soup out of the pot and strain through a damp-cloth–lined sieve. Leave the bulk of the raft in the pot, and do not push down on any solids in the sieve; just allow to drain naturally. Season with the salt.

Serve hot for a delicious elegant first course, or chill for at least 3 hours, or overnight, for a gelled soup.

MAKES 9 CUPS (2.25 L); 8 FIRST-COURSE SERVINGS

jellied borscht
WITH CAVIAR

WELL, NO, caviar isn't essential. The sour cream topping can be topped with thin shreds of the cooked beets and some tufts of dill. But think of the colors and flavors of the acid-sweet ruby red soup, the stark white sour cream, and the pearly, lightly salty, black pop of the caviar.

The soup can easily be made vegetarian by substituting agar-agar for the gelatin. Rossl (page 176) can be substituted for the beets.

In any case, there will be beets left over. Grate and make them into a salad that is good with cold meats or fish. Use a lemon vinaigrette and some chopped dill. The beets could be added to a cucumber salad. If planning to make the Cauliflower Soup (page 376), peel the beets and cube them. They can be refrigerated for two to three days or frozen.

Citric acid in crystals or powder used to be easily available. Vitamin C is citric acid: Crushed tablets can be used.

1 pound (450 g) beets, all but 1 inch (2.5 cm) of the stems removed, scrubbed well

5 teaspoons gelatin or 3 teaspoons finely ground agar-agar

2 tablespoons fresh lemon juice

2½ teaspoons white vinegar

¾ teaspoon citric acid powder

8 to 10 tablespoons (95 to 125 g) sugar

2¼ teaspoons kosher salt

for serving

Sour cream

Caviar or chopped dill

IN A MEDIUM SAUCEPAN, bring the beets and 5 cups (1.25 l) water to a boil. Cover. Lower the heat and cook at a low boil for 20 to 40 minutes, or until the beets can easily be pierced with a skewer (cooking time depends on the size and age of the beets).

Strain the liquid through a fine-mesh sieve set over a small saucepan. Reserve the beets for another use. Measure the liquid and add enough water to make 4 cups (1 l).

If using gelatin, sprinkle it over the liquid and let it sit for 2 minutes to soften. Whisk to combine. Heat the soup to just under a boil, stirring frequently. If using agar-agar, combine it with the liquid and bring to a boil, lower the heat, and simmer for 5 minutes.

continued

Stir in the lemon juice, vinegar, citric acid, sugar, and salt and continue stirring until everything is dissolved. Remove from the heat. Correct the seasoning with salt, sugar, and lemon juice if necessary. The soup should be distinctly sweet and sour. (Remember that flavors fade when cold.) Refrigerate until set, about 6 hours.

Serve the soup chilled, topped with a dollop of sour cream and caviar or chopped dill.

MAKES ABOUT 4 CUPS (1 L); 4 FIRST-COURSE SERVINGS

gelled fish soup
WITH PEPPERED WHIPPED CREAM

QUITE A FEW YEARS AGO, Paula Wolfert and I did some work together. I had remembered this soup as being hers. When I called her to check, she remembered that it was her soup and my idea to gel it. She is still a wonderful cook, and I still like gelled soups.

This soup is full of my favorite Riviera fish soup flavors. The saffron and vegetables give it a luscious golden color. I doubt if I would often make only four portions; I would be more likely to double the recipe, as I often have a lot of fish stock on hand.

½ pound (120 g) cod fillet

½ small onion, quartered

1 small carrot, peeled and cut up

1 small rib celery, cut up

One 3-inch (7.5-cm) piece fennel stalk

2 medium plum tomatoes, cut up

3 sprigs parsley

One 2-inch (5-cm) piece orange peel

4 cups (1 l) Basic Fish Stock (page 362)

½ cup (125 ml) dry white wine

3 egg whites, plus shells from 3 eggs

¼ teaspoon fennel seed

½ bay leaf

1 teaspoon saffron threads
1 teaspoon Pernod
Pinch of dried thyme
2 teaspoons kosher salt
¼ teaspoon freshly ground black pepper
Peppered Whipped Cream (recipe follows), for serving

IN A FOOD PROCESSOR, chop the fish, onion, carrot, celery, fennel stalk, tomatoes, parsley, and orange peel. Pour into a medium non-aluminum saucepan. Stir in the stock and wine.

Combine the remaining ingredients (except the cream) in a bowl, lightly beating to break up the egg whites. Stir into the fish stock. Slowly bring the mixture to a boil, stirring occasionally. A mass, or "raft," will form on the top. Simmer over very low heat for 1 hour without stirring or otherwise disturbing the mixture.

Carefully lift the mass off and discard it. Ladle the clear liquid through a damp-cloth–lined sieve into a clear glass serving bowl; or, if you prefer, pour the soup into soup bowls and chill in those. Refrigerate overnight to set thoroughly.

Serve chilled, with peppered whipped cream.

MAKES 4 CUPS (1 L); 4 FIRST-COURSE SERVINGS

peppered whipped cream

THIS CAN ALSO be used with smoked fish or another, blander gelled soup.

½ cup (125 ml) heavy cream
¼ teaspoon freshly ground black pepper

PLACE THE CREAM in a bowl. Add the pepper, cover, and refrigerate overnight.

Strain the cream through a fine-mesh sieve into a metal bowl. Discard the pepper. Beat the cream until it has thickened and soft peaks form. Serve immediately.

MAKES 1 CUP (250 ML)

How to gel

THE TWO TYPES OF GELLING agents that are ordinarily added to set soups and other foods are agar-agar, which is vegetarian and made from seaweed, and what is normally called gelatin, made from bones.

Besides being vegetarian, agar-agar has the advantage of not needing to be cold to retain its firming qualities. It is available in health food stores. It comes in flakes, long strips, sheets, or powder. It is easiest to use in the powdered form. If the powder is unavailable, grind it in a spice mill (coffee grinder).

One package (28 g) of flakes contains about ¾ cup (28 g); ¼ cup (9.5 g) flakes will make about 4 full teaspoons of powder, enough to gel 4 cups (1 l) of liquid.

To substitute gelatin for agar-agar or agar-agar for gelatin, note that 2 tablespoons flakes or 2 full teaspoons ground (5 g) will gel the same amount as 1 package, or 1 tablespoon (9 g), of gelatin.

For soups and purées, the agar-agar or gelatin is dissolved in a small amount of the liquid and then stirred into the whole. To ensure even distribution in stocks, it is best to dissolve agar-agar in the entire amount of liquid; gelatin should be sprinkled in a small amount of the liquid before being stirred into the whole.

To dissolve agar-agar in a microwave: Combine the agar-agar and liquid as called for in the recipe in a 2-cup (.5-l) glass measure or bowl. Cook, uncovered, at 100% power in a high-wattage oven for 2 minutes or in a low-wattage oven for 3 minutes. If using gelatin, allow to soak in the liquid for 2 minutes. Cover and cook in a high-wattage oven for 30 seconds or in a low-wattage oven for 1 minute.

To dissolve agar-agar on top of the stove: Combine the agar-agar and liquid in a small saucepan. Bring to a boil. Lower the heat and simmer for 5 minutes, or until dissolved. If using gelatin, allow it to soften in ¼ to ½ cup (69 to 125 ml) of the liquid for 2 minutes, then heat it in the remaining liquid until dissolved.

tomato dill soup

THINK OF THIS MORE as a cabochon ruby than a clear red gem. We are leaving the translucent-soups world for another group of very good gelled soups that are fairly opaque.

This soup can be vegetarian if the vegetable stock and agar-agar are used.

1 tablespoon gelatin or 2 teaspoons finely ground agar-agar

1 cup (250 ml) Basic Chicken Stock (page 345) or Vegetable Broth (page 380)

2 cups (500 ml) Tomato Purée (page 384), canned tomato purée, or sterile-pack strained tomatoes

1½ teaspoons coarsely chopped dill

1½ teaspoons kosher salt

1 small clove garlic, smashed, peeled, and very finely chopped

⅛ teaspoon hot red pepper sauce

⅛ teaspoon celery seeds

2 tablespoons sour cream

2 tablespoons tomato paste

Celery leaves, chopped, optional

IF USING GELATIN, sprinkle it over the chicken stock and let stand until softened, 2 minutes. If using agar-agar, in a small saucepan, bring the stock and agar-agar to a boil. Lower the heat. Simmer for 5 minutes. Remove from the heat.

In a medium saucepan, combine the tomatoes, dill, salt, garlic, hot red pepper sauce, and celery seed. Cook over very low heat until steaming but not boiling. Scrape the gelatin or agar-agar mixture into the tomato mixture and stir until dissolved. Do not bring to a boil.

Remove the soup from the heat and cool until just warm to the touch. Stir together the sour cream and tomato paste. Slowly whisk into the cooled soup. Refrigerate, covered, for 3 hours, or up to 2 days.

Top each portion with some celery leaves, if using.

MAKES 3 CUPS (750 ML); 4 FIRST-COURSE SERVINGS

cauliflower soup
GELLED OR HOT

YEARS AGO when Joël Robuchon's restaurant, Jamin, was still on the Rue de Longchamp, I had one of the most sensational gelled soups of my life. It became one of his specialties. I think it must have been of great help in getting his three stars.

The top was a creamy white layer that was cauliflower. As my spoon slipped through that, it came to a softly gelled layer of beef consommé that in turn blanketed a layer of caviar. That is a little rich for my usual wallet. To try to emulate it, first buy some really good caviar. For each portion, put 2½ tablespoons in the bottom of a large bowl. Cover the caviar with a 1-cup layer (250-ml) of Beef Consommé (page 354) that has not yet gelled. Refrigerate. After about 2 hours, add a 1½-cup (375-ml) layer of the following cauliflower soup. Refrigerate.

This is my imitation of the cauliflower layer of the Robuchon soup. With more work, and spectacular results, it can be layered with the Spinach and Mint Soup (page 378). If not layering it, sprinkle with diced, cooked beets (page 371). The soup is equally good hot, and I like to toss on some Cubed Croutons (page 430).

Without chicken stock but with vegetable broth and agar-agar, this is vegetarian.

4 cups (1 l) Extra-Rich Chicken Stock (page 349), Basic Chicken Stock
    (page 345), or Vegetable Broth (page 380)
2 tablespoons gelatin for a gelled soup or 2 tablespoons finely ground
    agar-agar for vegetarian gelled soup, if using Basic Chicken Stock
1½ pounds (675 g) cauliflower florets (from about 1½ medium heads)
1 medium onion, cut into ¼-inch (.5-cm) dice, for hot soup only
1½ cups (375 ml) heavy cream for gelled soup, 2 to 4 tablespoons
    for hot soup
1 tablespoon kosher salt, or to taste

IN A MEDIUM SAUCEPAN, bring the stock (reserve ¾ cup [180 ml] if using gelatin or agar-agar), cauliflower, and, if using, the onion to a boil. Lower the heat and simmer, partially covered, for 15 minutes, or until the cauliflower is soft. Strain, reserving the solids and liquid separately.

In a blender, working in batches of no more than 2 cups (500 ml), purée the cauliflower with a little of the cooking liquid. Scrape the purée into a medium saucepan. Whisk in the remaining cooking liquid and the cream. Season with the salt. If serving hot, heat through and serve.

If using gelatin, in a small bowl, sprinkle the gelatin over the reserved ¾ cup (180 ml) stock. Let sit for 2 minutes to soften. Scrape the gelatin into the soup and heat over medium heat, stirring, until dissolved. If using the agar-agar, in a small saucepan, stir the agar-agar into the reserved ¾ cup (180 ml) broth. Bring to a boil. Lower the heat and simmer for 5 minutes, or until dissolved. Scrape and stir the agar-agar mixture into the soup until thoroughly combined.

For the chilled layered soup, cool slightly. Remove the plastic from the top of the chilled spinach soup. Pour the cauliflower soup carefully over the top of the gelled spinach soup. Chill for l hour. Press a layer of plastic wrap directly onto the surface of the soup, so the soup doesn't form a skin as it is chilling. Chill for an additional 2 hours, or overnight. Or, if serving the soup chilled on its own, divide the soup among six bowls. Chill for 1 hour, cover with plastic wrap as above, and chill until set, about 2 hours longer, or overnight.

MAKES 6 TO 7 CUPS (1.5 TO 1.75 L); 6 FIRST-COURSE SERVINGS OR 8 TO 10 SERVINGS
WHEN SERVED CHILLED WITH CHILLED SPINACH AND MINT SOUP (PAGE 378)

spinach and mint soup

I DEVELOPED THIS SOUP when I was playing with the Cauliflower Soup (page 376). In emulation of a great chef, Joël Robuchon, I wanted to make a beautiful layered cold soup based on creamy white cauliflower. Looking for a good contrast in color and flavor, I came up with the idea of spinach. It worked very well but is no threat to my memories of Robuchon. However, the spinach soup is good on its own. I have served it topped with sour cream or whipped cream and a mint leaf.

This is another good vegetarian soup when set with agar-agar.

4 cups (1 l) Extra-Rich Chicken Stock (page 349), Basic Chicken Stock (page 345), or Vegetable Broth (page 380)

2 tablespoons gelatin if using Basic Chicken Stock for a gelled soup or 2 tablespoons finely ground agar-agar for vegetarian gelled soup

1 large shallot, very finely chopped

16 sprigs mint

3 pounds (1.4 kg) spinach, stemmed and washed well

1 tablespoon kosher salt, or to taste

for serving

Cauliflower Soup (page 376); or 6 tablespoons (90 g) sour cream or whipped cream and 6 mint leaves

IN A MEDIUM SAUCEPAN, bring the stock (reserving ¾ cup [180 ml] if using gelatin or agar-agar), shallot, and mint to a boil. Lower the heat and simmer for 10 minutes, or until the shallot is soft.

Meanwhile, in a medium stockpot over medium heat, cook the spinach, with just the water that clings to the leaves after washing, turning frequently, for 4 to 5 minutes, or until the spinach wilts. Drain and discard any liquid.

Skim the shallots from the stock and add them to the drained spinach. Reserve the shallot cooking liquid. In a blender, working in batches of no more than 2 cups (500 ml), purée the spinach and shallots with a little of the cooking liquid. Whisk the puréed vegetables into the remaining shallot cooking liquid. Season with the salt.

If using gelatin, in a small saucepan, sprinkle the gelatin over the reserved ¾ cup (180 ml) stock. Let sit for 2 minutes to soften. Heat, stirring, until the gelatin dissolves. If using the agar-agar, in a small saucepan, stir the agar-agar into the reserved ¾ cup (180 ml) broth. Bring to a boil. Lower the heat and simmer for 5 minutes, or until dissolved. Scrape and stir the gelatin or agar-agar mixture into the soup until thoroughly combined.

Divide the soup evenly among six bowls if serving on its own, or eight to ten bowls if serving with the cauliflower soup. Chill for 1 hour. If serving the soup on its own, press a layer of plastic wrap directly onto the surface of each serving so the soup doesn't form a skin as it is chilling. In either case, continue to chill until set, about 2 hours longer.

To serve with the cauliflower soup, top each portion with a layer of the soup. Return to the refrigerator and chill for an additional 3 hours, or overnight.

If serving without the cauliflower layer, top each serving with a tablespoon of sour cream and stick a mint leaf into it.

MAKES 6 CUPS (1.5 L); 6 FIRST-COURSE SERVINGS OR 8 TO 10 SERVINGS
WHEN SERVED CHILLED WITH CHILLED CAULIFLOWER SOUP (PAGE 376)

Vegetable stocks

Vegetables are an important component of many soups and consommés, but they can make good stocks on their own for vegetarian, meatless soups.

vegetable broth

FOR A SMOOTHER, more unctuous mouth feel, agar-agar or tapioca powder may be added to the finished broth.

This broth is used plain in Scallion Soup (page 60) and Red Pepper Soup (page 44). Use the roasted version for Curried Squash and Apple Soup (page 114).

2 cloves garlic, smashed and peeled

2 medium-to-large onions, quartered

3 medium carrots, peeled and cut into 1-inch (2.5-cm) lengths

3 medium tomatoes, coarsely chopped

3 medium leeks, white part only, cut in half lengthwise, washed well, and cut across into 1-inch (2.5-cm) lengths

2 tablespoons olive oil

1 medium bunch spinach, stemmed, washed well, and cut across into 2-inch (5-cm) strips

1 cup (60 g) celery leaves

Stems from 2 bunches parsley (reserve the leaves for another use)

2 bay leaves

8 cups (2 l) water

TO MAKE A ROASTED VEGETABLE BROTH, place a rack in the middle of oven and heat the oven to 500° F (260°C; highest gas mark; #9 British regulo).

In a large roasting pan, place the garlic, onions, carrots, tomatoes, and leeks. Add the olive oil and toss to coat. Roast for 15 minutes. Turn the vegetables and roast for 15 more minutes. Move the vegetables around in the pan and roast for 10 more minutes, or until all the vegetables are nicely browned and the tomatoes are collapsing.

Place the roasted vegetables in a tall narrow stockpot. Add the spinach, celery leaves, parsley stems, and bay leaves, and 7 cups (1.75 l) water. Place the roasting pan on top of the stove. Stir in the remaining water. Bring to a boil, scraping up any browned bits from the sides and bottom of the pan with a wooden spoon. Pour this liquid over the vegetables in the pot.

For a plain vegetable broth, place all the ingredients, including the water, in a tall narrow stockpot.

In either case, bring to a boil. Lower the heat and simmer, partially covered, for 45 minutes. Strain through a damp-cloth–lined sieve. Use immediately, or refrigerate for up to 3 days or freeze.

MAKES 8 CUPS (2 L)

Note: To add consistency, ½ cup (20 g) agar-agar flakes, 8 teaspoons powdered, or 5 tablespoons (35 g) tapioca powder may be added to the finished broth. Mix together the agar-agar, if using, and the broth and bring to a boil. Lower the heat and simmer until the agar-agar dissolves, about 5 minutes. If using tapioca, mix with ¾ cup (180 ml) cold broth. Bring the rest of the broth to a boil. Whisk in the tapioca. Return to a boil. Remove from the stove. Both of these are good. The agar-agar sets up at room temperature.

mushroom broth

TO MAKE THIS BASE INTO A SOUP, add 1 tablespoon salt. It is also nice with Mushroom Dumplings (page 416) and some chopped tarragon or dill. Use instead of water in Mushroom Barley Soup (page 333) and Winter Mushroom Soup (page 108).

1½ pounds (675 g) white mushrooms, broken into large chunks
½ ounce (15 g) dried porcini mushrooms (cèpes)
1 ounce (30 g) dried shiitake mushrooms
12 cups (3 l) water

IN A FOOD PROCESSOR, working in batches if necessary, chop the fresh mushrooms to a coarse paste, stopping a couple of times to scrape down the sides of the bowl.

In a tall narrow stockpot, bring the fresh and dried mushrooms and water to a boil. Lower the heat and simmer, uncovered, for 30 minutes.

Strain through a fine-mesh sieve, and then through a damp-cloth-lined sieve. Use immediately, or refrigerate for up to 3 days or freeze.

MAKES 9 CUPS (2.25 L)

konbu dashi

THE JAPANESE HAVE A GREAT TRADITION of vegetarian food. Dashi, the light Japanese stock, normally contains both kelp, dried konbu, available in Japanese markets, and bonito flakes. This is a traditional vegetarian alternative. Consider slivers of shiitake, rounds of cooked carrot, and sticks of daikon as additives for a light soup to sip with a Japanese meal.

Aside from kaiseki meals, which are composed of a succession of elegant little dishes and which were originally an outgrowth of the tea ceremony, Japanese meals tend to be made up of several dishes served at one time. Soup is normally one of these.

One 1.75-ounce (50 g) package konbu (kelp)
8⅔ cups (2.2 l) water

WIPE THE KONBU with a damp cloth. Cut it into 4-inch (10-cm) pieces and place in a medium saucepan with the water. Cover and bring to a boil. Lower the heat to medium-low and simmer, partially covered, for 1 hour, or until the liquid has reduced to about 4⅓ cups (1.1 l).

Strain through a fine-mesh sieve and discard solids. Use immediately, or refrigerate for up to 3 days or freeze.

MAKES 4⅓ CUPS (1 L)

Soup bases

Bases are not stocks, but they are a wonderful way of carrying the sun into winter, of using the prodigal produce of spring, summer, and fall when it is cheap and plentiful.

tomato purée

YES, TOMATO PURÉE comes in cans or, better, sterile-packed in cardboard boxes, but homemade is best. It is used in Tomato Dill Soup (page 375), Vegetable Curry Soup (page 116), Goulash Soup (page 182), and White Bean Soup with Confit and Tomato (page 160).

6 pounds (2.7 kg) ripe tomatoes, cored and quartered

IN A HEAVY MEDIUM STOCKPOT, cook the tomatoes over medium heat until steam forms. Lower the heat, cover the pot, and cook, stirring once in a while, until the tomatoes are very soft, about 45 minutes. Remove from the heat and cool slightly.

Pass the mixture through the fine disc of a food mill. Use immediately, or refrigerate for up to 3 days or freeze.

MAKES 8½ CUPS (2.1 L)

chunky tomato base

THIS WORKS WELL for peasanty-type soups like minestrone. It is used in Dal Soup (page 326), Beef Stew for a Spoon (page 184), Chili Pork Stew (page 204), Tripe Gumbo (page 214), Vegetable Gumbo with or Without Roux (page 118), Fresh Cranberry Bean Soup with Tomato (page 295), Michael's Fish Soup (page 16), Family Fish Soup with Orzo (page 265), Duck Gumbo (page 158), and Mussel and Tomato Soup (page 241), or any soup that calls for lightly crushed canned whole tomatoes.

2 medium onions, cut into ½-inch (1-cm) cubes

6 tablespoons (100 ml) olive oil

5 pounds (2.25 kg) ripe red tomatoes, cored and cut into 1-inch (2.5-cm) cubes

IN A MEDIUM STOCKPOT, cook the onions and olive oil over low heat, stirring occasionally, for 8 minutes, or until the onions are translucent.

Raise the heat and stir in the tomatoes. Bring to a boil. Lower the heat and simmer for 20 minutes, or until the tomatoes are soft and liquid.

Use immediately, or refrigerate for up to 3 days or freeze.

MAKES 10 CUPS (2.5 L)

plum tomato purée

I REALLY DISLIKE most canned plum tomatoes. They seem to taste of the tin and they are very salty. If buying them, try to get them without purée. For many purposes, canned ordinary tomatoes, if they are good, will have a less heavy flavor. Plum tomatoes are normally used for sauce, as they are meatier, with less liquid.

This is used in Tomato Basil Soup (page 67), Curry Tomato Soup (page 72), Southwestern Corn and Tomato Soup (page 113), and Celery-Tomato Soup (page 48). This base can be made with or without the garlic.

**5 pounds (2.25 kg) ripe plum tomatoes, cored and cut into
    1-inch (2.5-cm) cubes**
1 cup (250 ml) olive oil
12 medium cloves garlic, smashed and peeled, optional

IN A MEDIUM STOCKPOT, combine the tomatoes, olive oil and, if using, garlic, and place over high heat until steam forms. Cover and lower the heat. Cook, stirring occasionally, for 30 minutes, or until the tomatoes are very soft. Pass the tomatoes through the medium disc of a food mill. Return to the pot. Bring to a boil. Lower the heat and simmer, uncovered, stirring frequently to avoid scorching, for 1 hour, or until the mixture is thick.

Use immediately, or refrigerate for up to 3 days or freeze.

MAKES 8 CUPS (2 L)

zucchini purée

ZUCCHINI'S OVERPOPULATION of the home garden is proverbial. Make and freeze this, and the green multitude will no longer seem like unwanted children. The peeled version is milder and lighter.

This base is used for Cabbage-Dill Potage (page 103), Zucchini Gazpacho (page 46), and Chilled Zucchini and Parsley Soup (page 54). Once made, the unpeeled base easily makes a good zucchini soup. Heat one part defrosted base to one part chicken stock and season to taste with salt and pepper.

2 tablespoons (30 g) unsalted butter or olive oil

3 pounds (1.4 kg) medium zucchini, trimmed, peeled or unpeeled, quartered lengthwise, and cut across into ½-inch (1-cm) lengths

IN A MEDIUM STOCKPOT, heat the butter or oil over medium heat until bubbling. Stir in the zucchini. Lower the heat and cover the pot. Cook, stirring frequently, for 45 minutes or until the zucchini is very tender. Remove from the heat and cool slightly.

Pass through the fine disc of a food mill, or purée in a food processor. Use immediately, or refrigerate for up to 3 days or freeze.

MAKES 3¾ CUPS (ABOUT 1 L)

celery
SOUP BASE

CELERY IS RATHER STRINGY and so this base cannot be successfully puréed in a food processor. It must be passed through a food mill or a sieve. This is used in Celery Soup with Lima Beans, Asparagus, and Peas (page 66) and can be used in Celery-Tomato Soup (page 48).

2 cups (500 ml) water
2 teaspoons kosher salt
2 bunches celery, cut across into 1-inch (2.5-cm) lengths

IN A MEDIUM SAUCEPAN, bring the water and salt to a boil. Stir in the celery. Return to a boil. Lower the heat and simmer, partially covered, stirring occasionally, for 35 minutes.

Pass through the medium disc of a food mill. Use immediately, or refrigerate for up to 3 days or freeze.

MAKES 6 CUPS (1.5 L)

fresh green pea
SOUP BASE

PEAS ARE GOOD for a short period of time when freshly picked. I use their purée for Quick Pea Soup (page 61). I'm sure that good cooks will find other uses. Be warned, shelling the peas takes time.

6¾ pounds (3 kg) peas in the pod, shelled (6 cups [990 g])
5 cups (1.25 l) Basic Chicken Stock (page 345) or commercial chicken broth

IN A MEDIUM SAUCEPAN, bring the peas and stock to a boil. Lower the heat and simmer for 8 to 10 minutes, or until the peas are tender.

In a blender, working in batches of no more than 2 cups (500 ml), purée the mixture. Use immediately, or refrigerate for up to 3 days or freeze.

MAKES ABOUT 8 CUPS (2 L)

red pepper
SOUP BASE

I REALLY LOVE THIS BASE. I have used it instead of tomatoes as the start of a pasta sauce and seasoned it lightly to use with cooked chicken or fish. In this book, it is used for Vichyssoise of Red Pepper (page 45) and Red Pepper Soup (page 44).

While this version makes only 2½ cups (625 ml), it can easily be made in other quantities (see the Variations). Use a large wide pot with a footed cake cooling rack inside. Put in as many peppers as will fit with the lid on. Proceed as in the recipe.

2½ pounds (1.1 kg) red bell peppers, cored, seeded, deribbed, and cut into quarters

POUR 1 INCH (2.5 CM) OF WATER into a large wide pot. Place a steamer rack in the bottom of the pot and place the peppers on the rack. Cover. Bring to a boil. Lower the heat and simmer, covered, for 45 minutes, or until the peppers are very soft. Alternatively, place the peppers in a 2½-quart (2.9-l) soufflé dish. Cover tightly with microwave plastic wrap. Cook at 100% power in a 650- to 700-watt oven for 15 minutes (or cook in a 400- to 500-watt oven for 20 minutes). Prick the plastic to release steam. Remove from the oven and uncover.

Pass the peppers through the fine disc of a food mill. If not using a food mill, purée the peppers in a food processor and then force the mixture through a sieve to remove the skins, but the results will not be as silky.

Use immediately, or refrigerate for up to 3 days or freeze.

MAKES: 2 ½ CUPS (625 ML)

Variations: *To make 1 cup purée:* Core, seed, and derib 1 pound red bell peppers. Place in a 2½-quart, (2.5-l) soufflé dish. Cover tightly with microwave plastic wrap. Cook in a 650- to 700-watt oven at 100% power for 10 minutes; or cook in a 400- to 500-watt oven for 15 minutes.

To make 5¼ cups purée: Core, seed, and derib 5 pounds red bell peppers. Place in a 5-quart (5-l) casserole. Cover tightly with microwave plastic wrap. Cook in a 650- to 700-watt oven at 100% power for 22 minutes. (This quantity doesn't work well in 400- to 500-watt ovens.)

From stock to soup

NOODLES, DUMPLINGS, MEATBALLS,
SAUCES, AND OTHER GOOD THINGS

SOUP IS THE BEST DRESSED of foods, sporting sprigs of herbs, thin streams of olive oil, or plump grains of rice. Consommé or its precursor, stock, has a particularly rich assortment of furbelows. I use stock for many things, but I sometimes think that most people make it for the things they can put in it.

From stock to soup is a very short distance—a noodle's width, a vegetable's square, a dumpling's diameter, or a crouton's cube.

The Viennese have a word for these things, *einlagen,* or "inlay." As Lillian Langseth Christensen indicated in *Gourmet's Old Vienna Cookbook,* the word doesn't mean something from the dentist but rather garnishes for clear soup. These garnishes were variously placed neatly in the individual soup bowls before the soup was added, or put into a tureen along with the soup, or simply served in the soup.

Many of these things that float on or go in or next to soup are in this chapter. A few are Viennese, but there are also Russian, French, Italian, North American, Central American, South American, Chinese, and other Asian solids and sauces.

For the simplest additions, look at the vegetables on pages 447–451. Remember salt and pepper as well as herbs and spices. Fresh herbs such as tarragon, dill, lemongrass, basil, and parsley and spices such as ginger and galangal (a rhizome related to ginger) should be used fresh if at all possible. Frozen is the next-best alternative. Sprigs of tarragon can be frozen individually and then put in a plastic bag. The same can be done with stalks of lemongrass or chopped lemongrass. Dill does not freeze well. Instructions for freezing basil are on page 300.

When adding things that need cooking to a clear soup, cook them separately so as not to cloud the soup.

Noodles and filled pastas

Noodles come both dry and fresh. They are made with a great variety of grains. It used to be that all noodles were called "noodles" when they included eggs, and "macaroni" when they were Italian and were destined for tomato sauce. Today, we seem to have jumped the fence in the other direction, using the word *pasta* for everything, which is pretty silly when we are including Asian rice sticks in our ever-growing larder.

dry noodles

Many good things come in packages, not all of them small. I do love fresh noodles (pages 393–395), but that doesn't lessen the utility and pleasure of the dried kinds. As a child, I loved alphabet soup and would try to collect enough of the right letters to spell out my name. Two B's were hard. I also liked shapes that I could scoop up in a spoon: the tiny stars, the rice shapes, and the bits called peppercorns, acini di pepe. There were also baby bow ties, made with eggs.

Here, I give quantities and weights, dry and cooked, for various noodles. I usually allow about a ½ cup (about 70 g) of cooked noodles per person for a first course in a soup.

Generally speaking, more solid shapes such as macaroni and ditalini do better in chunkier soups, while egg noodles and orzo do better in clear or light soups.

Dry egg noodles: There are 8 uncooked cups (480 g) in a dry pound of fine noodles and 11 uncooked cups (660 g) in a pound of medium egg noodles. They should both be boiled in three times their volume of salted boiling water—5 minutes for fine and 7 minutes for medium—and then drained and chilled under cold running water unless being used immediately.

> 1 cup (45 g) medium egg noodles, uncooked = 1 cup (100 g) cooked
> 1 cup (60 g) fine egg noodles, uncooked = 1 cup (135 g) cooked
> *Baby Bow Ties:* 1 cup (120 g) cooked in boiling water for 6 to 7 minutes =
> 2 cups (225 g)

Dry pasta without eggs (*pasta secca*):
> *Stellette or Stars:* 1 cup (225 g) cooked in boiling water for 5 minutes =
> 2⅔ cups (540 g)
> *Acini di Pepe:* 1 cup (225 g) cooked in boiling water for 10 minutes =
> 3 cups (540 g)
> *Orzo (Riso):* 1 cup (180 g) dry cooked in boiling water for 12 to 14 minutes =
> 2 cups (360 g)
> *Alphabets:* 1 cup (135 g) cooked in boiling water for 10 minutes = 2 cups (300 g)

Macaroni: 1 cup (120 g) cooked in boiling water for 9 to 12 minutes =
    1½ cups (180 g)

Ditalini or Tubetti: 1 cup (225 g) cooked in boiling water for 9 to 10 minutes =
    2⅔ cups (450 g)

Bean Vermicelli or Rice Sticks: 1 package (1.7 ounce; 50 g) cut or broken across
    into 2-inch (5-cm) lengths, soaked for 15 minutes in 6 cups (1.5 l) warm
    water, and then cooked in boiling water for 1 to 2 minutes = 1 cup (65 g)

Udon: 1 package (7 ounces; 200 g) cooked in a large amount of lightly salted
    boiling water for 10 minutes = 3 cups (400 g)

fresh egg noodles

When I was a child, I knew a Hungarian family that had an extraordinarily fine cook. She was a large, softly round woman who seemed to have been bleached by the steam in the kitchen and all the flour with which she worked. Her most extraordinary feat was the stretching of strudel dough. The large wooden table in the center of the kitchen was covered with a spotless white tablecloth. Palms down, fingers curled under, she stretched the dough with the backs of her knuckles until it was tissue-thin. On other days, the same table was used to roll noodle dough, golden with egg yolks. The backs of chairs and a sort of clothesline across the kitchen were draped with drying noodles.

Some noodles couldn't be hung as they were cut into small shapes: squares, lozenges, triangles, and half-moons. The strip ones varied from very thin for consommé to almost an inch wide to be served with goulash. The long strips were all formed in the same way. The big rectangle of dough was rolled up loosely and then cut across so that ribbons would form when the rounds were shaken out.

It was many years before I saw Italian fresh pasta being rolled out, this time by the grandmother of a high school classmate. She was a tiny woman and had to stand on a box her son had made for her to reach the well-scrubbed board. She used what looked like a piece of a broom handle to roll out the dough made silky with the addition of olive oil. When its thinness met with her approbation, she either cut it in the way I knew or cut it into squares or circles for delicious fillings that burst with flavor in the mouth. She was from the north of Italy, and most meals started with some version of this pasta.

Gradually, I learned to make these noodles on my own, although I seldom roll them by hand and even have resorted to bought sheets of fresh pasta. I also learned the thin pancakes the Viennese cut into strips as noodles. I mastered straciatella (page 127), the flourless egg strips that serve as soup in a brodo, often with strips of spinach, made wontons, and I even invented a filling or two for cappelletti.

egg pasta dough

THIS IS SILKY ITALIAN egg pasta dough. It is used for filled pastas (pages 397–401) as well as noodles. It will need to be kneaded by hand; but this dough is soft and pleasant to work with. To knead, the dough should be formed into a ball, flattened with the heel of the hand, rotated a quarter turn, gathered up, and the task repeated until the dough is smooth. The dough will require less kneading if a machine is used, as the piece of dough can simply be put through the rollers several times. If using a board and a rolling pin, use a pin made of wood that is not absolutely smooth. It grabs the dough. Roll smoothly and lightly. If the dough starts snapping back, let it rest for a minute or two before proceeding.

If the dough seems too brittle on a cold winter's day, add a little water a teaspoonful at a time.

Knives or cutters for pasta should have sharp smooth edges so as not to tear the dough.

>   **2 cups (260 g) all-purpose flour**
>   **¼ teaspoon kosher salt**
>   **3 eggs, lightly beaten**
>   **2 tablespoons olive oil**

for rolling
>   **Extra flour**
>   **Cornmeal (coarse preferred)**

IN A MEDIUM BOWL, mix together the flour and salt. Stir in the eggs and olive oil. Continue to stir until the dough begins to come together around the spoon. Dump out onto a lightly floured surface and knead for 10 minutes, or until silky smooth. Wrap in plastic and let sit at room temperature for 30 minutes before rolling out.

Cut the pasta into four pieces and roll them out according to the following directions.

To roll the pasta by hand: Working on a lightly floured surface, roll the dough from the center toward the edges until the sheet of pasta is thin enough to easily read magazine print—don't use the traditional newspaper; the print will smear onto the dough—through the pasta. Rotate the piece of dough often to prevent crimping, and keep the work surface lightly floured. Cover the sheet of pasta with plastic wrap and a kitchen towel and repeat with the remaining pieces of dough.

To roll the pasta by machine: Form the pieces of pasta dough into rough rectangles about as long as the rollers of the pasta machine are wide. With the rollers at their widest setting, feed the rectangles through the rollers. Continue passing the dough pieces one at a time through the rollers, decreasing the thickness of the rollers by one setting each time, to setting #2. Keep the rolled-out pasta dough covered with plastic wrap and a clean kitchen towel. The thinner the dough, the more quickly it dries out.

To cut egg noodles by hand: Working with one sheet of pasta at a time, cut 3-inch (7.5-cm) wide strips of dough with a large chef's knife. Stack the strips one atop the other and cut them crosswise into wide noodles (¾ to 1 inch; 1.8 to 2.5 cm), medium noodles (½ inch; 1 cm), or thin noodles (about ⅛ inch; .3 cm). Or, working with one sheet at a time, roll up a whole sheet and cut it across.

Put the cut pasta on a cloth lightly dusted with cornmeal, shaking out the strips of pasta and lightly sprinkling them with more cornmeal. Before cooking, shake off the cornmeal.

To cut egg noodles by machine: Insert the roller with the crenellations that will make the desired-width noodles into the machine. Put a cloth dusted with cornmeal onto the counter where the noodles will emerge. Run the strips of pasta made by the machine through the rollers one at a time. As each batch of noodles is made, remove to a cornmeal-dusted cloth.

To use the dough for filled pastas: See the recipes on pages 397–401.

MAKES 1 POUND (450 G)—ABOUT 5½ CUPS UNCOOKED NOODLES, 4 CUPS COOKED;
4 MAIN-COURSE SERVINGS OR 8 FIRST-COURSE SERVINGS

sliced pancakes

THESE ARE A DELICIOUS Austrian conceit. They are a little lighter than egg noodles and can be put in salted Beef Stock (page 165) or Chicken Consommé (page 350) only at the last minute. They are variously called crêpes, frittaten, nudeln, or pfankuchen.

I first had these at my mother-in-law's table. She also made dessert variations with a little sugar and about a teaspoon of melted butter, the palacinky (page 22).

> 1 egg, lightly beaten
> ½ cup (60 g) all-purpose flour
> ¼ teaspoon kosher salt
> ½ cup (125 ml) milk
> Unsalted butter, for cooking

IN A MEDIUM BOWL, whisk together the eggs, flour, salt, and milk until smooth.

Heat a small (8-inch; 20-cm) omelet or crêpe pan over medium-low heat. Rub a paper towel in some butter and lightly grease the bottom of the pan with the towel. Pour 3 tablespoons of the batter into the pan, lifting, tilting, and turning the pan to spread the batter thinly and evenly. Cook for 45 seconds to 1 minute. Turn the crêpe with a spatula. Cook for 45 seconds to 1 minute more, or until the crêpe is just beginning to brown on the second side. Slide the crêpe out onto a plate and allow to cool slightly. Repeat with remaining batter. Roll up the crêpes and cut them across into ¼-inch (.5-cm) strips (if desired, these strips can be cut across into 1½-inch [3.5-cm] lengths).

MAKES 5 CRÊPES, OR 1½ CUPS (375 ML) ¼-INCH- (.5-CM-) WIDE STRIPS;
6 SERVINGS, EACH IN 1 CUP (250 ML) BROTH

When I was very young, I read someplace that at a witch trial the evidence for the prosecution was that the "witch" managed to get the filling into the pies. Even when I was about seven or so, this seemed very strange to me, but I am willing to consider the development of filled pastas as magic—white magic. It is interesting that analogous recipes exist in different parts of the world. It may be a matter of trade routes. Comparing ravioli and wontons, wontons and cappelletti, cappelletti and one form of kreplach does make me feel that more than chance is at play here.

Usually, the dough is cut into rounds or squares. The filling is placed in the center or just off center. If the filling is in the center, the dough around the filling is usually moistened with a little water and a second round or square placed on top. If the filling is off center and if the pasta is a square, it is treated as a diamond; a point of the square is folded over to the opposite point to form a triangle. A round of dough will be folded in half to form a half-moon.

More often than not, once the dough has been folded over, the two opposite points are then attached to each other, either like a child clasping its hands over its tummy, or they meet turned up and away from the third point and are rounded like the arms of a whirling ballerina.

Kreplachs are formed like the triangular arms-folded-over-the-belly type of pasta. There is a more particular kind that is more familiar to me. The filling is placed in the center of the dough round and the edges are folded up to form a tricorne hat.

There are more different doughs and fillings than there are shapes of filled pasta that go in soup.

cappelletti

CAPPELLETTI means "little hats," as they have the shape of bishop's miters. This cap (miter) shape is arrived at when the pasta has been folded. Very small ones are called the navel of Venus. While cappelletti can be made from either a round or a square of pasta, the one from the square, with its pointy top, looks more like the bishop's hat. I prefer those made from rounds, as there is a little less dough so that they are more delicate.

There is often a confusion with tortellini. Tortellini are sometimes used in soup, but the form is usually the simple round—no larger than 1½ inches (3.5 cm) in diameter—folded over to make a half-moon.

continued

While the most common filling is meat-based, Vincenzo Buonassisi gives in his *Il Codice della Pasta* numerous fillings made of cheese or chicken, as well as more complex ones that may include brains, pork, mortadella, sausage, and prosciutto in addition to cheese and chicken breast or pork. I like the simple filling in this recipe but any of the ravioli or kreplach fillings could be used equally easily—and in any shape that amuses.

If making pasta seems too daunting, it is possible to buy fresh sheets of pasta or fresh lasagne noodles and then cut them into squares. They will not be as thin and tender as homemade.

The brodo used ideally would be a mixed one such as that left from making Bollito Misto (page 221). Alternatively, I suggest using Basic Chicken Stock (page 345), Roasted Turkey Stock (page 352), or the lighter Beef Stock (page 165).

for the pasta dough (1 recipe egg pasta dough, page 394, may be substituted)

2 eggs

1 tablespoon olive oil

Approximately 1½ cups (200 g) all-purpose flour

Water, as needed

for the filling

2 tablespoons (30 g) unsalted butter

1 bone-in pork chop (about ¾ pound [360 g])

1 small boneless skinless chicken breast (about ½ pound [225 g])

1 cup (90 g) freshly grated Parmesan cheese

4 egg yolks

½ cup (125 ml) heavy cream

Kosher salt, to taste

Freshly ground black pepper, to taste

Freshly grated Parmesan cheese, for serving

FOR THE DOUGH, in a small bowl, beat the eggs and oil. Put 1¼ cups (165 g) flour in a food processor. With the machine running, pour the egg and oil through the feed tube. Process until a stiff dough forms. Add 2 to 3 tablespoons (16 to 25 g) more flour if necessary. If a dough does not form, add a little water, 1 tablespoon at a time. Remove the dough to a lightly floured board. Knead for about 5 minutes, until the dough is very smooth and elastic; add 2 to 3 tablespoons (16 to 25 g) flour if necessary to keep the dough from sticking. Wrap the dough in plastic and let it rest at room temperature for 15 minutes.

For the filling, in a small frying pan, melt the butter over medium-low heat. Add the pork chop and cook for 6 minutes. Turn and cook for 6 more minutes; no pink should remain in the meat. Remove the chop from the pan and set aside to cool.

In the same skillet, cook the chicken breast over medium heat for 3 minutes. Turn and cook for 3 more minutes; the center should remain barely pink. Place the chicken with the pork to cool.

Cut the pork away from the bone and trim the fat. With a sharp knife, mince the pork and chicken. Do not use a food processor, as it will create mush.

In a small bowl, stir together the meat, Parmesan, egg yolks, heavy cream, salt, and pepper. Cover and set aside.

To make the cappelletti, divide the dough into six pieces. Work with one piece of dough at a time. Keep the rest covered with plastic. Roll out each piece by hand or by machine according to the directions on pages 394–395. With a glass or a sharp cookie cutter, cut the pasta into 2-inch (5-cm) rounds, as close together as possible. Leave the rounds flat on the counter. Quickly, reroll and cut the scraps.

Place 1 teaspoon of the filling in the center of each circle. Brush the edges very lightly with water. Fold the circle over the filling to form a half-moon and press the edges of the dough together to seal. Pick up the half-moon and pinch the enclosed filling lightly between forefinger and thumb. Bring one end of the half-moon around your thumb to meet the other end. You have formed a cappelletto; slip it off your thumb. Firmly pinch the two ends together to seal. Set the finished cappelletto on a lightly floured kitchen towel. Repeat with the remaining circles of dough.

At this point, the cappelletti may be cooked, put aside, uncooked and covered, for up to an hour, or frozen (see Note).

To cook the cappelletti, bring a large pot of salted water to a boil. Slip the cappelletti into the pot a few at a time until as many as desired, or all are in the pot. Stir gently until the water returns to a boil. Boil until the pasta is tender but firm, about 3 minutes. Drain thoroughly in a colander. Serve with Parmesan cheese.

MAKES 6 DOZEN CAPPELLETTI; 9 FIRST-COURSE SERVINGS, EACH IN 1½ CUPS (375 ML) BROTH OR 5 MAIN-COURSE SERVINGS, EACH IN 2 CUPS (500 ML) BROTH

Note: To freeze uncooked cappelletti, place them on a baking sheet in a single layer. Freeze until just solid, about 1 hour. Transfer to plastic freezer bags and seal tightly. Frozen cappelletti can be stored for up to 3 months. They should be cooked right out of the freezer, without defrosting. In that case, add about 1 minute to the cooking time.

duck or goose
CONFIT RAVIOLI

WHEN I MAKE QUICK CONFIT, I often have extra. When I get the energy, I make up a batch or two of these ravioli and use them for a very elegant dinner or freeze them for another time.

Sometimes I substitute cooked beef left from making beef stock.

Serve this delicate ravioli in duck stock seasoned with salt and pepper and a few blanched hair-thin strips of lemon zest. Beware! These ravioli are so good, thirty-six are really enough for only four people. If serving more people, double the filling and use a whole recipe of pasta.

¼ pound (120 g) torn meat from Quick Duck Confit (page 402) or
    Quick Goose Confit (page 404) or other cooked duck or goose, or
    even beef left from making stock (about ¾ cup)
Zest of ¼ lemon removed with a peeler in strips, blanched for 1 minute,
    run under cold water, and very finely chopped
¼ teaspoon finely chopped sage
¼ teaspoon kosher salt
A few grinds of black pepper
½ recipe Egg Pasta Dough (page 394)

IF USING CONFIT, CAREFULLY blot with paper towels to remove excess fat. With a sharp knife, chop the confit or meat fine. Do not use a food processor, as it will turn the meat to a paste. Mix together the meat, lemon zest, sage, salt, and pepper.

Cut the pasta into two pieces and wrap one in plastic. Working with one piece at a time, roll out the pasta by hand or by machine according to the directions on pages 394–395. (If rolling by hand, roll the dough thin enough to *easily* read magazine print through it. If using a machine, roll to the thinnest setting.) Cut the dough into 2½-inch (6.25-cm) rounds. The pasta is so thin it dries out very quickly, so cut only 2 or 3 at a time, and keep the uncut rolled-out dough covered with plastic wrap and a clean kitchen towel. Place ½ teaspoon of the filling in the center of each round. Brush the edges of the dough with a tiny bit of water. Fold the dough over the filling to form a half-moon. Press the edges of the dough together to seal. Place the formed ravioli on a parchment paper–lined cookie sheet and cover with plastic wrap. When the first strip of dough is used up, roll out the second piece and continue making ravioli until all the filling is used.

These ravioli can be used immediately, refrigerated for up to 3 hours, or frozen on the cookie sheet, then removed and stored in plastic freezer bags until ready to use.

Cook the ravioli in a large pot of boiling lightly salted water for 1 to 2 minutes, or until the pasta is cooked through. If the ravioli are frozen, do not defrost before boiling; simply cook a few minutes longer.

MAKES 36 RAVIOLI; 4 ELEGANT FIRST-COURSE SERVINGS, EACH IN 1½ CUPS (375 ML) SEASONED DUCK STOCK (PAGE 353), OR BEEF STOCK (PAGE 165), IF USING BEEF

quick confit

ORIGINALLY, confit was a southwestern French mode of preserving meats for the winter, in the days before refrigeration. Now it is prepared for the resulting unctuous and delicious meat. Pork, duck, and goose, as well as bird gizzards, are salted, seasoned, and cooked. Then they are packed in rendered fat and put to mellow in a wine cellar or other dark place—or, today, the refrigerator.

Confit is a wonderful ingredient for soups and salads and it can be bought, but often with some difficulty. It takes time to make but is well worthwhile.

I use it for what I call Garburesque of Goose or Duck (page 161), Cabbage and Goose Confit Soup (page 21), and White Bean Soup with Confit and Tomato (page 160). This recipe and the one for Quick Goose Confit that follows have the advantage of not needing a long curing and ripening process. However, because they aren't cured, they should definitely be eaten sooner than traditional confit. They can be frozen, however, which gives them a long life. This will not improve their flavor in the way a refrigerated aging does. These confits are refrigerated only briefly, so people don't have to wait forever to have a decent confit.

The first time making confit is the most difficult: rendering the fat and wondering if it will be enough to cover the meat. After the first time, there is the added advantage of all the fat saved from previous confits. This relieves some anxiety and makes the work a breeze.

When the meat from the confit has been used, put the fat into a plastic container in the freezer. Any fat left when the confit has been used makes the most delicious frying medium for potatoes and/or onions, and a very little bit added to a soup can give a wallop of flavor. The fat can be kept for another bout of confit.

The rendering process described in the recipes also gives a dividend of cracklings. They are addictive just sprinkled with salt, but they also make a fine topping for soups .

Cutting up the ducks or goose for confit will result in extra necks, wing tips, backs, and gizzards, all of which can be used to make Duck or Goose Stock (page 253).

quick duck confit

WHEN MAKING CONFIT, keep out the breasts for eating fresh. Confit, rewarmed, is good in salad.

Two 5-pound (2.25-kg) ducks, excess fat removed, including skin and fat from back, fat and skin cut into ½-inch (1-cm) pieces and duck cut into 8 servings (see page 122; backs, necks, wing tips, and gizzards reserved for stock)

2 tablespoons kosher salt

1 medium clove garlic, smashed, peeled, and coarsely chopped

1 medium shallot, finely chopped

2 teaspoons crushed black pepper

2 tablespoons coarsely chopped parsley

1 bay leaf, crumbled

1 head garlic, cut in half crosswise

2 whole cloves

PLACE THE CUT-UP FAT in a medium saucepan with 3 tablespoons water. Cook over low heat for about 1 hour, or until all the fat is rendered and the pieces of skin are golden brown, crisp, and floating on top of the fat.

While the fat is cooking, rub the duck pieces on all sides with the salt, the chopped garlic, the shallots, pepper, parsley, and bay leaf.

Place a rack in the upper third of the oven. Heat the oven to 500° (260°C; highest gas mark; #9 British regulo).

After 30 minutes, wipe the excess herbs off the duck. Place the duck pieces skin side up in a large roasting pan. Roast for 15 minutes, turn pieces over, and roast for 10 minutes longer. The skin of the duck should start to brown and quite a bit of fat should have been rendered.

Meanwhile, skim the cracklings (crisp skin) from the rendered fat. Drain on paper towels and serve warm, sprinkled with salt, or use to top a soup. Strain the fat through a fine-mesh sieve into a tall narrow stockpot. Set the pot over low heat, add the halved garlic and the cloves, and simmer for 5 minutes. Remove from the heat and allow to stop bubbling.

Remove the duck from the oven. Arrange the duck pieces compactly in the stockpot with the fat and garlic. Strain the fat from the roasting pan into the pot; the fat will not fully cover the duck. Return the pot to the stove over very low heat. After about 15 minutes, enough fat should have been rendered to cover the duck. Cook over low heat for 2 hours, or until the duck is very tender when pierced with a knife.

Remove from the stove. Cool completely in the fat.

The duck can be used right away or stored in the fat, refrigerated, for up to 1 week. For longer storage, freeze.

MAKES 2 WHOLE DUCKS (16 PIECES); 2 POUNDS (900 G) OR 4 ½ CUPS (1.25 L) TORN MEAT

quick goose confit

AS WHEN MAKING DUCK CONFIT, always save the back, neck, wing tips, and gizzards to make a stock. The goose will also provide the leg bone ends. The cracklings from this can be used in Navy Bean Purée (page 312).

One 12-pound (5.5-kg) goose, excess fat removed, including skin and fat from back, fat cut into ½-inch (1-cm) pieces and goose cut into 14 serving pieces (see page 122; back, neck, wing tips, and bony leg ends reserved for stock)

3 tablespoons kosher salt

2 medium cloves garlic, smashed, peeled, and very finely chopped

1 medium shallot, very finely chopped

2 teaspoons crushed black pepper

2 tablespoons chopped parsley

1 bay leaf, crumbled

1 medium head garlic, cut in half crosswise

2 whole cloves

PLACE THE CUT-UP FAT in a medium saucepan with 3 tablespoons water. Cook over low heat for one hour, or until all the fat is rendered and the pieces of skin are golden brown, crisp, and floating on top of the fat.

While the fat is cooking, rub the goose pieces on all sides with the salt, chopped garlic, the shallot, pepper, parsley, and bay leaf.

Place a rack in the upper third of the oven. Heat the oven to 500°F (260°C; highest gas mark; #9 British regulo).

After 30 minutes, wipe the excess herbs off the goose. Place the goose pieces skin side up in a large roasting pan. Roast for 15 minutes, turn the pieces over, and roast for 10 minutes longer. The skin of the goose should start to brown and quite a bit of fat should have been rendered.

Meanwhile, skim the cracklings (crisp skin) from rendered fat. Drain on paper towels and serve warm, sprinkled with salt, or use to top a soup. Strain the fat through a fine-mesh sieve into a tall narrow stockpot.

Set the pot over low heat, add the halved garlic and the cloves and simmer for 5 minutes. Remove from the heat and allow to stop bubbling.

Remove the goose from the oven. Place the pieces compactly in the stockpot with the fat and garlic. Strain the fat from the roasting pan into the pot; the fat will not fully cover the goose. Place the pot back on the stove over very low heat. After about 10 minutes, enough fat should have been rendered to completely cover the goose pieces. Cook over low heat for 2 hours, or until the goose is very tender when pierced with a knife.

Remove from the stove. Cool completely in the fat.

The goose can be used right away or stored in the fat, refrigerated, for up to 1 week. For longer storage, freeze.

MAKES 1 WHOLE GOOSE (14 PIECES)

pelmenyi

ORIGINALLY, pelmenyi were a Siberian specialty made at the end of summer with meat from animals that it would be too expensive to winter over. The little filled dough pockets were left outside to freeze. When they were wanted, a block was hacked off and they were poached either in broth or water.

The Russian Tea Room used to serve these, Wednesdays at lunch only, in chicken broth with the cooked gizzards, dill, and sour cream. Many Russians also serve them on a plate with butter and a side choice of sour cream or vinegar—surprisingly good. They still freeze well. A few can be added to any European-style chicken soup.

If there are any cooked gizzards left from making the chicken stock, chop them up and add them to the stock while the pelmenyi are cooking. Pelmenyi dough has no egg and is a little more robust than egg noodle dough. The cooking method is also an exception, as the pelmenyi are cooked right in the broth.

for the dough

> 2 cups (260 g) sifted all-purpose flour
>
> ½ teaspoon kosher salt
>
> ¼ cup (180 ml) water

for the filling

> ½ pound (225 g) ground beef
>
> ½ pound (225 g) ground pork—half fat, half lean
>
> 1 medium onion, very finely chopped
>
> 1 teaspoon water
>
> 1 teaspoon kosher salt
>
> Freshly ground black pepper, to taste
>
> 1 egg white, beaten, for egg wash

for cooking the pelmenyi

> 10 cups (2.5 l) lightly seasoned Extra-Rich Chicken Broth (page 349)
>   or Basic Chicken Stock (page 345)
>
> Finely chopped fully cooked chicken gizzards, optional

for serving

> Sour cream
>
> Chopped dill

FOR THE DOUGH, in a food processor, whirl together the flour and salt to combine and aerate. With the machine on, pour in the water in a thin stream. The dough will form very small kernels and some will begin to collect into a ball. Turn the dough out onto a floured work surface and knead just until smooth. Form into a flattish round. Wrap in plastic and refrigerate for 1 to 2 hours.

For the filling, in a medium bowl, lightly mix the beef, pork, and onion together. Stir in the water, salt, and pepper. Test the seasoning by sautéing a small patty, and adjust if necessary.

Roll the dough out by hand or by machine according to the directions on pages 394–395: Roll by hand to 1/16 inch (.25 cm) thick; by machine, to the #3 setting. Cut into circles using a 1½-inch (3.75-cm) round, preferably scalloped, cutter. Mound ½ teaspoon filling in the center of half the rounds. Brush the remaining rounds with a thin wash of egg white. Place egg wash side down on top of the filled rounds, pressing the seal tightly. Place on a cookie sheet lined with a tea towel. If time allows, and to replicate the frigid winter climate of Siberia, freeze overnight according to the directions in the Note following the recipe for cappelletti on page 399 before cooking; otherwise, allow to dry uncovered in the refrigerator for at least 2 hours.

Heat the chicken broth to a gentle boil in a 4- to 5-quart (4- to 5-l) pot. Add the pelmenyi a few at a time, until all are in the pot, and stir gently until the broth returns to a boil. Stir in the giblets, if using. Cook, stirring occasionally, until the pelmenyi are tender, about 5 minutes, 6 if frozen. Ladle the pelmenyi and broth into warm bowls and top each serving with a dollop of sour cream and a sprinkling of chopped fresh dill.

MAKES 70 TO 75 DUMPLINGS; 9 FIRST-COURSE SERVINGS, EACH IN 1¼ CUPS (310 ML) BROTH, OR 6 MAIN-COURSE SERVINGS, EACH IN 1½ CUPS (375 ML) BROTH

kreplach

Shortly after World War II, when there were still Yiddish-speaking grandmothers and psychoanalysis was the new science and therapy—to be idolized, feared, and made fun of—there was a kreplach joke. Grandma is upset because Ben, her little grandson, won't eat her famous kreplach. Her friend Becky says that there is a new doctor in the neighborhood, a psychoanalyst, and maybe he can help. Grandma goes to see the doctor and tells her sad story. The doctor says, "It's very simple: The child sees the kreplach and it's a mystery, frightening. Go home. Show him how it's made and everything will be fine."

Grandma goes home and calls Ben to come into the kitchen. She sits him on a stool next to the worktable and puts some flour on the table. "See, isn't that beautiful white flour?" "Yes, Grandma, it's beautiful." She sprinkles some salt and water on the flour and, gathering it up with her hands, kneads it into a smooth ball of dough. "Look, Ben, isn't it smooth and nice? It's dough." "Yes, Grandma, it's beautiful." She takes some meat and chops it with her knife, chops some onions and carrots. "Doesn't that look nice?" Then she panfries the meat and vegetables. "Gee, Grandma, that smells wonderful." She rolls out the dough and cuts it into rounds. "See, Ben, I take a little bit of the meat and I put it in the middle of the round." "Oh, that looks good." "Now I pick up one side of the dough, and the second side of the dough." "Oh, Grandma, I can't wait." "And I pick up the third side and bring them together." "OY! Kreplach!"

Nevertheless, I like kreplach. Esti, who works with me and is a Sabra, fondly remembers the chicken liver, cheese, and meat kreplach that her mother used to make. Some were fried and served with fried onions on top and others were made for soup. Her mother made them as if they were round ravioli, with two pieces of dough—which shows that authentic is a family's memory.

The dough used here is the same simple one that is used for pelmenyi, but any egg noodle dough can be substituted and rolled more thinly than the pelmenyi dough.

While chicken kreplach and chicken liver kreplach were both probably made to use up the rest of the chicken from making chicken soup, I am particularly fond of the beef version, using up some of the meat from making beef stock.

for the dough

2 cups (225 g) all-purpose flour
½ teaspoon kosher salt

2½ tablespoons vegetable oil or rendered chicken or goose fat

¾ small onion, very finely chopped

1 small carrot, peeled and very finely chopped

1 small clove garlic, smashed, peeled, and very finely chopped

1½ cups (180 g) finely chopped (but not so fine as to be puréed)
   beef boiled on its own or left from making stock (page 165)

1 tablespoon plus 2 teaspoons very finely chopped parsley

1½ teaspoons kosher salt, or to taste

Freshly ground black pepper, to taste

1 egg plus 1 egg yolk, lightly beaten

FOR THE DOUGH, in a food processor, pulse the flour with the salt to aerate. With the machine running, slowly pour ¾ cup (180 ml) water through the feed tube. The dough will form very small kernels and some will begin to collect into a ball. Turn the dough out onto a floured work surface and knead just until smooth. Form into a flattish round. Wrap in plastic wrap and refrigerate for 1 to 2 hours.

For the filling, in a small frying pan, heat the oil or fat over medium heat. Stir in the onion and carrot. Cook, stirring, for 4 minutes, or until the vegetables are beginning to soften. Stir in the garlic and cook for 1 minute. Stir in the meat, parsley, salt, and pepper. Cook, stirring, for 2 minutes. Remove to a small bowl. Allow the filling to cool slightly. Add the beaten egg and stir thoroughly to combine.

Cut the dough into four pieces. Work with one piece at a time and keep the rest covered with plastic wrap. On a lightly floured surface, roll the dough out to a little less than ⅛ inch (.3 cm) thick. Cut the dough into rounds with a 2¾-inch (7-cm) cookie cutter. Gather together the scraps, roll to the same thickness, and cut out more rounds.

Place 1 level teaspoon of filling in the center of each round. Lift three edges of the dough up over the filling so that the base forms a triangle. Press the edges of the dough together to seal and form the tricorne hat. Place the finished kreplach on a parchment or waxed paper–lined baking sheet and cover with a kitchen towel. Use immediately, or freeze on the sheet and then transfer to freezer bags.

Bring a large pot of lightly salted water to a boil. Working in batches, so as not to crowd the pot, slide the fresh or frozen kreplach into the boiling water. Reduce the heat and cook at a low boil for about 7 to 9 minutes, or until the dough is cooked through and the filling hot. With a slotted spoon, remove from the pot, drain on paper towels, and keep warm in a little of the broth.

MAKES 45 DUMPLINGS; 15 FIRST-COURSE SERVINGS,
EACH IN 1¼ CUPS (310 ML) SEASONED BROTH

chicken and pork

AS LIFE HAS GOTTEN TRENDIER and our foods—at least in restaurants—more exotic, that semi-ubiquitous standby of old Chinese restaurants, wonton soup, is disappearing, which is too bad as good wontons are delicious.

I am a bit lazy and tend to use premade wonton skins (wrappers) that I can buy. Eileen Yin-Fei Lo's *The Dim Sum Dumpling Book* gives a recipe for making them from scratch. They are not very different from noodle dough except that they have baking soda added. Wontons are shaped like cappelletti, but are slightly larger.

It is a good idea to double this recipe and freeze any extras. Make sure to remove as much sinew as possible from the pork, as it will not break down in the food processor.

for the filling

**3 ounces (90 g) skinless boneless chicken breast,
cut into 1-inch (2.5-cm) pieces**

**¼ pound (120 g) pork shoulder, including fat and lean,
sinew removed and cut into 1-inch (2.5-cm) pieces**

1 tablespoon mirin (sweet rice wine)

½ teaspoon peeled grated ginger

½ teaspoon toasted sesame oil

1 teaspoon soy sauce

A few grinds of black pepper

27 wonton skins (3 inches [7.5 cm] square)

IN A FOOD PROCESSOR, combine all the filling ingredients. Pulse about forty times to chop medium-fine. Remove to a bowl and stir a few times with a wooden spoon to ensure that the mixture is properly amalgamated.

Work with a few wrappers at a time and keep the rest covered with plastic wrap to avoid drying. Have a cup of water handy.

Place a wrapper on the counter at an angle, to form a diamond. Place 1 level teaspoon of filling in the center. Moisten the edges with a little water. Fold over the far point to the near point to make a triangle. Press the edges together to seal. Lift the points at the ends of the long side of the triangle and wrap over the mound of filling, so that they slightly overlap. Put a dab of water between the points and press together. Place the finished wonton on a waxed paper–lined cookie sheet. Repeat with the remaining wrappers and filling, keeping the finished wontons covered with a towel. Use immediately, or freeze on the sheet and transfer to freezer bags.

Bring a large pot of water to a boil. Carefully drop the fresh or frozen wontons into the boiling water. Lower the heat slightly, keeping the water at a low boil. Cook the wontons for about 4 minutes if fresh and 5 minutes if frozen, or until the filling is cooked through. With a slotted spoon, skim the wontons out and drain on a kitchen towel.

MAKES 27 WONTONS; 9 FIRST-COURSE SERVINGS, EACH IN 1½ CUPS (375 ML) BROTH

...ail onion, cut into ¼-inch (.5-cm) ...
6 cups (1.5 l) Roasted Pork Stock (page 000)
½ cup (100 g) pearl barley
1 medium rib celery, peeled and cut into ¼-inch (.5-cm
20 sage leaves, cut across into narrow strips
1 large bunch flat-leaf parsley, leaves only, coarsely chop,
2½ teaspoons kosher salt
Fresh   d black pepper to taste

shrimp and pork
WONTONS

THE FILLING FOR THESE WONTONS is more colorful but milder than the one on page 410, so that the shrimp flavor can shine.

for the filling

⅓ pound (150 g) spinach, stemmed and well washed

¼ pound (120 g) pork shoulder, including lean and fat, sinew removed and cut into 1-inch (2.5-cm) pieces

4 large shrimp, peeled, deveined, and cut across into 4 pieces

1 tablespoon soy sauce

1 egg white

½ teaspoon kosher salt

A few grinds of black pepper

1 medium scallion, trimmed and finely chopped

40 wonton skins (3 inches [7.5 cm] squared)

PLACE THE SPINACH, with the water clinging to it from washing, in a medium frying pan over medium-low heat. Cover and cook for about 30 seconds, or until the spinach loses a little volume. Uncover and continue to cook, stirring, for 1 to 2 more minutes, or until the spinach is completely wilted. Or to cook in the microwave, place the spinach in a microwave-safe container and cover with plastic wrap. Cook for 1½ minutes. Remove from the oven and carefully uncover.

With either method, allow the spinach to cool a little. Squeeze the spinach well to rid it of any excess liquid. There should be about 2 tablespoons.

In a food processor, combine the spinach and all the remaining filling ingredients except the scallions. Pulse about forty times to combine and chop medium-fine. Remove to a bowl and stir a few times with a wooden spoon to ensure that the mixture is properly amalgamated. Stir in the chopped scallion.

Work with a few wrappers at a time and keep the rest covered with plastic wrap to avoid drying. Have a cup of water handy.

Place a wrapper on the counter at an angle to form a diamond. Place 1 level tea-spoon of filling in the center. Moisten the edges with a little water. Fold over the far point to the near point to make a triangle. Press the edges together to seal. Lift the points at the ends of the long side of the triangle and wrap over the mound of filling, so that the points slightly overlap. Put a dab of water between the points and press together. Place the finished wonton on a waxed paper–lined cookie sheet. Repeat with the remaining wrappers and filling, keeping the finished wontons covered with a towel. Use immediately, or freeze on the sheet and transfer to freezer bags.

Bring a large pot of water to a boil. Carefully drop the fresh or frozen wontons into the boiling water. Lower the heat slightly, keeping the water at a low boil. Cook the wontons for about 4 minutes if fresh and 5 minutes if frozen, or until the filling is cooked through. With a slotted spoon, skim the wontons out and drain on a kitchen towel.

MAKES 40 WONTONS; 12 TO 14 FIRST-COURSE SERVINGS,
EACH IN 1½ CUPS (375 ML) BROTH

Bobblers and sitters with soup

Like noodles and filled pasta, most of these can be added to seasoned stock or con-sommé to make a first course. Some are served when the soup or broth turns into a meal with vegetables or other foods.

cornmeal dumplings

THERE ARE TRADITIONAL POLENTA GNOCCHI for soup, but they are much heavier than these dumplings. To stay within the Italian tradition, use the Parmesan cheese and black pepper. For a Southwestern fillip, use the cilantro and jala-peño instead.

The recipe is easily doubled. As these dumplings are largish, two per person should be adequate. Use the broth from Bollito Misto (page 221), or seasoned Beef Stock (page 165) or Basic Chicken Stock (page 345).

> 6 tablespoons (45 g) cornmeal, plus ½ cup (60 g) for rolling dumplings
>
> 1 teaspoon olive oil
>
> ½ teaspoon kosher salt
>
> 6 tablespoons (45 g) all-purpose flour
>
> ½ teaspoon baking powder
>
> 1 egg, separated, plus 1 egg yolk
>
> 1 medium jalapeño pepper, seeded, deribbed, and minced, or 2 tablespoons freshly grated Parmesan cheese
>
> 3 tablespoons coarsely chopped cilantro, if using the jalapeño, or freshly ground black pepper, to taste, if using the Parmesan

IN A SMALL SAUCEPAN, bring the 6 tablespoons (45 g) cornmeal and 1 cup (250 ml) water to a boil, whisking with a wire whisk. Continue cooking, stirring vigorously with a wooden spoon, for about 3 minutes, or until the polenta is very thick and dry. Stir in the oil and salt. Remove from the stove and cool to room temperature.

Combine the flour and baking powder. Stir the egg yolks and the flour and baking powder into the cooled polenta. In a small bowl, whip the egg white until stiff but not dry. Stir one third of the egg white into the polenta to lighten the mixture, then fold in the rest. Stir in the cilantro and jalapeño, or the cheese and pepper.

Spread the ½ cup (60 g) cornmeal on a plate. Scoop out heaping tablespoons of the batter, drop into the cornmeal and shape into dumplings, rolling in the cornmeal and patting into balls.

Bring a large pot of lightly salted water to a boil. Drop in the dumplings and simmer for 6 minutes. Turn the dumplings and simmer for 6 to 8 minutes more, or until cooked through. With a slotted spoon, remove to a paper towel to drain.

MAKES 8 DUMPLINGS; 4 FIRST-COURSE SERVINGS,
EACH IN 1 CUP (250 ML) BROTH

Note: The dumpling mixture can be made ahead and refrigerated overnight. The dumplings can also be shaped and cooked ahead, then refrigerated. Reheat in simmering water or stock for about 6 minutes.

mushroom dumplings

I THINK these are a fine creation. Serve them in Mushroom Broth (page 382) or sea-soned Beef Stock (page 165).

1 tablespoon (15 g) unsalted butter

2 medium shallots, very finely chopped

½ pound (225 g) white button mushrooms, trimmed, wiped clean,
   and finely chopped

1¼ teaspoons kosher salt

1 tablespoon finely minced flat-leaf parsley

½ cup (120 g) whole-milk ricotta

½ cup (65 g) all-purpose flour, plus 2 to 3 tablespoons
   (16 to 25g) for rolling

2 egg yolks

Freshly ground black pepper, to taste

IN A MEDIUM FRYING PAN, melt the butter over medium heat. Stir in the shallots and cook for 5 minutes, or until they are wilted. Stir in the mushrooms and salt. Cook, stirring occasionally, for 10 minutes. Stir in the parsley. Continue cooking, stirring frequently, for 15 minutes, or until the mushrooms and shallots are dark golden brown and dry. Remove the mixture to a bowl and allow to cool to room temperature.

Add the ricotta, the ½ cup (65 g) flour, the egg yolks, and pepper to the mushroom mixture and mix thoroughly to create a very moist dough.

Sprinkle a work surface with 2 tablespoons (16 g) flour. Divide the dough in two. Roll each piece into a log approximately 15 inches (37.5 cm) long and 1 inch (2.5 cm) in diameter, using additional flour as necessary to keep the dough from sticking. Cut across into small dumplings about ½ inch (1 cm) thick.

Bring a large pot of lightly salted water to a boil. Working in batches if necessary, simmer the dumplings for 5 minutes, or until they are floating and the centers are cooked; the dumplings will be moist in the center and slightly chewy.

MAKES 60 DUMPLINGS; 6 TO 8 FIRST-COURSE SERVINGS,
EACH IN 1½ CUPS (375 ML) BROTH

tarragon dumplings

THIS IS A TYPICAL GERMAN RECIPE that I have lightened with extra egg whites and flavored with tarragon, lovely if a bit far afield from tradition. These dumplings are pretty filling, so the recipe is ample for four or five people. It can easily be multiplied. Serve in seasoned Beef Stock (page 165) or Extra-Rich Chicken Stock (page 349), and consider adding some whole tarragon leaves to the finished soup.

The batter must be refrigerated for at least 1 hour, or preferably overnight, or it will be too soft to form. In any case, the forming should be done with hands thoroughly wet with cold water.

> 2 tablespoons (30 g) unsalted butter
>
> 1 cup (250 ml) milk
>
> ½ cup (90 g) instant Cream of Wheat (farina)
>
> 2 eggs, separated, plus 2 egg whites
>
> 1 teaspoon kosher salt
>
> Freshly ground black pepper, to taste
>
> 2 tablespoons tarragon leaves, finely chopped

IN A SMALL SAUCEPAN, melt the butter. Stir in the milk and bring to a simmer. Add the Cream of Wheat in a slow steady stream, stirring constantly. Cook, stirring, until thick and smooth, about 1 minute. Remove from the stove and let cool.

Stir the egg yolks into the cooled mixture. In a large bowl, whip the egg whites until stiff but not dry. Stir one third of the egg whites into the Cream of Wheat mixture. Fold in the remaining egg whites. Season with the salt, pepper, and tarragon. Refrigerate for at least 1 hour, or overnight.

Bring a large pot of lightly salted water to a boil. Wet or oil hands. Scoop out mounded tablespoons of the batter and shape the dumplings by tossing gently back and forth. Drop as many dumplings as will fit without crowding into the boiling water. Lower the heat and simmer for 5 to 10 minutes (depending on the temperature of the batter), turning once, until cooked through. With a slotted spoon, remove the dumplings to a plate and keep warm while cooking the remaining dumplings.

MAKES 16 DUMPLINGS; 4 TO 5 FIRST-COURSE SERVINGS,
EACH IN 1¼ CUPS (310 ML) BROTH

parsley dumplings

I ADAPTED THESE TYPICAL Southern dumplings from *Hoppin' John's Charleston, Beaufort, and Savannah Cookbook,* by John Martin Taylor. He graciously gave me permission to use them. These are used for Chicken with Dumplings (page 140). They would also be good made half-size and cooked for 8 minutes before turning and then 8 minutes longer.

This is basically a biscuit dough and can be baked following any standard instructions.

1⅓ cups (170 g) cake (weak) flour

1½ teaspoons baking powder

¾ teaspoon kosher salt

3½ tablespoons (50 g) cold unsalted butter

6 tablespoons (25 g) coarsely chopped parsley

6 tablespoons (90 ml) milk

Seasoned stock for cooking, optional

SIFT THE DRY INGREDIENTS together into a bowl. Using a pastry cutter, two knives, or fingers, cut in the butter until the mixture resembles coarse meal. Do not overwork the mixture. Stir in the parsley.

Make a well in the center of the flour mixture and pour in the milk. Quickly incorporate the milk with a wooden spoon. Dump the mixture onto a lightly floured surface and, using your fingertips, lightly knead until a soft dough is formed.

If not using in Chicken with Dumplings, bring 3 quarts (3 l) salted water or broth to a boil in a wide pot; reduce the heat to a simmer. Cut the dough into 12 or 24 equal pieces and form into flattish rounds. When the liquid returns to a simmer, cook on top of the simmering liquid, covered, for 10 minutes. Turn the dumplings over and continue to cook, covered, for 10 more minutes, or until cooked through. For smaller dumplings, see the introduction; if making the half-size dumplings, cook in two batches.

MAKES 12 DUMPLINGS

liver-rich dumplings

THESE ARE BASED on a typical Viennese recipe for dumplings that are traditionally served in kraft süppe, Beef Consommé (page 354). They are usually made with calf's liver and are less delicate in texture. Calf's liver can be substituted for chicken livers if desired.

4½ slices white sandwich bread, crusts removed

¾ pound (360 g) chicken livers, rinsed and connective tissue removed

3 tablespoons finely chopped onion

½ small bunch flat-leaf parsley, leaves only, finely chopped

2 teaspoons kosher salt

6 grinds black pepper

3 tablespoons all-purpose flour

IN A FOOD PROCESSOR, pulse the bread to fine crumbs. Transfer to a bowl.

In the food processor, pulse the livers, onion, parsley, salt, and pepper to combine; stop once to scrape down the sides of the bowl. Scrape the mixture into a medium bowl with a rubber spatula. Stir in 1¼ cups (140 g) bread crumbs. Add the flour and stir until fully incorporated.

Meanwhile, bring 8 cups (2 l) lightly salted water to a boil.

Shape the dumplings either by pushing 1½ tablespoon quantities that are more or less round into the water (they will look a little messy) or by forming them with two soup spoons into elongated ovals, like quenelles. Keep spoons wet so the mixture does not stick to them, and gently place as many formed dumplings as will fit without crowding into the lightly boiling water. Immediately lower the heat so that the water simmers. Cook for 5 minutes, or until cooked through. Remove the dumplings with a slotted spoon to paper towels as they are cooked. Cover and keep warm. Continue to make and cook dumplings until all the mixture is used.

MAKES 20 TO 22 DUMPLINGS; 4 TO 6 FIRST-COURSE SERVINGS,
EACH IN 1¼ CUPS (310 ML) BROTH

albóndigas

COPELAND MARKS IS AS FINE a collector of recipes as he has been a collector of textiles for a wide variety of museums. His *False Tongues and Sunday Bread,* about the food of Guatemala and the difficulties he experienced in collecting recipes there, is splendid. With his permission, I have adapted the following recipe from his book.

I prefer these meatballs served simply in broth such as roasted turkey stock, seasoned with salt and pepper. In Guatemala, they are often served with a variety of vegetables and some pasta is added to the poaching liquid. They can also be fried to serve with cocktails. The recipe can be halved.

2 slices white bread, crusts removed, slightly moistened with water, wrung out, and torn into pieces

2 tablespoons coarsely chopped mint

1 small onion, coarsely chopped

1 medium jalapeño pepper, seeded, deribbed, and coarsely chopped

2 medium cloves garlic, smashed and peeled

1 small tomato, coarsely chopped

1 tablespoon coarsely chopped cilantro

1 pound (450 g) lean ground beef

1 tablespoon kosher salt

Freshly ground black pepper, to taste

15 cups (3.75 l) Roasted Turkey Stock (page 352) or other savory stock, seasoned with salt and pepper

IN A FOOD PROCESSOR, pulse the bread, mint, onion, jalapeño, and garlic to purée. Add the tomato and cilantro. Pulse until the tomato is finely chopped. Remove to a medium bowl.

Mix in the ground meat, salt, and pepper.

Roll the mixture by rounded teaspoonfuls into 1-inch (2.5-cm) balls. In a large pot wider than it is deep, bring the stock to a boil. Working in batches, if necessary, to keep from crowding the pan, drop the meatballs into the boiling liquid and return to a boil. Lower the heat and simmer for 4 to 6 minutes. If working in batches, with a slotted spoon, remove the cooked meatballs to paper towels. When all of the meatballs are done, return the drained meatballs to the broth briefly to heat through. Ladle the meatballs and broth into bowls.

MAKES SEVENTY-TWO 1-INCH (2.5-CM) MEATBALLS; 8 TO 10 FIRST-COURSE SERVINGS, EACH IN 1¼ TO 1½ CUPS (310 TO 375 ML) BROTH

pâte à choux

THIS IS THE CLASSIC cream puff recipe. Small puffs are sometimes floated in soup on their own or are served next to a particularly elegant consommé, such as Oxtail (page 357), stuffed with cooked foie gras.

> 1 cup (250 ml) water
> 8 tablespoons (120 g) unsalted butter, cut into ½-inch (1-cm) pieces
> ½ teaspoon kosher salt
> 1 cup (120 g) all-purpose flour
> 4 eggs

IN A MEDIUM SAUCEPAN, place the water, butter, and salt. Bring to a simmer over medium heat. When the butter has melted, reduce the heat to very low. Stir in the flour and whisk until the mixture is smooth and shiny and forms a ball around the whisk. Remove from the heat.

Beat in the eggs one at a time, making sure each is thoroughly incorporated before adding the next. (If making gougères, see page 422.)

Preheat the oven to 425°F (218°C; between #6 and #8 gas mark; #7 British regulo). Line two baking sheets (not air-cushioned) with parchment paper.

Using a pastry bag with a number 8 (plain round ⅜-inch [1-cm]) tip, pipe the pâte à choux onto the baking sheets in ½-inch (1-cm) mounds. Bake for 15 minutes. Rotate sheets, turn the oven temperature down to 300°F (149°C; gas mark #2; between #1 and #2 British regulo), and bake the puffs until golden brown and very lightweight, about 20 minutes. Using a skewer, poke a hole in the side of each puff to release steam. Place on a rack to cool.

When the choux puffs are completely cool, slit them in half horizontally almost all the way through. Scoop out any uncooked dough in the middle.

MAKES 96 MINIATURE PUFFS

gougères

THESE ARE THE CHEESE VERSION of pâte à choux. They are typical of Burgundy, where they make a hot bite before the meal. I like them served next to soups. A little cayenne pepper can give extra zing. Only by tasting the cheese can one tell if extra salt is needed.

The gougères can be made ahead and refrigerated or frozen. To reheat, preheat the oven to 350°F (177°C; gas mark #4; between #3 and #4 British regulo) and bake on a cookie sheet for 8 minutes.

> **1 cup (60 g) freshly grated Gruyère or Parmesan cheese; or 1 cup (60 g) grated Cheddar cheese and 16 thick slices bacon, cut into ¼-inch (.5-cm) dice**
>
> **1 recipe Pâte à Choux prepared through the addition of the eggs (page 421), still warm**

HEAT THE OVEN TO 425°F (218°C; between gas mark #6 and #8; #7 British regulo). Line two baking sheets (not air-cushioned) with parchment paper.

If using the Cheddar and bacon, cook the bacon in a medium frying pan over medium heat until crisp. Remove the bacon with a slotted spoon to paper towels to drain.

Stir the cheese and the bacon, if using, into the warm pâte à choux. Using a pastry bag with a number 8 (plain round ⅜-inch [1-cm]) tip, pipe the dough onto the baking sheets in 1¼-inch (3-cm) mounds. Or, drop by rounded tablespoons onto the sheets.

Bake for 15 minutes. Rotate the baking sheets, turn the oven temperature down to 300°F (149°C; gas mark #2; between #1 and #2 British regulo), and bake the puffs until golden brown and lightweight, about 20 minutes. Serve hot or place on a rack to cool. If cooled, serve as they are or reheat as directed in the headnote.

MAKES ABOUT 50 PUFFS

puff pastry
CHEESE STRAWS

AT FANCY FRENCH DINNER PARTIES, two-handled consommé cups often arrive filled with clear broth and their saucers adorned with cheese straws. These are often bought at a pastry shop, but they can easily be made with store-bought puff pastry.

> **One 8- to 9-ounce (225- to 255-g) sheet frozen puff pastry, defrosted**
>
> **2 to 3 tablespoons grated Parmesan, Cheddar, Gruyère, pecorino, or caciocavallo cheese**
>
> **1 egg, lightly beaten with 2 tablespoons water, for egg wash**

HEAT THE OVEN TO 425°F (218°C; between gas mark #6 and #8; #7 British regulo).

Place the pastry on a lightly floured surface, opening it if folded. It should be about 9½ × 9 inches (23.75 × 22.5 cm). If the sheet is smaller, roll it out to the proper dimensions.

Sprinkle 2 tablespoons of the cheese in a wide band across the center third of the pastry. Fold one third of the dough over the center and sprinkle with the remaining cheese, if using. Fold the other third over to form a new rectangle, aligning the edges. With a roll of the pin, seal the ends of the rectangle so that the cheese will not fall out. Then roll back and forth from one sealed edge toward the other to form a rectangle about 12 × 8 inches (30 × 20 cm).

Trim the edges of the dough and cut across into ¼-inch- (.5-cm-) wide strips. Carefully twist each strip five or six times to form long Shirley Temple corkscrew curls and place about 1 inch (2.5 cm) apart on an ungreased parchment paper–lined baking sheet (not air-cushioned), pushing down the ends of each curl of dough to keep them twisted. If necessary, use two or more baking sheets, but bake one at a time. Brush the curls with a little egg wash and bake for ten minutes. Transfer to a wire rack and cool completely.

MAKES 25 TO 30 STRAWS

piroshki

No matter how filling or light the soup, Russians, Poles, Ukrainians, and many others from Central and Eastern European countries make savory turnovers to serve with it. There are as many names as countries; piroshki may be the best known. I have often tried to find a strict correlation between name—pirogen, for example—and dough or filling, to no avail. All of the turnovers, except those made with puff pastry, can be fried or baked. Some doughs are yeast-raised; I prefer them. I also give a dough for those who don't like to work with yeast, or whose memories it doesn't match.

Jewish knishes use a dough like this but are usually filled with highly seasoned mashed potatoes. A Russian form known as rastegai is usually filled with a fish mixture. The dough circle has the filling placed right in the center and both sides of the dough are brought up and pinched together, making an oval with a raised welt going down the center.

Once I make piroshki, I make a lot, as they keep well and can also be used as an hors d'oeuvre. Allow one to three per person with soup.

**Yeast-Raised Piroshki Dough (page 426) or Piroshki Dough
Without Yeast (page 425)**
**1½ cups (375 ml) Chicken Liver Piroshki Filling (page 427) or Beef and Pork
Piroshki Filling (page 428)**
3 egg yolks, beaten with 3 tablespoons cold water, for egg wash
Vegetable oil, if deep-frying

On a lightly floured surface, roll out the dough to about ¹⁄₁₆ inch (15 mm) thick. Cut out rounds with a 3-inch (7.5-cm) cookie cutter. Reroll scraps and cut out more rounds to use up the dough.

Place 1 level teaspoon of filling in the center of each round. Lightly brush some egg wash halfway around the edge. Fold the half of the lower pastry to form a turnover. Pinch the edges together to seal securely.

To bake the piroshki: Heat the oven to 350°F (177°C; gas mark #4; between #3 and #4 British regulo).

Place the piroshki on baking sheets (not air-cushioned) lined with parchment paper. Brush the tops lightly with egg wash and bake until golden brown, about 12 minutes. Remove from the oven. Allow to cool slightly before serving.

To deep-fat fry: In a 12- to 14-inch (30- to 35-cm) diameter wok with a stand (ring), heat 6 cups (1.5 l) oil to 375°F (190°C). If a wok is not available, use a medium stockpot with enough oil to come to a depth of at least 2 inches (5 cm). This will require more than 6 cups (1.5 l) of oil.

Working in batches, allowing plenty of room for the piroshki to float freely, slip the piroshki carefully into the hot oil. Fry until dark golden brown, about 4 to 5 minutes, turning halfway through the cooking time. With a slotted spoon, remove to a tray lined with a paper towel or brown paper bag. If desired, keep the cooked piroshki warm in a 200°F (93°C; lowest gas mark or British regulo) oven while cooking the rest.

Allow the oil to return to 375°F (190°C) before beginning the next batch.

To store and reheat: The turnovers can be made 1 to 2 days ahead and stored in airtight containers. Reheat on baking sheets in a 350°F (177°C; gas mark #4; between #3 and #4 British regulo) oven for 5 minutes. They can also be made 3 to 4 weeks ahead, tightly wrapped, and frozen. Reheat as above for 10 minutes.

MAKES ABOUT 75 TURNOVERS

piroshki dough
WITHOUT YEAST

2 cups (225 g) sifted all-purpose flour

1 teaspoon kosher salt

8 tablespoons (120 g) unsalted butter, at room temperature,
    cut into ½-inch (1-cm) pieces

5 tablespoons sour cream

1 egg yolk

2 tablespoons ice water

IN A MEDIUM BOWL, combine the flour and salt. Add the butter and rub into the flour until the mixture resembles coarse meal. Stir in the sour cream.

Beat the egg yolk and water together. Stir into the flour mixture to form a dough. Wrap the dough in plastic wrap and refrigerate for at least 1 hour.

MAKES 1 POUND (450 G); ENOUGH FOR 38 TURNOVERS

yeast-raised piroshki dough

THE NUMBER OF PEOPLE SERVED when the piroshki are used as a soup accompaniment will be between twenty-five and seventy-five. Relax; the piroshki freeze.

> 1 package (7 g) active dry yeast
> ¾ cup (180 ml) warm milk
> 3⅔ to 4 cups (370 to 450 g) all-purpose flour
> 2 eggs
> 1 teaspoon kosher salt
> 8 tablespoons (120 g) unsalted butter, at room temperature

IN A SMALL BOWL, combine the yeast and warm milk. Let stand for 5 minutes, or until foamy.

Stir in ⅔ cup (80 g) flour to form a smooth batter. Cover the bowl with plastic wrap and let stand for about 1 hour and 30 minutes, or until doubled in volume.

Pour the batter into a food processor or electric mixer. Add the eggs and salt and pulse, or mix, to combine. Begin adding the remaining flour about ½ cup (65 g) at a time, mixing well with each addition. When the mixture forms a dough that is beginning to leave the sides of the bowl, add the butter and mix well until thoroughly combined. Add enough of the remaining flour so that the mixture forms a soft dough that is not sticky.

Transfer the dough from the food processor to a bowl or leave in the electric mixer bowl. Cover with plastic wrap and allow to stand in a warm place for at least 1 hour and 30 minutes, or until the dough has doubled in volume.

Punch down the dough. Divide the dough into four portions and wrap each one in plastic wrap. Refrigerate for at least 1 hour so that the dough is easier to handle.

MAKES 1¾ POUNDS (790 G); ENOUGH FOR 75 TURNOVERS

chicken liver

6 tablespoons (90 g) unsalted butter

1 small onion, finely chopped

¼ pound (120 g) white mushrooms, wiped clean and coarsely chopped
   in a food processor

½ pound (225 g) chicken livers, cleaned

1½ tablespoons vodka

½ cup (15 g) loosely packed flat-leaf parsley leaves, coarsely chopped

1¼ teaspoons kosher salt

Freshly ground black pepper, to taste

IN A MEDIUM FRYING PAN, melt 3 tablespoons (45 g) butter over low heat. Stir in the onion and cook until soft, about 10 minutes. Stir in the remaining butter and the mushrooms. Cook for 2 minutes. Raise the heat to medium, stir in the chicken livers, and cook until browned

Meanwhile, gently heat the vodka in a small saucepan. Carefully ignite with a match and pour over the liver mixture. Reduce the heat and allow the flame to die naturally. Stir in the parsley, salt, and pepper. Cook 5 minutes longer.

Scrape the mixture into a food processor. Pulse just until finely chopped. Scrape into a small bowl and allow to cool.

MAKES 1½ CUPS (375 ML); ENOUGH FOR 75 TURNOVERS

beef and pork
PIROSHKI FILLING

2 tablespoons (30 g) unsalted butter

1 small onion, finely chopped

¼ pound (120 g) lean ground beef

¼ pound (120 g) lean ground pork

2 tablespoons coarsely chopped dill

1 teaspoon kosher salt

Freshly ground black pepper, to taste

1 hard-boiled egg, coarsely chopped

IN A MEDIUM FRYING PAN, melt the butter over low heat. Stir in the onion, beef, and pork. Cook, stirring occasionally, until the meat is no longer pink and the onions are soft, about 5 minutes. Stir in the dill, salt, and pepper. Cook for 2 minutes. Stir in the egg. Remove from the heat and allow to cool.

MAKES 1½ CUPS (375 ML); ENOUGH FOR 75 TURNOVERS

croutons

OR CROSTINI

THESE ARE THIN, flat croutons that the British used to call "sippets" and cut into fanciful—hearts and diamonds—shapes. When made with olive oil, they turn into Italian crostini. They can go on top of a wide variety of soups or be served on the side for people to add as wanted. For Mediterranean fish soups, they are frequently rubbed with raw garlic and topped with Rouille (page 433) or Aïoli (page 432). They are sometimes floated on Beef Consommé (page 354), topped with some of the marrow from the bones used to make the stock.

They show up in Cucumber Gazpacho (page 34), Great Green Soup (page 101), Bourride of Monkfish (page 260), Brandade Soup (page 264), and Michael's Fish Soup (page 16).

1 narrowish loaf good Italian bread, cut across on a slight diagonal into ¼-inch (.5-cm) slices
About ½ cup (125 ml) good olive oil

PLACE A RACK IN THE CENTER of the oven and heat to 350°F (175°C; gas mark #4; #4 British regulo).

Place half of the bread slices on a noninsulated cookie sheet. Brush the tops with a generous amount of olive oil. Toast for 15 to 17 minutes, or until the bread is brown around the edges and crisp. Let cool.

Repeat with the remaining bread.

MAKES ABOUT 48 CROUTONS

cubed croutons

CUBED CROUTONS ARE MORE TYPICALLY French. They are sprinkled on cream soups like Tomato Soup with Cream (page 69) or Hot Cauliflower Soup (page 376), where they provide a satisfying contrast of crunch.

Cubed croutons can be baked or fried and different fats can be used. The fried croutons yield a fattier, more satisfying product; the baked are leaner. Suit the fat chosen to that of the soup they are to go with.

3 cups (750 ml) vegetable oil if frying the croutons; or, for the baked, 2 tablespoons (30 g) unsalted butter, melted, or 2 tablespoons olive oil

6 slices white sandwich bread, crusts removed and cut into ½ inch (1-cm) squares

TO FRY THE CROUTONS, in a medium saucepan, heat the oil to 375°F (190°C). Working in small batches, fry the bread cubes for 20 to 25 seconds, turning once, until golden brown. Remove with a slotted spoon and drain on paper towels.

To bake the croutons, heat the oven to 350°F (177°C; gas mark #4; between #3 and #4 British regulo). Toss the bread cubes in butter or oil and spread in a single layer on a baking sheet. Bake for 7 minutes. Turn the croutons and bake for 8 more minutes, or until golden brown. Let cool.

MAKES 2 CUPS (500 ML) FRIED CROUTONS, 1¾ CUPS (440 ML) BAKED

creamy polenta

POLENTA, or cornmeal mush, is certainly not a classic component of soups, but many of my soups are more stew-like than classic soups. A large kitchen spoonful of polenta in the middle of each dish may be just what is wanted to make a soup into complete meals; or pass the polenta in a separate bowl and let people take what they want, as I do with the Goat Soup with Haricots Verts (page 218). It would go equally well with the Veal Soup with Fennel (page 27) and Beef Stew for a Spoon (page 184).

2 teaspoons kosher salt, or more to taste
1 cup yellow cornmeal
¾ to 1 cup (180 to 250 ml) heavy cream
6 tablespoons (90 g) unsalted butter
Freshly ground black pepper, to taste

IN A MEDIUM SAUCEPAN, bring 5 cups (1.25 l) water to a boil. Stir in the salt. In a large bowl, stir the cornmeal into 1½ cups (375 ml) cold water. Pour the cold water and cornmeal all at once into the boiling water. Return to a boil. Simmer, stirring frequently, for 30 minutes, or until the mixture pulls away from the sides of the pan and is able to hold its shape.

Over low heat, stir in the cream and butter. Continue to stir until the polenta is smooth and creamy. Season with pepper and additional salt, if desired.

MAKES ABOUT 6 CUPS (1.5 L); 6 SERVINGS

The somethings extra

This is the last and, as a group, the least logical section of the book. It is made up of sauces that are served alongside soups, preparations that are required before the soup is made, and a few condiments that are served with the soups.

aïoli

AÏOLI DEFINES PROVENCE. There are other garlic sauces along the Mediterranean coast, but not ones using eggs. Other versions of this sauce are bound only with bread or potatoes and they are closer to the garlic sauces of Spain and Italy. There is even a dish called the Grand Aïoli, which is like a bollito misto without the soup and with a broader selection of vegetables and snails. It is a Christmas or New Year's dish.

I use aïoli in Bourride of Monkfish (page 260) and Red Vinegar Seafood Stew (page 274). The taste develops with time; aïoli is best made a day ahead.

To make as rouille with a mortar and pestle, see page 433.

4 large garlic cloves, smashed and peeled
1 large slice French bread, crust removed
¼ cup (65 ml) milk
3 egg yolks
Kosher salt, to taste
Cayenne pepper, to taste
1½ cups (375 ml) olive oil
Fresh lemon juice, to taste

PLACE THE GARLIC IN A FOOD PROCESSOR. Soak the bread in the milk. Squeeze out the excess moisture and add the squeezed bread to the garlic. Process, scraping the sides of the work bowl once or twice, until the mixture is pasty and very smooth. Add the egg yolks and salt and cayenne to taste. Process until well blended and smooth. With the machine running, add the olive oil, a few drops at a time at first. As the sauce begins to look like mayonnaise, continue to add the oil in a slow steady stream until it is all incorporated. Add a drop of lemon juice and readjust the seasoning with salt and cayenne.

MAKES 3 CUPS (750 ML)

rouille

ROUILLE MEANS "RUST-COLORED," as *tâches de rousseur* are my freckles. The sauce is wonderful served with French Mediterranean fish soups. I have been known to slather it on bread and eat it with a salad.

Conventionally, it is used in Michael's Fish Soup (page 16), Bouillabiasse (page 268), and Fall Fish Stew (page 257). This sauce—and any mayonnaise-type sauce—needs to be added at the end of the cooking to assure that it doesn't break from too much heat. If small hot peppers in their dried form are unavailable, use the flakes that come in a jar.

Traditionally, this is made with a mortar and pestle, first pulverizing the solids and then slowly adding the oil as the pestle is rotated in one direction.

4 egg yolks

1 teaspoon kosher salt

¼ teaspoon dry mustard

2 teaspoons white wine vinegar

12 medium cloves garlic, smashed, peeled, and cut into chunks

3 small dried hot red peppers

1 cup (250 ml) extra virgin olive oil

1 cup (250 ml) vegetable oil

¼ cup (65 ml) bottled roasted red peppers, drained and coarsely chopped

½ cup (125 ml) fish soup, optional

IN A FOOD PROCESSOR, pulse the yolks, salt, mustard, vinegar, garlic, and dried peppers to combine. With the machine running, pour in the oil, a few drops at a time at first. As the sauce begins to look like mayonnaise, continue to add the oil in a slow steady stream and process until the oil is incorporated and sauce is thick. Add the red peppers and process until smooth. If using, add the fish soup.

MAKES 3 ½ CUPS (875 ML)

pesto sauce

PISTOU

PESTO IS ITALIAN, pistou is French. For a longer discussion, also of technique, see page 302. Either can be made with or without pine nuts and cheese. It depends on the dish, tradition, and personal preference. In soup, it is usually without nuts or cheese.

One version or another is used for Green Soup (page 75), Black Bean and Pistou Soup (page 304), Minestrone (page 115), and Simple White Bean and Pesto Soup (page 301). For soup, I tend to favor the nutless, cheeseless version.

2 tablespoons pine nuts, optional
2 large bunches basil, leaves only, washed well and dried
2 medium cloves garlic, peeled
¼ cup (65 ml) olive oil
3 tablespoons freshly grated Parmesan cheese, optional

IN A SMALL SKILLET, toast the pine nuts, if using, over medium-low heat for about 4 minutes, tossing frequently, until they are evenly lightly browned. Immediately remove them from the pan and cool completely.

In a food processor, finely chop the basil and garlic. With the machine running, pour the olive oil through the feed tube in a slow steady stream. Add the cheese and pine nuts, if using. Process until fairly smooth in texture.

MAKES ¾ CUP (180 ML)

peanut butter

I OFTEN USE PEANUT BUTTER from a jar; but it is easy to make at home in either a chunky or smooth version. It can be used in Spicy Peanut Butter Soup (page 314) and Chicken Stew with Peanut Butter (page 138). When using homemade peanut butters, it may be a good idea to add a little more salt to the finished recipe as these peanut butters have none.

> 2 cups (300 g) roasted unsalted peanuts
> ¼ cup (65 ml) peanut oil
> Kosher salt, to taste, optional

TO MAKE THE PEANUT BUTTER in a food processor, coarsely grind the peanuts until they are just starting to become oily. While the machine is running, pour the oil through the feed tube and continue to process until the desired consistency is achieved, 5 to 10 seconds for crunchy, 1 to 2 minutes for smooth.

To make the peanut butter in a blender, coarsely chop the peanuts. Stop the machine and pour in the oil. Turn the machine on and process until the desired consistency is achieved, stopping occasionally to scrape down the sides of the jar, 30 seconds to 2 minutes.

Season with salt, if desired. For a firmer butter, refrigerate for at least 1 hour before using. Keeps refrigerated for 2 weeks. If the peanut butter separates during storage, simply stir the oil back in.

MAKES 1 CUP (270 G)

quatre épices

A CLASSIC FRENCH CONDIMENT often used in sausages and pâtés, quatre épices turns up in White Bean Soup with Confit and Tomato (page 160).

> ½ cup plus 1 tablespoon (70 g) freshly ground white pepper
> 2¼ teaspoons ground cloves
> 1 tablespoon plus 2¼ teaspoons powdered ginger
> 2 tablespoons freshly grated nutmeg

COMBINE ALL THE SPICES and store in a tightly sealed jar for up to 6 months.

MAKES 1¾ CUPS (210 G)

On pages 220–223, there are instructions for making Bollito Misto, Pot-au-Feu, and Cocido. Each soup-making area has its own sauces. The Piedmont, home of Bollito Misto, has two excellent and typical sauces called, in the regional dialect, Bagnèt Verd and Bagnèt Ross. The Enriched Vinaigrette is typical of France and the Horseradish Sauce and Fresh Horseradish Condiment would be more Austrian and German.

enriched vinaigrette

THIS IS A DELICIOUS SAUCE to go with boiled meats and chicken or simple poached fish.

> 10 sprigs flat-leaf parsley, leaves only, coarsely chopped
>
> 2 teaspoons anchovy paste
>
> 1½ teaspoons Dijon mustard
>
> ½ teaspoon kosher salt
>
> ½ teaspoon freshly ground black pepper
>
> ¼ cup red wine vinegar
>
> 1 cup (250 ml) olive oil
>
> 2 tablespoons capers, coarsely chopped
>
> 1 hard-boiled egg, finely chopped

IN A FOOD PROCESSOR, pulse the parsley, anchovy paste, mustard, salt, pepper, and vinegar to combine. With the machine running, slowly pour in the oil. Remove to a small bowl. Stir in the capers and egg. This can be refrigerated for up to 3 days. Remove from the refrigerator 1 hour before serving, to allow the olive oil to liquefy.

MAKES 1½ CUPS (360 ML)

bagnèt verd

THERE ARE TWO CLASSIC SAUCES from the Piedmont for Bollito Misto (page 221), a red (page 438) and a green. This is the green. It is so good that it deserves outings on crudités and Croutons (page 429).

2 tablespoons white wine vinegar

2 tablespoons water, or as needed

1 cup (45 g) coarsely torn crustless stale bread (about 2 slices)

1 cup (40 g) chopped flat-leaf parsley

2 medium cloves garlic, smashed, peeled, and minced

2 teaspoons anchovy paste or 2 oil-packed anchovies, rinsed and minced

6 tablespoons (100 ml) extra virgin olive oil

¼ cup (40 g) minced green bell pepper

Yolk of hard-boiled egg

2 teaspoons minced seeded jalapeño pepper, optional

¾ teaspoon kosher salt

Freshly ground black pepper, to taste

IN A MEDIUM BOWL, pour the vinegar and 2 tablespoons water over the bread. Let stand until the liquid is absorbed and the bread is thoroughly soft. If all the liquid is absorbed before the bread is softened, add another tablespoon of water.

Mash the bread with a fork until smooth. Add the parsley, garlic, and anchovy paste and stir until thoroughly mixed with the bread paste. Gradually add the olive oil, stirring constantly with the fork until it is completely incorporated. Stir in the bell pepper, egg yolk, jalapeño, salt, and pepper. Let stand at room temperature for 30 minutes before serving.

The sauce can be stored covered in the refrigerator up to a week; allow it to stand at room temperature for 30 minutes before serving.

MAKES ABOUT 2 CUPS (400 ML); 6 SERVINGS

bagnèt ross

THIS IS THE RED SAUCE for Bollito Misto (page 221). The green one is on page 437. This makes a savory pasta sauce, or serve it over poached fish.

2¼ pounds (1 kg) plum tomatoes, coarsely chopped

2 medium onions, coarsely chopped

2 medium carrots, coarsely chopped

3 medium cloves garlic, smashed, peeled, and minced

1 small piece fresh or dried hot red pepper

1 medium rib celery, optional

A few sprigs of parsley, optional

2 teaspoons sugar

¾ cup (180 ml) red wine vinegar

Kosher salt, to taste

3 tablespoons very good olive oil

IN A MEDIUM SAUCEPAN combine the tomatoes, onions, carrots, garlic, hot pepper, and, if using, the celery and parsley over medium heat. Cover and cook, stirring occasionally, until the tomatoes are collapsed and bubbling. Lower the heat and simmer, partially covered and stirring occasionally, for 30 minutes.

Stir in sugar, vinegar, and salt, and return to a boil. Lower the heat and simmer, partially covered and stirring occasionally for 2 hours.

Adjust the seasoning between sweet and sour. Simmer for 30 minutes.

Stir in the olive oil and pass through a coarse sieve or the medium disc of a food mill.

The sauce can be made 1 day ahead and refrigerated. Serve at room temperature.

MAKES ABOUT 4 CUPS (1 L); 6 SERVINGS

horseradish sauce

THE EASIEST WAY TO SERVE horseradish is simply to spoon it out of a jar. The next easiest is to use prepared horseradish—white, not the red, which is sweet—and combine it with whipped cream or sour cream. I am particularly fond of the whipped cream version, which is less caloric because of all the air beaten in. The slight sweetness of the cream also tempers the bite of the horseradish.

One 4-ounce (113-g) bottle prepared horseradish
1 cup (250 ml) heavy cream or sour cream

PLACE THE HORSERADISH in a fine-mesh sieve and let drain for 15 minutes.

If using heavy cream, whip to stiff peaks. With a fork, gently combine the whipped cream or sour cream with the horseradish. If making more than an hour ahead, refrigerate.

MAKES 2 CUPS (250 ML) WITH WHIPPED CREAM, 1¾ CUPS (310 ML) WITH SOUR CREAM

fresh horseradish
CONDIMENT

THIS IS MORE WORK THAN THE PRECEDING SAUCE, but I make it every year when it is time to dig the horseradish. There is a special bite to fresh horseradish that is addictive. The Poles often simply sliver peeled horseradish—a vegetable peeler is the best way—and sprinkle the slivers on the hot meat or even into the broth, which may have a tarragon dumpling or two in it.

⅓ pound (150 g) horseradish, trimmed, peeled, and coarsely grated (use the large teardrop holes of a box grater)

4 teaspoons distilled white vinegar

1 teaspoon sugar

¼ teaspoon kosher salt

IN A SMALL BOWL, combine all the ingredients. Refrigerate overnight before using.

MAKES 1 CUP (90G)

ecuadorian ingredients

The wonderful vegetarian soups of the Ecuadorians rely on a few simple, basic made ingredients and a relish or two, such as Ground Roasted Peanuts (page 335) and Pickled Onions (page 446).

tamarillo sauce

THIS ECUADORIAN SAUCE is a great delight in both flavor and color. I have used it in Thick Potato Soup with Favas (page 296) and Hominy Soup (page 337). Once tried, it calls out for other inventions. Cooks without tamarillos can use Tomato Plum Sauce (page 442).

> 2 tamarillos (10 ounces; 300 g total)
> 1 teaspoon kosher salt
> 2 tablespoons very finely chopped white onion
> 1 tablespoon finely chopped cilantro
> 1 teaspoon canola oil
> 2 medium jalapeño peppers, seeded, deribbed, and finely chopped, optional

BRING A SMALL SAUCEPAN of water to a boil. Add the tamarillos and boil until the skins burst, 5 to 7 minutes. Remove with a slotted spoon, cool, and peel. Pass through the medium disc of a food mill.

In a food processor, purée the tamarillos and ¼ cup (65 ml) water. Add the remaining ingredients and process until well blended.

The sauce will keep tightly covered in the refrigerator or freezer for 2 weeks.

MAKES 1½ CUPS (375 ML)

tomato plum sauce

NOT ALL OF US HAVE ready access to tamarillos. I developed this in a T. S. Eliot "dry month" as a substitute for the prior recipe.

  3 vine-ripened plum tomatoes, peeled

  1 medium red plum, peeled

  2 tablespoons fresh lemon juice

  1 teaspoon kosher salt

  2 tablespoons very finely chopped onion

  2 tablespoons chopped cilantro

  1 teaspoon canola or vegetable oil

  2 jalapeño peppers, seeded, deribbed, and finely chopped, optional

IN A FOOD PROCESSOR, purée the tomatoes and plum with ¼ cup (65 ml) water. Pass through a coarse sieve into a medium bowl. Stir in the remaining ingredients.

This keeps in the refrigerator for 2 weeks.

MAKES 1 ½ CUPS (375 ML)

criolla sauce

THIS JOLT OF SPICE comes from Ecuador; but if it is on hand, it can liven up any number of dishes.

4 medium jalapeño peppers, seeded, deveined, and cut into ¼-inch
   (.5-cm) dice
1 teaspoon kosher salt
5 tablespoons fresh lime juice
1 tablespoon canola oil
1 small white onion, very finely chopped
1 tablespoon chopped fresh cilantro

IN A BLENDER OR FOOD PROCESSOR, purée the jalapeños with 2 tablespoons water. Pour the mixture into a small bowl, making sure to scrape out all of the purée with a spatula. Stir in the remaining ingredients.

This will keep tightly covered in the refrigerator for 2 weeks.

MAKES ¾ CUP (180 ML)

aliño

THIS ECUADORIAN CONDIMENT will keep virtually forever. Make the whole amount and store it in a glass jar in the refrigerator to have on hand for soups such as Lentil Soup from Ecuador (page 318) and Repé (page 108).

5 teaspoons (15 g) black peppercorns
3 tablespoons (15 g) cumin seed
1 medium red onion, thinly sliced
1 medium head garlic, smashed and peeled
⅓ cup (15 g) dried oregano
2 tablespoons canola oil

IN A SMALL DRY FRYING PAN over low heat, cook the peppercorns and cumin seeds until aromatic. Lower the heat slightly, cover, and continue to cook, shaking occasionally, for 5 minutes. Remove from the heat.

Grind the peppercorns and cumin in a spice mill or crush with a mortar and pestle. In a food processor, pulse the ground spices with the remaining ingredients until well combined; the onions and garlic should still be crunchy. Do not purée.

Aliño will keep tightly covered in the refrigerator for 2 months, or until I get tired of seeing it.

MAKES 1 ½ CUPS (360 G)

annatto butter

THIS FLAVORED BUTTER (or oil) begins almost every Ecuadorian recipe, including Thick Potato Soup with Favas (page 296), Lentil Soup from Ecuador (page 318), and Quinoa Soup (page 334). I double or triple the recipe, as I am fond of the soups. See pages 319–321 for using other fats.

> ½ cup (125 ml) annatto (achiote) seeds
> 8 tablespoons (120 g) unsalted butter or ½ cup (130 ml) oil

IN A SMALL SAUCEPAN, combine the annatto and 2 tablespoons butter or oil. Cook over low heat for 5 minutes. Strain through a fine-mesh sieve into a small heatproof bowl.

Repeat the process three more times, using the same annatto and 2 tablespoons of the remaining unseasoned butter or oil each time. Heat the mixture a little less each time to avoid burning, and strain the butter or oil into the same bowl. Refrigerate until needed.

MAKES ABOUT ⅓ CUP (100 G)

pickled onions

THESE ARE SERVED WITH Thick Potato Soup with Favas (page 296) and Hominy Soup (page 337) from Ecuador.

> 2 medium red onions, thinly sliced
> 2 teaspoons kosher salt
> 1 teaspoon lemon juice
> ¼ teaspoon sugar

TOSS THE ONIONS WITH THE SALT. Allow to sit until the salt penetrates the onion, about 20 minutes. Rinse to remove the salt.

In a small bowl, combine the onions with the lemon juice and sugar. Let sit until pink. These keep, refrigerated, for 1 month.

MAKES 2 ½ CUPS (675 ML)

refrito

USE IN ANY ECUADORIAN soup recipe to replace the refrito given.

> 1 teaspoon unsalted butter
> ½ teaspoon annatto (achiote) seeds
> 1 medium onion, cut into ¼-inch (.5-cm) dice
> Kosher salt, to taste
> Freshly ground black pepper, to taste

IN A SMALL SAUCEPAN, heat the butter and annatto over low heat until the butter melts. Stir in the onions and cook for 10 minutes, or until translucent. Season with salt and pepper.

MAKES ½ CUP (125 ML)

Vegetables

Often vegetables are all that is needed to turn a stock into a soup. Timings follow. Whenever cooking, it is important to know the sizes of the vegetables being used. These are the approximate sizes of the vegetables used in this book.

	Small	Medium	Large
Carrot	2 ounces (60 g)	3 to 5 ounces (90 to 150 g)	6 to 8 ounces (180 to 225g)
Celery	1 ounce (30 g)	2 to 3 ounces (60 to 90 g)	4 ounces (120 g)
Cucumber, Kirby	1 to 2 ounces (30 to 60 g)	3 to 4 ounces (90 to 120 g)	5 ounces (150 g)
Cucumber, regular	3 ounces (90 g)	6 ounces (180 g)	8 ounces (225 g)
Leek	2 to 4 ounces (60 to 120 g)	5 to 7 ounces (150 to 210 g)	8 ounces and over (225 g)
Onion	2 to 3 ounces (60 to 90 g)	4 to 5 ounces (120 to 210 g)	6 to 8 ounces (225 to 300 g)
Potato, firm*	3 to 4 ounces (90 to 120 g)	7 to 8 ounces (210 to 225 g)	over 8 ounces (225 g)
Potato, mashing	4 to 6 ounces (120 to 180 g)	8 ounces (225 g)	9 to 10 ounces (270 to 300 g)
Potato, sweet	6 to 7 ounces (180 to 210 g)	8 to 10 ounces (225 to 300 g)	10 to 12 ounces (300 to 360 g)
Pepper, bell	3 to 4 ounces (90 to 120 g)	5 to 7 ounces (150 to 210 g)	8 ounces (225 g)
Pepper, jalapeño	½ ounce (15 g)	1 ounce (30 g)	over 1 ounce (over 30 g)
Scallion	¼ ounce (7 g)	¾ to 1 ounce (21 to 30 g)	na
Shallot	less than 1 ounce (30 g)	1 to 2 ounces (30 to 60 g)	3 ounces (90 g)
Tomato, plum	2 ounces (60 g)	3 to 4 ounces (180 to 210 g)	5 ounces (150 g)
Tomato, regular	3 to 4 ounces (90 to 120 g)	5 to 7 ounces (150 to 210 g)	8 to 10 ounces (225 to 300 g)
Turnip	3 to 5 ounces (90 to 150 g)	6 to 7 ounces (180 to 210 g)	8 to 10 ounces (225 to 300 g)

*Firm potatoes, when very small, weigh 1 to 2 ounces (30 to 60g).

One cup of cooked, solid vegetable will increase the volume of 4 cups (1 l) of liquid by about ¾ cup (180 ml).

Asparagus: 1 pound (450 g) cut into 2-inch (5-cm) lengths = 2 cups (225 g) raw = 1¾ cups cooked = 1 cup purée. Simmer for 5 minutes.

Basil: 1 bunch (3.5 ounces; 90 g), leaves only = 1.75 ounces (55 g) = 2 cups = ¼ cup raw purée.

Beans:
Dry: See pages 293–294.
Fresh cranberry: ¾ pound (360 g) in the shell = 1 cup (170 g) shelled raw = 1¼ cups cooked. Simmer for 20 minutes.
Green and wax: ¼ pound (120 g), tipped and tailed = 1¼ cups raw = 1 cup cooked. Simmer for 6 to 10 minutes.
Haricots verts: ¼ pound (120 g), tipped and tailed = 1 cup raw = ¾ cooked. Simmer for 5 minutes.

Broccoli:
Florets: 5 ounces (150 g) = 2 cups raw = 1 cup cooked = ½ cup purée. Boil 5 to 10 minutes.
Stems: ½ pound (225 g) coins or matchsticks = 2 cups raw = 1 cup cooked = ⅔ cup purée. Boil for 5 to 10 minutes.

Broccoli di Rape:
1 bunch (12 ounces; 340 g), trimmed = 10 ounces (300 g) = 3 cups raw = 2 cups cooked. Boil for 10 minutes.

Cabbage: (white): ½ pound (225 g), shredded = 2 cups raw = 1 cup cooked. Simmer 15 to 20 minutes. Or, 1 medium cabbage, cut into 6 wedges. Simmer for 20 to 30 minutes uncovered.

Carrot:
Regular: 12 ounces (360 g), trimmed and cut into 1-inch (2.5-cm) pieces = 1½ cups (315 g) raw = 1 cup cooked = ⅔ cup purée. Simmer for 12 minutes. Large carrots, cut across into 2-inch lengths. Simmer thick parts for 17 to 20 minutes, middle parts for 13 to 15 minutes, thin parts for 10 minutes.
White baby: Simmer for 15 minutes.

Cauliflower: ½ small head (12 ounces; 360 g), trimmed and cored = 9 ounces (250 g) = 2½ cups raw florets = 2¼ cups cooked florets = 1 cup purée. Steam or simmer for 15 to 20 minutes.

Celery: 4 ribs (½ pound; 225 g), trimmed and cut into ½-inch (1-cm) lengths = 2 cups (200 g) raw = 1 cup cooked. Simmer for 10 minutes.

Celery root: 1 medium (10 ounces; 300 g), trimmed, peeled, and cut into ½-inch (1-cm) cubes = 1⅔ cups (180 g) raw = 1 cup cooked = ⅔ cup purée. Simmer for 10 minutes. 1 medium, trimmed, peeled, and quartered. For purée, simmer for 20 to 25 minutes; cut into eighths, simmer for 15 to 20 minutes.

Corn: 2 ears (20 ounces; 560 g) = 6 ounces (180 g) kernels = 1 cup raw; one 10-ounce (300-g) box frozen corn = 1½ cups. Simmer for 2 to 5 minutes.

Escarole: 1 whole (about 1 pound; 450 g). Simmer for 20 to 30 minutes.

Fava Beans: 2¾ pounds (1.25 kg), shelled = 1 pound (450 g) = 3 cups raw; blanched 1 minute and peeled = 9 ounce (270 g) = 1½ cups. For 1 cup, start with 1 pound 14 ounces. Simmer for 5 minutes.

Fennel: 1 medium bulb (⅔ pounds; 320 g), trimmed, cored, and cut into 1-inch (2.5-cm) cubes = 2½ cups (260 g) raw = 1¾ cups cooked. Simmer for 20 to 25 minutes. 1 medium bulb, halved. Simmer for 16 to 20 minutes; quartered, simmer for 10 to 15 minutes.

Kale: 1 bunch (10 ounces; 300 g), trimmed and cut into 2-inch pieces = 5 cups (240 g) raw = 1½ cups cooked. Simmer for 20 minutes.

Leek: 4 medium (1 pound; 450 g), white and light green parts only, cut across into ⅛-inch- (30-mm-) thick slices = 2½ cups (225 g) raw = 1 cup cooked. Sauté for 15 minutes over medium heat or simmer for 10 minutes. 1 medium leek, white and light green parts only, simmer for 10 to 15 minutes; 1 small leek, white and light green parts only, simmer for 7 to 10 minutes.

Lentils: See pages 293–294.

Mushrooms:

Shiitake caps, dry: ½ ounce (15 g) = ⅓ cup dry = ⅓ cup (30 g) soaked for 15 minutes in 1 cup (250 ml) warm water, drained, and squeezed dry = ⅓ cup ⅛-inch (30 mm) slices.

White button, caps: ⅓ pound (150 g), cut into ¼-inch (.5-cm) slices = 2 cups = 1 cup cooked. Sauté in oil or butter or simmer for 10 minutes.

White button, whole: 16 medium (½ pound; 225 g), cut into ¼-inch (.5-cm)
   slices = 2 cups raw = 1 cup cooked (plus 3 tablespoons liquid for sautéed
   version). Sauté in oil or butter or simmer for 10 minutes.

Wood ear, dry: ½ ounce (15 g) = ½ cup dry = 1 cup (65 g) soaked for 30 minutes
   in 1 cup (250 ml) warm water.

Napa (Chinese) Cabbage: 11 ounces (310 g), shredded = 2¾ (310 g) raw =
   1 cup cooked. Simmer for 5 minutes.

Okra: 3 ounces (90 g), cut into ¼-inch slices = 1 cup (85 g) = ¾ cup cooked. Simmer
   for 8 minutes.

Onion: 1 medium (¼ pound; 120 g), coarsely chopped = 1 cup (110 g) = ¼ cup cooked.
   Sauté in oil or butter or simmer for 10 to 15 minutes.

Parsley Root: ½ pound (225 g), peeled and cut into ½-inch (1-cm) cubes = 1⅔ cups
   (180 g) raw = 1 cup cooked. Simmer for 6 minutes.

Parsnip: 1 medium (¼ pound; 120 g), peeled and cut into ½-inch (1-cm) rounds =
   1 cup (100 g) raw = ½ cup purée. Simmer for 20 minutes.

Peas: 1½ to 2¼ pounds (675 g to 1 kg) in the shell, depending on the size of the peas
   and the thickness of a shell, shelled = 11 ounces (330 g) = 2 cups raw = 1⅔ cups
   cooked. Simmer for 8 to 10 minutes. One 10-ounce (300 g) package frozen peas =
   1⅔ cups. Simmer for 3 to 5 minutes.

Potatoes:

Mashing (Idaho or russet): 1 medium (½ pound; 225 g), cut into ½-inch (1-cm)
      cubes = 1½ cups (212 g) raw = 1 cup cooked. Simmer for 15 to 20 minutes.

Very small firm (such as new Red Bliss or white): Simmer for 15 to 20 minutes.

Radish: ¼ pound (120 g), trimmed and cut into ⅛-inch (30-mm) slices = 1 cup (110 g)
   raw = ¾ cup cooked. Simmer for 5 to 6 minutes.

Rice: See page 294.

Scallion: 12 whole (about ½ pound; 225 g), trimmed and cut across into ¼-inch (.5-cm)
   slices = 1 cup (170 g) raw = ⅓ cup cooked. Sauté in butter or oil or simmer for 5
   minutes.

Sorrel: 1 pound (450 g), stemmed and cut across into narrow strips = 8 cups (225 g) = 1
   cup cooked. Melted in butter or oil for 3 to 5 minutes.

Spinach: 12 ounces (360 g), stemmed = 4½ cups (180 g) raw = 1 cup cooked. Wilt in butter or oil or simmer for 2 to 5 minutes.

Squash:

Summer: 2 small (10 ounces; 300 g), trimmed and cut into ¼-inch (.5-cm) slices or into matchstick strips = 2 cups (280 mg) raw = 1 cup cooked. Sauté in butter or oil for 8 minutes.

Winter: 1 acorn squash (1 pound; 450 g), peeled, seeded, and cut into 2-inch (5-cm) chunks = 2½ cups (225 g) raw = 1¾ cups cooked = 1 cup purée. Simmer for 15 to 20 minutes.

Tomatoes:

Canned, not plum: one 14.5-ounce (400-g) can = 1½ cups (375 ml) whole = 1½ cups (375 ml) puréed.

Canned plum: one 33.5-ounce (940-g) can = 4 cups (1 l) whole = 4 cups (1 l) coarse chunks = 2½ cups (625 ml) without juice = 2 cups (500 ml) puréed.

Fresh: ½ pound (225 g), cut into ½-inch (1-cm) dice = 2 cups (200 g) raw = 1 cup cooked. Sauté in butter or oil or simmer for 5 to 15 minutes.

Sterile-pack, chopped: one 26.5-ounce (750 g) package = 3 cups (750 ml).

Sterile-pack, strained: one 35.25-ounce (1-kg) package = 4 cups (1 l).

Turnip: ½ pound (225 g), peeled and cut into ½-inch (1-cm) dice = 2 cups (180 g) raw = 1 cup cooked. Simmer for 20 to 25 minutes. 1 small turnip, halved, simmer for 15 to 20 minutes; 1 large, quartered, simmer for 15 to 20 minutes.

Index